. Koprivnica

. Sisak

Osijek

SLAVONIA AND
BARANJA

Đakovo .

. Slavonski Brod

SLAVONIA AND BARANJA
See pp178–195

**THE NORTHERN
COUNTIES**
See pp196–213

CENTRAL CROATIA
See pp164–177

. Split

. Dubrovnik

| 0 kilometres | 50 |
| 0 miles | 30 |

EYEWITNESS TRAVEL GUIDES

CROATIA

EYEWITNESS TRAVEL GUIDES

CROATIA

DORLING KINDERSLEY

LONDON • NEW YORK • MUNICH

MELBOURNE • DELHI

www.dk.com

A Dorling Kindersley Book

www.dk.com

Produced by Fabio Ratti Editoria Srl, Milan, Italy

Project Editor Donatella Ceriani
Art Editor Oriana Bianchetti

Editors Sara Cattel, Emanuela Damiani, Alessandra Lombardi
Giovanna Morselli, Federica Romagnoli

Main Contributors Leandro Zoppé,
Gian Enrico Venturini (Travel Information and Practical Guide)

Other Contributors
Božidarka Boža Gligorijević, Iva Grgic, Sanja Rojić

Photographer Lucio Rossi

Cartographers
Grafema Cartografia Srl, Novara
LS International Cartography snc, Milano

Illustrators
Modi Artistici

English Translation
Susan Andrews

Dorling Kindersley Limited
Editor Fiona Wild
Consultant Jane Foster
Senior DTP Designer Jason Little
Production Melanie Dowland

Reproduced by Fabio Ratti Editoria Srl, Milan
and in Singapore by Colourscan
Printed and bound by Graphicom, Italy

First published in Great Britain in 2003
by Dorling Kindersley Limited
80 Strand, London WC2R 0RL

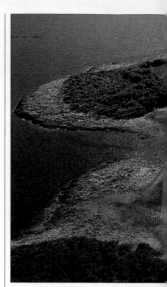

A lovely bay on the island of Mljet

Contents

Woodcutters by Mijo Kovačić,
Museum of Naive Art, Zagreb

◁ The splendid golden beach of Bol, on the island of Brač

Buzara, a typical Dalmatian dish, scampi in tomato sauce

The bustling harbour of Makarska

The Roman amphitheatre in Pula

The church of St Donat in Zadar

HOW TO USE THIS GUIDE

THE DETAILED INFORMATION and tips given in this guide will help you to get the most out of your visit to Croatia. *Introducing Croatia* maps the country and sets it in its historical and cultural context. The six sections, one dedicated to Zagreb, describe the main sights using maps, photographs and illustrations. In Istria, Kvarner and part of Dalmatia, two languages are spoken (Croat and Italian) and two place names may refer to the same town. Where both names are officially recognized, the Croat name is given first, then the Italian in brackets. Restaurant and hotel recommendations can be found in the section *Travellers' Needs*, together with information about shopping and entertainment. The *Survival Guide* has tips on everything from transport to making a phone call, as well as other practical matters.

CROATIA AREA BY AREA

Croatia has been divided into six main areas, each one identified by its own colour code. On the inside front cover is a general map of the country showing these six areas. All the most interesting places to visit are located on the *Pictorial Map* in each chapter.

Each area can be easily identified by its colour-coded thumb tab.

1 Introduction
This section describes the character and history of each area, highlighting its development over the centuries and what it has to offer the visitor today.

2 Pictorial Map
This shows the road network and provides an illustrated overview of the whole region. The most interesting places to visit are numbered, and there are useful tips on getting around the region by car and public transport.

3 Detailed Information
All the important towns and other places to visit are described individually. They are listed in order and follow the numbering shown on the Pictorial Map. Detailed information is given about the most important sights.

The Visitors' Checklist
provides practical information
about transport, opening times,
events and the closing dates of
places of particular interest.

**4 Detailed Information
on Each Sight**
*The main attractions are listed
for each place. A map shows
the main towns, villages and
beaches on the larger islands.*

5 Main Towns
*All the main towns have an
individual section where the
museums, monuments and
other places of interest are listed.
All the sights of major interest
are located on the town map.*

The town map shows
the main roads, stations,
car parking areas and
tourist offices.

6 Street-by-Street Map
*This gives a bird's-eye view
of the key areas of interest in
the main towns and cities with
photographs and captions
describing the sights.*

7 Croatia's Top Sights
*These are given two full
pages. There are cutaways or
reconstructions of historic
buildings, maps of national
parks with information about
trails and facilities available,
and there are floorplans of the
major museums. There are also
photographs of the main sights.*

Stars indicate the sights
that no visitor should miss.

INTRODUCING
CROATIA

Putting Croatia on the Map

COVERING AN AREA OF 56,542 sq km (21,825 sq miles), Croatia has a population of around 4,535,000 with an average of 80 inhabitants per square kilometre. Since the break-up of the former Yugoslavia, and Croat independence, the country has been bordered by Slovenia, Hungary, the Union of Serbia and Montenegro, and Bosnia-Herzegovina. It is not a large country, but it has a wide variety of natural and man-made environments. From a topographical point of view the country is made up of three types of terrain. Much is mountainous, with peaks up to 2,000 m (6,560 ft) high, mostly covered with forest and pasture. The vast Pannonian Plain lies between the rivers Drava, Sava and the Danube. Coastal Croatia is nearly 600 km (372 miles) long, but over 2,000 km (1,242 miles) long when the indented coastline is taken into account, and twice that when the hundreds of islands are included.

Satellite view of Croatia

CROATIA AND EUROPE

FINLAND

NORWAY   SWEDEN   ESTONIA

ATLANTIC

UNITED
KINGDOM   DENMARK   LATVIA

IRELAND   LITHUANIA

BOSNIA

OCEAN   NETHERLANDS   BELORUSSIA

BELGIUM   GERMANY   POLAND

LUXEMBOURG   CZECH   UKRAINE
REPUBLIC   SLOVAKIA

FRANCE   AUSTRIA

SWITZERLAND   UNGHERIA

SLOVENIA   ROMANIA

PORTUGAL   ANDORRA   Zagreb

CORSICA   CROATIA   BOSNIA
HERZEGOVINA   YUGOSLAVIA   BULGARIA

SPAIN

SARDINIA   ALBANIA

ITALY   GREECE

MOROCCO   ALGERIA   TUNISIA

Győr

HUNGARY

Lake
Balaton

Čakovec

Varaždin

Koprivnica

ZAGREB

Bjelovar

Cazma   Virovitica

Daruvar   Našice   Osijek

vac

Sisak   Kutina   UNION OF
SERBIA AND
MONTENEGRO

Glina   Požega   Đakovo   Vukovar

Nova Gradiška   Vinkovci   Novi Sad

Slavonski
Brod

Banja Luka

BOSNIA
HERZEGOVINA

Knin

Drniš

Šibenik   Sinj   SARAJEVO

Split

Šolta   Brač

Hvar   Mostar

Hvar

Vis   Opuzen

Korčula

Lastovo   Mljet National
Park   Dubrovnik

KEY

✈ International airport

⛴ Ferry terminal

▬ Motorway

▬ Major road

— Railway line

⚊⚊ International border

--- Ferry route

0 kilometres   75

0 miles   50

Bari   Igoumenitsa

A PORTRAIT OF CROATIA

CROATIA FORMS A MEETING POINT *between the Mediterranean and central Europe, and between the Alps and the Pannonian Plain. Its relatively small territory is made up of a wide variety of landscapes. A stunningly beautiful country, it is slowly re-emerging from the difficult years of conflict and regaining its role as a popular holiday destination.*

Croatia seceded from the Federal Socialist Republic of Yugoslavia in 1990, following the first free elections since World War II. However, brutal conflict quickly followed. The economy collapsed and many historic monuments and treasures were damaged or destroyed in the shelling. The United Nations administered disputed territories until 1995, and the last region, Eastern Slavonia, was returned to Croatian administration only in January 1998.

The resolution of the conflict recreated a country which had lost its autonomy long ago in 1097, when the killing of King Zvonimir brought an end to the Croatian dynasty. Under King Koloman, Croatia became part of Hungary

The flags of Croatia and the European Union

and remained so for 900 years, until 1918. At the end of World War I, Croatia declared independence but, under pressure from greater powers, agreed to become part of the kingdom of Yugoslavia. From the ruins of the Habsburg empire emerged Yugoslavia: a new state of Serbs, Croats and Slovenes.

Few people live in the steep mountainous areas and as a result the forests of this region, among the most beautiful in southern Europe, are unspoilt. The coast and larger islands are more densely populated and the income from tourism is important to many. The political upheavals of the last decade of the 20th century have caused a shifting of the population and many Serbs have moved away.

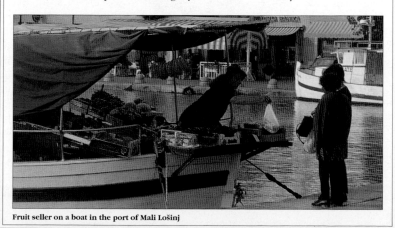

Fruit seller on a boat in the port of Mali Lošinj

◁ People strolling along Krešimirova ulica in the busy centre of Split

Fisherman mending his nets in the port of Fažana

POPULATION

According to a census carried out in early 2000 (complete statistics are not yet available), Croatia has a population of 4,535,054, of which 4,381,352 are resident. Compared with the census of 1991 there has been a 5.2 per cent fall in the population and a 7 per cent decrease in those resident. These figures, a reflection of the upheavals of the 1990s, reduce the numbers to 1968 levels. Two different factors were responsible for these changes. Firstly, the departure of about 400,000 Serbs (partially offset by the return of Croats resident in other parts of former Yugoslavia), and secondly, the emigration of many young people in search of work in other countries in Europe, America or Australia.

The tragic events of the 1990s have also altered the distribution of the population, emptying villages and concentrating populations in large urban centres. Changes to the size of many towns and cities, the result of enlarging their territorial boundaries, make detailed analysis difficult, particularly with regard to Zagreb, Rijeka, Split, Osijek and Zadar, where the population appears to have nearly doubled.

Woman in the typical costume of Konavle

ECONOMY

Manufacturing industries are concentrated in the larger cities and employ 20 per cent of the population. The service industry is being overhauled and provides employment for an increasing number of workers, mainly in the tourist sector, which has recovered after a decade of crisis: 7 per cent of the population is employed in this area.

Demand for fresh fish to supply the tourist resorts means that the fishing industry has revived and mussel farming has also expanded, in particular along the Limski Channel and around Ston. The privatization of much agricultural land, and the introduction of modern machinery and the rationalization of crops, have reduced the number of farm workers. However, the production of fruit and wine grapes has recovered, and overall quality is improving.

The urgent need to rebuild public and privately-owned buildings damaged during the recent conflict and the increasing need for tourist facilities keeps the numbers employed in the building trade high: 7 per cent of the work force.

However, in spite of an improved standard of living for most of the population, unemployment is still high. Croatia hopes to resolve most of its employment problems by joining the European Union, and by providing land, energy and labour at competitive costs. The building of a modern road network with the construction of new motorways, the modernization of the railways and plans to improve the ports will also help to alleviate high unemployment levels.

TRADITIONS AND CUSTOMS

Since the rebirth of the independent state, all kinds of traditional festivals have reappeared. These festivals, ceremonies or games commemorate historical, religious and military events. Some festivals are expressions of primitive or ancient faith, and mix Christianity with ancient pagan rites, others are linked to the religious calendar. Traditional costumes and jewellery, carefully preserved by the older generation, are worn on these occasions. The materials may sometimes be new but the designs stay faithfully traditional.

Other expressions of popular culture are the rites linked to the rhythms of farming: harvesting, bringing flocks down from the mountains, felling trees. The Feast of St Blaise, the patron saint of Dubrovnik, is magnificent. People from local and surrounding parishes gather, dressed in splendid costumes and displaying ancient banners in honour of the saint. Even the communists were unable to suppress this tradition. Another spectacular festivity is the Olympics of Ancient Sports in Brodanci, when young people parade in gold-embroidered costumes, followed by groups of musicians. Other important events are the Festival of the Bumbari in Vodnjan with its donkey race, the

One of many religious events in Split

Folk Festival in Đakovo and the Moreška and Kumpanija festivals in Korčula, commemorating battles against the Ottoman Turks.

LANGUAGE

The attempt to fuse the Croatian and Serbian languages lasted more than a century, but in 1991 the official language of Croatia became Croat, and this is now part of the constitution. The language has always been a fundamental part of Croatian identity, even under foreign domination. The people continue to use three basic dialects, štokavski in southern Croatia, čakavski around Zagreb and in the north, and kajkavski in Dalmatia. A dialect similar to Venetian is spoken along the coast.

RELIGION

Religious feeling has always been important to Croats. Religion was relegated to a secondary role during the communist period but the great sanctuaries are once again centres of spirituality. In the 1991 census, almost 90 per cent declared they were Christian (77 per cent Catholic, 11 per cent Orthodox), with a Muslim minority, mostly Bosnians, and a Protestant minority, mostly Hungarians. The Orthodox community has shrunk due to the fall in the number of Serbs.

The lively centre of Split, a popular meeting place

The Landscape and Wildlife of Croatia

A WIDE VARIETY OF LANDSCAPES can be found in Croatia, from wild uninhabited craggy gorges to steep river valleys and a stunningly beautiful indented coastline stretching into the lower Adriatic, dotted with hundreds of islands. A plateau stretches from the Istrian peninsula towards Gorski Kotar and ends in the hilly vine-growing region of Zagorje. The geological formations produced by the porous limestone terrain called karst are found in Gorski Kotar and continue to nearby Istria and the Velebit mountains, where the combination of wind, rain and rock has created strange shapes called *kukovi*. Nicknames and legends have been created by folklore for these rock formations, and for the thousands of rocky islands off the coast, remnants of an ancient mountain chain.

Seagull perched on a rocky outcrop near the island of Pag

MOUNTAINS

Mountains form 40 per cent of Croatia and rise to nearly 2,000 m (6,560 ft) high. The higher land is given over to sheep farming and the breeding of livestock. The forests are mixed, with pine, fir, chestnut and beech, depending on altitude and microclimate. The wildlife includes bears, wolves, wild boar, lynxes, badgers, foxes, roebucks and chamois. Forestry management aims to control deforestation.

The forests are a precious resource in Croatia. Thick vegetation covers more than 30 per cent of the country.

The chamois was thought to have disappeared from Croatia but there are now a dozen or so animals originating from Slovenia.

THE PLAIN

The plain is bordered by wide rivers which also define Croatia's borders for much of their length. The vast Pannonian Plain is the breadbasket of Croatia. Maize, wheat, soya and tobacco are grown here and at the fringes are vine-covered hills. At one time there were forests here, dominated by the Slavonian oak, much sought-after in Europe for the quality of its wood. A few isolated remnants of these forests can still be seen.

The oak of Slavonia, famous since ancient times, was used to build most of the ships in the Venetian and Dubrovnik fleets, because of its extraordinary strength.

The Croatian plain is one of the most fertile areas in Europe. Some agricultural produce is exported.

NATIONAL PARKS

Croatia began protecting wildlife areas of particular importance in 1949 by setting up the Plitvice Lakes National Park on the Lika plateau. A few years later, the Risnjak National Park was founded north of Rijeka, followed by the Krka National Park north of Šibenik. The Paklenica National Park, at the heart of the Velebit mountain chain, dates from 1959. In 1978 it was declared a world biosphere reserve by UNESCO and later included in the World Heritage List. It is home to over 2,400 species of plant. There are three national parks in the Adriatic: the Mljet National Park, founded in 1949, the Kornati National Park (1980) and the Brijuni National Park which dates from 1983. There are also nature reserves, oases, biotopes (environments characterized by particular conditions) and two marshes: Kopački Rit and Lonjsko Polje. This conservation policy has been richly rewarded as these reserves form some of the country's greatest tourist attractions.

Risnjak National Park with its thick forests of fir and beech

THE COAST

The coast's appearance is determined by the extent of its exposure to the fierce, northeast bora wind. Mediterranean flora flourishes on the sheltered side, with olives, lemon trees and vines. Low-growing vines are cultivated along the central part of the coast and on some of the islands, sheltered from the wind by stone walls. Two common plants along the coast and on the islands are lavender, particularly on Hvar, and broom.

The marine life is extraordinarily varied, with a wide range of species including sea-horses.

Broom *is a common sight in Croatia. In spring, it bears bright yellow flowers.*

LAKES AND RIVERS

The lakes of Croatia are not large, but some are truly spectacular, as for example those of Plitvice and those formed by the River Krka. The rivers are another of Croatia's valuable resources. The Danube, Drava, Sava, Kupa and Mura are all navigable and form international transport routes (although traffic is currently partly interrupted). The rivers abound with a variety of fish and are a big attraction for fishing enthusiasts.

Waterlilies *are in flower in late spring, particularly in Lonjsko Polje and Kopački Rit.*

Storks *live near the rivers as well as in protected nature reserves in Croatia. The wetlands make an ideal habitat for the rare black stork.*

Art and Artists in Croatia

FOR CENTURIES Croatian art has combined elements from eastern and western Europe. The coast was ruled by Venice for 400 years, and between the Middle Ages and the 17th century, Croatia was in regular contact with the other side of the Adriatic. Italian artists came to the islands to work, and the Dalmatians crossed the sea and brought Romanesque, Gothic and Renaissance styles back to their country. After the expulsion of the Turks at the end of the 17th century, many churches were rebuilt in the Baroque style, and acquired rich ornamentation. The 20th century saw the advent of Naive painting, an important artistic trend, and sculptor Ivan Meštrović was confirmed as Croatia's most famous contemporary artist *(see p155)*.

***Maria Banac*, sculpture by Ivan Meštrović**

SCULPTURE

THE ART OF SCULPTURE in Croatia has ancient origins and may have been inspired by the local stone, used to construct some of the most important Roman monuments in Pula and Split, which became models for future generations of Adriatic sculptors.

Sculpture and stone carving reached the height of expression with the Romanesque style. Dating from this time are the cathedral doors of Trogir and Split, the rose windows of Zadar and Rab, the capitals in the cloisters in Dubrovnik and Zadar, and much church statuary. The technical skills of the Renaissance period are documented in Šibenik cathedral, with masterpieces by Juraj Dalmatinac, Nikola Firentinac and Andrija Aleši.

The stonemasons should also be remembered, particularly those of Korčula. Decades of skilled work went into Korčula cathedral and the masons' work can be seen in hundreds of other towns and cities in Croatia.

Sculpture again reached a peak in the 20th century with Ivan Meštrović, the chief figure in a group of great artists which included Antun Augustinčić.

ANDREA BUVINA

All that is known of this sculptor is that he was born

Wooden panel by Andrea Buvina in Split cathedral

in Split and lived in the 13th century. The great door of the cathedral of his native city is testament to his skill. This masterpiece from 1214 consists of 28 wooden panels depicting the life of Christ, and uses simple lines allied to a wealth of detail.

MASTER RADOVAN

The sculptor Master Radovan was of Dalmatian origin and lived in the 13th century. His name appears on the door of

The door of the cathedral of Trogir by Master Radovan

the cathedral in Trogir, which he started in about 1240 and which was later completed by other artists. This complex masterpiece has columns, arches, sculpted relief figures and rich decoration. It is possible to discern scenes from the life of Christ such as the Annunciation, the Flight to Egypt, and the Martyrdom on Golgotha, while other sculptures represent the months of the year. The artist's expressive skill is revealed in the figures of Adam and Eve in particular.

JURAJ DALMATINAC

Juraj Dalmatinac, also known as Giorgio Orsini, was an ambassador for Dalmatian art, which was greatly influenced by Venice. The artist was born in Zadar in about 1400 and died in 1475. He was active in Dalmatia and in Italy as a sculptor and an architect.

Face by Dalmatinac in the cathedral of Šibenik

The cathedral of St James in Šibenik *(see pp106–7)*, to which he contributed, is regarded as one of the masterpieces of the Croatian Renaissance. Dalmatinac sculpted the faces on the upper part of the base of the apses and also the statues of Adam and Eve at either side of the Door of Lions.

ARTISTS

P AINTING IN CROATIA cannot
boast a history equal to
that of sculpture since it was
only after contact with the
Venetian school at the end
of the 16th century that
Croatian painting emerged
in Istria and Dalmatia. The
monasteries and cathedrals
commissioned Venetian
masters to make altarpieces
and in emulating these
models the great artists of
Dubrovnik developed.

In the late 17th–18th
centuries, the Baroque style
predominated in inland
Croatia in architecture as
well as art. Baroque
originated in German-
speaking areas and inspired
local artists; the Austrian
artist Ivan Ranger *(see p204)*
was a key figure. Interest in
religious paintings then
dwindled, and in the 19th
century, young artists were
inspired by pan-European
culture. In the 1930s and
40s Naive Art developed.

**Polyptych by Lovro Dobričević in
the church of St Mary of Dance**

VINCENT OD KASTAV

One of the most expressive
cycles of frescoes in Istria
bears the signature of this
Istrian painter, Vincent od
Kastav (Vincenzo da Castua),
who lived in the 15th
century. The frescoes are
hidden away in the small
church of St Mary (Sv. Marija
na Škriljinah) in Beram. The
brightly coloured frescoes, on
the side walls and the inside
façade, were painted in about
1471 with assistants and
have a primitive but vigorous
style. The *Life of
Christ and the Virgin*
has figures of saints;
the best-known
work is the *Dance
of Death,* where
Death, holding a
scythe, punishes
sinners, here
represented by all
the most powerful

people on earth (from the
pope to lords of the manor).

LOVRO DOBRIČEVIĆ

Little is known of Lovro
Marinov Dobričević (Lorenzo
De Boninis), pupil of Paolo
Veneziano, who lived in the
15th century and is regarded
as one of the most significant
exponents of the Dubrovnik
school. Two of his great
works are in Dubrovnik: the
Baptism of Christ (c.1448) is
in the Dominican Museum
and the polyptych *Virgin,
Christ and the Saints Julian
and Nicholas* (1465) is in the
church of St Mary of Dance
(Sv. Marije na Dančama).

JULIJE KLOVI

Julije Klovi (Giulio Clovio)
was one of the most famous
Renaissance
miniaturists. A
native of Croatia
(he was born
in Grižane in
1498), his most
significant works
are found
outside the
country. The
painter
developed his
craft in Venice,
and was then
summoned to work in
Rome, Mantua, Perugia and
numerous monasteries. He
died in Rome in 1578.

**Miniature
by Klovi**

Dance of Death **by Vincent od Kastav**

THE HLEBINE SCHOOL

Krsto Hegedušić (1901–75), Expressionist painter and later a Naive artist, founded a
group of artists called Zemlja ("Earth"). He encouraged the work of two amateur painters
from the village of Hlebine, near Koprivnica: Ivan Generalić and Franjo Mraz, who
depicted their local world on glass and canvas in fresh, vivid style. Together with Mirko
Virius they founded the Hlebine school which flourished from 1930 to the beginning of
World War II. Many other painters,
including Ivan Večenaj, Dragan
Gaži, Franjo Filipović and Josip
Generalić, followed their ideas,
concentrating on depicting the
lives of outcasts, the poor, and
working folk. The Hlebine school
became a worldwide phenomenon
with the 1952 Venice Biennale and
exhibitions in Brazil and Brussels.
Naive works are on show at the
Hlebine Gallery in Koprivnica and

Woodcutters **by Generalić, Museum of Naive Art, Zagreb**   the Museum of Naive Art in Zagreb.

Architecture in Croatia

CROATIAN ARCHITECTURE, LIKE ITS ART, has also been influenced by Croatia's position in Europe. Secular and religious buildings display a fusion of elements from nearby Italy and Germany and other forms originating in the Byzantine or Slavic worlds. This blending of influences was first noticeable in the time of the Romans and still continues today. Some styles became particularly important: for example the impressive cathedrals of the Adriatic coast, the legacy of many centuries of Venetian rule. In inland Croatia Baroque architecture prevails, characterized by exuberant decoration and expansive forms.

The Byzantine basilica of Euphrasius in Poreč

PRE-ROMANESQUE AND ROMANESQUE

True Croatian architecture begins with pre-Romanesque and dates back to the time of Duke Branimir (879–92), who created the first state of Croatia. Contact with the Byzantine world influenced the look of religious buildings in Istria and Dalmatia but some decorative elements reveal the first signs of Romanesque: small churches with irregular ground-plans appear in areas inhabited by Croatian tribes. The founding of Šibenik (1066) saw the first Romanesque buildings, introduced by the Cistercians. The style spread and remained popular until the end of the 16th century, and three-aisle cathedrals with apses were built as well as monasteries with cloisters, public buildings, town halls and loggias.

The façade consists of vertical and horizontal lines: the upper order is decorated with blind arcades and rose windows.

The church of St Anastasia in Zadar (see p92), *founded in the 9th century but rebuilt in the 12th–13th, shows the links between Croatian and Italian Romanesque, particularly in the façade, similar to churches found in Pisa and Lucca in Italy.*

Romanesque rose window

The arched main door, richly decorated

The church of the Holy Cross in Nin (see p98), *one of the most interesting examples of pre-Romanesque, and also Croatia's first cathedral, was built in the 9th century. It has a Greek cross ground-plan with three apses. It is positioned to ensure that the sun's rays fall in pre-planned positions on the floor and act as a clock.*

GOTHIC

The Gothic style, more than any other in Croatia, is lasting evidence of the long rule of the Venetians along the Istrian and Dalmatian coasts. It developed following the Venetian conquest of the Adriatic coast (1420) and is a fundamental expression of the close contact that was established. Venetian Gothic not only influenced the design of Dalmatian and Istrian churches but also mansions in Pula, Rab, Pag, Zadar, Šibenik and Split.

The door with an ogival arch is decorated with thin spiral columns and has two lions on the corbel.

Rose window

Façade of the Town Hall in Split

The cathedral of St Mark in Korčula (see p130) *is of Romanesque origins – the bell tower is evidence of this. The façade shows similarities with churches in Puglia in southern Italy. Gothic elements include the pointed arches over the entrance door, which was the work of Bonino of Milan.*

RENAISSANCE

The Renaissance style was only able to develop in those parts of the country which did not fall under Turkish rule. The most important architects and artists of the time were Juraj Dalmatinac *(see p18)*, Nikola Firentinac and Andrija Aleši, who worked mainly along the Adriatic coast. They were all involved in the construction of churches and public buildings. The cathedral of St James in Šibenik *(see pp106–7)* became a model for the churches of St Stephen in Hvar, St Mary in Zadar and St Saviour in Dubrovnik. Renaissance buildings also appeared in the north of Croatia, both in the form of private residences (Varaždin and Čakovec) and castles (Trakošćan and Veliki Tabor).

The second storey, with windows and a statue of the city's patron saint, St Blaise, in the centre, was a later addition.

The windows in Venetian Gothic symbolize the ties between Dubrovnik and Venice.

Sponza Palace in Dubrovnik (see p142) *has both Gothic and Renaissance elements, a reflection of the time it took to build. It was begun in 1312 (the beautiful Gothic windows on the first floor date from this period) and remodelled in 1516–22, when the Renaissance arcaded loggia on the ground floor was added.*

BAROQUE

This was the style that characterized the legitimization of Christian worship in Croatia after the expulsion of the Turks at the end of the 17th century. The signs of Ottoman rule were eradicated and architects, mainly of German extraction, constructed public and private buildings, enriching them with ornate decorations equal to those of the churches, castles and sanctuaries. The most notable examples of the Baroque style can be found in Varaždin, Požega, Osijek, Križevci, Ludbreg and Krapina.

Vojković-Oršić Palace, *now home of the Museum of Croatian History* (see p156), *is one of many fine Baroque buildings in Zagreb. The façade and interior have the sumptuous decorations of the time with elegant columns, scalloped windows and a decorated tympanum.*

MODERNISM

By the 19th century Zagreb had become the centre of political and cultural life in Croatia, which gave it a prominent role as leader in the architectural field. Much experimentation took place in the following century in the capital, inspired first by the Viennese Secession style and later by Modernism. The church of St Blaise and Villa Krauss are interesting examples of the latter style.

The Neo-Renaissance Mimara Museum in Zagreb

This typically elegant building is functional and symmetrical

The decorations in Secession style are stylized and not figurative.

On the façade are sculptures and bas reliefs by the Croatian artists Robert Frangeš-Mihanović and Rudolf Valdec.

The former National and University Library *in the centre of Marulić Square in Zagreb was designed by a local architect, Rudolf Lubinsky. It is regarded as the most significant work in the Secession style in Croatia.*

CROATIA THROUGH THE YEAR

THE UPHEAVALS of the decade from 1991–2000 inevitably affected the calendar of events which characterizes the cultural life of Croatia. However, concerts, theatre seasons and sporting events have now largely been resumed along with religious festivals and events linked to local traditions. The different stages in the agricultural year, such as the grape

Typical costume of Pag

harvest, the threshing, fishing or hunting seasons, are also marked. In addition, every town celebrates its patron saint's day and the "town's day", which is linked to episodes in the town's history. Zagreb offers a rich calendar of cultural events all through the year, while the festivals in the towns and villages along the coast are generally held during the summer season.

SPRING

THE ARRIVAL of spring in Croatia coincides with a series of important dates in the religious calendar. Spring brings warmer weather and also sees the beginning of a series of festivals and events which continue throughout the summer. Catholic churches are especially busy around Easter time, with its associated rituals.

Procession during Holy Week on the island of Korčula

MARCH

Holy Week *(Easter)*. On Korčula Easter is celebrated with processions of brotherhoods performing mystery plays and singing.

APRIL

Sonnet Day of Hanibal Lucić, Hvar *(mid-Apr)*. Poetry reading dedicated to

the great 16th-century local poet. European and Croatian poets participate.
Musical Biennial of Zagreb *(second half of Apr)*. Festival of modern music.
St George's Day, Senj *(23 Apr)*.
St Vincent's Day, Korčula *(28 Apr)*. The Kumpanija dance which commemorates an ancient battle between enemy armies is performed. At the finale local girls in costume dance in a circle.

MAY

Regatta Rovinj–Pesaro–Rovinj, Rovinj.
Meeting of Puppet Theatres, Osijek *(early May)*. Performances of professional and amateur puppet theatre companies.
Tournament of Rab *(9 May)*. Parade of costumed riders with crossbows.
Festival of the Small Theatre, Rijeka *(first half of May)*. Groups from all over Europe participate.
Josip Štolcer Slavenski Memorial, Čakovec *(first half of May)*. Musical festival dedicated to the great 20th-century Croatian composer.
Festival of Croatian Tambour Music, Osijek *(mid-May)*. Festival of ancient music with period instruments, including the tambour.
International Choir Competition, Zadar *(end May)*. Groups from all over Europe participate.

Festival of Amateur Film and Video, Požega *(end May)*. Screenings of short amateur films and videos.

SUMMER

AS THIS IS THE SEASON when most tourists visit Croatia, particularly Istria and Dalmatia, this is also the period when the calendar of events is busiest. There are festivals dedicated to music, theatre and dance, as well as many traditional festivals. The folk festivals held throughout the summer are particularly colourful events.

JUNE

Pula Opera Festival, Pula *(all summer)*. Opera season in the Roman amphitheatre.
Festival of the Harmony of Dalmatia, Omiš. Celebration of ancient and traditional folk songs and music.
Brodsko Kolo, Slavonski Brod *(mid-Jun)*. Displays of folk dancing in costume, shows and exhibitions of regional produce.

The festival of Brodsko Kolo, Slavonski Brod

AVERAGE DAILY HOURS OF SUNSHINE

Hours

Jan Feb Mar Apr May Jun Jul Aug Sep Oct Nov Dec

Sunshine
The Dalmatian coast is one of the sunniest parts of Europe, and the island of Hvar holds the record with its 2,700 hours of sun a year. The summers along the coast are hot and dry, while the inland areas have a continental climate with hot summers and cold winters.

Djakovski Vezovi, a folklore and embroidery festival in Đakovo

International Youth Festival of Music, Grožnjan *(mid-Jun–mid-Sep)*. Young artists from every country participate, not just musicians.
Summer Festival, Hvar *(second half of Jun–end Sep)*. Music, theatre, folklore and dancing.
Summer of Margherita, Bakar *(last week of Jun)*. Concerts and performances in the čakavski dialect.
International Children's Festival, Šibenik *(end Jun–beginning Jul)*. Festival dedicated to the creativity of the very young. Music, dance, theatre and film.

JULY

Labin Summer Festival, Labin *(Jul–Aug)*. Classical concerts, folk music.
Concerts in the Basilica of Euphrasius, Poreč *(Jul–mid Sep)*. Performances of church and secular music given by Croatian and European musicians.
Dance Week, Zagreb *(beginning Jul)*. International

festival of dance, movement and mime, organized in collaboration with European associations.
Tournament of Rab *(20 Jul)*. A re-enactment of a tournament with riders in costume and crossbow contests. The tournament is also held in May.
Music Festival, Zadar *(beginning Jul–beginning Aug)*. Church, theatre and instrumental music.
Djakovski Vezovi, Đakovo *(first week of Jul)*. Folklore displays and exhibition of local embroidery.
Festival of Satire, Zagreb *(first half of Jul)*. International festival celebrating the satirical.
Osor Music Festival, Osor *(mid-Jul–mid-Aug)*. Chamber music.
Split Summer *(mid-Jul–mid-Aug)*. A programme of opera, concerts, dance, theatre and performances of the first plays written in the Croatian language.
International Festival of Theatre, Pula *(mid-Jul–mid-Aug)*. Multimedia festival

with the participation of other European groups.
Dubrovnik Summer Festival, Dubrovnik *(mid-Jul–end Aug)*. The oldest international festival in Croatia: music, theatre, folklore, ballet, with performers from many countries.
Krk Summer Festival, Krk *(mid-Jul–end Aug)*. Music and prose, concerts, ballet, performances by young artists and folklore.
St Theodore's Day, Korčula *(27 Jul)*. The Moreška, a dance re-enacting a battle between Christians and Muslims.
International Tennis Tournament, Umag *(end Jul)*.
Pag Carnival, Pag *(last day of Jul)*. Traditional dancing, *kolo*, and various shows with the local people in traditional costumes.
International Folklore Festival, Zagreb *(end Jul)*. Croatian music and dance with international guests.

The Moreška dance,
St Theodore's Day, Korčula

AVERAGE MONTHLY RAINFALL

mm | | | | | | | | | | | | inches
300 | | | | | | | | | | | | 12
240 | | | | | | | | | | | | 10
180 | | | | | | | | | | | | 8
| | | | | | | | | | | | 6
120 | | | | | | | | | | | |
60 | | | | | | | | | | | | 4
| | | | | | | | | | | | 2
0 | | | | | | | | | | | | 0
Jan Feb Mar Apr May Jun Jul Aug Sep Oct Nov Dec

Rainfall
Rain is sparse along the coast, particularly in summer, when there is often the threat of drought. However, in the mountains, rain and snow are plentiful. In northeastern parts of the country there may be summer thunderstorms. Winter brings snow.

Costumed jousters on horseback during the folk festival, Sinj

AUGUST

Summer Carnival, Novi Vinodolski *(Aug)*.
Festival of the Bumbari, Vodnjan *(Aug)*. "Bumbari" is what the local people call themselves. A folk festival in costume with an unusual donkey race and the preparation of *crostoli*, cakes of Venetian origin.
Olympics of Ancient Sports, Brođanci *(Aug)*. Folk festival with traditional costumes and musicians playing in the streets.
Mediterranean Symposium of Sculpture, Labin *(Aug–Sep)*. A meeting place for artists from all over the world since the 1960s.
Baljanska Noć, Bale *(first Sun in Aug)*. Festival of the city.
Trka na prstenac, Barban *(first Sun in Aug)*. Jousting tournament, dating back as far as 1696.

Sinjska Alka, Sinj *(beginning Aug)*. Folklore festival commemorating victory over the Turks, with jousting competitions for horse riders. Parades, dancing, folk music and displays of regional produce.
St Roch's Day, Žrnovo and Postrana (on Korčula) *(16 Aug)*. Events include the Mostra, a traditional sword dance. At one time the festivities ended with the sacrifice of an ox.

Festival of Vinkovačke Jeseni, Vinkovci

AUTUMN

VISITING Croatia in this season means there are fewer crowds, even along the busy Adriatic coast. However this season also offers an unexpectedly rich and varied calendar of events. Many of the events are cultural but there are also several festivals celebrating wine and food – offering an ideal opportunity to discover some of the local produce of this country.

SEPTEMBER

International Doll Festival, Zagreb *(beginning Sep)*.
Vinkovačke Jeseni, Vinkovci *(Sep–Oct)*. Festival of music and folk traditions. Parades in costume.
Rovinj Art Programme, Rovinj *(second half of Sep)*. Multimedia festival with the participation of international artists.
Baroque Evenings in Varaždin, Varaždin cathedral *(second half of Sep–first half of Oct)*. Festival of Baroque music with the participation of top Croatian and European musicians.
Grape Festival, Buje *(last Sun in Sep)*.
Festival of New Cinema, Dubrovnik *(end Sep–beginning Oct)*. The presentation of new films and videos by amateur filmmakers.
Lace Exhibition, Lepoglava *(Sep)*.

AVERAGE MONTHLY TEMPERATURE

°C / °F

30 · 85
25 · 75
20 · 65
15 ·
10 · 55
5 · 45
0 · 32

Jan Feb Mar Apr May Jun Jul Aug Sep Oct Nov Dec

Temperature
The climate in Croatia is typically Mediterranean along the coast, with mild winters and hot, dry summers. Inland the climate is continental with hot summers and cold winters. The mountainous areas have an alpine climate.

Exhibition of traditional hand-made lace, still made according to ancient methods.

OCTOBER

Dora Pejačević Memorial, Našice *(Oct)*. Music festival commemorating this composer, with concerts, performances by artists and competitions.
Bela Nedeja, Kastav *(first Sun in Oct)*. Wine festival.
Maronada, Lovran *(first Sun in Oct)*. Chestnut festival.
Triennial of Ceramics, Zagreb *(mid-Oct–mid-Nov)*. Ceramics festival.

NOVEMBER

International Music Festival, Pula *(first half of Nov)*. Musicians from all over the world come to participate in this music festival.

The Town's Day, Lipik *(4 Nov)*. Traditional festival celebrating the town.

WINTER

THE COLD makes itself felt throughout Croatia, with the temperatures in Zagreb and Slavonia dropping well below freezing point and the cold bora wind sweeping across Istria and Dalmatia. But Croatians still love to go out and enjoy themselves and attend cultural events.

DECEMBER

The Town's Day, Osijek *(2 Dec)*. Celebration of Osijek's main feast day with music and dancing.

JANUARY

International Competition for Young Pianists, Osijek *(second half of Jan)*. For young musicians under 21.

FEBRUARY

Shrovetide Sezona, Kraljevica. Traditional masked ball.
Carnival of Rijeka, Rijeka. Colourful parade in elaborate costumes.
Carnival of the Riviera, Opatija.
International Competition for Young Violinists, Zagreb *(first half of Feb)*. For violinists under 30.
Carnival, Lastovo.
Feast of St Blaise, Dubrovnik *(2 Feb)*. Processions celebrating town's saint.

Costume at the Carnival of Lastovo

CROATIAN HOLIDAYS

New Year's Day 1 Jan
Epiphany 6 Jan
Easter Sunday and Monday Mar or Apr
Labour Day 1 May
Day of the Republic 30 May
Anti-Fascist Victory Day 22 Jun
National Independence Day 5 Aug
Assumption Day 15 Aug
All Saints' Day 1 Nov
Christmas 25 Dec
Boxing Day 26 Dec

A Baroque music ensemble playing in the cathedral, Varaždin

THE HISTORY OF CROATIA

S ITUATED BETWEEN *eastern and western Europe, Croatia has long been a land of passage but also a point of contact between different worlds and cultures. Diverse events and cultural influences have all contributed to the country's history. Croatia is particularly proud of its close ties to the West; for more than a century, parts of the country struggled to free themselves from harsh Turkish domination. The history of Croatia goes back almost as far as man's first appearance on earth.*

PREHISTORY

Early in the 19th century ancient human remains were found at Krapina in the north of Croatia. Dating from the Neanderthal period, "Krapina man" places human presence in Croatia in the middle-Palaeolithic. Other traces of prehistoric cultures have been found in Croatia. The richest site is probably Vučedol, near Vukovar, where the Neolithic "Vučedol Dove" *(see p186)* was found.

Clay vase found in Vučedol, 2800–2500 BC

THE ILLYRIANS

Around 1200 BC, tribes of Indo-European origin settled on the Pannonian Plain, the larger islands and along the coast. The tribes had different names (Istrians, Liburnians, Dalmatians, Japods) depending on where they settled, but the area was known under one name, Illyria. They traded amber and had dealings with other Mediterranean people and northern European traders. Traces of ancient walls on some hilltops confirm their presence.

THE CELTS

In the 4th century BC, the Celts began to search for new lands when Gaul became over-populated. Some tribes followed the River Danube to the present-day Bohemia, some went as far as the Greek border. In the same period the Greeks founded fortified colonies on some Dalmatian islands including Vis and Hvar and in the area of Trogir and Salona. Greek historians claim the Celts fought against Alexander the Great in 335 BC on the southern banks of the Danube. A century later, they attacked Delphi and on their return stopped at the Paludes Volcae, an area between the rivers Sava, Drava and Danube. These people were called Scordisci and mixed with the Illyrians. The Celts and Illyrians were defeated by the Romans in the 2nd century BC. After a number of rebellions, some people were expelled, but those remaining adopted Roman customs and gave Rome no fewer than six Emperors.

TIMELINE

50,000–30,000 BC
Homo sapiens neanderthalensis lives at Krapina

Krapina man, dating from the middle-Palaeolithic

1200 BC
Illyrian settlement in the Balkans

279 BC Celts, now settled in the Balkans, defeat the Greeks

6500 BC

3500 BC

500 BC

6000–2500 BC
Neolithic: sites of Danilo, Hvar, Butmir

2200-1800 BC
Aeneolithic: sites of Lasinje and Vučedol

Bronze cap 7th–6th centuries BC

390 BC Dionysius the Elder of Syracuse captures the island of Vis and founds an administrative post

◁ St Paul and St Blaise, patron saint of Dubrovnik, in a triptych by Nikola Božidarević

THE ROMAN CONQUEST

The Romans conquered Croatia at different times and in different ways. First, they wanted to put an end to attacks on their merchant ships, which were falling into the hands

Symbol of the Roman Empire, Sisak

of the Liburnians or the Dalmatians, so they subdued the coastal towns by landing Roman legions transported by the fleet. The first battle took place in 229 BC, when Teuta, the queen of the Illyrians, put to death a Roman ambassador who had tried to persuade her to put an end to the acts of piracy. Roman revenge was fierce and the towns of Epidaurum, Lissa and Pharos were attacked, conquered and forced to pay taxes to Rome. However, despite promises to the contrary, acts of piracy continued and Rome decided to deploy its legions based in Aquileia, east of Venice, a fortified town founded in 181 BC.

The legions succeeded in subduing Istria, a process completed by 177 BC. Twenty years later Publius Scipio Nasica inflicted the first defeat on the Dalmatians at Delminium and again on the Dalmatians and the Japods who inhabited the area of the delta of the River Neretva. In 107 BC the Romans defeated the Scordisci and the Illyrians and conquered the town of Segestica (Sisak). In 87 BC another war broke out between the Romans and the Illyrians which lasted for three years and was won by the Romans. In 48 BC the Illyrians sided with Pompey in the fight against Caesar, providing ships and men.

Pompey's defeat also at first appeared to be the decisive defeat of the Illyrians. However, many Illyrians, still determined to fight, fled to inland forests not occupied by the Romans. A few decades later, in 6 AD, the Illyrian people staged their greatest united rebellion yet, under the command of Batone. The first battles were won by the Illyrians who soon began to march towards Italy. After three further years of war, the Romans managed to get the better of Batone's exhausted, famished army, thanks to better military organization.

Over the years that followed, Caesar Augustus made the Balkans part of the Roman Empire. After a military campaign waged by Tiberius and completed in 12 AD, the Illyrian defences were dismantled and cities were founded, linked by roads wide enough for marching armies. The inhabitants became Roman citizens and were allowed to stand for public office. No fewer than six Roman emperors were of Illyrian origin, including Septimius Severus, Aurelian, Claudius II, Probus and Diocletian.

ROMAN ROADS

The roads were the first great public works built by the Romans. They allowed them to move legions

The Tabula Peutingeriana showing Roman roads

TIMELINE

229 BC The Roman army destroys Illyrian forts, subdues the Greek colonies of Lissa and Pharos and forces Illyrians to pay taxes

107 BC Decisive Roman victory over the Scordisci who are driven from the region; Rome owes the victory to Quintus Minucius Rufus

300 BC   200 BC   100 BC

177 BC The Roman fleet is attacked by Istrians; Rome sends an army which defeats them and drives them out

One of the many Roman fragments from the city of Sisak

119 BC The Dalmatian Lucius Metellus defeats the Scordisci and Dalmatian tribes near Segestica (Sisak); Romans settle in Salona and begin work on the Via Gabina from Salona to Andretium quickly and in fact the Roman road network remained the principal means of communication in this part of the Balkans for many centuries.

Two important arteries led from Aquileia: one towards the Istrian peninsula to Pula, the other in the direction of Aemona (Ljubljana). The main communication link in Dalmatia began in Aenona (Nin), went on to Zadar and continued, connecting Scardona (Skradin), Tragurium (Trogir), Salona, Narona, Epidaurum (Cavtat) and finally Catarum (Kotor). Other roads branched off inland from this coastal road: the busiest was that from Salona which went towards present-day Bosnia, through Klis and Sinj, near the town of Aequum (Čitluk). Another road followed the river Narenta (Neretva) to Sirmium, the present-day Sremska Mitrovica, which would become one of the capitals of the Roman Empire.

The inland roads were no less important: these followed the rivers Sava, Drava and the Danube. In the centre of Pannonia, one town which grew in importance was Siscia (Sisak), from which roads led towards Andautonia (Šćitarjevo), Mursa (Osijek), Cuccium (Ilok), Marsonia (Vinkovci) and the thermal spas of Aquae Salissae (Daruvar), Aquae Valissae (Lipik) and Aquae Iasae (Varaždinske Toplice), which were used by the emperors.

Pula in Roman times, in an engraving from 1819

Relief in the Baths in Varaždinske Toplice

the existing Illyrian towns on the main islands and along the coast were turned into Roman towns. The main towns were Senia (Senj), Aenona (Nin), Jadar (Zadar), Delminium (now a village east of Salona with few remains), Promona (a village near Makarska, with parts of the Roman walls), Burnum (the remains of the ancient town are near Kistanje along the road between Knin and Benkovac), Blandona (which no longer exists, near the lake of Vrana), Scardona (today Skradin), Narona (at the mouth of the Neretva near Vid), Tragurium (Trogir) and lastly, Salona (near Split). The towns had walls, forums, triumphal arches and aqueducts, the remains of which can often still be seen. The best-preserved aqueduct, built to serve Salona, was extended by Diocletian as far as Split and is, for the most part, still in use.

The principal Roman monuments remaining today in Croatia are in Pula, with its magnificent Roman amphitheatre *(see pp60–61)*, and in Split, site of the extraordinary Palace of Diocletian *(see pp118–119)*.

FOUNDING OF TOWNS

The Romans initially founded the Istrian towns of Poreč, Rovinj and Pula, which became a place of great importance in the 2nd century. Later

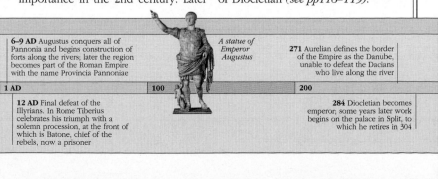

6–9 AD Augustus conquers all of Pannonia and begins construction of forts along the rivers; later the region becomes part of the Roman Empire with the name Provincia Pannoniae

A statue of Emperor Augustus

271 Aurelian defines the border of the Empire as the Danube, unable to defeat the Dacians who live along the river

| 1 AD | 100 | 200 |

12 AD Final defeat of the Illyrians. In Rome Tiberius celebrates his triumph with a solemn procession, at the front of which is Batone, chief of the rebels, now a prisoner

284 Diocletian becomes emperor; some years later work begins on the palace in Split, to which he retires in 304

Aerial view of the Roman ruins of the ancient city of Salona, destroyed in 614

THE BARBARIAN INVASIONS AND THE CRISIS OF THE ROMAN EMPIRE

In 378, after a century of relative peace, the Goths invaded Pannonia and then turned towards Italy. From that time, and for the entire 5th century, the Balkans were attacked by the Huns, Vandals, Visigoths and Longobards which finally caused the fall of the Roman empire in 476.

THE AVARS AND SLAVS IN THE BALKANS

The beginning of the 6th century saw invasion by the Avars, who were followed by other Slavic tribes. Those Roman inhabitants who did not manage to flee to the mountains or the islands were captured and sold as slaves. In 582 the Avars conquered and destroyed Sirmium (Sremska Mitrovica), one of the ancient capitals of the Roman Empire. Later they also subdued other nomadic tribes and organized a powerful army to

conquer Constantinople, but they were defeated by the Byzantines. Some of the troops returned to the Asiatic steppes, while others settled between the Danube and Tisza rivers, leaving the field clear for the Slavs who occupied Moravia and Bohemia to push southwards and towards the Adriatic, conquering all the Roman cities and destroying Salona (614). The Slavs settled in the countryside or in what remained of the sacked cities. These people cultivated the land and bred livestock and formed extended family groups *(zadruge)* with a *županj* at the head of each.

THE BULGARS AND THE BYZANTINE RECONQUEST

The Slavs' expansion to the south was halted by the Bulgars, a people of Turkish origin, who settled along the final stretch of the Danube. After the fall of the Western Empire, Byzantium attempted to reconquer

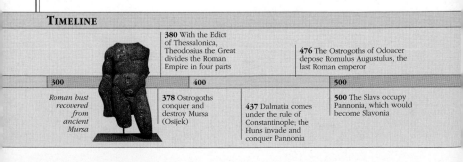

TIMELINE

380 With the Edict of Thessalonica, Theodosius the Great divides the Roman Empire in four parts

476 The Ostrogoths of Odoacer depose Romulus Augustulus, the last Roman emperor

| 300 | 400 | 500 |

Roman bust recovered from ancient Mursa

378 Ostrogoths conquer and destroy Mursa (Osijek)

437 Dalmatia comes under the rule of Constantinople; the Huns invade and conquer Pannonia

500 The Slavs occupy Pannonia, which would become Slavonia the Balkans and inflicted various defeats on the Slavs, while at the same time trying to make them part of the empire. The Byzantine fleet was able to move the army rapidly and in this way Greece, part of Macedonia and the Dalmatian islands and cities were retaken. Inland areas remained in Slav possession.

THE CROATS

At the beginning of the 7th century, perhaps summoned by the Byzantine emperor Heraclius, the Croats, a Slavic people possibly from what is now Iran, settled in upper Pannonia and Dalmatia, mixing with the native Roman people or refugees from the interior. In the inland regions, in the 8th and 9th centuries, the Croats set up territorial bases, while the coastal cities and the islands were governed by Byzantine officials with a fleet based in Zadar. In the 9th century, the Croats established a fledgling state in a hilly area now called Biskupija on the Dalmatian plateau, far from the Byzantine-controlled coast and away from central Croatia, subject to the Franks. Several churches were built here and the small settlement was named Pet Krikvah Polje. Recent archaeological digs have unearthed the foundations of religious buildings. The finds are now in Split and Knin.

THE FRANKS

Towards the end of the 8th century, the Franks led by Charlemagne succeeded in conquering what is now northern Croatia, Bohemia, Istria, Slovenia and part of

Foundations of one of the churches in Biskupija

Dalmatia. The area was divided into counties which were entrusted to loyal nobles or bishops. The Aquileian patriarch assumed particular importance for these lands when, in the 9th century, he sent monks and priests from Byzantium to spread the gospel and convert the Croats to Christianity. Among the priests were Cyril and Methodius, who devised Glagolitic script to spread the word in a language intelligible to the Slavs (*see pp32–3*).

THE FIRST CROATIAN TOWNS

During the 8th and early 9th centuries, the first Croatian towns were built next to the Byzantine-governed towns. Many (Dubrovnik, Zadar, Split and Trogir) were inhabited by people of mainly Roman origin. Biograd was founded near Zadar, and the town of Knin was repopulated by Croats under Prince Višeslav. Later, the town of Šibenik was founded. In Pannonia, the Roman town of Siscia (now Sisak) and the town of Mursa (Osijek) were revived by Prince Voinomir.

The baptismal font of Prince Višeslav, found near Nin

---

614 The Slavs and Avars conquer and destroy Salona; the Roman population seeks refuge in Split and the nearby islands

From 820 Croats found the cities of Biograd, Šibenik and Knin; Sinj and Osijek revive

600	700	800

Early 7th century The Croats settle in upper Pannonia and Dalmatia

799 Charlemagne defeats and subdues Croats in Laurana (Lovran); beginning of Croats' conversion to Christianity. Their cultural centre is in Aenona (Nin); first writing in Croat appears

Bust of Charlemagne (742–814)

Cyril and Methodius

THE TWO KEY FIGURES in the process of converting the Slav population to Christianity were the brothers Cyril (827–69) and Methodius (815–85). They were the sons of a Byzantine army officer and were born in Thessalonica, where they learnt several languages, including Slavic. The city, at that time Byzantine territory, was one of the most cosmopolitan in the Mediterranean. Initially, the two brothers took up different careers, but both eventually became monks. In 863 Emperor Michael III of Byzantium sent the two brothers to Moravia to spread the Slavonic (rather than Latin) liturgy among the people. The two men devised the Glagolitic alphabet to represent the Slav tongue, and translated religious texts. Croatian priests, especially along the coast, adopted Glagolitic and texts survive in a number of places. Glagolitic was a forerunner of Cyrillic script, named after Cyril.

The priests, Cyril and Methodius among them, were received in Rome by the pope with great solemnity.

Methodius *followed an administrative and military career, later entering a monastery. In 869 he was invited to Prague as the Archbishop of Moravia and Pannonia and the papal delegate to the Slav population. Here he undertook evangelical work, and completed the translation of the Bible into Slavonic.*

Methodius and his brother presented the pope with the relics of St Clement, the third Roman pope, who had died in the Crimea in the year 102.

The Glagolitic Alphabet *is composed of 40 letters, arranged in a sequence based on the Greek alphabet. Extra signs were added to represent particular sounds in the Slavic language, which are not found in Greek.*

The Croat population's acceptance *of Christianity soon became evident in the country's artworks and crafts. The working of stone and gold was already a traditional craft, but was now used for sacred objects. A primitive representation of the figure of Christ can be seen in this small cross from Zadar, dating from the 9th century.*

The use of Glagolitic script spread among the Slavonic clergy. Although banned from Roman-controlled territories, it was used for centuries in more far-flung monasteries.

Cyril and Methodius became patron saints of mainland Europe in 1979. Many churches, centres of religious studies, university institutions and libraries, including that of Bulgaria, are dedicated to Cyril, often with Methodius.

Cyril, whose real name was Constantine (he changed his name in Rome when he became a monk), dedicated himself to humanist studies. He was a teacher of philosophy and later responsible for the Library of Byzantium, becoming famous for his work. He died in Rome in 869.

CYRIL AND METHODIUS IN ROME

In 867, the two brothers were invited to Rome by Pope Hadrian II. Convinced by their cause, the pope approved the use of Slavonic language in liturgy. After his return to Moravia, Methodius had to face the hostility of the Aquileia patriarch and the Archbishop of Salzburg who wanted to reserve the Slavs' conversion to Christianity for priests of German origin. Methodius was arrested, tortured and only freed 15 months later after intervention by Pope John VIII.

TIMELINE

863 King Ratoslav invites Cyril and Methodius to Moravia to help convert the local population to Christianity

869 Cyril, sick, retires to a monastery in Rome where he dies shortly after. Methodius is nominated Archbishop of Pannonia and Moravia and the papal delegate to the Slav population. Methodius moves to Prague

893 Glagolitic is altered, introducing Greek characters: the new Cyrillic alphabet spreads among Serbs, Macedonians and Russians.

860	870	880	890

866 Cyril and Methodius translate the Gospel and sacred texts into Slavonic and devise Glagolitic script. Slavonic liturgy is introduced to Bohemia

867 Cyril and Methodius are invited to Rome by Pope Hadrian II, who agrees to the use of Slavonic in liturgy

885 Pope Stephen V forbids the use of the Slavonic language in liturgy

Mosaic on the tomb of Cyril

THE HUNGARIANS

The situation in the Balkans seemed stable enough towards the end of the 9th century. However, Hungarians from the Urals came to Europe and, under the leadership of King Arpad, settled along the middle stretches of the Danube and in the valleys of Transylvania, forcing out the Slavs and other tribes. They carried out military raids in Italy and Austria but were defeated in 955 by Emperor Otto II at Lechenfeld, on the plain near Ljubljana, and were forced to retreat to what are today the borders of Hungary and Transylvania. This Hungarian invasion was the last great invasion of the first millennium.

Monument to the first Croat king, Tomislav

THE KINGDOM OF THE CROATS

In the meantime, in 845, under Prince Trpimir, the Croats obtained a tacit autonomy from the Franks and formed a state which also controlled part of Dalmatia. This was recognized by the pope while Duke Branimir (879–92) was its leader. Prince Tomislav was crowned king in 925 and his death, in 928, was followed by years of anarchy until King Petar Krešimir IV (1058–74) came to power and united Croatia. Krešimir also conquered the

Relief of King Zvonimir in the baptistry of St John in Split

islands of Dalmatia. In 1054, with the schism of the Roman and Byzantine churches, Croatia sided with Rome. After the death of Petar Krešimir IV, his successor Zvonimir, who had married the sister of the Hungarian king Ladislaus, was crowned king by Pope Gregory VII and declared himself subject to Rome. The Croat nobles refused to accept this and killed Zvonimir in 1089.

THE UNION WITH HUNGARY

Claiming the right of succession, Koloman (1102–1116), the Hungarian king, came to power after Ladislaus. He conquered Croatia and was crowned king of Dalmatia and Croatia. In 1102 an agreement united the two states under one dynasty. A Croatian parliament (Sabor) was set up, to be ruled by a royally appointed Ban (governor), and the state was divided into counties governed by Croatian and Hungarian nobles. In the following century, to deal with the Tartar raids, King Bela IV reorganized the state into two parts (Croatia and Slavonia), each ruled by a Ban. New cities were founded and some were granted the privileges of a free city.

THE ROYAL FREE CITIES

These cities, defended by walls, moats and towers, were built mainly in Pannonia and the northern counties. Varaždin, founded at this time, became one of the area's busiest trading centres and, for a long period, the seat of the Sabor. The cities which emerged from the ruins

TIMELINE

896 Hungarians settle between the Tisza and the Danube	**901** Prince Tomislav defeats the Hungarians and forces them beyond the Sava. He obtains from Byzantium the authority to administer the cities of Dalmatia	**956** Branimir, prince of Croatia, rebels against the Byzantines. He obtains the title of king of Croatia with the pope's blessing

850	900	950	1000

899 Hungarians enter the Balkans and destroy the cities of the Croats, who seek refuge in Dalmatia	**930** The Byzantines renew the union with the coastal towns and cities who pay taxes to the emperor **925** Tomislav becomes king of the Croats with the pope's blessing	**1000** Venice's first armed naval expedition against pirates near mouth of Neretva river; towns on islands and coast of Istria and Dalmatia declare allegiance to Venice

The Golden Bull of 1242 declaring Zagreb (Gradec) a Free Royal City

Croatia, was enlarged and given a fort, as were Klis, Knin and Sinj in Dalmatia. Several noble families were also given the task of building and manning forts, as was the case with the Bribir counts, who moved to Zrin (taking the name of Zrinski). This intense programme strengthened a state which was threatened on many sides: after the danger of the Tartars had passed, threat of a Turkish invasion loomed.

of old Roman towns were fortified: as in Križevci, proclaimed a royal city in 1252, Koprivnica, declared a free town in 1356, and Ludbreg, which became a free town in 1320 and played an important role in the region's defences. The lower stretch of the Drava was strengthened, with a rebuilt Sisak and, further south, a new Slavonski Brod. Zagreb became a free royal city and seat of the Sabor in 1242; Vukovar became a free town in 1231. Thanks to tax advantages and non-subjection to feudal lords, these towns grew in importance and began to attract foreign merchants and artisans.

THE DEFENCES

King Bela IV built forts in strategic positions which were directly dependent on royal power or granted to the great feudal lords. Impressive ruins remain of these forts, including the famous one of Ružica near Orahovica in Slavonia. Samobor, in central

VENICE, ISTRIA AND DALMATIA

The Adriatic coast fared differently; its fate was linked to that of Venice. Much of Istria belonged to the Aquileian patriarchate, which held civil and ecclesiastical jurisdiction. From the year 1000, many coastal towns had agreements of mutual assistance with Venice, which had a powerful fleet for defence against attacks by pirates. Venice needed the Istrian cities, which often had fortified ports, for mooring their merchant fleets which plied the Croatian coast on their expeditions to the East. In the 13th century, some cities asked to come under Venetian rule for defence reasons, a process which in most cases took place peacefully. In Zadar, however, two warring factions forced Venice to employ crusaders on their way to the Holy Land to subdue the city (1202). In 1204 Zadar surrendered, and a year later Venice also conquered Istria and the city of Dubrovnik.

The taking of Zadar by the Venetians depicted by Andrea Vicentino

THE REPUBLIC OF RAGUSA

The story of the city of Dubrovnik, for a long time known as Ragusa, takes up an entire chapter in Croatia's history. The city was founded by exiles from Epidaurum which had been destroyed by the

The Republic of Ragusa in a contemporary illustration

Avars. It became an important trading port thanks to its central position in the Adriatic, and its safe mooring. In 1205, it came under Venetian rule. This lasted for 150 years and resulted in the city's current appearance. In 1358, Hungary's Louis I of Anjou defeated the Venetians and reunited the Croatian territories, but in 1382 Ragusa bought its freedom by means of a treaty with the king of Hungary. It became an independent republic and flourished as a great power and a thriving spiritual and cultural centre. In 1808, Napoleon Bonaparte's troops entered the city and the republic came to an end.

TURKISH DOMINATION

The Kingdom of Hungary went through a long period of dynastic crisis when the house of Arpad died out after the death of Andrew III in 1301. There were numerous contenders for the crown, provoking fierce battles until 1308 when Charles Robert of Anjou, of the Neapolitan royal family, came to the throne. Under the Angevin dynasty, with Matthias Corvinus (1470–90), the Hungarian-Croatian kingdom enjoyed a long period of prosperity, competing with Venice for possession of the coast and Adriatic

islands. However, a Turkish invasion was imminent and after the battle of Kosovo Polje in 1389, the Turks conquered nearby Bosnia and part of Serbia. In 1463, the Sultan Mohammed II began to invade Croatia from Bosnia. The Croatian army was defeated in 1493 at the battle of Krbavsko Polje. In the Battle of Mohács, on 29 August 1526, the Hungarian king, Louis II, died without heirs, leaving the way clear for the Turks of Suleyman II the Magnificent to conquer almost all of Croatia and much of Hungary.

Ottoman army in the Battle of Mohács

TIMELINE

1301–08 The Arpad dynasty dies out with the death of Andrew III. After lengthy controversy, Charles Robert of Anjou comes to the throne

Silver coin commemorating the Battle of Mohács

1527 The kingdom of Hungary and Croatia passes to the Habsburgs

1526 King Louis II dies in the Battle of Mohács against the Turks

1300	1350	1400	1450	1500

1409 After a costly war against Sigismund of Habsburg, Ladislaus of Anjou becomes king of Hungary and Croatia. He sells Dalmatia to Venice

1493 Croatian troops are defeated at Krbavsko Polje by Jacub, a Pasha of Bosnia

1520 Marko Marulić writes *Judita*, the first work written in Croat

View of Osijek at the time of liberation from the Turks in 1687

VENICE AND THE PURCHASE OF DALMATIA

The wars with Venice over coastal Dalmatia continued until 1409 when the Hungarian king, Ladislaus of Anjou, renounced all rights over Dalmatia and sold it for 100,000 gold ducats to Venice. The towns and islands stayed under Venetian rule from 1409 until 1797, when Venice surrendered to Napoleon. As well as the territories purchased by Venice, other towns wanted to become Venetian possessions. They were given a great deal of autonomy by Venice, whose principal interest was in the security of the ports and their defence, building the ramparts which today characterize these towns. During the wars of the early 18th century, Venice conquered the whole of Dalmatia, except for Dubrovnik, then an independent republic, and a small stretch of coast, extending its borders to the Velebit passes, which still separate Croatia from Bosnia-Herzegovina today.

Franjo Krsto Frankopan, beheaded in 1671

TIES WITH THE HABSBURGS

In 1527, Croatian and Hungarian nobles granted what remained of the kingdom to Archduke Ferdinand of Habsburg, who then concentrated all power in the court, depriving the nobility of control of the cities and border areas. In 1578, he established the Military Frontier (*Vojne Krajine*) which was administered by the military governor of Vienna. This was to serve as a buffer zone against the advancing Turks. To populate this frontier, Serb, Morlach and Bosnian refugees were brought in and integrated with the military garrisons. For some decades there was a truce, then the Turkish offensive against Vienna resumed, but the Turks were pushed back, first in 1664 and again in 1683. The slow retreat of the "infidels" from Croatia began at this point. Croatia was liberated ten years later, while Bosnia remained under the Turks. The liberated areas became border lands and remained so until 1881. Vienna's heavy taxation and centralization policy caused discontent, but the attempt to detach Croatia from Hungary and Vienna, begun in 1670 by some of Croatia's most influential families (Frankopans and Zrinskis) *(see p175)*, resulted in the beheading of two rebels in 1671, the Ban Petar Zrinski and Franjo Krsto Frankopan, halting any attempt at revolt.

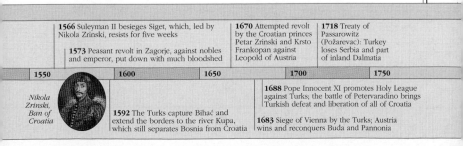

1566 Suleyman II besieges Siget, which, led by Nikola Zrinski, resists for five weeks

1573 Peasant revolt in Zagorje, against nobles and emperor, put down with much bloodshed

1670 Attempted revolt by the Croatian princes Petar Zrinski and Krsto Frankopan against Leopold of Austria

1718 Treaty of Passarowitz (Požarevac): Turkey loses Serbia and part of inland Dalmatia

| 1550 | 1600 | 1650 | 1700 | 1750 |

Nikola Zrinski, Ban of Croatia

1592 The Turks capture Bihać and extend the borders to the river Kupa, which still separates Bosnia from Croatia

1688 Pope Innocent XI promotes Holy League against Turks; the battle of Petervaradino brings Turkish defeat and liberation of all of Croatia

1683 Siege of Vienna by the Turks; Austria wins and reconquers Buda and Pannonia

Drawing showing the Congress of Vienna

THE KINGDOM OF THE ILLYRIAN PROVINCES

The Napoleonic wars also affected Croatia, where the Kingdom of Illyrian Provinces was established in 1809, governed by the French marshal, Marmont. This relatively short period (five years) saw the introduction of important economic and legal reforms which left a deep impression on Croatian culture. With the mood of growing nationalism in Europe, people felt inspired to rebuild a united state. However, at the Congress of Vienna (1815), Croatia supported the expansionist aspirations of Austria, which annexed all the Istrian and Dalmatian territories which had belonged to Venice, and the Republic of Dubrovnik.

THE ILLYRIAN MOVEMENT

Croatian aspirations were apparent in movements which also influenced and politicized the newly emerging working class, a product of early industrialization. The origins of this nationalist trend can be dated to the 1834 writings of Ljudevit Gaj (1809–72),

known as "the Illyrian". Moving against this trend, however, was the expansion of Hungary, which tried to extend its influence in frontier zones by imposing the use of the Magyar language in administrative affairs and schools. In the former Venetian territories on the other hand, a pro-Italian nationalism, with ideas of unification, was spreading among the middle classes in the Dalmatian and Istrian cities. The Austrian government opposed all these movements and continued to govern without compromise. Indeed, they tried to introduce the teaching of German in schools. Any possible unification of Croatian territories was blocked by maintaining the *Krajine*, the military border, and by customs barriers between the various areas. Major public works, the expansion of the ports of Rijeka and Pula, which became a base for the Austrian fleet, and a renewed road network were all made to promote Austrian interests.

FROM THE REVOLT OF 1848 TO AUSTRO-HUNGARIAN REIGN

After 1847, when the Sabor (parliament) of Zagreb managed to proclaim Croat as the official language and abolished feudalism, the revolt of the Hungarian people and the hopes aroused by the Italian revolution in 1848 also involved Croatian political movements. The failure to understand the Hungarian rebels and ambiguous Austrian policy forced the Ban, Josip Jelačić, into war against Hungary, now ruled by

Ban Josip Jelačić, a Croatian national hero

rebels. The Austrian monarchy was saved but then became, if anything, even more keen on centralization. In 1867, Franz Joseph, the Austrian emperor, modified the structure of the state and established the Austro-Hungarian empire. Hungary was granted autonomy and a corridor to the sea. Rijeka and the hinterland became part of the Magyar state. However, under pressure from the Sabor, in 1868 the Austrian emperor granted Croatia the status of "a nation with territory within the Austro-Hungarian Empire", and Zagreb became its cultural and political centre. In 1863 the bishop of Đakovo, Josip Juraj Strossmayer, founded the Croatian Academy of the Arts and Sciences and the University (1874), the first in the Balkans.

Bishop Josip Juraj Strossmayer, founder of the University of Zagreb

Political contention continued to develop along different lines. Some people dreamed of a confederation of states within the Habsburg monarchy, others felt that the moment had come to unite the Slav peoples in one state, and lastly, others felt it was time for Croatian independence.

Tension increased in 1878 when Bosnia and Herzegovina came under Austrian rule, sparking reaction from the Kingdom of Serbia, which had been established in 1862 after the expulsion of the Turks. The Serbian ruling classes aspired to unify the southern Slavs and intended to extend their territories towards Dalmatia and Slavonia, which they regarded as Serbian land. In the last decade of the 19th century a political battle developed in Dalmatia and Istria. It formed between a movement supported by the bourgeoisie in the cities formerly under Venetian rule which pushed for autonomy, and other groups which aimed at a union with Serbia. Austria, which as always took advantage of these internal controversies, did not concede any form of autonomy.

WORLD WAR I

In 1914, with the assassination of Archduke Franz Ferdinand in Sarajevo, World War I broke out which caused the dissolution of the Habsburg Empire. Croatians paid dearly for their involvement in the war, as did many other countries, but finally the Croatian population was able to free itself from foreign rule.

Flag of the Hungarian-Croatian Imperial regiment

1860 Austrian emperor reinstates the Sabor

1885 Vienna dissolves the *Krajine* and those areas become part of the Croatian state again

1904 Antun and Stjepan Radić found the People's Peasant Party

1914 Assassination in Sarajevo and World War I begins

1860	1870	1880	1890	1900	1910

1868 Birth of United Kingdom of Croatia and Slovenia supported by Emperor Franz Joseph

Emperor Franz Joseph

1908 Austria annexes Bosnia and Herzegovina

1912 Slavko Cuvaj proclaimed Ban of Croatia, dissolves the Sabor and abolishes the Constitution

Assassination of King Alexander in Marseilles (1934)

FROM THE STATE OF SLOVENES, CROATS AND SERBS TO THE KINGDOM OF YUGOSLAVIA

Croatia proclaimed independence in 1918, but a few months later agreed to be part of a state formed by Slovenes and Serbs under the Serbian dynasty of Karađorđević. The Treaty of Rapallo (1920) allotted Istria, Zadar, the islands of Cres, Lošinj, Lastovo and Palagruža to Italy, followed in 1924 by Rijeka. The discontent of Croatians led many citizens to join the People's Peasant Party, led by Stjepan Radić until he was shot and fatally wounded in parliament in Belgrade in 1928. The revolts which broke out in Croatia were repressed and in 1929 King Alexander abolished the constitution and then

established the Kingdom of Yugoslavia. The assassination of the king in Marseilles (1934) by the Ustaše (Croatian fascists), led by Ante Pavelić, increased tension and in an attempt to suppress the uprising and placate the discontented, in 1939 the government of Belgrade established the Banovina of Croatia within the Kingdom of Yugoslavia. However, a few days later World War II began.

WORLD WAR II

Initially, Yugoslavia supported the Axis, but a military revolt removed the king of Yugoslavia, and the country was then invaded by Nazi troops. A kingdom of Croatia was established, which was to be governed by Aimone of Savoy, but in reality it was an independent state led by Pavelić. Italy took control of the islands and cities of the Dalmatian coast. Resistance gained ground in all of Yugoslavia led by the Communist Party and its chief, Marshal Tito: from 1941 to 1945 Croatia was bloodied by war and internal conflicts which caused hundreds of thousands of deaths.

Tito with his wife and son in a photo from 1927

MARSHAL TITO

At the end of the war the state of Yugoslavia was reunited, and regained land granted to Italy after World War I (see p47), as well as the area of Prekomurje and a part of Baranja, which were both Hungarian at the time.

In 1948, the break between the Yugoslav Communist Party and the Soviet Union led Marshal

TIMELINE

1919 Treaty of Paris: a country of Slovenes, Croats and Serbs is created, which later becomes the kingdom of Yugoslavia	**1932** Civil war breaks out in Yugoslavia **1934** King Alexander is killed in Marseilles; his son Paul takes power	**1948** Yugoslavia breaks away from Soviet influence and begins policy of non-alignment

1920	1930	1940	1950	1960

1929 King Alexander Karađorđević proclaims a dictatorship. Croat Ante Pavelić founds terrorist organization of Ustaše to fight the Serbs	**1939–41** World War II: Yugoslavia is conquered and divided, and Croatia nominally becomes a kingdom under Aimone of Savoy	**1947–48** Exodus of nearly all the Italians from Istria and Dalmatia **1945** The Yugoslav Federal state is founded

THE HISTORY OF CROATIA

Tito to employ a policy of mediation and neutrality between the opposing international factions of the Cold War. Tito held together the country's various ethnic groups with great difficulty and these ties showed signs of strain after he died in 1980. The reform of the constitution, aimed at weakening Serbia's dominance over the other states, did not alter the resentment of the Croats and Slovenes who sought support for opposition to the regime in religion and nationalism.

Stipe Mesić, elected president in 2000

THE DISSOLUTION OF THE SOCIALIST REPUBLIC OF YUGOSLAVIA

The fall of the Berlin Wall (November 1989) and the break-up of the Soviet Union at the end of 1991 convinced the governments of Slovenia, Croatia (under its first president, Franjo Tudjman) and Macedonia that they should dissolve federal ties and proclaim independence, after a referendum which was won by a wide margin by the secessionists (May 1991). However, a Serb faction, supported by the Yugoslav People's Army (JNA) from Belgrade, stirred up

rebellion and war broke out. In Slovenia the war lasted only six days, but the battle in Croatia was prolonged. Under the pretext of defending the Serbs, parts of Slavonia and Baranja were occupied by the JNA, and in Krajina the Serbian Republic of Krajina was created with Knin as its capital. A fifth of Croatia fell to Serb soldiers, and the city of Dubrovnik was held under a seven-month siege.

THE INDEPENDENT STATE OF CROATIA

Five years later the land occupied by the Serbs was liberated by the Croatian army and the Erdut Agreement (1995) sanctioned reunification, although the disputed territories (Slavonia and Krajina) were overseen by the UN until 1998.

In the spring of 2000 a general census was carried out but not all data are available. Elections held in December 2000 voted in a coalition of democratic parties and this government is viewed favourably by most European countries. Since then, steps have been taken for Croatia's entry into the European Union. Once the new government was installed, the break-up of the vast state machine began with the sale of the banking system, tourist hotels and facilities as well as some industries. The auction of Tito's fleet attracted the most attention. In March 2002, the Italian bank, UniCredito, bought the important Croatian bank, the Zagrebačka Bank, bringing it into the European circuit.

Bombed houses in Vukovar during the war of 1991–95

Monument to Marshal Tito in Kumrovec

1980 President Tito dies and conflict between the various nationalities begins

1999 In December president Franjo Tudjman dies and in the subsequent elections democratic parties win the majority

2000 On 7 February Stipe Mesić is elected President of the Republic

1970	1980	1990	2000

1991 Slovenia and Croatia abandon Republic, Croatian land inhabited by Serbs is occupied by Yugoslav People's Army: war between Serbia and Croatia begins

1995 Erdut Agreement: Slavonia and Krajina are administered by the United Nations

1998 With the restitution of Slavonia and Krajina, Croatia once again becomes a free united country

CROATIA
AREA BY AREA

Croatia at a Glance

CROATIA IS A FASCINATING COUNTRY with great ethnic, historical and architectural diversity as well as varied topography. The north had close ties with the former Austrian empire, and the bell towers alongside 19th-century Baroque churches and buildings have a Viennese look. The eastern side marks the start of the Hungarian plain with broad rivers and houses with overhanging roofs. The Adriatic coast is quite different, with its indented coastline fringed with lovely islands. The coastal cities reflect the centuries-old Venetian culture with churches, monasteries, palaces and forts testifying to the brilliance of the late Middle Ages and the greatness of the Renaissance period.

St Mark's Square (pp152–3), *with its Gothic church of the same name, is the heart of the Gornji Grad district in Zagreb and the city's oldest square.*

ZAGREB *(pp146–63)*

ISTRIA AND THE KVARNER AREA *(pp46–85)*

CENTRAL CROATIA *(pp164–77)*

Basilica of Euphrasius *in Poreč* (pp52–3) *has marvellous mosaics, some of the best preserved examples of Byzantine art in Croatia.*

Amphitheatre, Pula (pp60–61)

Plitvice Lakes National Park (pp84–5) *is one of nature's natural wonders with 16 lakes surrounded by woods. The cascading waterfalls create an impressive display of light and colour.*

DALMATIA *(pp86–145)*

Kornati National Park (pp96–7) *is made up of over 150 islands with underwater caves and sheltered coves. The park covers an area of about 300 sq km (115 sq miles) and is surrounded by clear seas. These wooded, rocky islands present an unforgettable sight.*

ADRIATIC SEA

◁ **Typical cultivated landscape in the north of Croatia**

Zagorje (pp198–9), *west of Varaždin, towards the border with Slovenia, is a fascinating area with vine-covered hills, thermal spa towns and castles.*

Kopački Rit Park (pp192–3) *is an oasis of great ornithological interest. In spring and summer the Danube overflows, transforming this area into a large lake attracting more than 200 bird species.*

0 kilometres 50

0 miles 50

THE NORTHERN COUNTIES *(pp196–213)*

SLAVONIA AND BARANJA *(pp178–95)*

Lonjsko Polje National Park *(p174)*

The Palace of Diocletian *in Split* (pp118–9) *was built by Emperor Diocletian at the end of the 3rd century. The city of Split grew up in and around it. Almost in its original state, it is the largest Roman building in the Adriatic.*

The Tvrđa in Osijek (pp190–91), *the fortified nucleus of the city, has 18th-century military buildings. Initially Roman, then Hungarian, Turkish and lastly Austrian, the city retains traces of most of these diverse cultures.*

The City of Dubrovnik (pp138–44) *is situated on the coast. It is surrounded by fortifications begun in the early 10th century and enlarged over the years.*

ISTRIA AND THE KVARNER AREA

THE ISTRIAN PENINSULA, *nestling at the northern end of the Adriatic Sea, and the islands that tumble down the Kvarner gulf are some of the most sought-after holiday destinations in Europe. The coast is spectacular and the towns and cities are fascinating. Three National Parks: the Brijuni Islands, the Plitvice Lakes and Risnjak preserve the natural charm of the area.*

Until 1000 BC, the region was inhabited by Illyrians. From 42 BC Istria became part of the Roman empire, when the Province of Dalmatia was founded. Cities were built along the coast and on the islands, and many traces of Roman presence remain. Pula has a well-preserved amphitheatre dating back to the 1st century, the sixth largest arena of its kind in the world.

Mosaic in the Basilica of Euphrasius in Poreč

With the fall of the western Roman empire, much of the eastern Adriatic coast came under the control of Byzantium. The intricate, well-preserved golden mosaics of the 6th-century basilica of St Euphrasius in Poreč survive from that time.

In 1420 the area came under Venetian rule, a situation which was to last until 1797, when Napoleon dissolved the Venetian Republic. Nearly 400 years of Venetian rule are recorded by 15th-century open air loggias, elegant bell towers and buildings with Venetian-Gothic windows, built by wealthy merchants.

With the Treaty of Vienna in 1815, Austria-Hungary extended its domain to include Venetian lands. Rijeka developed into an industrial port under Austro-Hungarian rule and is still today a hub for Croatian shipping. Close by in Opatija the Habsburgs built elegant villas and planted lush gardens for their winter holidays.

In 1918 Istria briefly became part of the new kingdom of Serbs, Croats and Slovenes, which subsequently became Yugoslavia in 1928.

Many Istrian towns have two official names, an Italian and a Croatian, a legacy from 1920, when Istria was given to Italy as a reward for having joined the Allies in World War I. During World War II, the region became a stronghold for Italian partisans. After 1945, most of Istria was given back to Yugoslavia.

The Roman amphitheatre at Pula, one of the best preserved Roman theatres in the world

◁ View over the sea from the city walls of Rab

Exploring Istria and the Kvarner Area

ISTRIA IS A TRIANGULAR PENINSULA, traditionally divided into three areas. White Istria is a central plateau of karst or limestone with sparse areas of oak, pine and ash trees; grey Istria consists of a strip of eroded limestone with rich soil, used for vines and olive trees; and red Istria is a plateau furrowed by the rivers Mirna and Rasa, farmed for cereals and vegetables. The most popular destinations in Istria are Poreč, Rovinj, Pula and the Brijuni National Park. The Kvarner area includes the city of Rijeka and the coastline as far as Jablanac. Woods cover the northern hinterland, with the Risnjak National Park to the north, and the Plitvice Lakes National Park to the southeast. The islands of Krk, Cres, Lošinj and Rab are delightful places to explore. Many of the towns on the coast have an Italianate appearance, a legacy from centuries of Venetian rule.

The cathedral of St Mary the Great on the island of Rab

GETTING AROUND

The roads are good and a motorway from Rijeka to Zagreb is under construction, as well as a main road from Pula to the border with Slovenia. The larger islands can be reached by ferry and there are frequent sailings in the summer season. Buses link all the main towns. The Trieste–Pula railway interconnects with the Ljubljana–Rijeka line and trains link Rijeka and Zagreb, with connections to the south of Croatia.

SIGHTS AT A GLANCE

LOCATOR MAP

KEY

✈	International airport
▬	Two-lane motorway, toll-free
▬	Major road
▬	Minor road
▬	Railway line
- -	Ferry route
�018	Viewpoint

The rocky coastline near Rovinj

SEE ALSO

• *Where to Stay* pp220–23
• *Where to Eat* pp234–6

Façade of the church of St Servelus, Buje

Buje (Buie) ❶

Map A2. ▓ 3,200.
▲ Pula, 70 km (43 miles) S.
▤ from Pula, Rijeka, Kopar, Trieste.
ℹ Istarska 2, (052) 773 353.
▨ Nights of Kanegra (Aug); Grape festival (Sep).

O**N AN ISOLATED HILL**, among flourishing vineyards, stands Buje, the ancient Roman settlement of Bullea. Formerly a Frankish feudal village, in 1102 it became part of the Patriarchate of Aquileia and in 1410 the town came under Venetian rule.

The town still retains the outline of the ancient walled castle and has kept its original medieval layout, with narrow alleys and lanes leading to the main square. The church of **St Servelus** (Sv. Servul) and its Aquileian bell tower stand here. The church was built in the 16th century over the remains of a Roman temple, of which a few pieces, columns and inscriptions survive.

Inside the church are wooden statues from the 14th and 15th centuries (*Madonna with Child* and *St Barbara*), sculptures representing St Servelus and St Sebastian (1737) by Giovanni Marchiori, and an organ by Gaetano Callido (1725–1813).

A 15th-century Venetian Gothic palace and a 16th-century loggia with a frescoed façade also face the square.

Outside the walls is the church of **St Mary** (Sv. Marija), erected in the 15th

century: a wooden statue of the Virgin and a *Pietà* are from the same period. Some of the paintings of biblical scenes are by Gasparo della Vecchia (early 18th century).

The **Civic Museum** houses an interesting collection of handicrafts and pieces made by local craftsmen.

⛫ Civic Museum
Trg Slobode. ℂ (052) 772 023.
◯ Jun–Sep: 4–8pm Mon, Wed, Fri; 9am–1pm Tue, Thu, Sat; Oct–May: by appt.

ENVIRONS: Perched on a hilltop, 8 km (5 miles) south-east of Buje, is the medieval town of **Grožnjan** (Grisignana).

In 1358 the Venetians bought the town from Baron Reiffenberg and since that time it has been the administrative and military centre of the surrounding area. A tower, some parts of the walls and two doors are all that remain of the old town.

Within the walls are a 16th-century loggia, in the main square, and the Baroque church of St Vitus and St Modest. The church has splendid altars and a marble choir.

After World War II, the inhabitants, nearly all of them Italian, abandoned the town. In 1965, however, it was declared a "City of Artists". Contemporary artists work and exhibit their art in the

various local galleries and workshops. In summer the town plays host to concerts and international musical events *(see p23)*.

Umag (Umago) ❷

Map A2.
▓ 4,900. ▲ Pula, 83 km (51 miles).
▤ Kolodvorska ulica, (052) 741 817.
ℹ Obala J B Tita 3, (052) 741 363.
▨ Feast of St Pilgrim (last Sun in May); International tennis tournament (end Jul); concerts in summer.
Ⓦ www.istra.com/umag

T**HIS TOWN** is located on a narrow peninsula which frames a small bay. It was founded by the Romans and given the name of Umacus. In 1268, it became an important port when it passed into Venetian hands. Later, in the the 14th century, a wall and towers were built, some of which remain.

The town still has many 15th- and 16th-century stone houses, some with ornate Gothic windows.

On the left outer wall of the 18th-century church of **St Mary** (Sv. Marija) is a relief of St Pilgrim and the fortified town of Umag, and inside the church is a 15th-century Venetian-school polyptych.

15th-century polyptych, church of St Mary, Umag

Today Umag is a busy sea-side resort with numerous hotels. It has become known for its well-equipped sports centres and major tennis tournaments are held here.

View of the ancient wall and port of Umag

Boats in the harbour at Poreč

Novigrad (Cittanova) ❸

Map A2. 🏠 *2,500.* ✈ *Pula, 60 km (37 miles).* 🚉 *Pazin, 41 km (25 miles).* 🚌 *(052) 757 660.* ℹ *Porporella 1, (052) 757 075, (052) 758 011.* 🎭 *Jazz music festival (Aug), Patron saint's day, St Pelagius (last weekend Aug).*

ORIGINALLY a Greek colony and later a Roman one called Aemonia, Novigrad stands at the mouth of the River Mirna. In the Byzantine period (6th century) when it was enlarged, it was called "New Town" (Neopolis). From the early Middle Ages until 1831 it was an episcopal seat. In 1277 it passed into Venetian hands and oak from Motovun Forest was shipped to Venetian dockyards.

In the 13th century the town was walled for defence, but it was unable to withstand a Turkish attack in 1687 and the town was partially destroyed along with many works of art.

Evidence of the Venetian period can be seen on the façades of the houses in the narrow lanes which lead to the main square (Trg Slobode). An 18th-century loggia stands here. Of the early Christian basilica of **St Pelagius** (Sv. Pelagij), rebuilt in the 16th century, only the Romanesque crypt from the 11th-century remains. In the present-day Baroque church are paintings from the Venetian school of the 18th century. Evidence of the Roman and medieval periods can be seen in the museum housed in the Urizzi Palace.

Poreč (Parenzo) ❹

Map A2. 🏠 *7,600.* ✈ *Pula, 53 km (33 miles).* 🚉 *Pazin, 32 km (20 miles).* 🚌 *Ulica K Hoguesa 2, (052) 432 153.* ℹ **Local:** *Zagrebačka 9, (052) 451 719;* **Regional:** *Pionirska 1, (052) 452 797.* 🎭 *Season of classical music (at St Euphrasius) and jazz festival (both Jul–Aug) .* 🌐 *www.istra.com/porec*

POREČ WAS A Roman town (Colonia Julia Parentium) which, after centuries of splendour, was sacked by the Goths and fell into decline. In 539 it was conquered by the Byzantines, who founded a bishopric around the year 800. The town then became part of the kingdom of the Franks, who gave it to the Patriarchate of Aquileia. In 1267 it was the first Istrian town to choose Venetian rule, and the town acquired a Venetian look as palaces, squares and religious buildings were built.

In 1354 it was destroyed by the Genoese and later, plague, pirates and a long war greatly reduced the population. During Austrian domination it became the seat of the Istrian Diet (parliament) and an important shipyard.

The old centre shelters on a narrow peninsula protected by rocks and the island of St Nicholas. Despite being a popular base for visitors to Istria, the old town has

Archaeological exhibit in the Poreč Museum

remained intact and Poreč invariably wins an annual award for "best-kept town".

The layout is based on the original Roman network, with a main road (Decumanus) and another main road at right angles (Cardo). The main monuments of the town line these roads.

Along the Decumanus stand many Gothic houses. At the easternmost point is the Baroque Sinčić Palace (17th century), which houses the **Poreč Museum** (Zavičajni Muzej Poreštine). It is dedicated to Roman and early Christian archaeology; an ethnographic section illustrates daily life in the Poreč region. Nearby in St Maurus Street (Sv. Mauro) is the House of Two Saints, all that is left of the abbey of St Cassius (12th century), with two Romanesque figures on the façade. To the west, the Decumanus leads to Trg Marafor, once the site of the forum, with houses from the 12th and 13th centuries and the remains of a pre-Roman temple.

North of the square is the church of **St Francis** (Sv. Frane, 12th–14th centuries), altered in the Baroque period. To the east is the parish house with an ornate Romanesque façade. From here there is a passage that leads to the Basilica of Euphrasius, which has marvellous Byzantine mosaics *(see pp52–3)*.

🏛 Poreč Museum
Sinčić Palace, Dekumanska 9.
📞 *(052) 431 585.* ⏰ *Jun–Sep: 10am–1pm, 6–9pm daily; Oct–May: by appt.* 📷 ♿ 📹

A typical trefoil window in Venetian Gothic style, Poreč

Poreč: Basilica of Euphrasius
Eufrazijeve Bazilike

A mosaic in
the apse

THIS 6TH-CENTURY CHURCH, a Byzantine masterpiece, is decorated with splendid mosaics on a gold background. The basilica of Euphrasius was built for Bishop Euphrasius between 539 and 553, by enlarging the existing 4th-century Oratory of St Maurus Martyr. Some of the original floor mosaics still survive. Over the centuries the building has undergone numerous alterations. In December 1997 the basilica was added to the UNESCO World Heritage List. Classical concerts are held in the church from May to September.

★ Ciborium
Dominating the presbytery is a beautiful 13th-century ciborium, supported by four marble columns. The canopy is decorated with mosaics.

★ Apse Mosaics
Mosaics from the 6th century cover the apse. On the triumphal arch are Christ and the Apostles (above), on the vault, the Virgin enthroned with Child and two Angels, to the left St Maurus, Bishop Euphrasius with a model of the basilica, and Deacon Claud with his son.

Remains of a 4th-century mosaic floor from the Oratory of St Maurus are in the garden.

Sacristy and the Votive Chapel
Past the sacristy's left wall is a triple-apsed chapel with a mosaic floor from the 6th century. Here lie the remains of the saints Maurus and Eleuterius.

STAR FEATURES

★ **Apse Mosaics**

★ **Ciborium**

Interior
The entrance leads to a large basilica with a central nave and two side aisles. The 18 Greek marble columns have carved capitals featuring animals, some of Byzantine origin and others Romanesque. All bear the monogram of Euphrasius.

Baptistry
This octagonal building dates from the 6th century. In the centre is a baptismal font and there are also fragments of mosaics; to the rear rises a 16th-century bell tower.

Atrium
This has a roughly square portico with two columns on each side. Tombstones and a variety of archaeological finds dating from the medieval period are displayed in this area.

The Bishop's Residence, a triple-aisled building dating from the 6th century, now houses several paintings by Antonio da Bassano, a polyptych by Antonio Vivarini and a painting by Palma il Giovane.

The church of St Anthony in Vrsar, built in the 15th century

Vrsar (Orsera) ❺

Map A3. 🏚 *1,700.* 🚊 *Pula, 41 km (25 miles).* 🚌 *Pazin, 42 km (26 miles).* ℹ️ *Rade Končara 46, (052) 441 187.* 🎭 *International sculpture exhibition, Montraker quarry (summer); classical music concerts (summer).* �W *www.istra.com/vrsar*

THE REMAINS OF a villa, a quarry and the foundations of an early Christian building all provide evidence that Romans once settled here. In documents preceding 1000 AD, this village is mentioned as the feudal territory of the bishop of Poreč, who owned a fortified summer residence here. Until 1172 it remained under the protection of the bishop and then came under Venetian rule.

The town had an outer wall and towers which have now almost disappeared except for the Sea Gate. Near the gate is the church of **St Mary** (Sv. Marija) from the 10th century, one of the most important Romanesque monuments in Istria. Inside are frescoes which are among the oldest in the region and a mosaic floor with floral motifs.

The town is dominated by the 18th-century **Vergotini Castle**, built by restructuring the bishop's former residence. Near the only remaining gate in the medieval wall is the small church of **St Anthony**, built in the 15th century with an open portico.

ENVIRONS: Just outside Vrsar lies **Koversada**, Europe's largest naturist resort.

To the south of Vrsar, towards Rovinj, is the **Limski** Channel, now a marine reserve. The channel is 9 km (5 miles) long, and 600 m (1,970 ft) wide with steep sides, perforated by limestone caves which have been lived in from time to time since the Neolithic Age. In the early 11th century, one of the caves was the home of the hermit St Romualdo, who founded the monastery of St Michael near Klostar.

Many of the restaurants in the area offer the oysters and mussels farmed in the channel.

Fishermen on the Limski Channel

Rovinj (Rovigno) ❻

Map A3. 🏚 *13,000.* 🚊 *Pula, 49 km (30 miles).* 🚌 *Pula.* 🚢 *Trg na Lokvi, (052) 811 514, 811 453.* ℹ️ *Obala P Budicina 12, (052) 811 566.* 🎭 *Modri Biser (Blue Pearl), International pop festival (summer); Grisia, International art exhibition (2nd Sun Aug); Patron St Euphemia's day (16 Sep).* �W *www.istra.com/rovinj*

THE ROMANS BUILT this port on an island, which was joined to the coast in 1763 by filling in the channel dividing Rovinj from the mainland.

Initially ruled by the Byzantines and the Franks, from 1283 until 1797 the town was under Venetian control.

Traces of a wall dating back to the Middle Ages can still be seen.

In the square in front of the pier is Balbi's Arch (1680), an ancient city gate, as well as a late-Renaissance clock tower. A loggia from 1680 is now the **Civic Museum**, housing 18th-century art from the Venetian school and works by modern Croatian artists.

In the roads branching off the square are Baroque and Renaissance buildings. The backs of many of these face the sea. The **cathedral**, dedicated to St Euphemia (Sv. Eufemije) dominates the town. Originating in early Christian times, it was rebuilt in 1736. The saint's remains are preserved in a Roman sarcophagus in the apse on the right of the three-aisle church. The adjacent bell tower is 61 m (200 ft) high, and was modelled on that of San Marco in Venice. It is crowned by a copper statue of St Euphemia.

In the east of the city is the 13th-century **Baptistry of the Holy Trinity** (Sv. Trojstvo). Along the waterfront is the Institute of Marine Biology. It was founded in the late 19th century and has an aquarium. Nearby, Red Island (Crveni otok), is in fact two islands linked by an embankment.

South of the town is Zlatni Rt, a park planted with cedars, pines and cypresses, with well laid-out trails.

🏛 **Civic Museum**
Trg M Tita 11. 📞 *(052) 840 471, 830 650.* ⬤ *Jun–Sep: 9am–12.30pm, 6.30–10pm Mon–Sat; Oct–May: 9am–12.30pm Tue–Sat.*

The port of Rovinj, dominated by the cathedral

The church of St Elizabeth inside the walls of Bale

Bale (Valle) ❼

Map A3. 🏘 *900.* 🛫 *Pula, 28 km (17 miles).* 🚉 *Pula, 25 km (15 miles).* 🚌 *Trg palih Boraca.* 🛈 *Trg palih Boraca 3, (052) 824 270, (052) 824 303.* 🎭 *Night of Bale, Baljanska Noć (first Sun in Aug); Castrum Vallis, art exhibition (Jul & Aug).*

O N A HILL of limestone, the Illyrians constructed a fort which dominated the surrounding countryside. The Romans also built a *castrum* (Castrum Vallis) on the same site, which was renovated when the place became a feudal estate of the Patriarchate of Aquileia. During Venetian rule, which began in 1332, the town grew in size and acquired its present layout of an elliptical wall with towers enclosing two parallel rows of houses. Interesting buildings include the Gothic-Venetian Magistrates' Court with coats of arms on the portico, the loggia, and the Gothic-Renaissance **Castle** dating from the 15th century, a residence for the Soardo Bembo family. Under one of the two side towers is a gate leading to the old town.

The church of **St Elizabeth** (Sv. Elizabete), of Romanesque origins, was reconstructed in the 16th century and again in the 19th. The church contains a splendid Romanesque crucifix, a sarcophagus, a polyptych and a crypt with a marble Renaissance altar.

There are two other churches in the town. One dates from the 14th century and is dedicated to St Anthony; the other, dedicated to the Holy Spirit, was built in the 15th century.

Vodnjan (Dignano) ❽

Map A3. 🏘 *3,700.* 🛫 *Pula, 11 km (7 miles).* 🚉 *Ulica Željeznička, (052) 511 538.* 🛈 *Narodni trg 3, (052) 511 700, 511 672.* 🎭 *Bumbari, a festival in costume based on the name given to the town's inhabitants (Aug).*

T HE TOWN OF Vodnjan stands on a hill among vineyards and olive groves. At one time it was an Illyrian fort and later, a Roman military post known as Vicus Atinianus. From 1331 until 1797 the town was under Venetian rule.

The old part of town still has various buildings in Venetian-Gothic style, including the Bettica Palace and the 18th-century church of **St Blaise** (Sv. Blaž). In the church are some splendid statues and about 20 paintings from the 17th to 19th centuries, as well as a *Last Supper* by G Contarini (1598) and an *Encounter of Saints* attributed to Palma il Vecchio.

Seven rooms of the church are given over to religious art (730 pieces): vestments, china and silver reliquaries, statues and paintings, and a fine polyptych by Paolo Veneziano from 1351 (*Portrait of the Blessed Leon Bembo*). There are also six mummies of saints, which have survived miraculously without being embalmed. The most revered is that of St Nicolosia.

🔓 **St Blaise**
Trg Zagreb. 🔆 *(052) 511 420.*
⭕ *9am–7pm daily.* **Collection of Religious Art** 🔆 *(052) 511 420.*
⭕ *Jun–Sep: 9am–7pm daily; Oct–May by appt.*

Fažana (Fasana) ❾

Map A3.
🏘 *2,800.* 🛫 *Pula, 8 km (5 miles).*
🚉 *Vodnjan, 5 km (3 miles).*
🚢 *to the Brijuni Islands.*

T HIS SMALL TOWN is known mainly as the embarkation point for the islands of the Brijuni National Park *(see pp56–7)*. Its ancient name, Vasianum, derives from the production of oil and wine amphorae during the Roman period. Facing the sea is the church of **SS Cosmas and Damian** (Sv. Kuzma i Damjan), which was founded in the 11th century and has undergone various reconstructions. Inside is a painting by Jurai Ventura of *The Last Supper* (1578), and in the sacristy are remains of frescoes by Italian artists from Friuli dating from the 15th–16th centuries.

To the side of the church is a seven-storey bell tower with an octagonal spire. The church of **Our Lady of Carmel** from the late 14th century has Gothic frescoes by unknown artists and a 17th-century loggia. Nearby is the church of **St Elys** from the 6th century, with a stone doorway and blind-arch windows, which preserves its Byzantine appearance from the 8th–9th centuries.

Thanks to the growth in numbers of visitors heading for the Brijuni Islands, the town has grown and new facilities have been built.

The façade of the church of SS Cosmas and Damian in Fažana

Brijuni National Park ⑩
Nacionalni Park Brijuni

THE BRIJUNI ARCHIPELAGO is made up of 14 islands and was declared a national park in 1983. The two largest islands have been inhabited since the Palaeolithic era. In Roman times there were aristocratic villas and later religious communities. The islands were abandoned in 1332 because of malaria, but people returned in the following century to work the stone quarries. In the late 19th century, the islands were bought by the Tyrolean industrialist Paul Kupelwieser. After World War II they were used as a summer residence by Marshal Tito, and were visited by heads of state. Visitors are only allowed on the two main islands, Veli Brijun and Mali Brijun.

SV. MARKO

GAZ

OKRUGLJAK

The Fort of Mali Brijun is situated on the second largest island in the archipelago. The Austro-Hungarian fort was built at the end of the 19th century.

MALI BRIJUN
LESSER BRIJUN

SUPIN

SUPINIĆ

Aerial View of the Brijuni Islands
The islands are covered with lush vegetation, much of it undisturbed by human habitation.

Barban

GALIJA

GRUNJ

Safari Park
Tito introduced many species of exotic animal, including zebra. Many were gifts from visiting heads of state.

KRASNICA

VRSAR

Native Animals
Numerous indigenous animals also live freely in the park: fallow deer, moufflon, roedeer, hares, peacocks and about 200 species of wild bird.

KEY

▬	Minor road
🚢	Ferry
🚊	Electric train
ℹ	Tourist information
⌂	Archaeological site

Ancient Trees
Hundreds of different plant species from all over the world were planted on Brijun. Many of the trees, like this ancient olive, are now fully mature and are regarded as living monuments.

Roman Villa
Excavations have unearthed the foundations of a Roman villa, its calidarium *(hot room) and a* frigidarium *(cold room). A large room where the family met for banquets and ceremonies is decorated with mosaics.*

The museum,
opened in 1955, contains cultural and archaeological finds from the island.

In the area around Brijuni harbour hotels and a golf course have been built.

VELI BRIJUN
GREATER BRIJUN

Brijuni

MADONA

Rt Ploče

Peneda

0 metres	800
0 yards	800

The Tegetthoff Fortress
is a ruined Austrian defence system which was built in the 19th century.

The White Villa (Bijela Vila) dates from the Venetian period. It was restored in 1721. This was Tito's summer residence and was used for receptions and political meetings.

Byzantine Castle
On the western coast, in the gulf of Dobrika, are the ruins of a complex of buildings dating from the Byzantine era (539–778), with towers and walls for defence.

Pula (Pola) ⑪

Vase,
Archaeological
Museum

PULA IS WELL-KNOWN for its magnificent monuments from the Roman era, when it was a colony known as Pietas Julia. It became an episcopal seat in 425 and still has the foundations of some 5th-century religious buildings. It was destroyed by the Ostrogoths, but flourished again when it became the main base for the Byzantine fleet in the 6th and 7th centuries: the cathedral and church of St Mary of Formosa date from this time. In 1334 it came under Venetian rule, but by mid-17th century the population had declined to 300. Revitalized in 1856 when Austria made it the base for its fleet, it is still one of the most important naval bases in Croatia. Today, Pula is a university town and, with Pazin (see pp62–3), the administrative centre of Istria.

The cathedral's interior, a combination of styles and periods

Arch of the Sergii, 1st century BC

⋔ Arch of the Sergii
Slavoluk obitelji Sergijevaca
Ulica Sergijevaca.
The arch was erected in the 1st century BC on the orders of Salvia Postuma Sergia, to honour three brothers who held important positions in the Roman Empire. The arch is small with fluted columns, a winged victory and Corinthian capitals. Its frieze has a bas-relief depicting a chariot pulled by horses.
    Next door is a bar named Uliks ("Ulysses"), in memory of James Joyce, who lived here for six months in 1904.

⛪ Church of St Mary of Formosa
Kapela Marije Formoze
Maksimilijanova ulica. ⬛ to public.
A small Byzantine church, built on a Greek cross plan, this was once a chapel, part of the large Basilica of St Mary of Formosa. Inside are remains of mosaics from the 6th century.

⛪ Church of St Francis
Sv. Frane
Ulica Sv. Frane. ☐ for mass.
Built at the same time as the adjacent monastery in the late 13th century, this white stone church has a fine doorway with a Gothic rose window. The interior is a single nave with three apses; on the main altar is a splendid wooden 15th-century polyptych by the Emilian school. Various exhibits from the Imperial Roman era can be seen in the monastery cloisters.

⋔ Temple of Romae and Augustus
Augustov hram
Forum. ☎ (052) 218 603.
☐ Jun–Sep: 9am–1pm, 6–9pm daily; Oct–May: by appt.
Built in the 1st century AD, this temple stands in the square which was once the site of the Roman forum. It is a splendid example of Roman architecture, built on simple lines. It is 17m (56 ft) long

Temple of Romae and Augustus, a jewel of Roman architecture

and 6m (20 ft) wide, with six plain columns and beautiful carved capitals.

⛪ Cathedral
Katedrala
Obala Maršala Tita. ☐ Jun–Sep 9am–noon, 6–9pm; Oct–May: for mass.
The cathedral, dedicated to the Blessed Virgin Mary, was founded in the 6th century after Pula became an episcopal seat. It was enlarged in the 10th century, but its present appearance dates from the 17th century. However, parts of the walls, some of the capitals and the windows are from the original building. On the right is a doorway from 1456, while the bell tower, built between 1671 and 1707, contains stone blocks from the amphitheatre.

⛪ Church of St Nicholas
Sv. Nikola
Castropola. ☐ by appt.
ℹ (052) 212 987 (Tourist office).
This church dates from the 6th century but was partially rebuilt in the 10th century. Towards the end of the 15th century it was assigned to the Orthodox community. Inside are some fine icons from the 15th and 16th centuries.

🏛 Castle and Historical Museum of Istria
Povijesni muzej Istre
Kaštel. ☎ (052) 211 740.
☐ summer: 8am–7pm daily; winter: 8am–4pm daily. 🅹
This star-shaped castle with four bastions houses the Historical Museum of Istria

and was built by the Venetians in the 14th century on the ruins of the Roman Capitol in the city centre. The walls linking the four towers offer splendid views over the city. Nearby are the remains of a 2nd-century theatre.

🏛 Archaeological Museum of Istria
Arheološki Muzej Istre
Carrarina 3. ☎ (052) 218 603. ◯ Jun–Sep: 9am–8pm daily; Oct–May: 9am–3pm Mon–Sat. ⚑
The Archaeological Museum is housed in the former German school, within a park which is reached from the Twin Gate. On display are finds from Pula and the surrounding area, with collections from the Prehistoric era to the Middle Ages. On the

Headless Statue, Archaeological Museum

ground floor are architectural remains, mosaics, altars and other exhibits from antiquity to medieval times.

The rooms on the first floor contain exhibits from the Neolithic to the Roman era. Three rooms on the second floor are dedicated to Roman antiquity (including a headless female statue found at Nesactium, near Pula). Two rooms have exhibits from the late-Classical to medieval periods. Of particular interest are pieces from Slavic tombs dating from the 7th to 12th centuries.

🏛 Twin Gate
Dvojna vrata
Carrarina.
The gate, from the 2nd–3rd centuries, has two arches with an ornate frieze. Nearby are parts of the wall which once encircled the city.

VISITORS' CHECKLIST

Map A3. 🏘 62,500. ✈ 8 km (5 miles), (052) 530 111. 🚢 (052) 211 878. 🚉 (052) 541 982. 🚌 Istarka ulica 3, (052) 219 074. 🛈 **Tourist office**, Forum 3, (052) 212 987. ☷ Pula Opera Festival, Pula Amphitheatre (summer), Croatian Film Festival (summer). 🆆 www.istra.com/pula

🏛 Gate of Hercules
Herculova vrata
Carrarina.
South of the Archaeological Museum stands the single-arched Gate of Hercules. Built in the 1st century BC, it is the oldest and best preserved Roman monument in the city. At the top of the arch is a carving of the head of Hercules with a club.

🏛 Amphitheatre
See pp60–61.

PULA TOWN CENTRE

Amphitheatre ⑪
Archaeological Museum of Istria ⑨
Arch of the Sergii ①
Castle and Historical Museum of Istria ⑦
Cathedral ⑤
Church of St Francis ③
Church of St Mary of Formosa ②
Church of St Nicholas ⑥
Gate of Hercules ⑩
Temple of Romae and Augustus ④
Twin Gate ⑧

TRIESTE RIJEKA
Railway station

0 metres 200
0 yards 200

KEY

🛈 Tourist information
✝ Church
🅿 Parking
🚢 Ferry
🚌 Bus station
⊠ Post office

Pula Amphitheatre
Amfiteatar

THE ELLIPTICAL ARENA IN PULA is one of the six largest Roman amphitheatres existing today. Originally a small amphitheatre built here by Claudius, it was enlarged by Vespasian in 79 AD for gladiator fights. The amphitheatre could hold 23,000 spectators and had about 20 entrances. It remained intact until the 15th century when some of the stone was used to construct the castle and other buildings in the city. It was restored, first by the French governor of the Illyrian provinces, General Marmont, and again more recently when it was adapted for musical events. It can seat 5,000 spectators and is a venue for concerts ranging from opera to rock as well as for an annual film festival.

View of the amphitheatre today

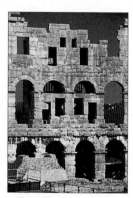

Four Towers
The roofs of the towers were designed to collect the scented water that was sprayed onto the stalls. It is also thought that there was a structure capable of supporting large awnings as protection from the sun and rain.

Amphitheatre Wall
The well-preserved external wall of the amphitheatre has three floors on the side facing the sea, and two on the opposite side, because it was constructed on an incline. At its highest point, the external wall measures 29.40 m (96 ft).

Interior of the Amphitheatre
When first built, the broad tiers could seat an audience of 23,000 people. Shows of every kind were performed, including naval battles. Today, during the summer season, operas, ballets and plays are put on here.

VISITORS' CHECKLIST

Flavijevska ulica. ☎ *(052) 219 028.* ☐ *summer: 9am–9pm daily; other seasons: 9am–4pm daily.* 🏛 🚻 *limited access.*

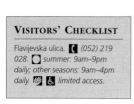

The various corridors which led to the seats allowed spectators to find their places efficiently.

RECONSTRUCTION

The main floor of the arena, 67.75 m (222 ft) long and 41.05 m (135 ft) wide, was originally framed by iron railings to separate spectators from the performance. Between the tiers of seats and the railings there was a space, 3m (10 ft) wide, reserved for staff. Along the main axis, under the arena, were underground corridors which were used by the gladiators and cages for animals. The animals were kept here before being sent into the stadium.

Today the southwest tower is one of the entrances.

Underground Area
Many archaeological finds from the amphitheatre and other Roman buildings are kept in the underground passages, where there were once cages and prisons.

Arches
The first two floors have 72 arches, the third has 64 large rectangular openings. The arches lit the internal corridors which enabled spectators to move from one sector of the amphitheatre to another.

Barban ⓬

Map B3. 🏙 *250.* 🚆 *Pula, 28 km
(17 miles).* 🚌 *Pula.* 🚊 *from Pula.*
ℹ️ **Regional:** *Pionirska 1, Poreč,
(052) 452 797.* 🎪 *Trka na prstenac,
Tournament of the Ring (Aug).*

A FREE TOWN in the late
Middle Ages, in
1334 Barban came
under the rule of the
county of Pazin, and
from 1420 until 1797
it was part of
Venetian territory. It
was granted to the
Loredan family in
1535, and many
buildings acquired
their current
Venetian look.
The town still has
some medieval
fortifications which now
incorporate several
Renaissance buildings.

The church of **St Nicholas**
(Sv. Nikola) faces the square,
which is reached through the
Great Gate (Vela Vrata). The
church has five marble Gothic
altars and many Venetian
paintings (16th–18th
centuries), one attributed to
the Italian artist Padovanino.

In the same square is the
Loredan Palace from 1606
and, towards the Small Gate
(Mala Vrata), the Town Hall
dating from 1555 with a
loggia and a clock tower.

Outside the Great Gate is
the 14th-century church of **St
Anthony** (Sv. Antun), with
some frescoes from the
15th century. In 1970, the
Tournament of the Ring was
revived and costumed lancers
on horses participate in this
traditional annual event.

🏛 **St Nicholas**
📞 *(052) 567 173.* ⭕ *by appt.*

Svetvinčenat ⓭

Map A3. 🏙 *300.* 🚆 *Pazin.* 🚊
from Pula. ℹ️ **Regional:** *Pionirska 1,
Poreč, (052) 452 797.*

T HIS WALLED VILLAGE was
built in the 10th century
on a small hill around a much
restructured fort. The main
square is one of the most
beautiful in Istria. Many of the

main buildings in the village
are found here, including
the 15th-century church of
the **Annunciation** which
contains two paintings
by Palma il Giovane and
an *Annunciation* by the artist
Giuseppe Salviati.

The **Castle** dates from the
13th century and is one of the
best preserved in the region.
It belonged to the
Venetian families of
Castropola, the
Morosini and the
Grimani. In
1589, the Grimani
commissioned the
architect Scamozzi to
convert one of the
square towers into a
residence for the
Venetian governors,
the other into a
prison. High walls connecting
the other two round towers
enclose a large internal
courtyard. This is reached
through the citadel's only
gate, which at one time had a
drawbridge. The town's coat
of arms and that of the
Grimani family can also
be seen here.

The town's name derives
from the Romanesque church
and cemetery of **St Vincent**
(Sv. Vinčenat), whose walls
were frescoed by an
unknown 15th-century artist.

🏛 **St Vincent**
Cemetery. 📞 *(052) 560 004.*
⭕ *by appt.*

ENVIRONS: About 10 km (6
miles) away are the ruins of
Dvidgrad (Duecastelli), an
atmospheric, abandoned
walled village, surrounded
by lush vegetation. Around

**Church of the
Annunciation,
Svetvinčenat**

1000 AD, two castles were
built on neighbouring hills
and were later enclosed by an
oval wall. A village of 200
inhabitants grew up inside the
wall around the basilica of St
Sophia, built between the
11th and 12th centuries.
Although attacked and burnt
by the Genoese in the 14th
century during the war with
Venice, the village soon
recovered. In the 17th century,
sacking by the Uskoks (*see
p79*) and a malaria epidemic
depopulated the village. It has
not been inhabited since then.

**Reconstruction of a room in the
Ethnographic Museum, Pazin**

Pazin ⓮

Map B2. 🏙 *5,300.*
🚆 *(052) 624 310.* 🚌 *(052) 624
437.* ℹ️ *Stari trg 8, (052) 622 460.*
🌐 *www.istra.com/pazin*

T HE TOWN OF Pazin
originated in the 9th
century as a fort and stands
on a cliff 130 m (426 ft) high.
One side of the cliff falls
away to an abyss called Fojba
which is 100 m (328 ft) deep
and about 20 m (65 ft) wide,
and is said to have inspired
Dante's description of the
Gateway to Hell in *Inferno.*

In the 14th century, Pazin
passed into the hands of the

The imposing, overgrown ruins of Dvidgrad

Habsburgs, who granted it to the Montecuccoli family as a reward for their services in the war against the Turks. The family maintained ownership of the castle after the end of the feudal regime.

The castle's present layout dates from the 16th century, when the wings were joined and a large tower was added. The tower is reached through a doorway in the façade made in 1786. Since 1955 it has housed the **Ethnographic Museum of Istria** (Etnografski muzej). In 1996 the **Civic Museum** was set up, with weaponry and finds from the castle on display.

The church of **St Francis** (Sv. Frane) and its 15th-century monastery were cultural centres for the area. The first schools to be set up in inland Istria were built here.

🏛 **Ethnographic Museum of Istria and Civic Museum**
Castle, Trg Istarskog razvoda 1.
🎫 *(052) 624 351.* ⬜ *May–Oct: 9am–6pm Mon–Sat, 9am–3pm Sun; Nov–Apr: 9am–4pm Mon–Sat.* 📷

Gračišće ⓯

Map B2. 🏃 *350.* 🚍 *Pazin, 7 km (4 miles).* 🚌 *Labin.* 🛈 *Aldo Negri 20, Labin, (052) 855 560.*

THE SMALL VILLAGE of Gračišće stands on a hill among woods and vineyards. At one time this was a strong military garrison, which stood on the borders of the Venetian Republic and the Habsburg empire. The town has some interesting buildings, such as the 15th-century **Salamon Palace** in Venetian-Gothic style and, to the side, the **Bishop's Chapel**, also in Venetian Gothic style, where the bishop of Pićan spent the summer.

The church of **St Mary** (Sv. Marije) was consecrated in 1425 and has a characteristic barrel vault and several frescoes. The Romanesque church of **St Euphemia** (Sv. Fumija) was rebuilt in the 16th century and still has a wooden crucifix from the 14th century. The loggia near the main gate dates from 1549.

The picturesque town of Pićan, once a bishop's see

Pićan ⓰

Map B2. 🏃 *316.* 🚍 *Pazin, 17 km (10 miles).* 🛈 *Aldo Negri 20, Labin, (052) 855 560.*

KNOWN AS Petena under the Romans, Pićan stands on a hilltop 350m (1,150 ft) high. It was a bishop's see from the 5th century to 1788, and has some intriguing medieval buildings. Inside the medieval walls is a cathedral dedicated to St Nicephorus, built in the 14th century, and rebuilt in the early 18th century after an earthquake. The story of the Christian martyr Nicephorus, whose remains were brought to Pićan by horse, are shown in a painting by Valentin Metzinger (1699–1759) in the cathedral. The Romanesque church of St Michael (Sv. Mihovil) in the cemetery has early 15th-century frescoes.

Labin ⓱

Map B3. 🏃 *320.* 🚍 *Rudarska ulica 5, (052) 855 022.* 🛈 *Aldo Negri 20, (052) 855 560, 851 486.* 🎵 *Classical music concerts (summer).*

THE OLD PART OF Labin is made up of the medieval part inside the walls, and the part from the Venetian period around Tito Square (Titov Trg). Here stand the 19th-century Town Hall, a 17th-century bastion, a loggia (1550) and the St Flora gate (1587) with a Lion of St Mark.

In the square called Stari Trg is the Gothic **Church of the Blessed Mary's Birth** (Rodjenje Marijino), built in the late 14th century but frequently renovated. A rose

window decorates the façade and inside are works by Venetian artists of the 16th and 17th centuries, including a painting by Palma il Giovane.

In the same square are the Magistrates' Court (1555), Scampicchio Palace (16th century) and the early 18th-century Baroque Lazzarini Palace, now the **Town Museum** with Roman and medieval finds, and a lifelike reconstruction of a coal mine. Labin was Croatia's most important coal mining town until the mines were closed down in 1999. In 1921, in opposition to rising Fascism in Italy, 2,000 coalminers set up the Labin Republic, a socialist mini-state that barely lasted a month.

🏛 **Town Museum**
Trg 1 Maja 6. 🎫 *(052) 852 477.*
⬜ *Jun–Sep: 10am–1pm, 5–7pm Mon–Sat; Oct–May: 7am–3pm Mon–Fri.*

ENVIRONS: About 4 km (2 miles) from Labin lies the popular seaside resort of Rabac.

Stepped road and ancient buildings, Labin

Detail of the altar in the church of St George the Younger, Plomin

Plomin ⑱

Map B3. 🏠 *140*. ✈ *Pula, 72 km (45 miles)*. 🚉 *Rijeka, 40 km (25 miles)*. 🏃 *Aldo Negri 20, Labin; (052) 855 560*; **Regional:** *Pionirska 1, Poreč, (052) 452 797*.

AN ANCIENT FORTIFIED town once stood here on the site of the Roman town Flanona, which was destroyed by the Avars in the 6th century. It was rebuilt after 1000 AD and took on its present look in the 13th century after it had become Venetian territory. Plomin, built on a sheer cliff 180 m (590 ft) above the bay of the same name, was once densely populated.

Houses take up nearly all the space inside the walls (from the 13th–14th centuries and only partially preserved). Worn, narrow roads climb towards the centre, where the 13th-century Romanesque church of **St George the Elder** (Sv. Jurai Stari) stands. Inside is a tablet in Glagolitic script *(see p33)* from between the 11th and 12th centuries, one of the oldest Croatian Glagolitic documents in Istria.

The church of **St George the Younger** (Sv. Jurai) also contains treasures of artistic merit. The church was consecrated in 1474, but was greatly altered in the 18th century. There are two Renaissance altars in carved, painted wood and a rich church treasury. Two frescoes by Robert, a German painter, were found on the wall during restoration work.

Mošćenice ⑲

Map B2. 🏠 *330*. ✈ *Rijeka, 53 km (33 miles), on the island of Krk*. 🚉 *Rijeka*. 🏃 *Aleja Slatina, Mošćenička Draga, (051) 737 533*.

THIS SMALL VILLAGE was founded by the Liburnians on a small hilltop. The structure of the medieval town is still evident, with houses pressed against the walls, narrow streets, small alleys and courtyards. There are lovely views over the Kvarner Gulf from the village.

In the main square is the church of **St Andrew** (Sv. Andrije), a building of medieval origin which was rebuilt in the Baroque style in the 17th century. Inside are some statues by the Paduan sculptor Jacopo Contieri, which adorn the beautiful 16th-century choir. The tall bell tower dominates the town. Just outside the walls are the small church of St Sebastian from the 16th century, and the 17th-century church of St Bartholomew.

The history of the area is documented in the **Ethnographic Museum** (Etnografski Muzej).

🏛 **Ethnographic Museum**
🕒 *(051) 737 551*.

ENVIRONS: A series of steps leads down to Mošćenička Draga (2 km/1 mile), where there is a large pebble beach.

Statue by Contieri, church of St Andrew, Mošćenice

Lovran ⑳

Map B2. 🏠 *3,640*. ✈ *Rijeka, 35 km (22 miles)*. 🚉 *Rijeka, 35 km (22 miles)*. 🚌 *Rijeka, 35 km (22 miles)*. 🏃 *Šetalište Maršala Tita 63, (051) 291 740*. 🎭 *Festival of St George (23 Apr); Marunada, chestnut festival (first Sun in Oct)*. 🌐 *www.tz-lovran.hr*

THE MODERN PART of Lovran (whose name derives from the laurel trees which are common in the area) is built on the slopes of the Gorica hill and extends along the coast until it meets the long seafront at Opatija *(see p65)*. The old part of the town stands on a small peninsula along the coast. The houses in the ancient fortified town lean against the enclosing walls, of which very few parts remain: just a tower and the Stubiza Gate. In the main square, as well as a medieval tower there are several houses with Venetian Gothic façades and the church of **St George** (Sv. Jurai), built in the 14th century and rebuilt in the Baroque period, along with a Romanesque bell tower. Inside the church, on the vault and the arch of the apse are some late Gothic frescoes (1470–79) representing the life of Christ and several saints. A building with a figure of St George stands in the main square.

Along the coastal promenade which extends

Old mill at the Ethnographic Museum, Mošćenice

The Villa Angiolina In Opatija, surrounded by a splendid park

between Lovran and Ika stand several beautiful early 20th-century Secessionist villas *(see p21)*, surrounded by lush gardens.

🏛 **St George**
📞 *(051) 291 611.* ⬜ *by appt.*

Tour of the Fortified Towns ㉑

See pp66–7.

Opatija ㉒

Map B2. 🏘 *9,000.* ✈ *Rijeka, 25 km (15 miles), island of Krk.* 🚉 *Rijeka.* 🚌 *Rijeka.* ℹ **Local:** *Nikole Tesle 2, (051) 271 710, 271 273;* **Regional:** *Park 1 maja, (051) 272 909, 272 988.* 🎭 *Karneval na Opatijskoj Rivijeri (Carnival); International regatta (May); Gastrofest (Mar).* 🌐 *www.opatija.hr*

THE TOURIST RESORT of Opatija takes its name from a 14th-century Benedictine abbey, around which a village was built. On the site of the monastery now stands the church of St James (Sv. Jakov), built in 1506 and enlarged in 1937.

Tourist interest began to grow in around 1845 when a nobleman from Rijeka, Iginio Scarpa, built the grand **Villa Angiolina** here. The villa is surrounded by a large park and became the first hotel.

A few years later the Austrian Empress Maria Anna stayed here and her visit was immediately followed by visits from other court dignitaries. More luxury hotels and villas were then built and the small town became a fashionable turn-of-the-century resort. Tourism in Opatija was given a boost by the construction of the railway line which linked Austria with Rijeka, with a tram line to Opatija.

The Emperor Franz Joseph also built a villa here, where he used to stay for long periods in the winter, so as to enjoy the mild climate of the area. Today the coast is still lined with luxury late 19th-century hotels and villas surrounded by parks and gardens. It is no longer the height of fashion, although older visitors are drawn by its comparative tranquillity.

Kastav ㉓

Map B2. 🏘 *930.* ✈ *Rijeka, 20 km (12 miles), island of Krk.* 🚉 *Rijeka, 11 km (7 miles).* 🚌 *Rijeka, 11 km (7 miles).* ℹ *Kastav 43, (051) 691 425.* 🎭 *Bela Nedeja, wine festival (first Sun in Oct).*

ON A HILL a short distance from Rijeka is the town of Kastav, which originated in the early Middle Ages. The castle was the residence of the local lord of the manor until the 16th century, and later the home of the Austrian governor. In Lovkine square stand the 17th-century church of St Helen of the Cross (Sv. Jelena Krizarica), the church of St Anthony of the Desert (15th century), and a loggia from 1571, restored in 1815. By the water trough a plaque recalls the drowning in 1666 of Captain Morello, guilty of imposing excessive taxes.

The harbour at Opatija, once a great favourite with the Habsburg royals

Tour of the Fortified Towns ㉑

Message box for denunciations

THE VILLAGES AND TOWNS OF ISTRIA were all fortified. The first people to build walls were the Istri (Illyrian tribes), who put up defences on the hilltops where they settled. There are 136 such fortified towns in Istria. Many were abandoned, but evidence in some shows continuous occupation from 1000 BC up to the present day. The walls were reinforced in Roman times and rebuilt in the late Middle Ages, then enlarged when the towns came under Austrian or Venetian rule. Documents written in the ancient Glagolitic script can be seen on a detour.

Hum ③
This small village is protected by an oval wall, reinforced by the Venetians. The church of St Jerome has splendid 12th-century Byzantine frescoes.

Buzet ④
An Illyrian fort and a Roman fortification (Pinguentum), Buzet belonged to the Venetians from 1420 onwards. They rebuilt the town wall with a Large Gate (1457) and a Small Gate. Today Buzet is known for its truffles.

Draguč ⑤
Medieval walls form the backs of the houses in this village. Ramparts were built by the Venetians after 1420. The 14th-century church of St Roch has a series of frescoes, including a Journey of the Magi.

KEY

▬▬	Tour route
▪ ▪	Trail of the Glagolitics
⋯⋯	Other roads
ℹ	Tourist information
☼	Viewpoint

Motovun ⑥
This medieval town stands on a hill dominating the valley. The old town is still encircled by an original 13th–14th-century wall. Later, a second wall was built around the suburbs. An internal gate, under a 15th-century tower, leads from the Lower Town to the Upper Town.

Roč ②

The wall around Roč was built by the Patriarchate of Aquileia in the 14th century. Towers were added in the 1500s. Roč was an important centre for Glagolitic writing and in the 1200s the alphabet was carved on a wall in the church of St Anthony Abbot. The Romanesque church of St Roch contains two fresco cycles.

TIPS FOR DRIVERS

Departure point: Boljun.
Distance: 77 km (48 miles) one way. **Stopping-off points:**
Motovun *Restaurant Mcotic, (052) 681 758;* **Hum** *Humska Konoba, (052) 660 005 (restaurant);* **Buzet** *Gostiona Most, (052) 662 867 (restaurant).*
🛈 **Buzet** *Trg Fontana, (052) 662 343.* **Poreč** *Head office for Istria, Pionirska 1, Poreč, (052) 452 797.*

0 kilometres   3

0 miles   3

Boljun ①

The village still has some of its medieval walls, the 16th-century ramparts, a tower and a water trough from 1697. The grain store, loggia and the Romanesque church of SS Cosmas and Damian are on the main road. Gothic paintings can be seen in the 14th-century church of St Peter.

THE TRAIL OF GLAGOLITIC DOCUMENTS

The "Trail of the Glagolitics" (Aleja Glagoljaša) winds between Roč and Hum. It is 7 km (4 miles) long and was created from 1977 to 1985 to commemorate this ancient Croatian script. Along the way are 11 significant Glagolitic documents recalling events and people who contributed to the spread of the writing, invented in the 11th century by the saints Cyril and Methodius to translate the scriptures *(see pp34–5)* into Slavonic.

Glagolitic document in stone on the trail to Roč

Rijeka ㉔

FOUNDED BY THE LIBURNIANS and conquered by the Celts, this town became a Roman city called Tarsatica. Over the centuries it frequently changed hands, and finally came under the rule of the Habsburgs. In 1719, to develop its maritime role, Ferdinand of Habsburg declared Rijeka a free town. The city became part of the kingdom of Hungary in 1769 and its economic importance continued to grow. Together with shipyards and industry, Rijeka is one of Croatia's main ports and a key rail and road junction. In February and March each year, Rijeka hosts Croatia's largest carnival celebrations.

Local handicraft *(see p244)*

The Korzo, a pedestrian avenue with 19th-century buildings

Exploring Rijeka

Over recent decades, the city has expanded, somewhat chaotically, along the coast and into the surrounding hills. However, its Central European atmosphere is still preserved in the majestic 19th-century buildings along the Korzo and the Riva, two broad avenues south of the Old Town (Stari Grad), built on land reclaimed from the sea. The Korzo is the heart of the city, lined with cafés, bars, restaurants and shops.

Church of the Capuchins
Kapucinska crkva
Kapucinske stube 5. ☎ *(051) 335 233.* ○ *before mass (7.30am, 7pm).*
North of Žabica Square (Trg Žabica) is the Capuchin Church, built between 1904 and 1929. The church is also known as the Madonna of Lourdes, because it was built on the 50th anniversary of the miracle of Lourdes.

Church of St Nicholas
Sv. Nikola
Ulica Ivana Zajca. ☎ *(051) 643 499.* ○ *before mass (7.30am, 7pm).*
The church of St Nicholas, built by the Orthodox community in 1786, contains fine icons from Vojvodina in Serbia.

Civic Tower
Gradski Toranj
About halfway along the Korzo is the Civic Tower. The tower is the result of alterations made to the gate of the Old Town from the 15th century. It was erected in the 18th century and the clock *(Pod Uriloj)* was also added. In 1890 the dome was built. An imposing building, it is decorated with coats of arms, including those of the city and the Habsburgs, and busts of the emperors Leopold I and Charles VI.

Detail of the Civic Tower

Town Hall
Municipij
Trg Riječke Rezolucije.
In 1883, the 14th-century Augustinian monastery was turned into the Town Hall. It takes up three sides of the square and is today the office of the University Rector.

Roman Arch
Stara Vrata
Trg Ivana Koblera.
In an alley leading from the north side of the square are the remains of a Roman arch, which was probably a gate to the city. It is a simple stone structure. Nearby, excavations have unearthed the foundations of a perimeter wall from the Roman period.

Church of the Assumption
Crkva Uznesenja Blažene Djevice Marije
Pavla Rittera Vitezovića 3. ☎ *(051) 214 177.* ○ *7am–noon, 4–7pm.*
The collegiate of the Assumption, once a cathedral, preserves little of its original 13th-century aspect. It was renovated in the Baroque style in 1695 and altered in 1726 with Rococo details, and a 16th-century rose window was inserted. Inside, the altars, some paintings and the chancel are from the Baroque period. The bell tower bears the date of its construction (1377); the upper part is in Gothic style.

Cathedral of St Vitus
Katedrala Sv. Vida
Trg Grivica. ○ *7am–noon, 4–7pm.*
The church of St Vitus, patron saint of the city, is now the cathedral. This large Baroque church was built between 1638 and 1742 by the Jesuits. Baroque altars, and a Gothic crucifix on the main altar from the 13th century, adorn the interior.

Maritime and Historical Museum of Coastal Croatia
Pomorski i Povijesni Muzej Hrvatskog Primorja
Muzejski trg 1/1. ☎ *(051) 213 578.* ○ *9am–1pm Tue–Sat.*
This is the oldest museum in Rijeka, founded in 1876, but

Gothic crucifix in the cathedral of St Vitus

since 1955 housed in the Governor's Palace built in 1896. The history of navigation is told through the collections of model ships, weapons and seafaring equipment from the 17th and 18th centuries. There are also rich archaeological collections from prehistory to the Middle Ages, displays of prints, furniture, paintings and an ethnographic collection.

🛕 Our Lady of Trsat
Gospa Trsatska

Frankopanski trg.
On the opposite bank of the Rječina river, above the centre of Rijeka, is Trsat. At the top of the 561 steps from Tito Square (Trg Titov) is the Sanctuary of Our Lady of Trsat. The church and Franciscan monastery were built in 1453 by Martin Frankopan on the site of a 12th-century church. It was in this church, from 1291 to 1294, that parts of the Holy House of Mary of Nazareth were preserved before being transferred to Loreto in Italy.

The altar of Our Lady of Trsat, with the painting of the Virgin

To compensate the local people for this loss, in 1367 Pope Urban V donated to them a *Virgin with Child*, painted by St Luke, which now stands on the main altar.

The sanctuary was visited by soldiers and sailors who left votive gifts, now kept in a chapel next to the cloisters. The church was remodelled in 1864 but retained the triumphal arch, the marble altar which sits underneath the painting of the Virgin, and many tombs of the Frankopan family.

VISITORS' CHECKLIST

Map B2. 🏠 168,000. ✈ Krk, (051) 842 040. 🚂 Krešimirova ulica, (051) 211 111. 🚌 Trg Žabice 1, (051) 660 360. 🚢 Riva, (051) 212 696; Adriatic: Verdijeva 6, (051) 214 300; Jadrolinija Riva 16, (051) 211 444. 🛈 Užarska 14, (051) 213 1456. 🎭 Biennial art exhibition (1 Jul–30 Sep), Summer Music.

🏰 Trsat Castle
Gradina Trsat

Ulica Zrinskog. 📞 (051) 217 714. ⏰ summer: 9am–10pm; winter: 9am–3pm. 🚻 🛒 🎵
The Sanctuary of Our Lady leads to a castle built by the Romans to defend Tarsatica, parts of which still survive. In the 13th century, Trsat was owned by the Frankopans, who built another castle on the same site. In the 19th century it was bought and renovated by an Austrian general, Laval Nugent, who lived and was buried here. There are fine views from the site over the Kvarner gulf.

RIJEKA TOWN CENTRE

Cathedral of St Vitus ⑦
Church of the Assumption ⑥
Church of the Capuchins ①
Church of St Nicholas ②
Civic Tower ③
Marine and Historical Museum of Coastal Croatia ⑧
Roman Arch ⑤
Town Hall ④

0 metres 200
0 yards 200

KEY

🛈 Tourist information

✝ Church

🅿 Parking

🚌 Bus station

✉ Post office

Cres ㉕

THE NARROW ISLAND OF CRES is 65 km (40 miles) long. In the north, a colony of native griffon vultures, protected by law since 1986, nests on a plateau swept by the dry, cold bora wind. The south is milder and olives and vines are grown. A single road travels from the north of Cres to the south of Lošinj, linking the islands by a bridge. Tourism focuses on just a few villages such as Cres, Osor, Martinšćica and Valun.

VISITORS' CHECKLIST

Map B3. 🚶 *3,200.* 🚌 *(051) 211 444.* **Cres** ℹ *Cons Ulica 11, (051) 571 535.* **Osor** ℹ *(051) 237 007.* �W *www.tzg-cres.hr*

Dry-stone walls and olive groves overlooking the town of Cres

Cres Town

Cres nestles in a bay sheltered by the hill behind. The town became important when the bishopric and governor's seat were transferred here from Osor.

The walls and the two gates with stone arches give the town a Venetian feel, and the church of Our Lady of the Snow has paintings by artists from the Venetian school. The 16th-century Town Hall, or Loggia, is now a fruit and vegetable market.

The old port is a lively place, bustling with fishermen and visitors. The Town Gate, a clock tower and several Renaissance buildings face the port. The church of St Isidore (the patron saint), dates from the 10th or 11th century.

Osor

Until the mid-15th century this was the main town on the island, with a port and a bishopric. It later declined and the capital was moved to Cres. Today the entire town is a museum, with Bronze Age remains and some splendid monuments, making it a centre of great artistic interest.

The beautiful 5th-century cathedral of the Assumption was renovated in 1497 and is built of honey-coloured stone. The façade has an arched tympanum above a doorway with a relief of the Virgin Mary. Inside the church there is a painting of SS Nicholas and Gaudentius on the altar.

The Archaeological Museum (Arheološki muzej) occupies the Town Hall and has stone inscriptions and interesting finds from the Illyrian and Roman periods, and the early Middle Ages. The façade of the Bishop's Palace (second half of the 15th century) bears coats of arms of the bishops and nobles of the island and the interior is richly decorated. Some walls, foundations and mosaics are all that remain of the cathedral of St Peter. Nearby are two Romanesque churches dedicated to St Plato and St Catherine.

🏛 Archaeological Museum

Arheološki musej
Town Hall, Palazzo Petrić.
📞 *(051) 571 127.* ⬤ *for restoration. Contact Tourist Office for information.*

KEY

▬	Minor road
▬	Scenic road
🚢	Ferry
ℹ	Tourist information
🏖	Beach with facilities
🔆	Viewpoint

0 kilometres   8

0 miles   8

Map labels: Porozina, Beli, Cres, Plavnik, Lubenice, CRES, Vidovići, Štivan, Belej, Nerezine, Osor, Pogana

Door of the Gothic church of Our Lady of the Snow, Cres

Lošinj (Lussino) ❷⑥

THE ISLAND OF LOŠINJ has a mild climate and sub-tropical vegetation with maritime pines, palms, oleanders and citrus trees. The main town, Mali Lošinj, was founded in the 6th century, when 12 Croat families landed here. The most famous beach is at Čikat bay, southwest of Mali Lošinj. It is 30 km (19 miles) long and a popular place for water sports.

**Interior of the church of
St Anthony Abbot, Veli Lošinj**

Mali Lošinj
This pretty town, which, like Cres, belonged to Venice for many centuries, has many buildings from the 18th and 19th centuries, when maritime activity was at its height. The oldest part of the town lies around the 18th-century church of St Mary. Large hotel complexes just outside the town cater for package holidaymakers at this popular and bustling resort.

Veli Lošinj
Quieter than Mali Lošinj, this is a lovely town with villas hidden among the lush vegetation. The church of St Anthony Abbot is from the 15th century but was rebuilt at a later date. It has a rich store of paintings, including examples by Bartolomeo Vivarini (1430–90), Bernardo Strozzi (1581–1644) and Francesco Hayez (1791–1882). The Baroque style is much in evidence on the seven altars.

There is a splendid view of the town and the coastline from the 16th-century tower of the Uskoks (see p79).

ENVIRONS: The island of **Susak** is renowned for its unusual geology: a 10-m (33-ft) layer of sand covering a calcareous platform. Vines grow well on this soil and all the islanders have vineyards; their wealth is measured by the number of vines they own. The vines, grown on terraces and protected by cane windbreaks, are further sheltered by dry-stone walls which are typical of the islands and the coastline of the upper Adriatic. The picturesque, brightly coloured women's costumes are famous. They are made by the islanders during the winter months and shown off at festivals.

The island of **Ilovik**, south of Lošinj, covers an area of nearly 6 sq km (2.3 sq miles) and is home of about 350 people, most of whom live in the village of Sv. Petar on the northeast coast. Vines, olives, fruit and flowers grow well in this mild climate. Nearby is the uninhabited island of Sv. Petar, where there are the ruins of a Venetian fortress and a Benedictine Abbey with a church and monastery. Prehistoric and Roman finds (mosaics, coins and other objects) have been discovered on Susak and Ilovik.

Unije is the largest of the lesser islands. It is hilly with little vegetation and a steep rocky coast on the western side, but there is a more accessible coast on the eastern side. The village is built around the church of St Andrew and its bell tower can be seen from a distance. The islanders tend to make their living from market gardening or fishing.

KEY

▬	Minor road
═	Path
🚢	Ferry
✈	Airport
ℹ	Tourist information
🏖	Beach with facilities
☀	Viewpoint

Overlooking the fishing harbour of Mali Lošinj

Risnjak National Park: The Leska Trail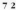
Risnjak Narodni Park

THE VAST GORSKI KOTOR PLATEAU, which separates Croatia from Slovenia, begins north of Rijeka. Part of the area has been declared a national park in order to protect the forests and natural environment and the ecological balance of the area. The park, set up in 1953, originally covered an area of 34 sq km (13 sq miles), but it is now double that size, most of it made up of forests and grasslands with many karst (limestone) features. The climatic conditions, caused by the territory's particular exposure and altitude, are very varied and about 20 different plant communities have been identified. The Leska trail was set up in 1995 to inform visitors about various aspects of this area.

▨ Park area

▨ The Leska trail

Silver Fir Forest ⑧
The silver fir, in great demand for boat building, has disappeared from many woods in Croatia; here it mingles with beech trees.

Chasm ⑦
Cold air from the chasm and the damp subsoil of this rocky fissure make the flora of great interest: plants which normally only grow at the higher altitudes of the park can be found here.

Feed Troughs ⑥
Feed troughs are set up here in winter to provide food for all the animals in the park.

Hranilište

⑥

685

Osmatračnica
⑨
690   *Klada*

Gmajna

686

MARKOV BRLOG

Observatory ⑨
From this viewing platform the behaviour of animals such as bears, foxes, lynxes, martens and wild cats can be observed in the woods. There are also many birds, both non-migratory and birds of passage. Towards evening at certain times of the year, eagles, hawks and crows can also be seen.

707

⑫

⑩

Leska
⑪

Cultivating the Countryside ⑩
Only one house is inhabited in the village of Leska. It is used from spring to autumn by farmers, who come to grow potatoes, peas and beans on specially built terraces.

Springs ⑪
Water flows under the layers of impervious rock and springs are created where the water emerges.

Tree Trunks ⑫
Fungi thrive in the cracks of old tree trunks providing a source of food for insects too.

Beech and Fir Forests ⑤

The trail goes through woods of fir and beech trees; many of the trees are very large. The undergrowth consists of hazelnut, bilberry and elder bushes.

Mountain Meadows ④

The areas which were deforested for agriculture or grazing land for animals are now mountain meadows. In late spring they explode with the varied colours of heather, purple moor grass, fescue and other grasses.

685

③

④

②

686

686

①

Conservation of Trees ①

The protection of the older, larger plant species was one of the reasons the reserve was set up. Within the park are examples of enormous ancient beech, silver and spruce fir trees, and also some rarer trees, such as the mountain elm and maple.

0 metres 200

0 yards 200

CRNI LUG

Storm Damage ②

When strong winds blow down old or sick trees, they are left where they fall as they provide suitable growing conditions for microorganisms such as fungi.

KEY

■ Pedestrian trail

= Other roads

Karst Sinkholes ③

A karst sinkhole is a funnel-shaped hollow in the land. This feature is caused by water erosion of the rock and is characteristic of limestone areas.

Krk ㉘

Part of the Frankopan castle

THIS IS THE LARGEST of the Adriatic islands, with an area of 409 sq km (158 sq miles). A bridge links the island to the mainland, built to provide good connections to the island's international airport. Along the eastern coast the island looks almost ghostly, its white rocks swept by the bora wind. Inland and on the more protected western coast, there is rich, lush vegetation.

VISITORS' CHECKLIST

Map B3. 🏛 *16,500*. ✈ *(051) 842 132*. **Krk** 🚢 *(051) 863 170.* 🛈 *Trg Sv. Kvirina 1, (051) 221 359; Krk Vela Placa 1, (051) 222 583.* **Baška** 🚢 *(051) 856 821.* 🛈 *Kralja Zvonimira 114, (051) 856 544.* **Omišalj** 🛈 *Ribarska Obala 10, (051) 846 243.*

The crystal-clear waters surrounding the island of Krk

Krk was first inhabited by the Liburnians, followed by the Romans, who founded Curicum (the present-day Krk) and Fulfinum (now Omišalj). Traces of walls, baths and villas with floor mosaics still remain.

In the 6th century it came under Croatian rule and after the Frankish and Byzantine occupation it became part of the possessions of Venice. It was then granted to Dujmo, founder of the Frankopan family, and from 1480 to 1797 it was directly ruled by Venice.

Krk was a centre for Glagolitic script and the Baška Tablet, now in the Croatian Academy of Arts and Sciences in Zagreb, was found on the island.

Krk Town

The town of Krk developed in the Middle Ages on the site of the Roman town of Curicum. The wall and three Venetian city gates are still visible: the City Gate with a guard tower called Kamplin, the Sea Gate (Pisana) and the Upper Gate. Facing the main square are Renaissance-era buildings and in the area of the Roman baths is the cathedral of **Our Lady of the Assumption,** dating from the 1100s but modified since. The three-aisle church has a façade of light-coloured stone. Inside are four paintings (1706) by Cristoforo Tasca, and a wooden Baroque pulpit.

The treasury is in the adjacent Romanesque church of **St Quirinus** which houses the **Diocesan Museum**. This contains works from the cathedral and other churches on the island, including the silver Frankopan altarpiece depicting the *Virgin Mary in Glory* and a polyptych (1350) by Paolo Veneziano.

Behind the cathedral stands the Frankopan castle with four square towers from 1191, and a round tower from the Venetian period. Inside the walls are churches dedicated to Our Lady of Health and St Francis. The latter has an engraved wooden pulpit.

Omišalj

Omišalj lies on a headland near the site of Roman Fulfinum. The village (Castrum Musculum in the Middle Ages) was enclosed by walls, some of which

KEY

▬	Major road
▬	Minor road
▬	Scenic route
🚢	Ferry
✈	Airport
🛈	Tourist information
🏖	Beach with facilities

Map labels: Kraljevica, Omišalj, Rudine, Njivice, Klimno, Šilo, Porat, Glavotok, Šepići, Kozarin, Vrbnik, KRK, Krk, Košljun, Punat, Valbiska, Jurandvor, Baška, Stara Baška

0 kilometres   8

0 miles   8

◁ **The shingle beach of Stara Baška on the island of Krk**

survive. Narrow streets lead up to a square with a 17th-century Venetian loggia, the church of St Helen with reproductions of Glagolitic script, and the Romanesque church of St Mary (13th century) with a dome, bell tower and 16th-century choir, and a 15th-century triptych by Jacobello del Fiore.

Glagolitic inscription and rose window, St Mary, Omišalj

Baška

Stara Baška (Old Baška) is opposite Omišalj. Baška (New Baška) is on the coast and is a popular tourist resort with a beautiful beach, 2 km (1 mile) long, and clear sea. The church of the Holy Trinity (1772) stands in a small square; inside is a fine *Last Supper* by Palma il Giovane.

Behind Baška, around a castle destroyed in the 11th century, is Starigrad, with the Romanesque church of St John, rebuilt in 1723.

In the church of St Lucy in Jurandvor, a short distance from Baška, is a copy of the Baška Tablet (the original is in Zagreb), the oldest document in Croatia written in Glagolitic script.

Košljun

Since 1447 a Franciscan monastery has stood on this small island. In the cloisters are stone inscriptions from the Roman and medieval eras and the library has over 20,000 Glagolitic documents. In the church is a polyptych by Girolamo di Santacroce (1535) and a *Last Judgment* by Ughetto. The treasury and many sacred objects are in the church of St Bernard.

Bakar ㉙

Map B2.
🏠 *1,900.* 🚌 *(051) 761 214.*
ℹ *Primorje 39, (051) 761 411.*
🎭 *Daisy Summer, concerts and shows in the čakavski dialect (last week Jun).*

THE DEMOLITION of a refinery and a coke plant has brought visitors back to this village, which was once a popular destination for people attracted to the landscape of the area and curious about the phenomena of the fresh-water springs. These springs originate in underground sources and flow out to the coast.

The **Frankopan Castle** and surrounding fishing village are also worth a visit. The village stands on the site of the Roman Volcera. From the 15th century until 1778 it belonged to the Frankopans who, in 1530, built a triangular-shaped castle. It is still well-preserved with high windows which were salvaged when it was transformed into a palace for the Šubić-Zrinski family who lived in the property after the Frankopans.

The parish church has a painting of the *Holy Trinity* by Girolamo da Santacroce and a Crucifix from the 14th century. Evidence of the past is preserved in the **Civic Museum** which has many tombstones and sculptures dating from the Roman and early Middle Ages. Bakar keeps its naval traditions alive thanks to the prestigious Maritime Academy, which was founded in 1849.

The internal courtyard in the Frankopan castle, Kraljevica

Kraljevica ㉚

Map B2. 🏠 *3,000.* 🚊 *Rijeka.*
🚌 *(051) 281 330.* ℹ *Rovinj, (051) 282 078.* 🎭 *Shrovetide Sezona, traditional masked ball (carnival).*

A WELL-KNOWN tourist resort on the mainland, Kraljevica is linked to the island of Krk by a long bridge which also connects with Rijeka airport (on Krk). In the old town (Stari Grad) is a castle, built in the 16th century by the family of the counts of Šubić-Zrinski. The castle walls also shelter the small church of St Nicholas.

A village inhabited by families from the fortress of Hreljin developed around the castle. In the new district (Novi Grad), on a small promontory above the sea, is a castle built by the Frankopan family in 1650 in the late-Renaissance style. It has a square ground-plan with four round towers. It was turned into a magnificent palace in the middle of the 18th century.

In 1728, the Austrian emperor Charles VI began to create a sizeable port here, at the end of a road that went from Karlovac to the sea.

The Frankopan castle in Bakar, dominating the village

Crikvenica ㉛

Map B2. 🏘 *5,800.*
✈ *Rijeka, 16 km (10 miles), island of Krk.* 🚌 *Nike Veljačića 3, (051) 781 333.* 🛈 *Trg Stjepana Radića 1, (051) 241 867.* 🎪 *Trade fair of Croatian products (5–12 Jul); Town festival (Aug).* 🖳 www.tzg-crikvenica.com

A ROMAN STAGING POST called Ad Turres existed here at one time, with a port for trading in timber. In 1412 Nikola Frankopan (whose name derives from the noble Roman family of the Frangipani) built a castle here. It was later donated to the Pauline order, who set up a church, monastery and school. In the 16th century a wall and a round tower were built and, in 1659, the church was enlarged by adding a nave. The town, now a popular tourist resort, takes its name from the monastery. At the beginning of the 19th century, the Pauline order was dissolved and in 1893 the ancient monastery was turned into the Hotel Kastel (*see p220*).

The town has a long gravel beach and is one of the most popular tourist resorts along this stretch of coast. Thanks to its position, protected from the winds by the Velebit mountains, it enjoys a mild climate with dry summers and warm winters.

Gate of the former Pauline monastery, now a hotel, in Crikvenica

The altar in the church of SS Philip and James, Novi Vinodolski

Novi Vinodolski ㉜

Map B3. 🏘 *3,800.* ✈ *Rijeka, 28 km (17 miles), island of Krk.* 🚉 *Rijeka, 49 km (30 miles).* 🛈 *Ulica Kralja Tomislava 6, (051) 244 306.* 🎪 *Patron saints' day, Philip and James (May); Novi Vinodolski summer carnival (Aug).*

T HE OLD TOWN, built on a hill overlooking the Vinodol valley, holds an important place in Croatian history. On 6 January 1288, in the castle built by the Frankopan dukes, the Vinodol Codex, one of the oldest legislative Croatian texts in Glagolitic script (*see pp34–5*), was produced. The document is now in the National Library in Zagreb. It was signed by the representatives of nine communes, and established rules for the ownership and use of local land.

In 1988, the 700th anniversary of the Vinodol Codex, a fountain created by the sculptor Dorijan Sokolić was placed in the central square of Novi. The fountain bears the names of the places which participated in drawing up the laws.

The town is also remembered for the stratagem used by Bishop Kristofor to save the troops defeated by the Turks: the horses' shoes were put on backwards so as to foil their pursuers. Having reached the safety of Vinodol Castle, the bishop gave thanks by rebuilding the church of **SS Philip and James** (Sveti Filip i Jakov). He was buried here in 1499.

The church, decorated in the 17th century in the Baroque style, has a magnificent altar from that period. The side altar has a Gothic Virgin Mary from the 15th century.

The 13th-century **Frankopan Castle**, recently restored, is now a museum, with exhibits from the Roman and medieval periods and a rich, varied collection of traditional folk costumes.

Costume in the castle of Novi Vinodolski

Senj ㉝

Map C3.
🏘 *6,000.* ✈ *Rijeka, 52 km (32 miles).* 🚌 *Ulica Kralja Zvonimira 8, (053) 881 235.* 🛈 *Stara cesta 2, (053) 881 068.* 🎪 *Feast of St George (23 Apr).* 🖳 www.lickosenjska. com/senj

T HE COLD WIND known as the bora of Senj blows through a pass in the Velebit chain of mountains, making the town the chilliest place in the Adriatic. People have long been aware of it, yet despite this notoriety, Senj has always been inhabited, first by the Illyrians, then by the Romans who created a port at Senia.

THE USKOKS

In 1526, shortly before the Battle of Mohács, numbers of Christians from the hinterland fled to the safer coastal cities to escape the Turks. The refugees were called "Uskoks" (fugitives), and their main desire was to fight those who had taken their land. Initially they were organized by Venice around the fortress of Klis, from which they attacked the Turk-occupied land. In 1537 the Turkish government made a treaty of non-belligerence with Venice on condition that the Uskoks were removed from Klis. Some Uskoks went to Primosten, but the main nucleus settled in Senj, under the rule of the Habsburgs, who encouraged them to procure fast boats in order to plunder the heavy Turkish ships. When Austria also slowed down operations against the Turks, the Uskoks took up piracy and started sacking coastal towns. At the end of the war between Venice and the Ottoman empire in 1617, the emperor was forced to remove the Uskoks from the coast and they and their families were transported to the west of Zagreb, to the Žumberak mountains.

Relief in the Museum of the Uskoks, Senj

This soon became a bishopric and an important trading port for the transport of timber. After 1000 AD it was granted to the Templar Knights. It then passed to the Frankopans, and finally came under the direct rule of the King of Hungary. As defence against the Turks, the Habsburgs established the first station of the Military Frontier *(Vojna Krajina)* here. This stronghold had a powerful outer wall which is now only partially preserved.

Nehaj Castle, dominating the town of Senj

After the Battle of Mohács in 1526, many Uskoks from Sinj and Klis came to Senj, and were co-opted by the local Austrian governor in the fight against the Turks. Their presence is recorded in **Nehaj Castle**, a fortress built on a square plan, constructed in 1553–8 by the Uskok captain, Ivan Lenković, on a hill a short distance from the town. It was positioned so as to sight approaching ships. The well laid-out **Museum of the Uskoks** is on the first floor of the fort, and has an excellent view over the bay.

In the southern part of the wide bay is the main square, called Cilnica. Facing the square is the Frankopan palace, built in 1340 and altered in the 19th century. There are also large salt warehouses, and, further in, the **Cathedral of St Mary** (Sv. Marija), built in the 13th century and altered in the Baroque period. It has tombstones with Renaissance reliefs and Baroque works, including an altar decorated with four marble statues.

A short distance from the square is the Vukasović Palace which houses the **Civic Museum** (Gradski Muzej Senj), a museum of local history. The palace was once the residence of an Uskok captain. Flanking the roads of the town and in the Small Square (Mala Placa), also known as Campuzia, are Renaissance buildings such as

the Town Hall with its splendid loggia. Nearby is the Leonova Kula tower, dedicated to Pope Leo X, and the small, pretty church of St Mary. Senj is the departure point for ferries to Baška (on the island of Krk) and the island of Rab.

ENVIRONS: The small village of **Jablanac** lies 37 km (23 miles) south of Senj. This bustling place is also a departure point for ferries to the island of Rab, and a good starting point for visiting the Velebit massif.

Jablanac is worth an unhurried visit so as to enjoy the well-preserved town, the harbour houses and the numerous archaeological finds scattered over the area. Jablanac was a county seat and its representatives met in the medieval castle. The castle was built by the Ban (governor) Stjepan Subić, as was the church and its cemetery, both known from documents from 1251. The castle is now in ruins.

Jablanac, south of Senj, departure point for the island of Rab

Rab ❸

A window in the Prince's Palace in Rab town

THE ISLAND OF RAB lies parallel to the Velebit massif, creating a channel which was much dreaded by sailors because it forms a tunnel for the cold, dry bora wind which makes this part of the coast rocky and barren. The opposite, western side of the island is protected from the wind and the climate is mild. Here the landscape is much greener and maquis alternates with woods of pine, oak and holm oak. The Romans knew the island by the name of Arba, or Scadurna, and, after its conquest, built a settlement on the site of the present-day town of Rab. This island is a popular holiday destination with its sandy beaches, rocky coves and mild climate.

Rab Town

The main town, Rab, which gives its name to the island, became a bishopric in the early Christian period and was inhabited by Slavic people in the 6th century. After it had been conquered by the Franks, it was administered by Venice and a treaty of mutual defence was agreed upon which lasted until 1000 AD. Rab was at times under the rule of the Hungarian kings until 1409, when it became Venetian territory. Venice ruled the island until 1797.

The town, famous for its four bell towers which make it look like a ship with four masts, has some lovely Venetian architecture. Along the three main streets are fine aristocratic buildings with Romanesque doorways, such as the Nimira, Tudorin, Kukulić, Galzigna and Cassio Palaces. The ancient medieval

View of Rab with its four bell towers

walls around the Old Town (Kalbanat) on the southern point of the peninsula were destroyed, and in the 15th century a wall was built which also enclosed the New Town, called Varos. Part of this wall is well-preserved, particularly the stretch facing the bay of St Euphemia.

🏛 Loggia

Ulica Sdreanja, Rab.
Where the main road, Ulica Sdreanja, widens out, there is a beautiful Venetian loggia, built in 1506 in Renaissance style, and a granary *(fondak)*. To the left is the Sea Gate (Morska Vrata), a tower from the 14th century. Through the gate is the town square.

🏛 Prince's Palace

Knežev Dvor
Trg Municipium Arba, Rab. ◐ *to the public.*
The port and the town square are the heart of Rab, and this is also where the Prince's Palace was built in the 13th century in the Romanesque style. It was later enlarged in the Gothic style and then rebuilt in the Renaissance style. It has Venetian Gothic

The Sea Gate, one of the ways into the town of Rab

windows and Renaissance mullioned windows. In the courtyard are some Roman and medieval remains.

🔒 Monastery and Church of St Andrew

Sv. Andrija
Ulica Ivana Rabljanina, Rab.
This small Romanesque church is annexed to a Benedictine convent founded in 1118. The bell tower, the oldest in Rab, is from the following century. The belfry has trefoil windows.

🔒 Cathedral of St Mary the Great

Katedrala Sv. Marija Velika
Ulica Ivana Rabljanina, Rab.
This splendid Romanesque building was consecrated by Pope Alexander III in 1177. The façade has alternating layers of pink and white stone and above the portal is a sculpted *Deposition* by Petar Trogiranin dating from 1514. The three-aisle interior, divided by columns, has a beautiful baptismal font made by the same sculptor in 1497, and a polyptych by Paolo Veneziano (1350) on the altar.

In the presbytery is a splendid altar canopy with marble columns and on the main altar, surrounded by an ornate wooden choir, is a reliquary from the 12th century with the remains of St Christopher.

The 13th-century bell tower stands 70 m (230 ft) away from the cathedral. It is the tallest of all the bell towers on the island.

The bell tower of the Cathedral of St Mary the Great

🔓 Chapel of St Anthony of Padua
Sv. Antun

Ulica Ribara, Rab.
The small church of St Anthony, dating from 1675, is a good example of religious Baroque architecture. Inside is a marble inlaid altar and a 17th-century painting from the Venetian school.

🔓 Franciscan Convent of St Anthony Abbot
Sv. Antun Opat

Rab. 🔵 *to the public.*
The church and convent of St Anthony Abbot stand behind the cathedral at the end of the promontory. This convent, built for a closed order of nuns, was founded in 1497 by the noblewoman Magdalena Budrišić.

🔓 Church of St Francis
Sv. Frane

Parco Komrcar, Rab.
The church dates from 1491 and stands to the north of the town in Komrcar Park. It is a blend of Gothic and Renaissance and has an original façade with three sculpted shells.

The altar in the Renaissance church of St Justine in Rab

🔓 Convent and Church of St Justine
Sv. Justa

Gornja Ulica, Rab. ⬜ *9am–noon, 6–8pm Jul & Aug; 7.30am–9pm Jun–Sep.*
The convent and church were consecrated in 1578, and were intended for nuns from non-noble families. The bell tower with its onion dome dates from 1672. The church now houses a Museum of Holy Art, with the crucifix of King Koloman from 1112, and the reliquary of St Christopher

VISITORS' CHECKLIST

Map B3. 🏛 *9,200.* **Rab** 🚢 *from Rijeka, Senj, Pag, Zadar;* (051) 742 112. 🚢 *Mali Palid.* (051) 724 189. ℹ️ *Donja ulica 2,* (051) 724 064. 🎵 *musical evenings, Church of the Holy Cross (Jun–Sep); Tournament of Rab, (9 May, 7 Jul).* 🌐 *www.tzg-rab.hr*

(12th century), protector of the town. Also on display are paintings and panels, including a polyptych by Paolo Veneziano (1350), Gospels and illuminated books in Glagolitic script.

Kampor
Kampor lies at the end of a long bay (Kamporska Draga) and has preserved its stone houses and terraces of olives and vines. Many private holiday houses have sprung up around the village.

The Franciscan convent of St Euphemia, with a small adjacent Romanesque church, is near the church of St Bernard. The church contains two panels by Bartolomeo and Antonio Vivarini, a Byzantine panel (14th century) and other works. In the cloister there are various tombs and the sarcophagus of Magdalena Budrišić, the noblewoman who founded the convent of St Anthony Abbot in Rab.

Lopar
The village of Lopar is at the end of a rocky peninsula. It is a popular spot thanks to the sandy beaches fringed by pinewoods and the leisure facilities on offer (tennis, football and mini-golf).

SV. GRGUR

GOLI
Goli

Lopar

0 kilometres   5

0 miles   5

Supertaska Draga
Kampor

105

R A B

Rab 🚢ℹ️

KEY

━━ Major road

━━ Minor road

🚢 Ferry

ℹ️ Tourist information

🏖 Beach with facilities

☼ Viewpoint

Barbat na Rabu

105

DOLIN   Pudariča
                Mišnjak

Polyptych by the Vivarini, church of St Bernard, Kampor

One of the spectacular waterfalls at the Plitvice Lakes ▷

Plitvice Lakes National Park ㉟
Nacionalni Park Plitvička Jezera

T HE PLITVICE LAKES NATIONAL PARK, located in the heart of Croatia, was founded in 1949. This area of 300 sq km (115 sq miles), covered in lakes and forest, has been part of the UNESCO World Heritage list since 1979. It is particularly known for its spectacular waterfalls. There are 16 lakes within the park and visitors can move around by following the paths along the shores or by using footbridges. Electric buses take people to the starting points of the trails and to the hotels in the park. The largest lake can be toured by electric boat. There are no towns or villages in the reserve, only hotels.

A hut by the lake shore

The bird life is extremely varied: 160 species have been recorded, including the eagle, marsh harrier, peregrine falcon, hoopoe, kingfisher, heron, little owl, and tawny owl.

Footbridges
Numerous footbridges and rowing boats enable visitors to get from one shore of a lake to another and are a lovely way to get in and explore the fir, pine and beech forests.

OTOČ

Ciginovak

Proščansko jezero

Okrugliak

Labudovac

S T U B I C A

Galovac

Gradinsko jezero

Isola

P R I J E K A
K O S A

Gliborita draga

0 metres   500

0 yards   500

Velika Poljana

Entrance 2

ZARA

Dense Forests
The forests alongside the waters are home to some of the largest European species of animal, including wolves, lynxes, foxes, wild boar, roebucks, wild cats, otters and badgers.

VISITORS' CHECKLIST

Map C3. ▮ *(053) 751 014, 751
015.* ◯ *summer: 8am–sunset
daily; winter: 9am–4pm daily.*
▨ � *limited access.*
Ⓦ *www.np-plitvice.tel.hr/np-
plitvice*

Flora
*The park flora is very varied, from waterlilies on the
lakes to forests of gigantic trees. There is also a rich
undergrowth of shrubs, a source of food for wildlife.*

Waterfalls
*It is possible to follow
signposted routes and
walk behind the
waterfalls to watch
the rushing waters as
they cascade from
the lake above.*

The park vehicles,
electric buses, take
visitors around the area
on special routes.

Entrance 1

KEY

▬	Major road
▬	Route for park vehicles
■ ■	Footpath
- - -	Boat route
⛴	Electric boat
▮	Tourist information
Ⓟ	Parking

View of the River Korana
*Along the banks of the River Korana, into which the
lakes drain, are a few shepherds' huts and several
sawmills which are run on hydraulic power. The
river flows between steep cliffs in a spectacular
natural landscape.*

DALMATIA

······································

*D*ALMATIA IS THE MOST VISITED *region of Croatia. Although tourism collapsed in the 1990s because of the war, visitors are again flocking to the rocky coastline and sandy beaches, the deserted islands and the splendid cities of this Adriatic region. As a consequence of relationships and trade with Italy, an Adriatic culture developed here which has given Dalmatia an Italianate feel.*

In the 1st century BC, after two centuries of war, the Romans managed to conquer the Dalmatian and Liburnian tribes and integrate them into their system. For over three centuries the region enjoyed a period of prosperity which was eventually brought to an end by the arrival of peoples from Asia, including the Slavs in the 7th century.

In 915, after a long period of wars and unrest, the first Croatian kings founded a new state, blessed by papal authority. New public and religious buildings, walls and town halls were built, the arts began to flourish, and trading with the Italian coast increased. This was a period of great cultural vitality, which survived the collapse of the Croatian state and its integration into the Kingdom of Hungary in the 12th century. In 1409, after a long series of conflicts, the Hungarian king sold the islands and

**The Lion of St Mark
on the Land Gate in Zadar**

many of the coastal cities to Venice. In the 16th century, there followed a second flowering of the arts, and the sculptors, architects, painters, writers and scholars of this period laid the foundations for the future development of Croatian culture, art and literature.

In late spring, when the Jadranska Magistrala coast road has yet to be invaded by heavy summer traffic, this must be one of the loveliest parts of Europe. From Karlobag the road winds along the edge of the Velebit mountain chain and the Dalmatian and the Biokovo plateaux. Seawards is the long, lunar-surfaced island of Pag and further along are the islands around Zadar, those around Split, and finally the lovely island of Mljet, set in an azure sea. Behind are hillsides covered in vineyards and maquis vegetation, dominated by the bright yellow flowers of broom.

View of the city of Šibenik with the white dome of the Cathedral of St James

◁ **Lavender flowering on the island of Hvar**

Exploring Dalmatia

To the north is zadar, with its exceptional monuments, and the islands of the Zadar archipelago, the southern part of which is designated the Kornati National Park. The road travels on to Šibenik, with its perfectly preserved old town centre and splendid cathedral, and Trogir, an architectural jewel. The ruins of the Roman town of Salona are just outside the city of Split, which developed within the Palace of Emperor Diocletian. The coastal road turns inland to cross the delta of the Neretva and reaches Ston, a point of access to the peninsula of Pelješac. Finally, on a rocky spur stands the medieval city of Dubrovnik, once known as Ragusa, now a UNESCO World Heritage Site.

Bell tower of the cathedral, Zadar

KEY

✈ International airport

▬ Major road

▬ Minor road

⚊ Railway

- - Ferry route

✲ Viewpoint

GETTING AROUND

The most comfortable way of visiting Dalmatia is by car, which allows you to stop when and where you like. Traffic is always heavier during the summer holiday months. Cities and towns are not directly connected by railway, but buses are frequent and run between almost all the towns. The main coastal towns and the more important islands are linked by frequent ferry connections (see pp270–71). Yachts can be hired for cruising along the coast (see p250).

Karlovac

Senj
Karlovac

KARLOBAG
PAG ⑥

Rijeka

PAKLENICA NATIONAL PARK ⑤

GRAČAC

ZADAR ARCHIPELAGO ②

④ LJUBAC

NIN

OBROVAC

NOVIGRAD

Ancona

① ZADAR

KNIN ⑩

BISKUPIJA

KRKA NATIONAL PARK ⑦

DRNIŠ ⑨

OTAVICE

SINJ ①

③

KORNATI NATIONAL PARK

ŠIBENIK ⑧

KLI ⑫

SALONA ⑯

SOLI ⑰

⑬

MARINA ⑭ ⑮

SPLIT

PRIMOŠTEN

TROGIR

Ancona

Ancona

⑱

ŠOLTA

Pescara

HVAR

PAKLENI ISLANDS

VIS ⑳

BIŠEVO

0 kilometres   30

0 miles   30

The imposing 15th-century Minčeta Tower in Dubrovnik

LOCATOR MAP

SIGHTS AT A GLANCE

The island of Dugi Otok, in the Zadar Archipelago

SEE ALSO

• **Where to Stay** pp223–5

• **Where to Eat** pp236–9

Zadar ❶

ORIGINALLY ILLYRIANS INHABITED this narrow peninsula, but its present layout dates back to Roman rule, when the straight roads and forum were built. It became an important *municipium*, and a port for the trading of timber and wine. In the Middle Ages it was the main base for the Byzantine fleet. Venice and the king of Hungary fought over Zadar in the 12th–13th centuries but in 1409, King Ladislaus of Hungary sold his Dalmatian islands and cities to Venice for 100,000 ducats. Zadar became Zara and enjoyed a spell of prosperity; churches and palaces were built. After World War I, Zadar was ceded to Italy by the Treaty of Rapallo, but many Italians left after the forming of Yugoslavia in 1947. Zadar was repeatedly bombed during World War II and suffered considerable damage.

The Sea Gate, rebuilt from a Roman arch

The medieval tower, Bablja Kula, with part of the ancient wall

🛡 Land Gate and Walls
Kopnena Vrata
The Land Gate was built in 1543 by the great Veronese architect Michele Sanmicheli as the entrance to the city. The gate has a large central aperture and two smaller openings at the sides, divided by four white stone pilasters supporting four half-columns.

Above the main gate is a relief of St Chrysogonus on horseback and the lion of St Mark, symbol of Venetian rule. Beyond the gate are a few remains of the ancient walls, the former Venetian arsenal, and Liberation Square (Trg Zoranića) with a Roman column in the centre.

On one side of the square stands the medieval tower of Bablja Kula. At the base of the tower are five fountains (Trg Pet Bunara), which once supplied water to the city of Zadar.

🛡 Church of St Simeon
Sv. Šime
Trg Šime Budinića. 📞 *(023) 211 705.*
⬜ *before mass.*
Originally constructed in Romanesque style, the church was rebuilt after 1632 to house the remains of the saint, which are kept in a silver reliquary. This impressive work is nearly 2 m (6 ft) long and was made between 1377 and 1380 by Francesco da Milano and bears reliefs showing scenes of St Simeon's life.

Among the other works, of note is an altarpiece depicting the *Virgin and Saints*, the work of a Venetian artist. It was covered with silver leaf by a local goldsmith in 1546.

🏛 People's Square
Narodni trg
Heart of the medieval city, the site of political debate and the business district, the square is still the centre of public life today. The Town Hall, which was built in 1938, faces the square, as does the Renaissance City Loggia (Gradska loža) built by Michele Sanmicheli in 1565 as the city courts. It is now used for exhibitions.

Nearby, the 16th-century Town Guard Palace, with a clock tower dating from 1798, houses the Ethnographic Museum, with collections of costumes and objects from the entire county.

🏛 Sea Gate
Vrata Sv. Krševana
This complex construction is the result of rebuilding work carried out by Michele Sanmicheli in 1573 on a Roman arch dedicated to the Sergi family. On the seaward side is the lion of St Mark and a memorial stone recalling the Battle of Lepanto (1571). On the inner side of the gate is a stone commemorating Pope Alexander III's visit in 1177.

🛡 Church of St Chrysogonus
Sv. Krševan
Poljana Pape Aleksandra III.
⬜ *during the concert season.*
Prior to 1000 AD a church and monastery were built by Benedictines on the site of the Roman market. While the church, rebuilt in 1175, has survived with few alterations, the monastery was destroyed in World War II. At the height of the monastery's splendour it possessed a rich library and a *scriptorium*, famous for its transcribed and illuminated

The apse of the church of St Chrysogonus

works. The three-aisle church, divided by columns (salvaged from a previous building), has a simple Romanesque appearance, except for the Baroque main altar with statues of Zadar's four patron saints: Chrysogonus, Zoilus, Simeon and Anastasia. The apse is the best-preserved part, with some 13th-century frescoes and a Romanesque crucifix on the altar.

🏛 Archaeological Museum
Arheološki Muzej

Trg opatice Čike 1. 📞 (023) 250 516. ⏰ summer: 9am–1pm, 5–8pm Mon–Fri, 9–1pm Sat, 5–8pm Sun; winter: 10am–1pm, 4.30–6.30pm Mon–Fri, 9am–1pm Sat. 📷 📹 by appt. 🚻

The Archaeological Museum is housed in a new building near the old Roman Forum. The collections date from prehistory to recent times and come from the entire Zadar area and the islands. Of particular interest is glass from the Roman period and the early Christian and medieval liturgical objects.

The beautiful Renaissance façade of the church of St Mary

⚓ Church of St Mary and Museum of Sacred Art
Sv. Marija i Zlato i Srebro Zadra

Zeleni trg. 📞 (023) 250 496. ⏰ summer: 10am–12.30pm, 6-8pm Mon–Sat, 10am–12.30pm Sun; winter: 10am–12.30pm, 5–6.30pm Mon–Sat. 📷 📹 🚫 🚻

On one side of the square called Zeleni trg stand a Romanesque bell

Sculpture, Museum of Sacred Art

VISITORS' CHECKLIST

Map C4. 🏠 76,500. ✈ Zemunik 12 km (7 miles), (023) 313 311. 🚌 (023) 212 555. ⛴ A Starčevića 1, (023) 211 555. ⛴ Jadrolinija: (023) 254 800. ℹ **City:** Ilije Smiljanića, (023) 212 222, 212 412; **Regional:** Sv. Leopolda Mandića 1, (023) 315 316, 315 107. 🌐 www.zadar.hr 🎵 Musical evenings at St Donat (Jul & Aug), Summer theatre.

tower, built for King Koloman in 1105, and the church of St Mary. The church, built in 1066, has undergone various alterations and now has a Renaissance façade. The three-aisle interior has a large women's gallery; the stucco-work is from 1744. The monastery next door is now the Museum of Sacred Art: on the ground floor are gold pieces; on the upper floor are paintings and statues, including a polyptych by Vittore Carpaccio (1487).

ZADAR TOWN CENTRE

Archaeological Museum ⑥
Cathedral of St Anastasia ⑩
Church of St Chrysogonus ⑤
Church of St Donat *p93* ⑨
Church of St Mary and Museum of Sacred Art ⑦
Church of St Simeon ②
Forum ⑧
Land Gate and Walls ①
People's Square ③
Sea Gate ④

0 metres 300
0 yards 300

KEY

ℹ	Tourist information
✝	Church
🅿	Parking
⛴	Ferry
⊠	Post office

🏛 Forum

The main square of the ancient Roman city of Jadar was built between the 1st and 3rd centuries. The Forum, 90 m (295 ft) long and 45 m (147 ft) wide, was bordered on three sides by porticoes with marble columns. In the present square, Zeleni trg, are the foundations of public buildings, including a meeting hall, some of the original paving, several *tabernae* (to the south) and a Corinthian column on the western side.

Rose window, St Anastasia

The Romanesque façade of the Cathedral of St Anastasia

🏛 Cathedral of St Anastasia

Katedrala Sv. Stošije

Forum. 📞 *(023) 251 708.*

🕐 *7am–8pm daily.*

The magnificent cathedral of St Anastasia also stands on the site of the Forum. It was founded by the Byzantines in the 9th century and rebuilt in the Romanesque style in the 12–13th centuries. It has a rectangular ground-plan with a large semicircular apse.

The harmonious façade with three doors, completed in 1324, is divided in half horizontally with the upper part characterized by arches and columns and two splendid rose windows. The main window is Romanesque and the other is Gothic.

Statues adorn the outside of the central door; above are five orders of small columns culminating at the top in a semicircle and enclosing a rectangular stone door carved with festoons: above is a relief of the *Annunciation.*

The three-aisle interior is divided by two rows of columns and pilasters which support the high arcades. At the sides of the raised presbytery are engraved wooden choir stalls, the work

The right-hand altar inside the Cathedral of St Anastasia

of the Venetian Matteo Moronzoni (early 15th century). The ciborium with four Corinthian columns is decorated with different motifs (1332). Underneath is a small sarcophagus containing the remains of St Anastasia, dating from the 9th century.

The altars are mostly Baroque; on one there is a lovely painting by Palma il Giovane. In the right-hand nave is an imposing Baroque altar dedicated to the Holy Sacrament; just beyond is the hexagonal baptistry. The bell tower, which stands to one side of the cathedral, was begun in 1452. It was eventually completed in the 19th century by the British architect Thomas G Jackson.

PLAN OF THE CATHEDRAL OF ST ANASTASIA

KEY

① Altar of the Holy Sacrament
② Baptistry
③ Roman pilaster
④ Sacristy
⑤ Choir stalls
⑥ Main altar and ciborium
⑦ Bishop's chair
⑧ Chapel of St Anastasia
⑨ Souls of Purgatory altar
⑩ Bell tower

0 metres   15

0 yards   15

Zadar: Church of St Donat
Sv. Donat

THE CHURCH OF THE HOLY TRINITY, which later took the name of its founder Bishop Donat, is one of the finest examples of Byzantine architecture in Dalmatia. It was built in the early 9th century on the paving stones of the Roman Forum and has a circular ground-plan with three circular apses. Inside is a women's gallery which goes all the way around the church and creates an upper storey. St Donat has not been used as a church since 1797, but because of the good acoustics, concerts are often held here.

Dome
The cylindrical-conical dome rises in the centre of the church to a height of 27 m (88 ft).

Exterior
The church is built of honey-coloured Dalmatian stone, much of which came from the old Roman Forum.

One of the three apses with blind arches. At one time the altar was situated in the central apse.

The Women's Gallery
The interior of the church has a matroneum, or women's gallery, supported by six pilasters and two Roman columns which border the circular nave and divide the structure into two floors.

The internal walls are completely bare. Probably the original decorations, frescoes or mosaics, have been lost.

Roman Fragments
Stones from the Roman Forum were used for the paving; other Roman material is visible in the walls, entrance and gallery.

Zadar Archipelago ❷

Crucifix in SS Cosmas and Damian, Pašman

THE ZADAR ARCHIPELAGO is made up of more than 300 islands surrounded by crystal-clear waters. The larger islands are covered in Mediterranean scrub and olive trees. The archipelago is what remains of a mountain chain which once ran parallel to the Velebit mountains, but which is now almost submerged. Only about a dozen of the islands are inhabited, and the small communities live by fishing, farming and rearing animals. There are a few hotels on the larger islands closer to Zadar, and private accommodation can be found on all the others. Daily ferry services link Zadar with the main islands.

Dugi Otok, the largest island in the Zadar archipelago

Dugi Otok

Covering an area of 124 sq km (48 sq miles), this is the largest island in the archipelago. The inhabitants live in about ten villages. Fishing and farming takes place in the northern part of the island and on the flatter areas of the island, while the southern, hillier terrain is given over to sheep farming. The western coast is steep and desolate but beaches and bays punctuate the eastern coast.

Proximity to Zadar means that since Roman times it has been a popular place for the city nobles to build holiday villas. In the Renaissance period more summer residences were built here, particularly in **Sali**. This is the largest town and port on the island and there are some houses in the flamboyant Gothic style. The Renaissance church of St Mary of the Assumption has some paintings from the same period by Juraj Čulinović.

The fishing village of **Božava**, at the northernmost point, is also a popular yacht marina. It has a small church, dedicated to St Nicholas, which dates from the 10th century. Inside the church a sculpture depicts Arab saints.

The long bay of **Telašćica**, to the south, is a natural harbour and was once used by the Venetian fleet. One side ends in a sheer cliff and the other in thick pine woods. This area is being reforested after a disastrous fire in 1995. The southern part of the island is part of the Kornati National Park (see pp96–7).

Ugljan

This lush, green island is 22 km (13 miles) long and covers an area of 50 sq km (19 sq miles). It has a population of 7,600 and the small villages lie along the eastern coast of the island. In the main village, Ugljan, is the Franciscan monastery of St Jerome, built in the 15th century. It has a pretty cloister and the library contains numerous works written in Glagolitic script.

A more newly built village is **Preko**, where the wealthier citizens of Zadar own villas. There are also hotels, camping sites and rooms in private houses. The village is dominated by the large Venetian fortress of St Michael which stands on a hill 265 m (869 ft) high. A bridge links the island to Pašman.

View from the fortress of St Michael, Preko

OLIB

SILBA

PREMUDA
Premuda

ŠKARDA

IST
Ist

MOLAT
Zapuntel Brgulje Molat

SESTRUNJE
Sestrunj

Veli Rat

Božava Dragove

DUGI OTOK

0 kilometres 10

0 miles 10

The Monastery of SS Cosmas and Damian in Pašman

Pašman

This wild, unspoilt island has a population of 3,500, who live in villages on the coast facing the mainland. There are fewer tourists than on Ugljan. The western side is given over to vineyards, while the eastern part has thick maquis right down to the coastline, where there are also some pebble beaches.

South of **Pašman**, a fishing village and the main centre on the island, is **Tkon**, an embarkation point for ferries. On Mount Čokovac, north of Tkon, is the Benedictine **Monastery of SS Cosmas and Damian** (Sv. Kuzma i Damjan). Built in 1125, it became a centre of Glagolitic culture and has a well-stocked library with Glagolitic texts. In the 15th century the church and monastery were rebuilt in the Gothic style when they were taken over by the Franciscan order. The church (14th–15th century) has some good sculptures, including a painted crucifix.

Premuda

This island covers an area of 9 sq km (3 sq miles) and has fewer than 100 inhabitants, all of whom live in the village of Premuda. It is the most isolated of the islands in the archipelago. There are no hotels but visitors can find rooms in private houses.

In Italy, the island is remembered for a naval battle between Italy and Austria which took place on 10 June 1918 during World War I.

The island has beautiful beaches and thick pine woods, and as there are no private cars it is also very peaceful. There are several weekly connections to Zadar.

Molat

The three villages on Molat support several hundred people, who depend on fishing and farming. There are two ports, Zapuntel, the main ferry port, and Brgulje, which is used when the main port is inaccessible.

For centuries the island belonged to Venice, which fostered the establishment of a community of monks and local people, who set about re-establishing the woods which had disappeared with over-exploitation. Over the last decade an intense reforestation programme has been under way.

The church of St Andrew is all that remains of the monastery. There are no hotels on the island but accommodation can be found in private houses in Molat, Zapuntel and Brgulje. There are many coves along the low, jagged coastline.

Olib

About 700 people live here in the village of Olib, where buildings include several 16th-century houses and a tower. The church of St Anastasia is from the same period and was once part of a monastery. In the parsonage are manuscripts and sacred books written in Glagolitic, as well as many stone remains, which confirm the presence of a community here in Roman times. The sea is delightful, and rocky cliffs alternate with coves and sandy beaches. Rooms can be found in private houses.

Goat on the peaceful island of Olib

Ugljan — 110 — Preko — Kuklijica — 110 — Banj — Nevidane — Pašman — Tkon

UGLJAN — PAŠMAN

IŽ
Veli Iž — Malj Iž

109 — Sali

KEY

━━ Minor road
— Path
⊠ Ferry
▉ Tourist information
⯅ Beach with facilities
� Viewpoint

Kornati National Park ❸
Nacionalni Park Kornati

IN 1980 THE SOUTHERN PART of the Zadar Archipelago was declared a national park. The name Kornati derives from the name of the main island in the group, Kornat. The park was set up to protect the waters, to allow all kinds of marine life to flourish, and to stop people building on the islands. The park is 36 km (22 miles) in length and 6 km (4 miles) wide and is made up of 147 islands of white stone. Nearly all the islands are uninhabited and have little or no vegetation. The islands are surrounded by clear blue sea, with jagged coastlines, hidden coves and underwater caves.

One of the few houses on the Kornati Islands

Exploring Kornati National Park

The Kornati Islands were the peaks of a mountain chain about 20,000 years ago. When this area was part of the Roman empire, the main islands were holiday resorts, popular with the prosperous inhabitants of Zadar. Beautiful Roman villas with mosaic floors as well as fishponds and baths were built.

During the long period under Venetian rule the islands, which were then covered with rich vegetation, were used as a base for the Venetian fleet. At present the Kornati Islands belong to the inhabitants of Murter, to the east, who bought them around the end of the 19th century to use as grazing for sheep and goats.

The islands are bare and arid and are characterized by steep cliffs, stony ground and sinkholes typical of a karst (limestone) landscape. Sheep farming has impoverished the flora of these islands. In fact, the vegetation disappeared when the shepherds of Murter cut down the trees and burnt the scrub in order to grow grass for their livestock, which were left here to graze freely from spring to autumn. Dry-stone walls were built between the plots of land to form pens for the animals.

On some of the islands near the coast there are small cottages. Each has a stable at the side with an outdoor hearth for making cheese. Many also have a small jetty.

The Kornati Islands have become a popular destination for scuba divers and sailors. The marine life is varied with around 350 plant species and 300 animals. To conserve this diversity, fishing is prohibited throughout the entire Kornati National Park.

Besides dozens of rocky outcrops, the islands of Kornat, Levrnaka, Piškera, Lavsa, Kasela, Mana and Katina make up the park, as well as the southern part of Dugi Otok (see p94), with the bay of Telašćica the only wooded area. The best way to visit is by sailing boat, and there are organized day trips from Murter and Zadar.

Aerial view of the Kornati Islands

DUGI OTOK
Sali
Mala Proversa
Telašćica
KATINA
SVRŠATA
KORNAT
Lučica
Vrulje
MANA
PIŠKER

KEY

═══ Path

──── Borders of the park

Ferry

Beach with facilities

Viewpoint

0 kilometres   10

0 miles   10

The steep chalk cliffs on the island of Kornat

Kornat

The island of Kornat is the largest island in the park. There is a small medieval church dedicated to the Virgin Mary here. There is also a look-out tower with the Venetian name of Toreta dating from the 6th century, an example of Byzantine military architecture. Near the old village of Vrulje, the main village in the archipelago, is **Vela Ploča**, where there is a spectacular chalk cliff leaning at a 40-degree angle over the sea, measuring 200 m (656 ft) long and 150 m (492 ft) high.

Mala Proversa

At Mala Proversa, the straits which divide Dugi Otok from the island of **Katina**, it is possible to see some interesting Roman remains: the ruins of a villa, a fishpond and a huge tank for water, which was distributed to the villa's rooms. The few mosaics found here are now in the Archaeological Museum in Zadar (see p91).

Lavsa

This island with its pretty bays and coves is a popular tourist destination. The ruins of a partly submerged wall are all that remain of an ancient Roman salt works.

Piškera

There are also traces of Roman presence in Piškera. Once there was a village here with about 50 houses, a warehouse for fish and a tower for the tax collector. The houses and tower are now almost all in ruins. However, the church from 1560 is still standing.

Svršata

On the small island of Svršata there are two walls that go down to the sea and continue into the water, where they join up with another wall. It is thought that this square tank was a Roman construction for keeping fish fresh.

Mana

The island of Mana is famous for its semicircular cliffs. Spray from the waves breaking on the cliffs can reach up to a height of 40 m (131 ft). On top of the cliffs are the ruins of a Greek-style fishing village, built for the film *The Raging Sea* in 1961.

VISITORS' CHECKLIST

Map C4. 🚢 from Murter, Zadar, Šibenik. **Kornati National Park** 🚩 (022) 434 662. W www.kornati.hr 📧 **Murter** 🚩 (022) 434 995. **Zadar** 🚩 (023) 212 222, 212 412 (excursions from Zadar).

THE KORNATI ISLANDS BY BOAT

The archipelago of the Kornati Islands is a real paradise for sailors. These are beautiful, mysterious islands where the only sounds are those of the sea and the wind. There is only one small port, Piškera, which is open from May to September; electricity and fresh water are rationed. The natural beauty of the area makes sailing here unforgettable.

A typical island of white rock, bare of vegetation

SMOKVICA

LAVSA

KURBA VELA

Kornati National Park, a paradise for sailing

Nin ④

Map C4. 🏘 *1,700*. ✈ *Zadar, 24 km (15 miles)*. 🚉 *Zadar, 36 km (22 miles)*. 🚌 *Zadar, 36 km (22 miles)*. 🛈 *Trg hrvatskih branitelja 1, (023) 264 280*.

FOUNDED BY the Liburnians, the town was important in Roman times, when it was called Aenona. It later became one of the first permanent Croat settlements. The use of Glagolitic script spread from here when it became a Bishop's see in the 9th century. It was the centre of a long controversy between the local Church and the Pope over the use of the Croatian language in liturgy.

Malaria and the difficulty of defending the town caused it to be abandoned once again, and the bishopric was abolished in the 12th century. The few remaining monuments date from this glorious period (9th–12th centuries): the churches of the Holy Cross, St Anselm and St Ambrose. The cathedral of St Anselm, where the kings of Croatia were crowned, no longer exists.

Inside the town walls is the small 9th-century church of the **Holy Cross** (Sv. Križ), one of the finest examples of pre-Romanesque churches in typical Croatian style *(see p20)*. The name of its founder, the prefect Gladeslaus, is engraved on the lintel. The church's small size, harmony and beauty encapsulate the spirituality of the era.

Nearby is the 18th-century church of **St Anselm** (Sv. Anselm). It has a rich treasury with silver reliquaries from the 9th to 15th centuries. Near the church stands a large statue by Ivan Meštrović of Bishop Gregory of Nin, promoter of Glagolitic script. Also inside the walls is the church of **St Ambrose** (Sv. Ambroz), built in the 12th century in the Romanesque style with Gothic additions.

At the end of the main road, Zadraska ulica, is a small Archaeological Museum with prehistoric, Roman and medieval remains.

The small Romanesque church of St Mary in Ljubač, near Nin

🏛 Church of the Holy Cross, of St Anselm and of St Ambrose
🛈 *(023) 264 160, 264 162 (Archaeological Museum).* ⭘ *by appt.*

ENVIRONS: A short way southwest of Nin stands the church of St Nicholas (Sv. Nikola) in Prahulje. This unusual building, constructed on an Illyrian tumulus, has a dome with an octagonal watch tower from the 16th century on top of it, added during the Turkish invasion. Dating from the 9th century, the church is built on a trefoil plan and once held inscriptions and tombs of

members of the court of Princes Višeslav and Branimir, now in the archaeological museum in Zadar. The church is a well-preserved example of primitive Croatian art.

Ljubač is 13 km (8 miles) northeast of Nin and the site of some ruins: the wall, central buildings and towers of the medieval Castrum Ljubae, built by the Templar Knights. It fell into ruin after the order was dissolved. Still standing is the 12th-century Romanesque church of **St Mary**, noted for its three semicircular apses. Near the village is the small church of St John from the Middle Ages.

🏛 Church of St Nicholas
🔔 *(023) 264 160.* ⭘ *by appt.*

The church of St Nicholas in Prahulje, not far from Nin

Statue of Gregory of Nin, by Ivan Meštrović

A LAND OF SALT WORKS

Salt trading was a very lucrative business in the Middle Ages. Three areas were suitable for its production in the upper Adriatic: the mouth of the River Dragonja, today the border between Slovenia and Croatia, the bay of Pag, and the lowlands around Nin. The salt works of Pag, of Roman origin, which were protected by two ranges of hills, were the largest and most profitable, unlike those of Nin. The possession of these salt flats, still profitable today, has been the cause of various wars ever since.

The salt works on Pag, of Roman origin, still in use today

Paklenica National Park ❺

Nacionalni Park Paklenica

Map C4. 🏠 *Starigrad Paklenica, (023) 369 202, 369 155.*
🕐 *8am–4pm daily.* 🏷
W *www.tel.hr/paklenica*

Lilies in the Botanical Garden in Paklenica National Park

SITUATED IN the imposing Velebit massif, Paklenica National Park was founded in 1949. The entrance is east of Starigrad Paklenica, on the Magistrala coastal road (E65), halfway between Karlobag and Zadar.

The park covers an area of 36 sq km (14 sq miles), and is formed by two gorges, Velika Paklenica (Big Paklenica) and Mala Paklenica (Small Paklenica), which cut into the limestone mountains. The gorges were eroded by two rivers and parts of the canyon walls are more than 400 m (1,312 ft) high.

The rock faces are pierced by numerous caves, but they are not easily accessible. Only the Manita cave can be visited, accompanied by a guide. The bare rock faces of Velika Paklenica are popular with rock climbers.

High up, majestic birds of prey make their nests, in an ideal habitat for breeding. Golden eagles, vultures, hawks, and especially peregrine falcons can be seen here. In the forests there are bears, wild boar, foxes, roebucks and hares. A path in the valley penetrates far into the interior of the park to a cliff edge where there is a magnificent view of the wooded Vaganski Vrh mountain, the highest in the Velebit chain.

The **Velebit** mountain chain is nearly 150 km (93 miles) long. The terrain is karst (limestone) with many sink holes and plateaux separated by deep fissures. In 1978 UNESCO listed Velebit as a biological reserve for humanity with the aim of protecting this wild environment, with its 2,700 plant species and numerous colonies of large birds of prey. The *kukovi* – strange, impressive rock formations sculpted by wind and water – are also protected.

One of many birds of prey in the park

The park is also home to an interesting **Botanical Garden** (Botanički Vrt), founded in 1966 on the slopes of Mount Zavisan at an altitude of 1,576 m (5,169 ft).

Near Gradac are the Cerovac caves, discovered in 1912 during the construction of a railway line. They are dedicated to Turkalj, the engineer who discovered them. The two large caves are called Upper Grotto, 1,250 m (4,100 ft) long, and Lower Grotto, 2,500 m (8,200 ft) long. The caves have typical karst (limestone) formations with stalactites and stalagmites, small lakes and waterfalls.

A good starting point for visiting the caves and the botanical garden is the bridge of Maslenica.

One of the paths leading into Paklenica National Park

Pag ❻

T HE ISLAND OF PAG IS 63 km (39 miles) long and has two mountain chains running parallel to the coast: at the southern end cliffs frame a deep bay with numerous inlets. The island was inhabited in the Neolithic Age, and was occupied by the Liburnians in around 1200 BC. When Dalmatia was conquered by Publius Cornelius Scipio in the 1st century AD, the Romans built the town of Cissa and the fortified port of Navalia here. In the Imperial period, villas were built and some mosaic floors and an aqueduct still survive. The Slavs settled in Pag in the 6th century and became sheep farmers. After 1000 AD Zadar and Venice fought over the island to gain control of the salt pans *(see p98)*. When Cissa was destroyed by the inhabitants of Zadar, the islanders chose a new location for a village, Stari Grad, which was fortified by the Venetians in 1192.

Sheep grazing on Pag

in maquis, olive groves and aromatic herbs, particularly sage. As well as the production of olive oil and a distinctive wine called Žutica, sheep farming is one of the main occupations on the island. Pag is famous for its sheep's cheese *(paški sir)*, which has a distinctive taste thanks to the aromatic herbs in the grazing. The cheeses are coated with olive oil, and undergo lengthy maturation.

Pag Town

The small main island town occupies a sheltered bay facing the mainland. It was granted the status of a free town by King Bela IV in 1244, but rivalry with Zadar brought about its destruction. The walls, the castle, a monastery and the church of St Mary in the old town are in ruins. In 1409, Pag came definitively under the rule of Venice.

The dry, barren east-facing coast, swept by the bora wind

Exploring Pag

The island, connected by a bridge to the Magistrala coast road (E65) at its eastern tip, just beyond Dinjiška, is dry and barren, with only a few areas cultivated with vines and olive trees. The coastline facing the mainland, rocky and jagged and white in colour, is exposed to the

bora wind and bears little vegetation. The typical dry-stone walls were built to protect the land from the wind and to separate the flocks of sheep belonging to different farmers. The southwest coast is a little flatter with some small beaches. Here the land is covered

---

KEY

▬	Major road
▬	Minor road
▭	Scenic route
🚢	Ferry
🛈	Tourist information
🏖	Beach with facilities

Tovarnele
Magistrala coast road
Kovači
Žiglien
Stara Novalja
107
106
Karlobag 🛈
PAG
Metajna
Novalja 🛈 🏖
Pag 🛈
Goric
106
Mandre
Košljun
ŠKRDA
MAUN

0 kilometres 5
0 miles 5

LACE, SYMBOL OF THE TRADITIONS OF PAG

Pag is renowned for its clean waters and its delicious sheep's cheese, but it is also well-known for its lace. For centuries this lace has been created by the patient hands of the women of the island who, in warm weather, sit by their doorsteps intent on creating this intricate lace. Made using a special stitch, the lace is used to decorate blouses, bedlinen, altar cloths and table centrepieces. Some decades ago a school was established here to train new lacemakers. A collection of antique lace was left to the school by former lacemakers and the examples are used as models. Lace is sold here and some of the rooms are set up as a museum.

Typical Pag lace

VISITORS' CHECKLIST

Map C4.
🏠 *8,000.* 🚢 *Prizna-Žigljen.*
Pag ℹ *Ulica od spitala, (023) 611 301.* 🎭 *Lace exhibition (summer); Carnival of Pag, traditional kolo dance and traditional costumes (31 Jul).*
W *www.pag.hr*
Novalja ℹ *(053) 661 404.*
W *www.novalja.hr*
Karlobag ℹ *dr. Tudmana 2, (053) 694 251.*

The Duke's Palace in the main square, Pag

In 1443 the Venetian rulers, with the assistance of local nobles, entrusted the design of a new town to the famous architect Juraj Dalmatinac (Giorgio Orsini). It took several decades to build what is now the present-day Pag.

Venetian rule brought a long period of peace and prosperity, bolstered by the income from the productive salt works. Between the 15th and 18th centuries, important public buildings and a parish church, locally called the cathedral, were built.

The town has preserved its original structure with two main roads intersecting in the main square, and minor roads running parallel.

The high walls with eight towers and four gates were demolished at the end of the 19th century, but some traces (a gate and two bastions) still remain. The 15th-century Duke's Palace (Kneževa Palača), which has been altered, and the unfinished Bishop's Palace by Juraj Dalmatinac face the main square.

A monument to Dalmatinac by Ivan Meštrović and the church of **St Mary of the Assumption** (1443–1448) stand in the same square. The church is a blend of Romanesque and Gothic, with three aisles divided by white stone columns with carved capitals. The façade has a rose window and there is a lunette above the door. Numerous works of art are preserved here, including a wooden 12th-century crucifix, a *Virgin of the Rosary* by Giovanni Battista Pittoni, an organ, and a treasury.

Novalja

Located at the beginning of the narrow peninsula of Lun, Novalja is the second town on the island. It makes its living entirely by tourism, thanks to its level beach. In the centre of the town are the remains of an early Christian basilica and a pre-Romanesque church dating from the 9th–10th centuries.

A new ferry service connects the island to the mainland, running from Novalja to Prizna.

ENVIRONS: Boat excursions to Pag leave from **Karlobag** on the mainland. Karlobag lies in a pretty bay and takes its name from the fortress that the Archduke of Austria, Charles Augustus of Habsburg, built in 1579 on the site of a village destroyed by the Turks.

The fortress lost its importance after the Turkish threat had passed and was abandoned. Its attractive stones were then used to build the houses in the village. Still visible are some of the massive walls and the remains of a monastery, which once had a famous library and a church.

The harsh but fascinating landscape, characteristic of the island of Pag

Krka National Park ➐
Nacionalni Park Krka

THE PARK COVERS AN AREA of 142 sq km (55 sq miles) and was established in 1985 to protect the middle and lower stretches of the River Krka, which flows into the bay of Šibenik. The source of the river is near Knin, and the river begins its journey of 75 km (47 miles) inside a canyon on the limestone plateau behind Šibenik. It finally spills over into the spectacular Roški Slap and Skradinski Buk waterfalls, forming a series of lakes and rapids surrounded by vegetation. The bird life in the park is very varied.

Monastery of Visovac
In the middle of the lake is the monastery of Visovac. It was founded by Franciscans in 1445 who were joined by Franciscans from Bosnia in 1576. They brought books, illuminated manuscripts and sacred vestments with them.

Skradin
Once a settlement of Illyrian and Liburnian tribes, then a Roman town, Skradin was a bishop's see from the 4th century. It is one of the main access points to the park; boats go upriver from here to the waterfalls.

Around the lake families of egrets and night herons can be seen perched on the branches of the willows or hidden among the reeds. About 200 species of bird have been counted here.

Skradinski Buk
From a height of 45 m (147 ft), this impressive waterfall cascades down 17 steps over a distance of 800 m (2,624 ft). Some of the park paths, sprayed by the falls, pass next to what is one of the most spectacular natural displays in Croatia.

The lower basin becomes a pool of emerald-green water in the summer and is an attractive place to sunbathe or picnic.

Map labels:
ÆEVRS
ÆEVRSKE
Smrdelje
56
Ičev
BRIBIRSKE MOSTINE
BRIBIRSKE MOSTINE
Bratiškovci
Ru
Entrance 2
Prukljan
Visovačko Jezero
311 Dubravice
Prukljansko Jezero
Skradin ℹ
Raslina
311
ℹ Lozovac
ŠIBENIK
Entrance 1
8
ŠIBENIK

Roški Slap
Here the river widens and deepens within the forest before finally cascading from between the trees, producing waterfalls over 25 m (82 ft).

VISITORS' CHECKLIST

Map C–D4. **Park** ⓘ *Trg Ivana Pavla II br 5, Šibenik, (022) 217 720.* Ⓦ *www.npkrka.hr* ⏰ *summer: 8am–8pm; winter: 9am–5pm. The park can be visited by car or coach entering at Lozovac or Skradin.* 🅿️ **Monastery of Visovac:** *can be visited on organized boat trips from Roški Slap.*

Krka monastery, first mentioned in 1402.

GRAČAC

509

Brljansko Jezero

Kistanje

Knin

Vrbnik

33

Nečmen

DRNIŠ

Citluk

Mratovo

Oklaj

0 kilometres 5

0 miles 5

Lake Visovac is at the heart of the park. After the waterfalls, the river flows through a narrow valley and then widens to form the lake. Some stretches of the banks are steep and others hilly with oak woods.

DRNIŠ

River Cikola
After Lake Visovac, the Krka is joined by the River Čikola and from here the river flows towards the Skradinski Buk and then on to the sea.

56

Širitovci

Monastery Visovac

Drinovci

DRNIŠ

Čikola

s Kalik

ŠIBENIK DRNIŠ

KEY

— Major road

— Minor road

═ Scenic route

ⓘ Tourist information

★ Waterfall

VISITING THE PARK

The protected area begins at the Knin valley and continues to the bridge of Šibenik. Road signs mark the entrances to the park; each has a parking area, a tourist information centre, and a ticket office. Cars can enter from Lozovac, while the Roški Slap

View of Krka Park

waterfalls can be reached from Miljevci or Skradin. About 15 km (9 miles) from Burnum, other road signs indicate the entrance to the area of the Roški Slap waterfalls. Boats leave from Skradin for trips to the Skradinski Buk waterfalls and from here it is possible to take a short cruise to the Roški Slap falls, crossing the lake of Visovac and visiting the monastery on the island.

Šibenik ❽

Statue of Juraj Dalmatinac

THE TOWN IS FIRST DOCUMENTED in 1066 as Castrum Sebenici, when King Petar Krešimir IV described it as a triangular fortified town. In the 12th century it came under Hungarian-Croat rule. Between 1412 and 1797 it was ruled by the Venetians, and the old centre acquired grand buildings and three large forts as well as bastions on the island of St Nicholas. It was a prosperous time, the arts flourished and Šibenik became one of the liveliest cultural centres in Renaissance Croatia.

Venetian rule gave way to a brief period of French occupation until Austria took over and ruled until 1917. The recent war brought about the collapse of local industry however, and mass unemployment.

Aerial view of the Cathedral of St James

🏛 Church of St Francis

Sv. Frane

Trg Nikole Tomaszea 1. 【 *(022) 214 241.* ☐ *by appt.*

Along the busy seafront, on the southern edge of the old town centre, once stood the monastery and church of St Francis, founded in 1229 and destroyed during a raid in 1321. Some capitals, a few statues, and parts of the arches in the cloister remain of the original structure. Towards the middle of the 15th century several new chapels were added on.

The buildings were completely rebuilt in the Baroque style around the middle of the 18th century. The church underwent complete renovation: the wooden ceiling and the sumptuous gilded carved wooden altars were remade, and every wall was decorated with paintings.

Inside, in the first chapel on the left, is a great organ from 1762, made by Petar Nakić.

The large cloister has kept its 14th-century structure and there is a library with manuscripts and liturgical material in the monastery.

🏛 Church of St Barbara

Sv. Barbara

Kralja Tomislava.

The small church of St Barbara, behind the apse of the cathedral of St James, was built around the middle of the 15th century, and conserves parts of an older building. Irregular openings make the façade unusual: the lunette on the main door has a statue of St Nicholas from the workshop of Bonino of Milan (1430). Inside is an altar made by a youthful pupil of Juraj Dalmatinac, Giovanni da Pribislao, who was obliged to match another altar which had been saved from the previous church.

The church also houses a rich and interesting collection of religious art, with paintings, sculptures and illuminated texts dating from the 14th to 16th centuries.

🏛 Count's Palace – Civic Museum

Muzej Grada Šibenika

Gradska Vrata 3. 【 *(022) 213 880.* ☐ *summer: 10am–1pm, 6–10pm; winter: 10am–1pm, 5–7pm daily.*

This palace takes its name from the Venetian Count Niccolò Marcello who built it in the first decade of the 17th century. It was the Venetian governor's residence and is now a Civic Museum. This late-Renaissance building houses coin collections, archaeological finds from the Neolithic to Roman periods, tomb finds, early Croatian sculptures (7th–9th centuries), and a rich archive of historical documents about the town and its territory, many from the medieval period. There is a statue of the count (1609–11) on the façade next to the entrance doorway.

🏛 Cathedral of St James

Katedrala Sv. Jakova

See pp106–7.

🏛 Old Loggia

Gradska vijećnica

Trg Republike Hrvatske.

In front of the cathedral's Door of Lions stands the Old Loggia, formerly the seat of the town council, built between 1532 and 1543 to a design by Michele Sanmicheli, and restored after it was damaged during World War II.

This is a two-storey structure: the ground floor is an open portico with nine large arches, the upper floor is a loggia, with a balustrade.

The 16th-century Old Loggia, designed by Michele Sanmicheli

🏛 Foscolo Palace

Palača Fosclo

Andrije Kačića.

The Venetian governor, Leonardo Foscolo, built this palace in the Venetian Gothic style in around 1450.

The façade was decorated with Renaissance reliefs by Juraj Dalmatinac's pupils (15th century), and another relief, attributed to the master, has two putti supporting the coats of arms of the noble family, at the side of the entrance door.

View of Šibenik from the medieval Fort of St Anne

⛫ Fort of St Anne
Tvrdava Sv. Ana
ℹ️ *Civic Museum, (022) 213 880.*
The fort is of medieval origins and the oldest defensive structure in Šibenik. It was destroyed after lightning struck the powder magazine. When it was rebuilt, account was taken of the town's altered defence needs, and the towers were omitted. Its present appearance dates from the 16th–17th centuries. Now officially renamed St Michele, it offers magnificent views over the islands.

⛫ Fort of St John
Tvrdava Sv. Ivan
ℹ️ *Civic Museum, (022) 213 880.*
Standing on a hill 125 m (410 ft) high, the fort, originally 15th century, was rebuilt in a star shape after the town was attacked by the Turks in 1649.

⛫ Šubićevac Fort
Tvrdava Šubićevac
ℹ️ *Civic Museum, (022) 213 880.*
The third large fort called Šubićevac, or Baron's Fort, was constructed rapidly in 1646, in the face of an imminent Turkish attack. The fort, in fact, greatly contributed to the defeat of the Turks in 1647. After a long siege, large parts of it had to be rebuilt. The present structure dates from the middle of the 17th century and a pretty garden is laid out in front of the bastions.

⛫ Fort of St Nicholas
Tvrdava Sv. Nikola
ℹ️ *Civic Museum, (022) 213 880.*
The fort was planned by the Italian architect Gian Girolamo Sanmicheli, and

built between 1540 and 1547 on a cliff overlooking the city. It is a fine example of military architecture, both for its strength and for the beauty of the decorations above the entrance gate, in the apertures, in the rooms, and along the corridors. The fort was often used as a prison.

The Fort of St Nicholas, outside the entrance of Šibenik harbour

ŠIBENIK TOWN CENTRE

Cathedral of St James pp106–7 ④
Church of St Barbara ②
Church of St Francis ①
Count's Palace – Civic Museum ③
Fort of St Anne ⑦
Foscolo Palace ⑥
Old Loggia ⑤

0 metres   200
0 yards   200

KEY

ℹ️	Tourist information
✝	Church
✝	Orthodox church

Šibenik: Cathedral of St James
Katedrala Sv. Jakova

A face on the cornice of the apse

IT HAS TAKEN CROATIAN and international experts several years to restore Šibenik's cathedral since its shelling in 1991. Its original construction by renowned Dalmatian and Italian artists began in 1432 and was completed in 1555. The original project was entrusted to the Venetian, Antonio Dalle Masegne, who built the lower Gothic level. His successor, Juraj Dalmatinac (see p18), designed the upper Renaissance part, the sculptures by the doors, with Adam and Eve by the Door of Lions, the 72 faces on the outside of the apse, many of the capitals, the tomb of Juraj Šižgorić and, along with Andrija Aleši, the beautiful baptistry. On Dalmatinac's death in 1475, the work was continued by Nikola Firentinac, who built the splendid presbytery with the choir, the dome, the galleries and vaulted roof.

The Dome, a unique structure built of interlocking slabs of stone, was badly damaged in 1991.

Transept
The transept is supported by a square structure; on three sides is an arch surmounted by a statue. The stones were worked in such a way that they fitted together without the need for mortar.

★ Presbytery
The finely worked stone stalls were made by Juraj Dalmatinac and Nikola Firentinac. Other sculpted reliefs adorn the upper parts.

The exterior is decorated with 72 sculpted human faces on the cornice, the work of Juraj Dalmatinac and his assistants.

Door of Lions
This door is named after the two stone lions which support statues of Adam and Eve. The doorway is framed by slim, finely carved columns.

STAR FEATURES

★ **Baptistry**

★ **Presbytery**

★ Baptistry
At the end of the right aisle is an impressive baptistry with many statues and reliefs sculpted by Juraj Dalmatinac, Nikola Firentinac and Andrija Aleši. The fine baptismal font is supported by three putti.

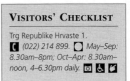

Façade
The symmetrical façade has an arched tympanum in the centre. The taller central section has a rose window in the centre and a smaller one above on the tympanum. The façade is framed by two pilasters and has only one door.

The cathedral was built entirely in local stone and is a tribute to the great technical skill of the stone-cutters.

The Gothic doorway is decorated with groups of sculptures of saints ascending the arch, which is framed by two spires.

Interior
The three-aisle interior is divided by columns with carved capitals supporting pointed arches. The tall central nave has a frieze and women's gallery.

Drniš **9**

Map D4. **👤** 4,700.
🚉 Šibenik, 25 km (15 miles), (022)
333 699. **🚌** Šibenik, (022) 212 087.
ℹ (022) 212 346.

T HE TOWN OF DRNIŠ first
appears in documents
towards the end of the 15th
century, as the site of a fort
built to stop a Turkish
invasion, at the point where
the River Čikola cuts into
the valley and flows down
towards Šibenik.

In 1526 the fort was
captured and enlarged by the
Turks, who made it one of
their outposts. A village
with a mosque and baths
developed around the fort,
but during the wars between
Venice and the Ottoman
empire, from 1640 to 1650,
the fort and the village were
almost entirely destroyed by
the Venetians.

In the reconstruction that
followed the mosque was
remodelled and became the
church of St Anthony. The
minaret became the bell
tower of the church of St
Roch. Serbs populated the
town and it became part of
the Krajina territory.

Along the road from Drniš
to Šibenik, the ruins of
defence structures with high
walls and a tower can be seen.

ENVIRONS: Some 9 km (5
miles) east of Drniš is the
village of **Otavice**, the
birthplace of Ivan Meštrović's
parents. The great sculptor
(see p155) built a **Mausoleum**
here for himself and his
family. It is simply designed
in the form of a stone cube
with a shallow dome.

**Meštrović Mausoleum in Otavice,
near Drniš**

Knin **10**

Map D4.
👤 12,000. **🚉** (022) 663 722.
ℹ (022) 212 346.

A TOWN on the main road
from Zagreb to Split,
Knin has long played an
important role in Dalmatia's
history. It occupies a strategic
position on the plateau, and
there have been defences
of some kind here since
prehistoric times. In the 10th
century, when the town was
known as Ad Tenen, the **Fort
of St Saviour** (Sveti Spas),
was built here. It was used by
reigning Croat monarchs, who
often stayed in the nearby
town of Biskupija and held
coronations here.

Early in the 11th century
Knin became a bishopric and
the residence of several
aristocratic Croatian families.
Occupied by the Turks in the
early 16th century, in 1688
Knin fell to the Venetians.

The Morlachs, in the pay of
Venice, distinguished themselves in the battle to retake
the fort by scaling the walls.
Afterwards they rebuilt the
fort and settled in the town.

In 1991, the Serbian army
used the fort when most of
the inhabitants of Croat origin
were forced out. It became a
focus for the Serb rebellion
and the Republic of the Serb
Krajina, of which Knin was
the capital, was created. In
August 1995 the territory was
returned to the Croats.

ENVIRONS: About 5 km (3
miles) away is **Biskupija**,
once known as the "Field of
five churches", for its religious
buildings (9th–11th centuries)
attended by the Croat kings.
King Zvonimir was killed here
by Croat nobles who did not
accept his allegiance to the
pope. By the main building
is a church designed by
Ivan Meštrović and frescoed
by Jozo Kljaković.

The imposing fort of St Saviour in Knin, on Mount Spas

Sinj ⓫

Map D5. 👥 *11,500.* 🚆 *Split.*
🚌 *Split.* ℹ️ *Vrlicka ulica 50, (021)
826 352.* 🎭 *Sinjska Alka, jousting
tournament in costume (1st Sun Aug).*

O N THE CETINA plateau
the Romans founded
Aequum, the present-day
Čitluk, on the road towards
Bosnia, but the unhealthy
area and malaria forced the
inhabitants to abandon the
town and move to a nearby
hill called Castrum Zyn. This
was safer and easier to defend
and they built a fort here.

At the end of the 1400s
some Franciscan monks, who
had fled from a monastery in
Rama, a Bosnian town, came
here, bringing with them an
image of the Virgin believed
to be miraculous and they
built a **Franciscan
Monastery** (Franjevacki
Samostan) and a church.

The town, by
now called
Sinj, was
captured
by the Turks in 1513
and remained in
their possession
until 1699 when it
was liberated by the
Venetians. Its strategic
position urged the
Turks to attempt
to recapture it
in 1715, but an
unexpected attack
by 600 horsemen, citizens
of the town, against the
Ottoman troops prevented
its capture.

**Sculpture of
the jousting
tournament, Sinj**

This historical event is
commemorated every year on
the first Sunday in August
with a jousting tournament
(Sinjska Alka), when expert
riders take part in a
competition to capture
a shield, the symbol of
victory. A bronze sculpture
representing the joust stands
in the public gardens.

The Franciscan church,
rebuilt at various times, is a
popular pilgrimage site. The
monastery has recently been
renovated and some of the
rooms house archaeological
finds from ancient Aequum.

🏛️ **Franciscan Monastery**
A Stepinca 1. 📞 *(021) 707 010.*

Primošten, once an island but now linked to the mainland

Klis ⓬

Map D5.
👥 *2,300.* 🚆 *Split.* 🚌 *Split.*
ℹ️ *Megdan ulica 57, (021) 240 578.*

T HE LITTLE VILLAGE of Klis is
dominated by an imposing
Fort which consists of three
concentric walls. It was
founded by the Romans on a
hill above a mountain pass
which led from the plateau
onto the plain. The
Venetians strengthened
the fort and enlisted
the Uskoks to help
fight off the Turks,
who however finally
captured it in 1537.
The Turks enlarged
the fort, building a
mosque and a minaret
and from here they
menaced the city of
Split until 1648
when they were
driven off by
Venetian troops. The
fort was in use until
the Austrians took over. The
mosque was turned into a
church and the minaret
was demolished.

The town's restaurants are
particularly known for their
excellent spit-roasted lamb.

**The Fort of Klis, the scene of
many bloody battles**

Primošten ⓭

Map D5. 👥 *1,750.*
🚆 *Split.* 🚌 *Split (021) 338 483.*
🚤 *Marina (022) 570 068.*
ℹ️ *Rudina Biskupa J. Arnerica 2,
(022) 571 111.* 🎭 *Wine
exhibition "Babic" (Oct).*

O RIGINALLY an isolated
island, Primošten is now
connected to the mainland by
a bridge and a causeway. The
name Primošten means
"brought closer by a bridge".
The island was inhabited in
prehistoric times, and was
settled by Bosnian refugees
fleeing from the Turks. Under
Venetian rule, walls were
built around the town.

The top of the town is
dominated by the church of
St George, built in the late
15th century and enlarged
around 1760. Inside is an icon
of the Virgin on a silver
panel, and a Baroque altar.

A popular resort with
pebbly beaches, Primošten is
also famous for its vineyards
(see p127) and a good red
wine called Babić.

Marina ⓮

Map D5. 👥 *900.*
ℹ️ *(021) 889 015.*

T HIS SMALL HOLIDAY resort lies
in a sheltered bay and has
a marina and a pretty beach.
The village has been
inhabited since the 15th
century. In 1495 the Bishop
of Trogir built a massive
tower in the port, now the
Hotel Kaštil.

The two churches in the
village, St Luke and St John,
were built in the 15th century
and restructured at various
times by the Sobota family,
the feudal lords of the village.

Trogir **⑮**

S ET ON A SMALL ISLAND just off the mainland, Trogir is one of the jewels of the Dalmatian coast, with many splendid monuments. The Greeks of Issa (now Vis) first settled here in 380 BC, when they founded the fortified town of Tragyrion (island of goats) which became Tragurium under the Romans in 78 AD. In the Middle Ages Trogir was protected by the Byzantine fleet, but in 1123 it was attacked and destroyed by the Saracens, and abandoned by the few surviving inhabitants. It revived again 70 years later and a period of extraordinary artistic growth ensued, first under the kings of Hungary and, from 1420, under Venetian rule. In 1997 Trogir was listed as a UNESCO World Heritage site.

The seafront of Trogir, with Kamerlengo castle in the distance

Most of the old historic centre of the town is on an island and is encircled by a wall with two gates. A bridge now joins the island to the mainland and another links it to the island of Čiovo. Tourism is important to the town: ice-cream parlours, restaurants and pizzerias line the small squares. The main public and religious monuments, and other important buildings, have been the subject of restoration for some years.

⚏ Land Gate
Kopnena Vrata
Rebuilt in the 16th century, this gate was made from a tall doorway in pale rusticated stone, with grooves which once supported a drawbridge. On the cornice above the arch stands the lion of St Mark and, above that, on a pedestal, stands a statue of the Blessed John of Trogir (Sv. Ivan Trogirski), one of the town's patron saints.

🏛 Civic Museum
Muzej Grada Trogira
Gradska vrata 4. **C** *(021) 881 406.*
◻ *Jun–Sep: 9am–noon, 6–9pm, Mon–Sat; Oct–May: 7am–3pm, Mon–Sat.* 📷 ▣
On the other side of the Land Gate is the Baroque Garagnin Fanfogna Palace, now the Civic Museum, with 18th-century furnishings. There are archaeological collections, books, documents, drawings and antique clothes linked to the town's history.

⚏ Stafileo Palace
Palača Stafileo
Matije Gupca 20. ◐ *to the public.*
Stafileo Palace was built in the late 15th century. A series of five windows in Venetian Gothic style punctuates each of the two floors, the openings framed by pillars, capitals and carved arches. Around the arches are reliefs of flowers and leaves. The design is attributed to the school of Juraj Dalmatinac, who worked for many years in Trogir.

⛪ Cathedral of St Lawrence
Sv. Lovre
Trg Ivana Pavla II. **C** *(021) 881 426.*
◻ *8am–noon, 4.30–7pm daily.*
The cathedral stands on the site of an ancient church, destroyed by the Saracens. Construction started in 1193, but was prolonged for decades and involved dozens of artists. The three-aisle building has three semi-circular apses: the central nave is higher than the side aisles from which it is divided by eight columns.

There are two entrances. The side door, known as "the count's", is very simple, and dated 1123. The other entrance is a magnificent Romanesque door under an atrium, to the right of which stands a beautiful Venetian-Gothic bell tower, built between the early 15th century and the end of the 16th century. This door was carved in around 1240 by the Dalmatian sculptor Master Radovan *(see p18)*, and is the finest expression of Romanesque sculpture to be found in Dalmatia. Two stone lions support statues of Adam and Eve either side of the door. Scenes of the different months of the year are carved on the pilasters and on the second semicircle there are images of saints.

Above the door, in the large lunette, is a relief of the Nativity and in the semicircles are episodes from the Bible. The door is enclosed under a sloping roof with a corbel at the top with a statue of St Lawrence. In the atrium is a baptistry designed by Andrija Aleši in around 1460 with a relief of the Baptism of Christ.

The intricate Romanesque door of the Cathedral of St Lawrence

Aerial view of the square and the cathedral

statues of the apostles in shell-shaped niches and, in the centre, the sarcophagus of the Blessed Orsini, the first bishop of Trogir. The sculptures are by Nikola Firentinac, Andrija Aleši and Ivan Budislavić.

In the sacristy are paintings by Salvator Rosa and Gentile Bellini, cabinets carved by Grgur Vidov, and a Treasury with many gold pieces, reliquaries and paintings dating from the 17th-century.

The tall bell tower was built in the 14th century, but was partly destroyed during the wars early in the following century and only the ground floor remains of the original building. When Trogir became part of Venetian territory, the bell tower was rebuilt. The first floor with a balustrade by Matej Gojković (1422), is in the Venetian-Gothic style, with two narrow mullioned

VISITORS' CHECKLIST

Map D5. 👥 10,500. ✈ Split, 30 km (18 miles). 🚂 Split, 30 km (18 miles). 🚌 (021) 881 405. ℹ Obala bana Berislavića 12, (021) 881 412. 📠 (021) 881 508.

windows with a trefoil, surmounted by blind arches. The second level has two tall windows on each side: the north and south walls have mullioned windows with four trefoil eyes, those on the east and west walls are surmounted by fretwork grilles, with columns and capitals at the centre and corners, giving a feeling of lightness to the entire floor. Recent studies attribute this work to the Italian sculptor Lorenzo Pincino, who worked in Trogir and Dalmatia for many years, with the assistance of local craftsmen.

The third storey, from the late 16th century, was built by the sculptor Trifun Bokanić and has large arched openings.

The church interior contains an octagonal stone pulpit from the 13th century built and sculpted by Mauro, a choir with wooden stalls inlaid by Ivan Budislavić towards the mid-15th century, and a ciborium on the main altar with sculptures depicting the Annunciation. On the altars are paintings by Palma il Giovane and Padovanino.

Along the left aisle is the chapel of the Blessed Orsini, a masterpiece by Nikola Firentinac and Andrija Aleši made in 1468–72, with 12

TROGIR TOWN CENTRE

Cathedral of St Lawrence ④
Church of St Dominic ⑪
Church of
    St John the Baptist ⑧
Church of St Nicholas ⑩
Čipiko Palace ⑤
Civic Museum ②
Kamerlengo Castle
    and St Mark's Tower ⑫
Land Gate ①
Loggia and
    Clock Tower ⑦
Sea Gate and
    Fish Market ⑨

Stafileo Palace ③
Town Hall ⑥

KEY

ℹ Tourist information

✝ Church

⛴ Ferry

✉ Post office

0 metres   100
0 yards   100

Exploring Trogir

A GOOD TIME TO VISIT TROGIR is the late spring or early autumn, when the narrow streets, flanked by ancient stone houses, are not so busy with summer visitors, and there is space to stop and admire the ingenious architectural details that make this island so fascinating. A carved doorway, a coat of arms, or a mullioned window may decorate the façade of a building; the entrance to a courtyard may offer glimpses of scented gardens. These are all indications of a once widespread prosperity and also evidence of Trogir's cultural past, when it was an important centre for the arts. After many years of hardship and neglect, the town is now gradually being restored to its former glory.

The Clock Tower

supported by six columns with Roman capitals and dates from the 14th century. On the wall are two reliefs, one from 1471 sculpted by Nikola Firentinac (*Justice*), and one from 1950 by Ivan Meštrović (*Ban Berislavić*). The Clock Tower stands to the left of the Loggia. It supports a pavilion dome, salvaged in 1447 from the chapel of the oratory of St Sebastian. The saint's statue on the façade was sculpted by Nikola Firentinac.

A Renaissance well in the courtyard of Čipiko Palace

🏛 Čipiko Palace
Palača Čipiko
Gradska ulica. ● *to the public, except courtyard.*
An inscription indicates 1457 as the year of completion of the beautiful Čipiko Palace, built for Trogir's most illustrious family. Over a Renaissance doorway, distinguished by its columns with capitals, is a shell decoration above a finely worked cornice.

The first floor has a mullioned window with a balustrade in light coloured stone. In the centre, two columns with capitals support pointed arches and at the ends of the window are two thin pilasters surmounted by capitals with spiral decorations. Between the arches are four sculptures of angels. Two central ones hold a scroll with the coats of arms

of the Čipiko family. The second floor lacks a balustrade, and is similar in style to the lower floor, although its decorations are less ornate.

A second door, opening on to a side street, has a complex structure. Two fluted door jambs support capitals with carved foliage decoration and a stone cornice with two sculpted lions holding a coat of arms. These are flanked by two sculptures of angels in medallions.

🏛 Town Hall
Municipija
Trg Ivana Pavla II.
On the eastern side of the square is the Town Hall. This building originates from the 15th century and has three storeys with open arches and a beautiful mullioned window with a balustrade on the upper floor, which was restored in the 19th century. Numerous coats of arms decorate the façade which has three Renaissance doors framed by projecting stone. The pretty porticoed courtyard is open to the public. However, the interior, which has been altered at various times, has nothing of significant interest.

🏛 Loggia and Clock Tower
Gradska loža
Trg Ivana Pavla II. ● *daily.*
The Loggia and the Clock Tower face John Paul II Square (Trg Ivana Pavla II). The Loggia has a roof

🔒 Church of St John the Baptist
Sv. Ivan Krstitelj
◐ *for restoration.*
This small Romanesque church, built in the 13th century, is the pantheon of the powerful Čipiko family. The church houses an **Art Gallery** (Pinacoteca) with collections of medieval illuminated manuscripts, ornaments, paintings and precious gold pieces from various churches. The collection also includes a sculpture (*Deposition*) by Nikola Firentinac, organ panels by Gentile Bellini (*St Jerome* and *St John the Baptist*), two polyptychs by Blaise of Trogir and other paintings dating from the 15th–17th centuries.

The doorway of the Romanesque church of St John the Baptist

The Fish Market, housed in a 16th-century loggia

🏛 Sea Gate and Fish Market
Južna Vrata
Obala Bana Berislavića.

The Sea Gate was built at the end of the 16th century and has two beautiful columns made of blocks of light-coloured stone which frame the opening and support a projecting block on which stands the lion of St Mark.

Nearby is the Fish Market which is held in an open loggia with nine columns supporting the roof. It was built in 1527 and was formerly the customs house.

Ceremonial costumes made by the tailor Boris Burić Gena

BORIS BURIĆ GENA

As well as having a glorious artistic past, Trogir can also boast a present-day success story. This is thanks to the tailor Boris Burić Gena, who specializes in making antique-style clothes for ceremonies and parades. The careful choice of fabrics, meticulous design and precise matching of accessories have made this talented craftsman's name. His workshop now draws wealthy and famous clients from all over Europe.

🔒 Church of St Nicholas
Sv. Nikola
Gradska ulica 2. 📞 (021) 881 631.
🕐 summer: 8am–noon, 4–7pm daily.

The church and Benedictine convent date from the 11th century, but were rebuilt in the 16th century. The convent rooms now house the **Zbirka Umjetnina Kairos**, an art collection which includes the *Kairos*, a relief of Greek origins (1st century BC) depicting the god of opportunity, a Gothic Crucifix, and a Romanesque statue *(The Virgin with Child)*.

Relief depicting Kairos, St Nicholas

🔒 Church of St Dominic
Sv. Dominik
Obala Bana Berislavića.
🕐 summer: 8am–noon, 4–7pm daily.

The church and monastery of St Dominic are Romanesque-Gothic buildings constructed in the 14th century. They were renovated by Nikola Firentinac in the Renaissance style. The single-nave church contains the tomb of Giovanni Sobota, a lawyer, attributed to Nikola Firentinac (1469), and a splendid painting by Palma il Giovane *(Circumcision of Christ)*.

🏛 Kamerlengo Castle and St Mark's Tower
Kaštel Kamerlengo

In the southwest corner of the island stands Kamerlengo Castle, which was at one time the residence of the Venetian governor. It was built by the Venetians in about 1430, and is a four-sided structure with a hexagonal base. It faces the sea. High walls connect the three towers and the bastion. This imposing structure was once connected to St Mark's Tower (Kula svetog Marka).

The large open space inside the castle is used for outdoor theatre performances and concerts in the summer.

St Mark's Tower was built by the Venetians after the construction of the castle and has the typical structure of defences built in the Renaissance period. A circular tower stands on a truncated cone base and there is a long series of embrasures on the roof. Artillery was installed on the top level in readiness to defend the strip of water that separates the island from the mainland.

What was once the parade ground, between the castle and St Mark's Tower, is now the town's sports field.

The imposing St Mark's Tower, built for defence in 1470

Salona ⑯

Detail of the Tusculum

THE ANCIENT TOWN OF SALONA, 5 km (3 miles) from Split, is famous for its Roman ruins. The name Salona (or Salonae) derives from the salt (*sal* in Latin) works in the area. Originally an Illyrian settlement, it was then Greek, but did not become an important centre until the Romans built a town next to the Greek city. During the rule of Augustus it became a Roman colony called Martia Julia Salonae and later it was the capital of the province of Dalmatia. In the 1st century AD the Romans built an amphitheatre, theatres, temples, baths, a Forum and town walls reinforced with towers, and Salona became the richest and most populated city in the mid-Adriatic. In 614 the Avars and the Croats destroyed it and it fell into disuse. The buildings and the churches were stripped and the stone was used for new buildings.

Salona's main road

Ruins of the walls and triangular tower

Exploring Salona

At the end of the 19th century excavations began to bring to light the buried remains of this ancient settlement. The work has clearly shown that the town had two districts dating from different periods: the original, old centre (*Urbs vetus*) and a later part which dates from the Augustan era (*Urbs nova occidentalis* and *Urbs nova orientalis*). The excavations have uncovered only a part of the layout of the **Outer Walls**, which were frequently reinforced over the centuries. However, the foundations and the remains of towers with triangular or rectangular bases are visible.

A good place to begin a tour is the **Necropolis of Manastirine**, the burial area just outside the walls, north of the city (near the parking area). In the 4th century a religious building was constructed here to house the relics of the Salonian saints, victims of Diocletian's persecution of Christians. The ruins of the necropolis and the basilica are well preserved.

From Manastirine, after the entrance, you reach the **Tusculum**, a villa built in the last century for the distinguished archaeologist Frane Bulić, to enable him to study Salona. A scholar and director of the Archaeological Museum in Split, he devoted much of his life to researching the ancient ruins of this city. The building is now a small museum.

However, the most interesting material is now in the Archaeological Museum in Split (*see p121*).

Further on is the richest area of ruins with the foundations of early Christian basilicas, baths and the Caesarea Gate. The **Baths** were built in the 1st century when the city became the capital of the province of Dalmatia. In the early Christian period the buildings were probably transformed into religious buildings: the **Bishop's Complex** in the northeastern sector of Salona comprised basilicas, a baptistry and the bishop's residence. Before Christianity became widespread, early Christian martyrs were slayed here, including St Domnius (the patron saint of Split), Venantius and Anastasius.

The foundations of two basilicas have been excavated. One is known as the **Urban Basilica**, the other, called **Honorius' Basilica**, had a Greek cross

The Necropolis of Manastirine, just outside the walls

Basilica Urbana in the Bishop's Complex

plan. This is also the site of what remains of the **Caesarea Gate**: arches flanked by two octagonal towers, showing the building techniques used by the Romans in the Imperial era.

Going west along the walls you reach the **Necropolis of Kapljuć**, another early Christian burial site, and then the imposing ruins of the **Amphitheatre**, in the easternmost part of the city.

The amphitheatre, in brick, was probably covered in stone and stood in the newer part of the city on the northwest edge of *Urbs vetus* (Old Town) close to the walls. According to historians, the amphitheatre could seat 18,000–20,000 people. The foundations and a part of the lower tribune have been excavated and the discovery of a network of underground channels has led to the theory that simulated naval battles were held in the arena.

The amphitheatre's construction date was controversial for a long time,

but has now been established as the second half of the 2nd century AD.

From the amphi-theatre, another path leads to the **Theatre** at the edge of the old city. This was built in the first half of the 1st century AD and part of the stage and the foundations of the stalls have been excavated. Next to the theatre is the **Forum**, the political and commercial heart of the city. Unlike the Forum in Zadar *(see pp90–93)*, the paving was dismantled and only the foundations remain. In the Roman era some of the most important buildings stood around the Forum, which was begun in the 1st century AD and subsequently modified.

The best-preserved Roman construction in ancient Salona is the **Aqueduct**, built to bring water from the River

VISITORS' CHECKLIST

Map D5. 🚌 *from Split.*
🛈 *(021) 210 048.* ☉ *summer: 7am–7pm; winter: call to check opening times.*

Jadro to the city and extended in the time of Emperor Diocletian to reach his palace in Split *(see pp118–9)*. Repair work was carried out at the end of the 19th century and the southern part of the aque-duct is still in use. Alongside the walls it is possible to see some parts of the aqueduct above the surface – more evidence of the great skills of Roman civil engineers.

From the theatre you return to the Manastirine necropolis. North of this site is the **Necropolis of Marusinac**, built outside the city around the tomb of St Anastasius. In this area a few traces of a basilica dating from the 5th century are still visible.

The Amphitheatre, of which only a part of the lower tribune remains

THE RUINS OF SALONA

Amphitheatre ⑦
Baths ③
Bishop's Complex ④
Caesarea Gate ⑤
Forum ⑨
Necropolis of Kapljuć ⑥
Necropolis of Manastirine ①
Necropolis of Marusinac ⑩
Theatre ⑧
Tusculum ②

Snack bar

Walls and Aqueduct

Sinj

URBS NOVA ORIENTALIS

URBS NOVA OCCIDENTALIS

URBS VETUS

Modern town

Split

0 metres   500
0 yards   500

Motorway E65

Split ⑰

Detail of Papalić Palace

SHIPYARDS, FACTORIES and a busy port present the modern face of Split, which expanded unchecked after World War II. The old town centre is still full of charm however; it grew up in and around the Emperor Diocletian's vast Roman palace, one of the largest and best-preserved left from the Roman world. In 614, the palace took in refugees from Salona *(see p114)*, which had been razed by the Avars, and these newcomers began to use the Roman structure as housing. Among the refugees were the bishop and other religious dignitaries, who breathed new life into the bishopric of Split. After two centuries of Byzantine rule and the establishment of Croat communities, Split became part of the Venetian territories in 1409. Under the Venetians, new walls and the Gripe Fort were built and the arts flourished.

View of the port and the seafront of Split

🚻 Golden Gate
Zlatna Vrata

This was the main entrance to Diocletian's Palace *(see p118)*. It faces Salona and was the most impressive of the gates, with towers and decorations above the semicircular arches and on the bases of the statues. In the 11th century, the corridor between the palace and the gate was closed and turned into the church of **St Martin** (Sv. Martin). An inscription commemorates Father Dominic, the founder.

🏛 Museum of Split
Muzej Grada Splita

Papalićeva 1. 🄲 *(021) 341 240, 360 171.* ⭘ *Jun–Sep: 9am–noon, 6–9pm daily; Oct–May: 9am–4pm Tue–Fri, 10am–noon Sat & Sun.* 🖼
The Gothic Papalić Palace is

one of the most interesting of the 15th–16th-century buildings constructed in the abandoned parts of the Diocletian complex. It is now an exhibition area with artistic finds, 16th-century works, paintings and books illustrating the history of the city from the 12th to the 18th centuries.

🚻 Peristyle

The interior courtyard of the Roman complex is now a popular tourist meeting place with a busy café. The columns bordering three sides rest on a high plinth and have finely worked capitals. The access to the former private quarters of Diocletian has a tall arched tympanum and relief decorations.

🔒 Baptistry of St John
Sv. Ivan Krstitelj

🄲 *(021) 342 589.*
⭘ *for restoration.*
This small, beautiful building, consecrated in the 6th century, was the Palace's Temple of Jupiter. Inside, the baptismal font incorporates a pre-Romanesque panel representing King Zvonimir and other dignitaries. The statue of St John on the end wall is by Ivan Meštrović and was added before World War

Baptismal font in the Baptistry of St John, former Temple of Jupiter

II. The tomb of Bishop John is from the 8th century and the one in front of it, that of Bishop Lawrence, dates from the 11th century.

🔒 Cathedral of St Domnius
Katedrala Sv. Duje
See p119.

🚻 Silver Gate and Church of St Dominic
Srebrna Vrata i Sv. Dominik
Hrvojeva ulica. **Church of St Dominic** ⭘ *am.*
Near the Silver Gate there is a market, a wonderful chaos of seasonal fruit and vegetables, homemade cheeses, hams and dried herbs. Because of the open space, this also provides the best view of the Palace of Diocletian. It is still possible to distinguish the different structures of the complex, and part of the guards' corridor, on the walls, can be walked along.

In front of the gate is the Oratory of St Catherine, built in the Middle Ages. It was used by the Dominicans while they built their own monastery (1217). The oratory was almost entirely rebuilt in the 17th century and became the church of St Dominic (Sv. Dominik). Inside the church, which was enlarged in 1930, are a *Miracle in Surian* by Palma il Giovane and an *Apparition in the Temple*, attributed to his school.

🚻 Brass Gate
Brončana Vrata
Although this gate is plain and faces the sea and port

(it was in fact a service entrance), it opens on to the richest façade of the palace. The upper floor had a portico which was later enclosed to make living quarters.

🏛 Iron Gate
Željezna Vrata
The church of **Our Lady of the Belfry** (Gospa od Zvonika), named after the presence of the city's oldest

bell tower (1081), was made from the ambulatory of this entrance to the Palace.

🏛 People's Square
Narodni Trg (Pjaca)
Ethnographic Museum 📞 (021) 344 164. ⬜ 8am–1pm Mon–Wed, Fri & Sat; 8am–1pm, 5pm–7pm Thu; 10am–noon Sun.
This was the centre of business and administration from the 15th century and the nobility

erected prestigious buildings here. Examples are the Venetian-Gothic **Cambi Palace** and the Renaissance **Town Hall** (Općinski Dom), built in the first half of the 15th century, with a loggia with three arches on the ground floor and a Gothic window on the upper floor. This houses an **Ethnographic Museum** (Etnografski Muzej), including Dalmatian folk crafts: silver jewellery, weapons, wooden objects and costumes.

The Renaissance Town Hall on People's Square in the centre of Split

SPLIT TOWN CENTRE

Baptistry of St John ④
Braće Radića Square ⑩
Brass Gate ⑦
Cathedral of St Domnius ⑤
Church of St Francis ⑪
Golden Gate ①
Iron Gate ⑧
Museum of Split ②

People's Square ⑨
Peristyle ③
Silver Gate and Church of St Dominic ⑥

KEY

◼ Palace of Diocletian pp118–9
🛈 Tourist information
✝ Church
⊠ Post office

0 metres   100
0 yards   100

National Gallery
Archaeological Museum
Poljud Stadium
Our Lady of Grace in Paljud

ULICA KRALJA TOMISLAVA

KRUŽIĆEVA

MARMONTOVA ULICA

OBROVAČKA

ZADARSKA

MAJSTORA J.

DOMINISOVA

MARULIĆEVA

KREŠIMIROVA

HRVOJEVA

OBALA HRVATSKOG NARODNOG PREPORODA

Dubrovnik
Gripe Fort

Museum of Croatian
Archaeological
Monuments
Meštrović Gallery

Railway station
Bus station

Palace of Diocletian

DIOCLETIAN, probably a native of Salona, became emperor in 284 and set out to reorganize the immense Roman Empire, dividing it into two parts with an Augustus at the head of one half and a Caesar at the head of the other. After governing for 20 years, Diocletian retired from public life and in 305 moved to the palace which he had commissioned from the architects Filotas and Zotikos in the bay of Split. After Diocletian's death in 313, the palace was used as administrative offices and the governor's residence. In 615, crowds of refugees from Salona found shelter here after the destruction of their city by the Avars. The richest settled in the emperor's apartments, the poorer in the towers and above the gates. The corners of the palace were marked by four square towers, and four towers along the north, east and south sides, while the side facing the sea had a loggia with arches.

Iron Gate and the Clock Tower
This is the best preserved gate: beyond is the church of Our Lady of the Belfry with a 12th-century tower next to it.

Temple of Jupiter
This had an atrium with six columns. The body of the building had a coffered vault and rested on an underground crypt. In the early Middle Ages it was turned into the Baptistry of St John.

The Temples of Venus
and Cybele were circular outside and had a hexagonal ground-plan inside. A colonnaded corridor ran around the outside.

The Mausoleum of Diocletian, now the Cathedral of St Domnius

Peristyle
Near the crossroads where the Cardo and Decumanus intersected, the peristyle gave access to the sacred area. On one side were the temples of Venus and Cybele and, further back, that of Jupiter (now the Baptistry of St John); on the other side, the Mausoleum, now the cathedral.

Portrait of Diocletian
After reorganizing the empire, the emperor sought the spiritual unification of its citizens. The state religion, personified by the emperor, gained in importance, and temples were constructed bearing his image. Christians were subject to extremely violent persecution.

The Golden Gate, facing Salona, was the main entrance to the palace. This was the most imposing of the gates with two towers and many decorations.

The Silver Gate, or eastern gate, was a simpler copy of the Golden Gate.

RECONSTRUCTION OF DIOCLETIAN'S PALACE

The palace, shown here in its original form, was like a typical Roman military camp. It was 215 m (705 ft) long and 180 m (590 ft) wide and was enclosed by very thick walls, at times 28 m (92 ft) high. The four-sided stronghold was reinforced with towers on the north, east and west sides. There is a gate on each side, connected by two roads corresponding to the Roman *Cardo* and *Decumanus*.

⛪ Cathedral of St Domnius
Katedrala Sv. Duje
Kraj Sv. Duje 5. 📞 *(021) 342 589.*
🕐 *Jul & Aug: 8am–noon, 4–7pm daily; Sep–Jun: 10am–noon daily.*

Originally Diocletian's mausoleum, the cathedral was consecrated in the 7th century when the sarcophagus containing the body of Diocletian was removed and replaced by the remains of St Domnius. It was the archbishop of Split at the time who transformed the mausoleum into a Christian church. It has remained practically unaltered since that time except for the construction of a Romanesque bell tower (12th–16th centuries) and the addition of the 13th-century choir inside.

An ancient sphinx in black granite rests at the foot of the bell tower. The entrance doorway has wooden panels from 1214, with scenes from the Gospel in floral frames. The cathedral, built on an octagonal ground-plan, has a double order of Corinthian columns, most of them the Roman originals; above these is a frieze decorated with scenes of Eros hunting, supporting medallions with portraits of Diocletian and his wife Prisca. In the second niche on the right, with frescoes dating from 1428, is the

The 13th-century hexagonal pulpit, Cathedral of St Domnius

Altar of St Domnius, the work of Bonino of Milan (1427). The wooden choir stalls in the 17th-century presbytery are an example of Romanesque carving from the beginning of the 13th century.

To the side is a chapel housing the **Altar of St Anastasius**, designed in 1448 by Juraj Dalmatinac. The niche after this was altered in the 18th century to create the Baroque chapel of St Domnius. The 13th-century hexagonal **pulpit** is supported by thin columns with carved capitals. The 14th-century building behind the cathedral houses the sacristy and the name of one of the architects, Filotas, is inscribed by the entrance. In the sacristy, now the Cathedral Museum, are many works of art, including objects in gold and silver, ancient manuscripts, medieval icons and vestments. Of particular importance are the *Historia Saloniana* written by Archdeacon Toma in the 13th century and a 7th-century Gospel.

Detail of the Altar of St Anastasius, Cathedral

Exploring Split

A S WELL AS DIOCLETIAN'S PALACE, Split has much in the way of historical and artistic interest to offer. In the medieval period, villages were built near the walls and when the city became a free town these settlements were linked in a more orderly fashion. The present-day Braće Radića Square and the People's Square were built, along with the Cambi Palace and the Town Hall. After 1420, construction of the external defences began and town walls were built. Between Split and Trogir, castles built for defence against the Turks still survive.

The 15th-century Marina Tower, built by the Venetians

🚇 Braće Radića Square
Trg Braće Radića
This medieval square is at the southwest corner of Diocletian's Palace. The tall **Marina Tower** (Hrvojeva Kula) is the only evidence of the imposing castle built by the Venetians in the second half of the 15th century after the final defeat of Split. Built on an octagonal ground-plan, it stands on the southern side of the square.

On the northern side is the Baroque **Milesi Palace**, which dates from the 17th century. There is also a work by Ivan Meštrović in the centre of the square: the great monument to Marko Marulić, the writer and scholar (1450–1524) who was the founder of literature in the Croatian language. The imposing bronze statue dedicated to the writer has an inscription with some verses by the poet Tin Ujević.

Monument to Marko Marulić

🛐 Church of St Francis
Sv. Frane
Trg Republike. ▯ *(021) 355 088 (Tourist office).* ◯ *by appt.*
The church has been rebuilt in recent times but the small Romanesque-Gothic cloister, with thin columns enclosing a flower garden, is original.

The church, with mainly Baroque furnishings, has a 15th-century crucifix by Blaž Juriev Trogiranin. It also houses the tombs of the city's illustrious citizens, including that of Archdeacon Toma (the first Dalmatian historian), writer Marko Marulić and the well-known composer Ivan Lukačić.

🏛 Museum of Croatian Archaeological Monuments
Muzej Hrvatskih Arheoloških Spomenika
Šetalište Ivana Meštrovića. ▮ *(021) 358 420, 358 455.* ◯ *winter: 9am–3pm Tue–Sat, 10am–noon Sun; summer: 9am–3pm, 5–7pm Tue–Sat, 10am–noon Sun.* 🖼
Set up in 1975, this museum houses finds from the area around Split dating from the early Middle Ages. The collection also includes the works of early Croat sculptors, dating from 800. The stone fragments, salvaged from churches and castles, consist mainly of tombs, capitals, altar fronts, ciboria and windows. Highlights include Prince Višeslav's hexagonal baptismal font in marble, dating from the beginning of the 9th century, and the sarcophagus of Queen Jelena (10th century), discovered in the ancient Roman city of Salona.

***Distant Agreements* by Ivan Meštrović, Meštrović Gallery**

🏛 Meštrović Gallery
Galerija Meštrović
Šetalište Ivana Meštrovića 46. ▮ *(021) 358 450.* ◯ *Jun–Sep: 10am–6pm Tue–Sat, 10am–3pm Sun; Oct–May: 10am–4pm Tue–Sat, 10am–2pm Sun.* 🖼
The building housing this gallery was the residence of Ivan Meštrović in the early 1930s *(see p155)*. The sculptor himself designed the building with two low towers at the ends and a loggia with eight columns on the façade. His sculptures, including *Distant Agreements* and *The Robes*, decorate the garden and the interior. Among statues in marble, wood and bronze are *The Contemplation*, *The Vow* and *Psyche*. Part of the building still preserves the artist's apartments.

The **Kaštelet**, further down the road at No 39, can be visited with the same ticket. This 17th-century residence belonged to the Cavagnin family and was bought by Meštrović in 1932 to set up an exhibition hall. The artist also built a small church here to exhibit a series of reliefs called *New Testament*, now replaced by a different work, the *Author of the Apocalypse*.

🏛 National Art Gallery
Galerija Umjetnina
Lovretska 11. ▮ *(021) 480 149, 480 150.* ◯ *winter: 9am–noon, 4–6pm Mon–Sat; summer: 9am–noon, 5–7pm Mon–Sat.*
The gallery offers a broad overview of art in Split and the rest of Dalmatia from the 16th to the 20th centuries.

The Venetian masters have a place of honour in the gallery but there are also important icons from the so-called school of Bocche di Cattaro (18th–19th centuries) and more contemporary work, including works by Ivan Meštrović and Vlaho Bukovac. Temporary exhibitions are also held here.

🏛 Archaeological Museum
Arheološki Muzej
Zrinsko Frankopanska 25. 🔲 *(021) 318 720.* ⭘ *winter: 9am–1pm Tue–Sat, 10am–noon Sun; summer: 9am–1pm, 4–7pm Tue–Sat, 10am–noon Sun.*
🖼 ✔ ♿

The museum was founded in 1820 and has been on its present site since 1921. It contains a considerable number of finds from the Roman, early Christian and medieval periods

Sarcophagus, Archaeological Museum

which are exhibited in rotation. Of great interest are the finds from Roman Salona, including sculptures, capitals, sarcophagi (those from the 4th–5th century still have pagan reliefs), jewellery, coins, small objects in glazed terracotta and ceramics. There are also finds from the Roman town of Narona *(see p128).*

🏠 Our Lady of Grace in Poljud
Gospa od Poljuda
Poljudsko Šetalište 17. ℹ️ *(021) 355 088.* ⭘ *by appt.*
Towards Zrinsko-Frankopanska in the direction of the suburbs lies an area once

Polyptych by Girolamo da Santacroce, Our Lady of Grace

called the marsh *(poljud)*. In the 1400s, the Franciscans built a fortified monastery here with large lateral towers, and a church with a trussed roof. A polyptych by Girolamo da Santacroce from 1549 stands on the main altar, depicting the *Virgin and Saints*: the figure holding a model of the city is St Domnius, patron saint of Split.

Many works of art are on display, including a *Portrait of Bishop Tommaso Nigris* by Lorenzo Lotto (1527) and miniatures by Bone Razmilović.

Not far from the monastery is the stadium of the famous Hajduk football team, built in 1979 in the suburb of Poljud and designed by Boris Magaš.

🌿 Marjan Peninsula
This protected nature reserve is on the west side of town, and is reached by a winding flight of steps. On the way is the 13th-century church of St Nicholas (Sv. Nikola). A path leads out to the wooded

peninsula, from where there are fine views out to sea, with the islands of Šolta, Brač and Hvar clearly visible.

ENVIRONS: Seven Castles (Kaštela) is the name given to a series of fortifications built by the Venetian governor and local nobles to defend the town against the Turks between the end of the 15th century and the 16th century, along a large well-sheltered bay between Split and Trogir. A village now called Kaštela grew up around the complex. Five of the original castles are still preserved, as are the fortified villas which rose from their reconstruction.

St George's Castle (Kaštel Sućurac), the summer residence of the bishop of Split, was built at the end of the 14th century and strengthened the following century by building a wall, of which some traces remain.

Abbess Castle (Kaštel Gomilica) was built on an island which is now linked to the mainland.

Vitturi Castle (Kaštel Lukšić) was transformed into a large villa, keeping only the old external structure. It was built by the Vitturi family, who donated a sculpture by Juraj Dalmatinac to the church of St Raynerius (Sv. Arnir). **Kaštel Stari** has kept its original aspect; the sea-facing side looks like a palace with Gothic windows.

All that remains of the **New Castle** (Kaštel Novi) are the tower and the church of St Roch, which was built by the Čipiko family.

The stadium of the Hajduk football team, built in 1979 in the suburb of Poljud

Šolta ⑱

Map D5. 🏔 *1,400.* 🚢 *from Split.*
ℹ *Grohote, (021) 654 151.*

THIS LONG ISLAND, indented with bays and coves, covers an area of 52 sq km (20 sq miles). The economy is based on agriculture thanks to reasonably fertile soil and, over recent years, tourism has also become important. The Romans called the island Soletta and it was a holiday resort for the nobility of Salona. The ruins of many villas can be found in lovely locations on the island.

After the attack on Salona in 614, some of the refugees fled here and villages were built. Some still have small churches dating from the early Middle Ages. The island was later abandoned in favour of Split and after 1537 stayed uninhabited for over a century, due to constant Turkish raids. Near Stomorska, Grohote, Donje Selo and Nečujam, traces of defence towers can be seen.

Many people from Split have holiday homes here.

Brač ⑲

Map D5. 🏔 *14,000.*
✈ *(021) 523 330, 544 261.*
🚢 *to Supetar from Split.* 🚌 *(021) 631 122.* ℹ *Trg P Jakšića 17, (021) 630 551.* **Bol** ℹ *Porat bolskih pomoraca, (021) 635 638.*

THE THIRD LARGEST island in the Adriatic at 40 km/25 miles long and 15 km/9 miles wide, Brač has an interesting geological structure. In some

Bol's famous golden beach, changing with the tides

areas the ranges of limestone hills have sinkholes and are cut by deep ravines and gorges. In other areas a white, hard stone prevails. The stone has been quarried since ancient times *(see p132)* and is still much sought after as a quality building material. Extensive woods cover some parts of the island and other areas are cultivated.

Although Brač has always been inhabited, it was first subject to Salona (the rich Salonians built villas and also sought refuge here when their town was attacked by the Avars), and then to Split. Both Split and Brač came under Byzantine and then Venetian rule. Under the Venetians (1420–1797), villages were built in the interior but no defences were built to prevent the pirates and Turks landing.

Ferries from Split on the mainland dock at the old town of **Supetar**, which has some good beaches.

To the southwest lies the town of **Milna**, which was founded at the beginning of the 18th century and faces a sheltered bay. The exterior of the church of the Annunciation of Mary (Velika Gospa) is Baroque and the interior is decorated in the Rococo style.

Nerežišća, in the centre of the island, was for a long period the main town. The Governor's Palace, the Loggia and a pedestal with the lion of St Mark are signs of its former status.

The major attraction at **Bol**, on the southern coast, is its famous long beach (Zlatni Rat, meaning Golden Horn), a triangular spit of shingle

The town of Pučišća on the island of Brač

ŠOLTA
━━ *111*
Maslinica Grohote
Stomorska

KEY

━━ Major road
━━ Minor road
🚢 Ferry
✈ Airport
ℹ Tourist information
🏖 Beach with facilities

Supetar
Škrip
Milna *114* Nerežišća *113* Pučišća Povlja
Selca
BRAČ *113*
Sumartin
115
Bol

0 kilometres 10
0 miles 10

which reaches out into the sea and changes shape with the seasonal tides. It is a popular spot for windsurfing.

A Dominican monastery, founded in 1475, stands on a charming headland at the edge of the village. The beautiful church is decorated with paintings, including a *Virgin with Saints* attributed to Tintoretto. A rich treasury includes liturgical objects. From Bol you can climb up **Mount St Vitus** (Vidova Gora), a two-hour walk to one of the highest peaks in the Dalmatian islands (778 m/2,552 ft), near which a fortified monastery (Samostan Blaca) clings to rocks.

In **Selca** quarrymen can be seen at work and the Roman quarries where they extracted stone can also be visited. The blocks were loaded onto ships at the port of **Pučišća**, a charming, peaceful spot similar to **Sumartin**, further east, which was built around a monastery founded by Franciscans of Makarska in 1645. The monks brought with them a treasury and many of the paintings now preserved in the monastery.

Škrip is probably the site of the first settlement on the island and the presumed birthplace of Helen, mother of Emperor Constantine. The church and a painting by Palma il Giovane on the main altar are dedicated to Helen.

A fortified house houses **Brač Museum** and exhibits archaeological finds, evidence of mankind's ancient presence on the island.

🏛 **Brač Museum**
Škrip. ℹ️ *(021) 356 706.* ⭕ *by appt.*

The façade of the church of Our Lady of Spilica in Vis

Vis ⑳

Map D6.
🏘 *4,300.* **Vis** ⛴ *(021) 711 032.*
ℹ️ *Šetalište Stare Isse 2, (021) 717 017.* **Komiža** ℹ️ *(021) 713 455.*

FURTHER OUT IN THE Adriatic than the other Dalmatian islands, Vis was until 1989 a military base and closed to tourism. Now gradually being rediscovered by intrepid travellers, it has a jagged coastline with beaches, and an inland mountain chain with Mount Hum reaching a height of 587 m (1,925 ft).

The island was chosen by Dionysios of Syracuse as a base for Greek domination of the Adriatic. The Greeks founded the town of Issa here. Later the island was ruled by the Romans, then Byzantines and, from 1420, the Venetians.

The island played a key role during World War II – in 1944 Marshal Tito used it as a base for co-ordinating partisan military operations. The cave is still called "Tito's Cave". Crucial meetings between partisans, the Yugoslav government in exile and the Allies were also held on Vis.

The main town of **Vis** has Venetian Gothic buildings and the Renaissance church of Our Lady of Spilica (Gospa od Spilica), with a painting by Girolamo di Santacroce. In the town of **Komiža**, there is a castle built by the Venetians.

ENVIRONS: The **island of Biševo**, to the southwest of Vis, has a Blue Grotto (Modra Spilja), where, at midday, the water takes on beautiful colours. Day trips by boat to the cave depart from Komiža in the morning (contact the Tourist Office).

A monastery was built here around 1000 AD, which resisted raids by pirates and Saracens for 200 years. The ruins remain, along with a 12th-century church.

Part of the coastline near Komiža, on the island of Vis

Hvar ㉑

ART TREASURES, a mild climate, good beaches and fields of scented lavender make this island one of the treasures of the Adriatic. Limestone hills form the central ridge. Hvar's story begins in the 4th century BC when the Syracusans of Issa (now Vis) founded Pharos (the present-day Stari Grad) and Dimos (Hvar). Traces have been left by the Romans, the Byzantines, the Croatian sovereigns and the Venetians, who ruled from 1278 until 1797. After 1420, defences were built, and the capital was moved from Pharos to Hvar. In 1886, under Austria-Hungary, the "Hvar Hygienic Society" began to promote the town as a health resort. It is also the birthplace of a number of famous people: the painter Juraj Plančić (1900–30), and writer and art critic Tonko Marojević (b. 1941), a Croat intellectual.

Main square of Hvar, with the Cathedral of St Stephen

A peaceful bay on the island of Hvar

Hvar Town

This town is one of the most visited on the Dalmatian coast, thanks to the treasures within its walls (1278). During Venetian rule, governors and local nobles decided to make it a safe harbour for the fleets going to, or returning from, the Orient. They also transferred the bishopric and built monasteries.

Hvar has a long tradition of art and culture and one of the first theatres ever built in Europe is here. It was also the birthplace of the Renaissance poet Hanibal Lučić (c.1485–1553), and the playwright Martin Benetović (died 1607).

The town's most important buildings stand on three sides of the main square: the fourth is open to the sea. The Renaissance **Cathedral of St Stephen** (Katedrala Sv. Stjepana) has a trefoil pediment and a 17th-century bell tower standing to one side. The interior houses many works of art: *Virgin and Saints* by Palma il Giovane (1544–1628), *Pietà* by Juan Boschetus, *Virgin with Saints* by Domenico Uberti and a fine 16th-century wooden choir.

The **Clock Tower**, the **Civic Loggia** below and **Hektorović Palace** (Hektorovićeva Palača), recognizable by the beautiful Venetian-Gothic mullioned window, all date from the 15th century.

On the south side of the square is the **Arsenal**, which dates from the late 16th century. A theatre was built on the first floor in 1612, the first "public theatre" in the Balkans. People of all classes could come and see drama here, regardless of their social standing.

Outside the walls of the old town is the **Franciscan Monastery** (Franjevački Samostan) dating from 1461 and the church of **Our Lady of Charity** (Gospa od Milosti), with a relief on the façade by Nikola Firentinac. Inside are two paintings by Palma il Giovane (*St Francis receiving the Stigmata* and *St Diego*), three polyptychs by Francesco da Santacroce, a *Christ on the Cross* by Leandro da Bassano, and six scenes inspired by the

SVETI KLEMENT

116 Stari Grad Vrboska

Hvar

Jelsa

HVAR 116 Poljica

PAKLENI ISLANDS

Zavala

0 kilometres 5

0 miles 5

ŠĆEDRO

A field of lavender on the island of Hvar

VISITORS' CHECKLIST

Map D–E5. 11,500. from Split and Drvenik. **Hvar** (021) 741 007; Jadrolinija: (021) 741 132. Trg Sveti Stjepana, (021) 741 059. **Stari Grad** (021) 765 060; Jadrolinija: (021) 765 048. Nova Riva 2, (021) 765 763. **Sućuraj** (021) 773 228. (021) 773 229.

Passion of Christ by Martin Benetović. There are also many works of art in the rooms facing the cloister. The painting of the *Last Supper* in the refectory is of uncertain attribution – possibly Matteo Ingoli, Matteo Ponzone or the school of Palma il Giovane. There are splendid views from the 16th-century Španjola fort and from the Napoleon fort (1811).

The cloister of the Franciscan monastery, outside Hvar

Stari Grad

This town was originally called Pharos and was founded by the Syracusans in the 4th century BC (remains can be seen in Ciklopska ulica). Around Pod Dolom are the ruins of a Roman villa with mosaic floors. Stari Grad lies at the end of a long bay and the main sights are situated around the main square. Facing the square are the 17th-century church of **St Stephen** (Sv. Stjepan) and the

Baroque **Bianchini Palace** (Biankini Palača), the home of a **Nautical Collection**.

The heart of the town is dominated by **Kaštel Tvrdalj**, the fortified residence of Petar Hektorović which has a seawater fishpond. An Ethnographic Collection is now housed in the fort. Hektorović, a humanist poet, built the fort in around 1520. He was the author of the poem *Ribanje i ribarsko prigovaranje (Fishing and Fishermen's Conversation)* in which he vividly describes a fishing trip around the islands of Hvar, Brač and Šolta in which he took part.

The **Dominican Monastery** (Dominikanski Samostan), founded in 1482 and rebuilt and fortified after destruction by the Turks, has a rich library and a collection of paintings. In the town there is also an International School of Painting and Sculpture run by Professor Emil Tanay, for young people and postgraduates.

Kaštel Tvrdalj, Stari Grad

Dominican Monastery

(021) 765 442. Jun–Sep: 10am–1pm, 5–8pm; Oct–May: by appt.

Vrboska

The road leading to this small village offers a marvellous sight in June: vast fields of scented lavender.

Vrboska is home to the 16th-century church of **St Mary** (Sv. Marija), fortified in 1575 to provide shelter for villagers in the event of a siege. The Baroque church of **St Lawrence** (Sv. Lovro) has a polyptych on the main altar by Paolo Veronese (c.1570) and a *Virgin of the Rosary* by Leandro da Bassano.

Sućuraj

Lying in a sheltered bay is this village with the remains of a castle built by the Venetians in around 1630.

ENVIRONS: The **Pakleni Islands**, facing the town of Hvar, are uninhabited and mostly woodland. Their name derives from the resin *(paklina)* at one time extracted from the pines and used to waterproof boats. During the summer boat trips to the islands depart from Hvar. The nearest island, Jerolim, is given over to naturism.

The island of **Šćedro**, south of Hvar, is covered in pines and maquis. Illyrian tombs and parts of a Roman villa have been found here.

Bogomolje · 116 · Sućuraj

KEY

▬	Major road
▬	Minor road
⛴	Ferry
ℹ	Tourist information
🏖	Beach with facilities

Boating on the river in the Cetina Valley Nature Park

Omiš ②

Map D5.
🏠 *6,100.* 🚌 *(021) 864 210.*
🚌 *(021) 861 025.* ℹ *Trg Kneza Miroslava, (021) 861 350.*
🎭 *Klapa (Jul).*

IN THE LATE Middle Ages Omiš was known as the residence of the terrifying corsairs who fought against Venetian rule from the 12th century until 1444, when the town fell to Venice. Today it is a peaceful holiday resort with some industry along the coast, and the starting point for visits to the valley of the River Cetina.

In July, the Dalamatinksa Klapa festival attracts many visitors who come to hear Klapa, a kind of plainsong traditional to Dalmatia. It is still very popular, even among the young.

Only a few traces of the Roman *municipium* of Oeneum remain but many of the medieval defences built by the counts of Kačić and Bribir are still visible on a hill, once the site of the Old Town, or Starigrad. These consist of the walls going down to the River Cetina and also the ruins of a large fort (Fortica) with its distinctive high tower. From the fort, built between the 16th and the 17th centuries, there is a splendid view of Omiš and

The church of St Peter in Priko, a district of Omiš

the central Dalmatian islands. There are three interesting religious buildings in the town. One is the Renaissance church of **St Michael** (Sv. Mihovil) with a pointed bell tower, originally a defensive structure. Inside is a 16th-century wooden altar, a large 13th-century wooden cross and two paintings by Matteo Ingoli of Ravenna (1580–1631). At the end of the main road is the 16th-century **Oratory of the Holy Spirit** (Sv. Duh) with *Descent of the Holy Spirit* by Palma il Giovane (1544–1628).

However, the most fascinating monument here is in Priko, on the opposite bank of the River Cetina. This is the 10th-century church of **St Peter** (Sv. Petar), one of the most appealing pre-Romanesque churches in Dalmatia. It has a single nave, a dome and remains from the early Christian period incorporated into the walls.

ENVIRONS: The **Cetina Valley Nature Park**, immediately behind Omiš, shelters a river which flows into the artificial lake of Peruča. The river runs out of the lake and parallel to the coast for some distance and then, near Zadvarje, abruptly turns and cascades down before flowing into a narrow gorge. This beautiful natural environment, with its myriad bird species, can be explored on foot or by bicycle, but the most popular way to see it is to take one of the many boats through the park.

Makarska ②

Map E5. 🏠 *14,000.*
🚌 *Ante Starčevića ulica, (021) 612 333.* 🚌 *(021) 611 977.* ℹ *Obala Kralja Tomislava, (021) 616 288.*

THE MAKARSKA COAST extends from Brela to Živogošće and includes a long stretch of shore with lush vegetation sheltered by the Biokovo massif. Makarska, one of Dalmatia's most popular mainland resorts, lies within a bay sheltered by the peninsula of St Peter's. The town has ancient origins. It was the site of the Roman Muicurum which was destroyed by the Goths in

The Makarska coast, with white beaches and a mountainous backdrop

THE VINEYARDS OF DALMATIA

Vines are grown all along the coast of Dalmatia, and on many of the islands. Vineyards first start appearing around Primošten, near Trogir *(see p109)*, where the good quality red wine Babić is made, and become part of the landscape along the Makarska coast. Built on stony hillsides, these vineyards are often "fortified" with low dry-stone walls, painstakingly constructed with geometrical precision by peasant farmers. Low-growing vines cultivated inside the walls are protected from the cold north winds and kept cool in the hot summer months. A monument to human toil, the result of immense patience and effort, without these walls it would not be possible to cultivate this difficult ground.

Vines protected by dry-stone walls

The beach at Gradac, the longest in the eastern Adriatic

The Franciscan monastery, Makarska, now a museum

548, and rebuilt at a later date. It belonged to the Kingdom of Croatia until 1499, when it was conquered by the Turks, for whom it was a port and trading centre until 1646, the beginning of Venetian rule.

There are two ancient monasteries in Makarska. St Philip Neri (Sv. Filipa Nerija) was built in 1757, and has medieval and Roman-era fragments in the cloister. The Franciscan monastery (Franjevački Samostan), built in 1614 on the foundations of a 15th-century monastery, houses the **Malacological Museum** (Muzej Mala-kološki), with a collection of mollusc shells.

The centre of the modern town is the square called Brother Andrija Kačić Miošić

(1704–60), dedicated to the Dalmatian scholar and author of theological and philosophical works. Two seafront promenades extend towards the wide beaches and Kalelarga, where there are 18th-century buildings.

🏛 **Malacological Museum**
Franjevački Samostan put.
📞 *(021) 611 256.*

Gradac ㉔

Map E5. 🏙 *1,200.*
ℹ️ *Ulica Stjepana Radića 1, (021) 697 511.*

THIS TOWN'S FAME and popularity are due to the fact that it has the longest beach in the eastern Adriatic. Over 6 km (4 miles) long, the beach is lined with hotels and camping sites.

In the town itself there are two large 17th-century towers while nearby, in **Crkvine**, the remains of a Roman staging post between Muicurum (the present-day Makarska) and Narona *(see p128)* have been found. Gradac gets its name from the fort *(grad)* built in the 17th century to defend the town against the Turks.

ENVIRONS: In **Zaostrog**, 14 km (8 miles) northwest of Gradac, is a Franciscan monastery (Franjevački Samostan) founded in the 16th century and completed a century later. The façade of the church has an inscription written in Cyrillic script. In the rooms around the beautiful cloister there is a fascinating folklore collection, an art gallery, and a library and archive where documents about the period of Turkish occupation are kept. The scholar Andrjia Kačić Miošić *(see Makarska, p126)* lived and died in the monastery.

Around 20 km (12 miles) from Gradac, towards Makarska, is **Živogošće**, one of the oldest settlements on the Makarska coast. Today it is a busy tourist resort, but it was once famous for a spring which flowed from the rocks.

A Franciscan monastery was founded near this spring in 1776, and its beautiful church boasts an ornate Baroque altar. The monastery is famous for its well-stocked library and archives, which are the main source for the study of the area around the Biokovo massif.

Franciscan monastery, Zaostrog

The delta of the River Neretva in Opuzen, drained and turned into fertile fields

Opuzen ㉕

Map E6. ▨ *2,800.*
▤ *Metković, (020) 681 951.*
▮ *Stjepana Radica ulica 3, Metković, (020) 681 899.*

A T THE EDGES of the delta of the River Neretva, where the road leaves the Magistrala coast road (E65) and climbs the river valley, stands Opuzen. For centuries it was fortified and has always been considered something of a border town.

Towards the end of the 15th century, the Hungarian-Croat king, Matthias Corvinus, built the fort of Koš here. It was captured by the Turks in 1490 who ruled until 1686, when it came under Venetian rule. There are also traces of a 13th-century castle built by the Republic of Dubrovnik and the remains of a fort (Fortis Opus), built by the Venetians to defend the border of their territories. The town takes its name from this fort and the ruins can be seen on the eastern side of town.

In the entrance hall of the former Town Hall are some fragments discovered in the ancient town of Narona.

Narona ㉖

Map E6. ▤ *Metković, (020) 681 951.* ▮ *Stjepana Radica ulica 3, Metković, (020) 681 899.*

T HE ANCIENT Roman town of Colonia Julia Narona was founded by the Romans in the 2nd century BC. It was an important road junction and a trading centre with the Pannonian hinterland, and had temples, baths, a theatre and other buildings grouped around the Forum. A walled town, it was one of the first dioceses in the Balkans and flourished until the 7th century when it was occupied and destroyed by the Avars. It fell into disuse afterwards.

At the beginning of the 19th century, after a few chance discoveries, the Austrian archaeologist Karl Patsch began to carry out

Head of Emperor Vespasian, now in Vid's Museum

excavations. Work continued after World War II and uncovered numerous finds from pagan and Christian temples, houses and public works. Large parts of the area still have to be explored, but it is possible to get an idea of the importance of the town by visiting the Archaeological

Museum in **Vid**. This village stands on much of the site of ancient Narona, 3 km (2 miles) from Metković. In the museum are statues of gods and emperors, as well as weapons and jewels that were found in Narona. Other finds are in Split's Archaeological Museum *(see p121).*

The 16th-century church of St Vitus (Sv. Vid) stands just outside the town on the site of an old church, of which only parts of the apse remain.

Neum ㉗

Bosnia-Herzegovina. **Map** E6. ▨ *1,200.* ▤ *Metković, (020) 681 951.* ▮ *Stjepana Radica ulica 3, Metković, (020) 681 899.*

A LL THE BUSES running along the coastal road between Split and Dubrovnik pass through the 9-km (5-mile) stretch of coast that is part of Bosnia-Herzegovina. The main town is Neum, a holiday resort and Bosnia's only coastal town. Prices are cheaper here than in Croatia, and as a result it is a popular place for Croatians to stop off and go shopping.

Neum is a border town, and visitors should carry passports. There are several hotels and tourist facilities.

Pelješac Peninsula ㉘

Map E6. 🚌 *Metković, (020) 681 951.* **Ston** 🏛 *580.*
🚌 *(020) 754 026.* 🛈 *Pelješka Cesta, (020) 754 452.* **Orebić** 🏛 *1,600.*
🚌 *(020) 743 542.* 🛈 *Trg Mimbelli, (020) 713 718.*

THE PENINSULA of Pelješac juts out 65 km (40 miles) from the mainland, but it is only 7 km (4 miles) wide at its broadest point. A mountain chain forms its backbone, which peaks at Mount St Elijah (961 m/3,152 ft). The slopes and plain are covered with vineyards and fruit trees, and the shallow coastal waters are given over to oyster farming.

The peninsula was first colonized by the Greeks, then by the Romans and later by the Byzantines. From 1333 to 1808 it belonged to Dubrovnik.

The Pelješac coast, a centre for oyster farming

Ston

The town closest to the mainland, Ston was formerly called Stagnum because of its shallow waters. There have been salt pans here since the time of the Romans, who built a *castrum* on the site. It was enclosed by walls prior to 1000 AD.

The present defensive walls, still impressive above the town, were begun in the 14th century and completed in the 15th century on Dubrovnik's orders. There are more than 5 km (3 miles) of walls climbing from Veliki Ston, the main heart of the town, to St Michael's Mount and descending the opposite

slope until they reach Mali Ston. The 41 towers, seven bastions and two forts make this one of the largest and most interesting defensive structures in the Adriatic. Some of the best military architects such as Michelozzo Michelozzi, Župan Bunić, Bernardino of Parma, Juraj Dalmatinac and Paskoje Miličević contributed to its design and construction. The walls are still in good condition despite being bombed in 1991 and struck by an earthquake in 1996.

The main structures are at **Veliki Ston**, which is built on an irregular pentagonal ground plan. These are currently without decoration as the works of art are being restored. The buildings include the largest fort (Veliki Kastio), the neo-Gothic church of St Blaise (Sv. Vlaho), built in 1870 to replace a cathedral from the 16th century which was destroyed by the earthquake of 1850, the Governor's Palace (Knežev Dvor), enlarged in the same century and the Bishop's Palace (1573). The **Church and Franciscan Monastery of St Nicholas** (Sv. Nikola) was built between the end of the 14th century and the 16th century.

Mali Ston, the other focus of the town, is dominated by Fort Koruna, which dates from 1447, with two arsenals and a fortified warehouse for storing salt. There are wonderful views over the island of Korčula from here.

The Franciscan monastery between Orebić and Lovište

Orebić

Towards the tip of the peninsula, Orebić is the boarding point for ferries to Korčula. The town is also worth visiting for its **Maritime Museum** (Pomorski Muzej), which illustrates the history of its inhabitants, who were the most sought-after sea captains in the Mediterranean. At the end of their careers these seamen invested in villas along the coast or in the hills.

Just outside the village, towards Lovište, stands a massive **Franciscan Monastery** (Franjevački Samostan), founded in the 15th century. In the church alongside are two reliefs: one is a *Virgin with Child* by Nikola Firentinac (1501), who was a pupil of Donatello.

🏛 **Maritime Museum**
Trg Mimbelli. 📞 *(020) 713 009.*
🕐 *8am–noon, 6–8pm.* 🏷

Overlooking the circle of walls connecting the two parts of Ston

Korčula 29

DENSE FORESTS OF ALEPPO PINE, cypress and oak are found all over this island, one of the largest in the Adriatic at 47 km (29 miles) long. Mountains run the length of the island, reaching 560 m (1,837 ft) at their peak. Inhabited since prehistoric times, the Greeks named the island Korkyra Melaina (Black Corfu). After 1000 AD, it was fought over by Venice and the Croat kings and later by the Genoese and the Turks (in the 1298 naval battle between Genoa and Venice, the Genoese captured Marco Polo, said to be a native of the island). Today it is a popular holiday spot for its cliffs and sandy beaches, its villages and Korčula, its main town.

Gothic relief in All Saints' Church

VISITORS' CHECKLIST

Map E6. ﹩ 17,000. ☲ from Orebić, Split and Rijeka. **Korčula** ☲ (020) 711 216. ☲ (020) 715 410. ▯ Obala dr. Tuđmana 20, (020) 715 701, 715 867. ⊡ www.korcula.net ⬚ Moreška, 9pm every Thu in summer. **Lumbarda** ▯ (020) 712 005, 712 602. **Blato** ▯ Ulica 31 br 2, (020) 851 850. ⬚ Kumpanija (28 Apr). **Vela Luka** ☲ (020) 812 023. ▯ Ulica 41 br 11, (020) 813 619.

The Land Gate, main entrance to the old town of Korčula

Korčula Town

The town is perched on a peninsula, surrounded by strong 13th-century walls, reinforced with towers and bastions by the Venetians after 1420. The whole town is enchanting. The **Land Gate** (Kopnena Vrata) was fortified by a huge tower, the Revelin, which overlooked a canal dug by the Venetians to isolate the town. There are now steps in this area. Narrow streets branching off the main road are designed to lessen the impact of the bora wind.

Facing **Strossmayerov trg**, the central square, is the town's main monument: the 13th-century **Cathedral of St Mark** (Katedrala Sv. Marka), built in pale, honey-coloured stone. Most of it dates from the end of the 15th century. The skill of Korčula's sculptors and stone masons is evident in the door, where two lions guard the entrance, decorated with thin spiral columns and a lunette with the figure of St Mark, attributed to Bonino of Milan. Two further doors open onto the side aisles. On the left stands an imposing bell tower.

Inside are large columns with elaborately decorated capitals and several important sculptural works: a 15th-century holy water stoup, a font from the 17th century, and the tomb of Bishop Toma Malumbra, attributed to the workshop of Marco Andrijić, who also made the ciborium in the presbytery in 1481. There is also a statue of St Blaise by Ivan Meštrović. The paintings include *St Mark with St Jerome and St Bartholomew* by Tintoretto. On a wall are trophies recalling the Battle of Lepanto of 1571.

Next to the cathedral, in the Bishop's Palace, now the Abbot's House, is the **Abbey Treasury** (Opatska Riznica), which is particularly known for its Dalmatian and Venetian art, including a

Impressive entrance to the Gothic Cathedral of St Mark, Korčula

PROIZD

PRIGRADICA

Vela Luka

Potirna

Blato

Prižba

Brna

KEY

▬ Major road

▬ Minor road

☲ Ferry

▯ Tourist information

⬚ Beach with facilities

Korčula, the main town on the island, on an isthmus on the northeast coast

polyptych by Blaž of Trogir, two altar paintings by Pellegrino of San Daniele, a *Sacred Conversation* by Titian, a *Portrait of a Man* by Vittore Carpaccio and an *Annunciation* by Titian. A door by Bonino of Milan decorates the Gothic church of **St Peter** (Sv. Petar) to the left of the cathedral. Facing St Peter are the Gothic **Arneri Palace** and the Renaissance Gabriellis Palace (16th century). The latter has been the **Civic Museum** (Gradski Muzej) since 1957 and contains documents on Korčula's seafaring history, an interesting archaeological section covering the period from prehistoric to Roman times and other works of art, with many portraits of the local nobility.

Along the seafront is **All Saints' Church** (Svi Sveti), built in 1301 and remodelled in the Baroque style, which belongs to the oldest brotherhood on the island.

Inside is an 18th-century carved wooden *Pietà*, by the Austrian artist George Raphael Donner, and a 15th-century polyptych by Blaž of Trogir.

In the nearby quarters of the brotherhood is the **Icon Gallery** (Galerija Ikona), which is famous for its rich collection of Byzantine icons from the 13th to 15th centuries, many from Crete.

Outside the walls are the **Church and Monastery of St Nicholas** (Sv. Nikola), from the 15th century, with many paintings by Dalmatian and Italian artists.

🏛 **Abbey Treasury**
Trg Sv. Marka. 🛈 *(020) 715 701.*
🕐 *Jun–Aug: 9am–7pm; Sep–May: by appt.* 📷
🏛 **Civic Museum**
Trg Sv. Marka. 📞 *(020) 711 420.*
🕐 *Jun–Aug: 9am–1pm, 5–7pm; Sep–May: by appt.*
🏛 **Icon Gallery**
Trg Svihsvetih. 🛈 *(020) 715 701 (Tourist office).* 🕐 *Jun–Aug: 10am–1pm, 5–7pm; Sep–May: by appt.*

ANCIENT DANCES AND FESTIVALS

The Moreška and the Kumpanija are Korčula's two most noted folk festivals. Officially, the Moreška sword dance takes place in Korčula on 27 July, the patron saint's day (St Theodore). However, it is repeated on Thursdays during the summer as a tourist event. It commemorates the clash between Christians and Moors in the attempt to free a young girl kidnapped by the infidels. In Blato, the Kumpanija festival is dedicated to the patron saint, St Vincenza, and is celebrated with songs and music. At the end of the battle, girls in bright costumes appear, accompanied by pipes and drums. The festival takes place in front of the church on 28 April, but is repeated at other times in other towns on the island.

Actors performing the ancient Moreška sword dance

The sea and rocky coastline of Korčula

Lumbarda

Lumbarda is a village 6 km (4 miles) southeast of the town of Korčula and is thought to have been founded by Greeks from Vis. It was called Eraclea by the Romans. In the 16th century it became a holiday resort for the nobles of Korčula. Some inscriptions from the Greek period are now in the Archaeological Museum of Zagreb *(see pp160–61).*

Today this village is one of the centres of production for the liqueur-like wine called Grk, which is made from vines grown in the sand. The nearby small beaches are havens of tranquillity. It is also possible to rent cottages.

Blato

In the central square of Blato, a town where the festival of the Kumpanija *(see p131)* is held every April, are an 18th-century Baroque loggia,

the Renaissance **Arneri Castle**, where the Civic Museum documenting local history is being set up, and **All Saints' Church** (Svi Sveti), of medieval origin. This church was enlarged and rebuilt in the 17th century and has an altarpiece of the *Virgin with Child and Saints* on the main altar by Girolamo

di Santacroce (1540) and, in the chapel, the relics of the martyr St Vincenza, the object of veneration in the local community. The cemetery church of the **Holy Cross** and that of **St Jerome** date from the 14th century.

Vela Luka

Situated about 45 km (28 miles) west of Korčula is Vela Luka, called "the oldest and the newest town", because it was built at the beginning of the 19th century on the neolithic site of Vela Spilja. It is one of the largest towns on the island and industries coexist with attractive bays and numerous islands.

The hills surrounding the town shelter this area from the winds from the north and south. Vela Luka is also the main port on the island and there are regular ferry services to Split and Lastovo.

Lumbarda on the island of Korčula, one of the greenest in the Adriatic

The ancient Roman quarries, Brač

THE STONE OF DALMATIA

The excellent quality of the stone in the Dalmatian islands was known to the Romans, who used it to build the monuments of Salona and Diocletian's Palace in Split. On Brač, the old Roman quarries are still visible in Pučišća. Brač stone was used for the cathedral in Šibenik *(see pp106–7)*, for which Juraj Dalmatinac devised a method of cutting the stone so that blocks interlocked without mortar. Most of the palaces and churches in Venice are also made of Dalmatian stone. Further afield, part of the White House in Washington and the Royal Palace in Stockholm were faced with stone from Brač. In Korčula, quarrying ceased long ago, and stone cutting skills have largely died out. However, the quarries on the small island of Vrnik, facing Korčula, are still active and stone from here was used in the church of St Sophia in Istanbul, the Duke's Palace in Dubrovnik and the United Nations building in New York.

The Franciscan church and monastery on the island of Badija

Badija ③

Map E6.
🚤 *taxi-boats from Korčula.*

THIS IS THE LARGEST of the small islands, 1 sq km (0.4 sq m), surrounding the island of Korčula. It takes its name from the Franciscan monastery built here in 1392 for a community of monks who had fled from Bosnia. The monastery and church were enlarged in the following century and remained the property of the religious community until 1950, when Badija became a military site, and later a holiday resort for state employees.

The church, whose furnishings have been transferred to the Civic Museum and the cathedral in Korčula, has a façade in pale-coloured stone and a large central rose window.

The cloister is a good example of Gothic architecture at its most charming, with columns and arches.

The Loggia in the main square in Lastovo, venue for festivals

Lastovo ③

Map E6. 🏠 *1,200.*
🚤 *from Vela Luka (Island of Korčula) and from Split. Harbour Master: (020) 805 006.* 🛈 *(020) 801 018.*

THE ISLAND OF Lastovo, surrounded by about 40 small islands and rocky outcrops, was a military area until a few years ago and thus closed to tourists. The island is 9 km (5 miles) long and about 6 km (4 miles) wide. Although it is mostly mountainous terrain (Mount Hum reaches a height of 417 m/1,368 ft), vines, olives and fruit are cultivated on the terraced slopes. The coast is rocky apart from the bay close to the town of Lastovo.

Traces of the long period of rule by Dubrovnik (1252–1808) are visible in the upper part of the town and in the fort, built by the French in 1819 on the site of an earlier castle destroyed by Dubrovnik in 1606.

A church from the 14th century and a 16th-century loggia stand in the main square. Religious festivals are celebrated here.

Mention of the small church of **St Blaise** (Sv. Blaho), situated at the entrance to the village, is found in 12th-century documents. Also of ancient origins, in the cemetery, is the Romanesque **Oratory of Our Lady in the Field** (Gospa od Polja) from the 15th century. Some remnants of buildings and rustic villas testify to the presence of the Romans on the island. The lack of tourism has helped to preserve the old buildings.

Religious holidays are very popular and celebrated with traditional dances with antique musical instruments. The locals wear brightly coloured traditional costumes.

Some of the many uninhabited, unspoilt islands in the sea around the island of Lastovo

Mljet National Park �32
Nacionalni Park Mljet

THE ISLAND OF MLJET, called Melita by the Romans and Meleda by the Venetians, covers an area of 98 sq km (37 sq miles). It is mountainous, with two limestone depressions in which there are two saltwater lakes linked by a channel. In Roman times Mljet was the holiday resort of the wealthy of Salona, who built villas here. Some ruins can still be seen. In 1151, Duke Desa gave the island to the Benedictines of Pulsano in Gargano (Italy), who founded a monastery here. Two centuries later Stipan, the Ban (governor) of Bosnia, gave it to Dubrovnik, to which it belonged until 1815. In 1960 the western part was declared a national park to save the forest of Aleppo pine and holm oak.

Roman Palatium
Near Polače lie the ruins of a Roman settlement named Palatium, including the remains of a large villa and an early Christian basilica.

Pomena
Govedari
Polače
120
Kozarica
MLJET NATIONAL PARK
Soline
Blato
120

Monastery of St Mary
In the centre of Big Lake (Veliko Jezero) is a small island with a 12th-century Benedictine monastery, remodelled in the 1500s. It was a hotel from 1961 to 1991 and is now being restored.

Big Lake (Veliko Jezero)
The lake covers an area of 1.45 sq km (320 acres) and reaches a depth of 46 m (150 ft). A channel links the lake to the sea, and another channel links it to a smaller lake, Malo Jezero.

National Park
The area of 31 sq km (12 sq miles) is almost entirely forested. Mongooses, introduced here at the end of the 19th century to kill snakes, live in the forests.

0 kilometres   3

0 miles   3

Marine Life
*Dozens of species of fish, including grouper,
inhabit the underwater ravines and caves along
the coast. The most valued creature is the
endangered monk seal, protected in these waters.*

VISITORS' CHECKLIST

Map E6. 🏃 *1,300.* ⛴ *from
Dubrovnik.* **Govedari**
ℹ️ *Polače, (020) 744 086.*
National Park ℹ️ *(020) 744
041.* 📷 ☑️
🌐 *www.np-mljet.hr*
*The park can be visited on foot
or by bicycle following the trails.
Boats must be authorized – call
information office for details.*

The village of Babino Polje
was founded in around the
middle of the 10th century by
a group of refugees from the
mainland. The governor's
residence was built in 1333
when the island became part
of the territory of the Republic
of Ragusa (now Dubrovnik).

Saplunara
*Saplunara lies at the
southernmost point of
the island and boasts the
most beautiful beach in
the area. It has been
declared a nature
reserve for its lush
vegetation.*

Uninhabited Islands
*Nature is left undisturbed on these islands,
with woods of pine, holm oak and oak going
right down to the rocky shore.*

KEY

▬	Minor road
═	Path
—	Park border
⛴	Ferry
ℹ️	Tourist information
🏖	Beach with facilities

Fishing Villages
*The main coastal villages
are Polače and Pomena,
which are now inhabited
mainly by farmers and
fishermen. These villages
are lovely, tranquil places
in which to spend time.*

A secluded beach on the island of Mljet ▷

Street-by-Street: Dubrovnik ㉝

Detail of the door of the Rector's Palace

SET IN THE limpid waters of the Adriatic, Dubrovnik had been, until war broke out in 1991, one of the top international tourist destinations of Dalmatia, renowned for the beauty of its monuments, its magnificent walls and welcoming atmosphere. According to Emperor Constantine Porphyrogenitus it was founded by fugitives from Roman Epidaurum (now Cavtat) in the 7th century. It came under Byzantine, Venetian (1205–1358) and Hungarian rule, and attained formal independence after 1382, when it became the Republic of Ragusa. In the 15th and 16th centuries its fleet numbered over 500 ships. Artistically it flourished and its wealth was greatly influenced by the discovery of America and new trade routes. Much of the old town centre dates from the rebuilding that took place after the earthquake of 1667.

★ Rector's Palace
The highest level of city government met here. The rector lived here during his period of office, which was limited to one month.

★ Cathedral Treasury
The provenance of the objects here clearly demonstrates how the Dubrovnik merchants developed trading relations with the principal cities of the Mediterranean. The Treasury has works from the Byzantine, Middle Eastern, Apulian and Venetian schools. There are gold and enamel objects and also paintings by great artists.

LUČARICA

GUNDULIĆEVA POLJANA

PRED DVORO

POLJANA MARINA DRZICA

KNEZA DAMJANA JUDE

KEY

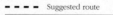

– – – Suggested route

View of Dubrovnik
Lovely views of Dubrovnik can be seen from the coast about 2 km (1 mile) to the south, where there is an elevated terrace. From here you can look over the entire city and its walls.

Church of St Blaise
This 16th-century church was rebuilt in the following century. At the beginning of the 18th century, it was redesigned by Marino Groppelli.

Sponza Palace

Originating in the 14th century, today the palace houses the State Archives. On the lintel is a Latin inscription: "Falsifying and cheating with the weights is forbidden. While I am weighing the goods, God is measuring me".

Franciscan Monastery and the Big Fountain of Onofrio

PLACA

PRIJEKO

The outer city walls

ZLATARSKA

SVETOG DOMINIKA

★ Dominican Monastery

Since its foundation in 1315, the monastery has played a leading role in cultural activities in the city. Important sculptors and architects played a part in its construction.

Ploče Gate

Next to the Dominican monastery is the Ploče Gate, which leads to the port. Goods arrived from, and were sent to, every port in the Mediterranean.

| 0 metres | 50 |
| 0 yards | 50 |

Fort of St John

To make the city impregnable, the governors employed the most important European architects of the time. This fortress was one of many bulwarks.

Exploring Dubrovnik

FROM THE AUTUMN OF 1991 until May 1992, Dubrovnik was the target of relentless, heavy bombing by Yugoslav troops. During this period over 2,000 bombs and guided missiles fell on Dubrovnik, damaging some of the most significant symbols of Dalmatian culture. Over half the houses and all the monuments were shelled. The war also hit the city's productivity, especially tourism, which suffered a dramatic decline for four years. Only after the Erdut Agreement of 1995 did life begin to return to normal. UNESCO and the European Union set up a special commission for the reconstruction of the city, and in a remarkably short space of time much of the damage has been repaired. Dubrovnik has now regained much of its former splendour and tourism is once again flourishing.

The solid Minčeta Tower, part of the wall defences

The splendid view from the impressive city walls

⛨ Walls
Gradske Zidine

🕐 summer: 9am–7pm daily; winter: 10am–3pm. Access to the walls near the Franciscan monastery in Poljana Paška Miličevića, the large square behind Pile Gate. 🎫 🎟 to hire a guide: (020) 420 192.

A symbol of Dubrovnik, the walls offer splendid views from the guards' walkway. They were built in the 10th century, with modifications in the 13th century. They were then reinforced at various times by great architects such as Michelozzo Michelozzi, Juraj Dalmatinac and Antonio Ferramolino.

The walls and ramparts are 1,940 m (6,363 ft) long and reach a height of 25 m (82 ft) in some parts. Those facing inland are up to 6 m (20 ft) wide and strengthened by an outer wall with ten semicircular bastions. Other towers and the Fort of St John defend the part facing the Adriatic and the port. Completing the defences to

the east and west of the city are two fortresses: the Revelin and the fortress of Lovrjenac.

⛨ Pile Gate
Gradska Vrata Pile

This is the main entrance to the old fortified centre. The stone bridge leading to Pile Gate is from 1537. The bridge crosses a moat which is now a garden. The gate is a strong

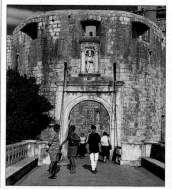

Pile Gate, leading to the old town

defensive structure built on different levels. In a niche above the ogival arch stands a small statue of St Blaise, the patron saint of Dubrovnik, by Ivan Meštrović. In the ramparts between the inner and outer walls is a Gothic door dating from 1460.

⛨ Minčeta Tower
Tvrđava Minčeta

This is the most visited of the walls' defensive structures. It was designed by Michelozzo Michelozzi in 1461 and completed by Juraj Dalmatinac three years later. The semicircular tower is crowned by a second tower with embrasures at the top.

⛨ Ploče Gate
Vrata od Ploča

The gate faces a small port and is preceded by the polygonal **Asimov Tower**. Dating from the 1300s, the gate is reached by an imposing stone bridge. It is a complex structure with a double defence system. A moat separates the gate and **Revelin Fort** (Tvrđava Revelin), designed in 1580 by Antonio Ferramolino. It was the last of the defences to be built. It is based on a pentagonal ground-plan and has massive walls enclosing three large rooms and a terrace. The city's art treasures were brought here for safety in times of difficulty because of the fort's strength.

🏰 Fort of St John
Tvrđa Sv. Ivana
Aquarium 🅒 *(020) 427 937.*
🕐 *Jun–Sep: 10am–6pm daily;*
Oct–May: 9am–1pm Mon–Sat. 🈺
Maritime Museum 🅒 *(020) 426*
465. 🕐 *9am–2pm Tue–Sun.* 🈺

A chain once helped to
defend the harbour, stretching
from this fort to the island in
front and then across to the
Tower of St Luke (Kula Sv.
Luke) along the walls.

The upper areas of the fort
house the **Maritime Museum**
(Pomorski Muzej), where
the seafaring history of
Dubrovnik is told through
model ships, standards, prints,
diaries and portraits.

On the lower level is an
Aquarium (Akvarij) with an
assortment of Mediterranean
marine life, including sea
horses, symbol of the
institution. At the top is
Bokar Fort (Tvrđava Bokar),
a circular bastion built by
Michelozzo Michelozzi.

🏰 Big Fountain of Onofrio
Velika Onofrijeva Fontana

This is one of the best-known
monuments in the city. It
stands in the square which

The Big Fountain of Onofrio (1438–44)

opens out immediately after
the Pile gate. It was built in
1438–44 by the Neapolitan
architect, Onofrio de la Cava,
who was also responsible for
designing the city's water
supply system. He
decided to draw
the water from the
River Dubrovačka
for this purpose. The
imposing fountain
once had two storeys,
but the upper level
was destroyed in the
earthquake of 1667.

Tucked between
the city walls and the
Franciscan monastery
is the **Church of St
Saviour** (Sv. Spas).
The façade of the
church is an example
of Venetian-Dalmatian
Renaissance
architecture, a style
dating from after
the earthquake
of 1520.

DUBROVNIK TOWN CENTRE

Big Fountain of Onofrio ⑥
Cathedral and Treasury ⑬
Church of St Blaise ⑪
Dominican Monastery ⑭
Fort of St John ⑤
Franciscan Monastery ⑦
Minčeta Tower ③
Pile Gate ②
Ploče Gate ④
Rector's Palace ⑫

Sponza Palace ⑩
Stradùn (Placa) ⑧
Square of the Loggia ⑨
Walls ①

KEY

▭ Street-by-Street: Dubrovnik *pp138–9*

⛴ Ferry

🅷 Tourist information

🈲 Church

🈲 Orthodox church

✉ Post office

Bus station
MAKARSKA

IZA GRADA
IZA GRADA
SPLIT
ŠIBENIK
PELINE
PRIJEKO
STRADÙN (PLACA)
ŠIROKA
OD
PUČA
OD RUPA
ZLATARSKA
DVROM
PRED
GUNDULIĆEVA
POLJANA
STROSMAJEROVA
OD KAŠTELA
CRIJEVIĆEVA
POLJANA
RUĐERA
BOŠKOVIĆA
OD MARGARITE
IZA
GRADA

0 metres   150
0 yards   150

The lovely late Romanesque cloister, Franciscan monastery

♙ Franciscan Monastery
Franjevački Samostan
Placa 2. 【 (020) 321 410. ○
9am–4pm daily. **Franciscan Museum**
○ 9am–3pm daily. 🖼 ☑
Construction of the monastery began in 1317 and was completed in the following century. It was almost entirely rebuilt after the earthquake in 1667, but the south door (1499), in Venetian Gothic decorated with a Pietà in the lunette, and a 15th-century marble pulpit escaped damage. The cloister, which was completely undamaged by the earthquake, reveals elements of the Romanesque and the Gothic style and has a fountain from the 15th century in the centre.

One side of the cloister leads to the **Pharmacy** (Stara Ljekarna), in use since 1317, where alembics, mortars, measuring apparatus and beautifully decorated jars are displayed on the old shelves.

The capitular room of the monastery houses the **Franciscan Museum** (Muzej Franjevačkog Samostana), which brings together religious works of art and objects belonging to the order. Instruments from the pharmaceutical laboratory are kept here and there is a valuable library.

♙ Stradùn (Placa)
This wide street, which crosses the city from east to west between two city gates, is known as Stradùn or Placa. It was constructed in the 12th century by draining and filling in the marshy channel which

Stradùn, the main street of Dubrovnik

separated the island of Ragusa from the mainland. The street was paved in 1468 and a series of stone houses was built after the earthquake of 1667. Today the street is lined with busy bars and cafés, and is a popular place for locals and visitors to gather in the evening.

♙ Square of the Loggia
Loža
This square, the political and economic heart of Dubrovnik, is situated at the eastern end of Stradùn and surrounded by important buildings. Today it is still a popular meeting place, in particular around **Orlando's Column**, which was built by the sculptor Antonio Ragusino (1418).

On the eastern side of the square is a **Clock Tower** (Gradski Zvonik). Repair work carried out in 1922 restored a 15th-century look to the Clock Tower. The nearby **Loggia of the Bell**, with four bells, dates from 1480. The bells were rung to call the citizens to gather whenever danger threatened.

Next to this stands the **Main Guard House**, rebuilt in 1706 after the earthquake of 1667. It has a large Baroque doorway, similar to a city gate, and is enlivened on the first floor by the Gothic mullioned windows, reminiscent of the earlier building which was built in the late 15th-century.

The **Small Fountain of Onofrio** (Mala Onofrijeva Cesma), dating from 1438, stands alongside the Guard House.

♙ Sponza Palace
Palača Sponza
【 (020) 321 032.
○ 8am–3pm, by appt.
To the left of the square is Sponza Palace. Remodelled in 1516–22, it has an elegantly sculpted Renaissance loggia on the ground floor and a beautiful Venetian Gothic three-mullioned window on the first floor, evidence of its 14th-

century origins, and a statue of St Blaise on the upper floor. It was the Mint in the 14th century and now houses the State Archives.

🏛 Church of St Blaise
Crkva Sv. Vlaha
Loža. 📞 *(020) 411 715.*
🕐 *8am–noon, 4.30–7pm daily.*
St Blaise was rebuilt in the early decades of the 18th century according to a 17th-century design and contains many Baroque works of art.

On the main altar stands a statue of the patron saint, Blaise. It was produced in the 15th century in gold-plated silver, and depicts the saint holding a model of the city in the Middle Ages.

Baroque façade of the church of St Blaise

🏛 Rector's Palace
Knežev Dvor
Knežev Dvor 1. 📞 *(020) 321 437.*
🕐 *9am–2pm Mon–Sat.* 💶
The Rector's Palace was for centuries the political and administrative centre of the Republic of Ragusa. It housed the Upper Council, as well as the rector's quarters and rooms for diplomatic meetings and official audiences. The building was designed by Onofrio de la Cava in 1435. In 1465 the portico was added, the work of Michelozzo Michelozzi, who also sculpted the capitals. The Gothic works are by Juraj Dalmatinac.

During the Festival of Dubrovnik concerts are held in the atmospheric internal courtyard. The arches and loggias were designed by Onofrio de la Cava.

The Rector's Palace, built in the 15th century as the administrative seat

The rooms of the palace house the **Museum of Dubrovnik** (Dubrovački Muzej), which offers an overview of the city's history through furniture, paintings by Venetian and Dalmatian artists (a *Venus and Adonis* by Paris Bordon and a *Baptism of Christ* by Mihajlo Hamzić), weights and measures, including the famous "Dubrovnik arm" (a unit of measurement), and coins from 1305 to 1803.

Over 15,000 works are on display, documenting the major periods of artistic and commercial vitality in the city. There are numerous uniforms, once worn by the governors and nobles. Also of great interest are the portraits of illustrious personalities who were born or lived in Dubrovnik, whose history is told through their heraldic coats of arms and commemorative medals.

Next door is the neo-Renaissance **Town Hall** (Skupština Općine), designed by Emilio Vecchietti in 1863. It is also the home of Gradska Kavana, a restaurant, and the Civic Theatre.

🏛 Cathedral and Treasury
Velika Gospa
Kneza Damjana Jude 1.
🕐 *9am–noon, 3–8pm daily.*
Cathedral Treasury 📞 *(020) 411 715.* 🕐 *9am–noon, 3–7pm daily.* 💶
The cathedral was built after the earthquake of 1667 by the Roman architects Andrea Buffalini and Paolo Andreotti. Inside are three aisles enclosed by three apses. Paintings by Italian and Dalmatian artists from the 16th–18th centuries decorate

the side altars, while an *Assumption* by Titian (c.1552) dominates the main altar.

Alongside the church is the **Cathedral Treasury** (Riznica Katedrale), famous for its collection of about 200 reliquaries. It includes the arm of St Blaise which dates from the 13th century, and a Holy Cross which contains a fragment of the cross on which Jesus was said to have been crucified. The tondo *Virgin of the Chair* is thought to have been painted by Raphael himself, and is a copy of the masterpiece which is now in Florence.

The treasury also has an extraordinary collection of sacred objects in gold, including a pitcher and basin in gold and silver with decoration that illustrates the flora and fauna of the area around Dubrovnik.

The great dome of Dubrovnik's Baroque cathedral

The church of St Dominic, inside the monastery

🔒 Dominican Monastery
Dominikanski Samostan Bijeli Fratri

Sv. Dominika 4. 📞 *(020) 321 423.* ⭘ *summer: 9am–6pm; winter: 9am–3pm.* 📷

Building began in 1315 and it soon became clear that because of the size of the complex, the city walls would have to be enlarged. The monastery was later rebuilt after the earthquake of 1667.

A long flight of steps with a stone balustrade leads up to the church. The door, the work of Bonino of Milan, is decorated with a Romanesque statue of St Dominic. The interior has a wide single nave and, hanging from the central arch, a splendid gilded panel *(Crucifix and Symbols of the Evangelists)* by Paolo Veneziano (14th century).

The various rooms of the monastery, arranged around the Gothic cloister by Maso di Bartolomeo (15th century), house the **Dominican Museum** (Muzej Dominikanskog Samostana). It contains an extraordinary collection of works from the so-called "Dubrovnik school", including a triptych and an *Annunciation* by Niccolò Ragusino, from the 16th century, and works from the Venetian school, including *St Blaise, St Mary Magdalene, the Angel Tobias and the Purchaser* by Titian, as well as precious reliquaries and objects in gold and silver.

ENVIRONS: The island of **Lokrum**, 700 m (2,296 ft) across the water from Dubrovnik, is a nature reserve set up to protect the exotic species of plants found here.

The first people to settle on the island were the Benedictines, who founded an abbey here in 1023. This was rebuilt in the 14th century, but later destroyed by the earthquake of 1667. In 1859, Archduke Maximilian of Habsburg built a palace here and renovated the cloister which later became the Natural History Museum.

There are good views from the fort, which was built by the French in 1808. Lokrum's beauty makes it a popular tourist destination.

In **Trsteno**, 20 km (12 miles) northwest of Dubrovnik, is an Arboretum. This was begun in 1502 in the park surrounding a villa built by Ivan Gučetić. The park has the typical layout of a Renaissance garden with grottoes and ancient ruins.

There are several Renaissance summer houses around Dubrovnik, including the **Villa Stay** in Rijeka Dubrovačka. It houses the Croatian Restoration Institute, an organization devoted to the conservation and restoration of paintings.

A statue in the Arboretum in Trsteno

Elaphite Islands ③④

Map F6. 🏛 *2,000.* 🚢 *from Dubrovnik.* ℹ️ *Dubrovnik regional tourist office (020) 324 222.*

LYING TO THE NORTH of Dubrovnik, the Elaphite islands (Elafitski otoci) can be reached from Dubrovnik by motorboat. There are several daily crossings. The islands were described by the natural historian Pliny the Elder, who named them after the fallow deer then found here.

Only three of the islands are inhabited: Šipan, Lopud and Koločep, while Jakljan is devoted to farming. Characteristics common to the islands are the woods of maritime pines and cypresses in the uncultivated areas and beautiful beaches and bays frequented by pleasure boats. The islands have long been popular with the aristocracy of Dubrovnik, who built villas here. Some islands had monasteries which were suppressed with the arrival of French troops in 1808. Many of the churches date from the pre-Romanesque period, but few, however, are still intact.

Koločep
This is the nearest island to Dubrovnik and for this reason has been a summer retreat since the 16th century for its

The island of Lokrum in front of Dubrovnik, a protected nature reserve

Sunj beach on the southeast coast of Lopud, one of the Elaphite islands

citizens. Most of the island is covered in maritime pines and subtropical undergrowth.

The churches of **St Anthony** and **St Nicholas** have pre-Romanesque origins, while the **Parish Church** dates from the 15th century.

Lopud
The island, measuring 4.6 sq km (1.7 sq miles), has a fertile valley sheltered from the cold winds by two ranges of hills. Most of the inhabitants live in **Lopud**, a village in a bay. The two forts, now in ruins, date from the 16th century and the Franciscan monastery is from 1483. The monastery church, **St Mary of Spilica** (Gospa od Spilica), contains a polyptych by Pietro di Giovanni (1520), a triptych by Nikola Božidarević, a painting by Leandro da Bassano, a triptych by Gerolamo di Santacroce and a carved choir from the 15th century.

Sunj, in the southeast, draws visitors because of its sandy beach, but the church is also worth visiting for its many works of art, including a painting by Palma il Giovane and a polyptych (1452) by Matko Junčić.

Šipan
This is the largest of the Elaphite Islands (15.5 sq km/6 sq miles) and there are two towns. In **Šipanska Luka** stands the pre-Romanesque church of St Michael and the ruins of a Benedictine monastery. In **Sudurad** there is a castle and the ruins of a bishop's palace.

Cavtat ㉟

Map F6.
🏛 1,900. 🚌 (020) 478 065. 🚢 from Dubrovnik. ℹ Tiha 3, (020) 478 025, 479 025. 🎭 Summer in Cavtat, Gospa od Cavtata (5 Aug).

CAVTAT IS the Croatian name for Civitas Vetus, the site of the Roman town of Epidaurum, destroyed by the Avars in the 7th century (occasional excavations have revealed the remains of a theatre, several tombs and parts of a road). The beauty of the area, the beaches, the luxuriant vegetation and the interesting monuments attract many visitors to the present-day village.

The **Baltazar Bogišić Collection**, assembled and donated by the scholar and jurist of the 19th century, is housed in the 16th-century

Count's Palace. The works of the painter Vlaho Bukovac are especially fine.

At the end of the seafront is the church of **St Blaise** (Sv. Vlaho) and a Franciscan monastery, both from the end of the 15th century. On the hilltop stands the **Račić Mausoleum** built by Ivan Meštrović (see p155) in 1922.

Konavle ㊱

Map F6.
ℹ Tiha 3, Cavtat, (020) 478 025, 479 025.

THE AREA SOUTHEAST of Cavtat occupies a narrow piece of land between the sea and the mountains of Bosnia-Herzegovina. Its name derives from the channels (konavle) which collected the water to supply the aqueduct – of which some traces remain – for the Roman town of Epidaurum.

The hilly areas are covered in vineyards and olive groves. The small villages maintain the old customs and traditional costumes are still worn by the inhabitants. Konavle was heavily damaged by bombing in 1991 and the houses are still being rebuilt. This area is also renowned for its excellent cuisine and there are numerous restaurants.

Traditional dress of Konavle, still used for festivals

One of the best known is **Konavoski Dvori**, housed in a watermill near the waterfalls of the River Ljuta.

The pretty seafront and port of Cavtat

ZAGREB

T HE CAPITAL OF CROATIA, *Zagreb is also the heart of the political, economic and cultural life of the country. Surrounded by woods and parks, the city lies between the slopes of Mount Medvednica to the north and the River Sava to the south. Located at the centre of continental Croatia, this Central European city constitutes a meeting point between eastern and western Europe.*

The political scientist Max Weber once declared that the quality of life in a city could be measured by the number of its cultural institutions. Zagreb has 20 museums, 16 theatres, 350 libraries, a university, and lively programmes of artistic and cultural events. This is not just because Zagreb is the capital (it has only been the capital since 1991), but is also due to the leading cultural and political role that Zagreb has played over the centuries.

History of Croatia by Ivan Meštrović, Meštrović Gallery

Zagreb was originally two separate medieval towns. Two settlements were built on two adjacent hilltops: Kaptol, the centre of religious power, and a bishopric from 1094, and Gradec (now part of Gornji Grad). In 1242, with the proclamation of a "Golden Bull", Gradec was given the title of royal free city by the Croat-Hungarian King Bela IV. This granted various economic and administrative privileges to the inhabitants. From the 16th century onwards Gradec was also where the Ban – the governor of Croatia delegated by the Hungarian kingdom – and the Croat parliament carried out their business and where Croat nobles met to govern this turbulent territory. The two towns were both fortified with ramparts, towers, moats and gates, and were separated by the river Medveščak. The river was often the site of violent clashes between Gradec and Kaptol, and that time is vividly recalled by the street called the Bridge of Blood (Krvavi Most).

In 1880, a terrible earthquake struck the city and many of the major monuments date from after this time.

The colourful Dolac market with fruit and vegetable stalls

◁ **View of the centre of Zagreb from Kralja Tomislava square**

Exploring Zagreb

THE CITY IS DIVIDED into two large sectors; the old town (Gornji Grad or Upper Town), which includes the two districts of Gradec and Kaptol, situated in the hills, and the modern area (Donji Grad or Lower Town) on the plain. The large square dedicated to the Croat governor Jelačić (Trg bana Jelačića) is where the upper and lower towns meet. The old town is home to the main centres of religious, political and administrative power. The more modern part developed after 1830 around a U-shaped series of parks and open spaces (known as the "horseshoe"). The major museums, including the Ethnographic Museum, Mimara Museum, Gallery of Old Masters and Gallery of Modern Art, are all located here, as well as the National Theatre. To the south of a series of gardens with sculptures lies the Botanical Garden. Around Jelačić square there are plenty of cafés with summer terraces.

LOCATOR MAP

SIGHTS AT A GLANCE

Museums and Galleries
Archaeological Museum ㉕
City Museum ➏
Croatian Historical Museum ⑫
Ethnographic Museum ⑳
Gallery of Modern Art ㉔
Gallery of Old Masters pp162–3 ㉓
Meštrović Gallery ➑
Mimara Museum ⑲
Museum of Arts and Crafts ⑱
National Museum of Naive Art ⑬
Natural History Museum ➐

Churches
Cathedral of St Stephen ➊
Church of St Catherine ⑯
Church of SS Cyril and Methodius ⑭
Church of St Francis ➌
Church of St Mark ➒
Church of St Mary ➍

Palaces and other Buildings
Archbishop's Palace ➋
Art Pavilion ㉒
Ban's Palace ⑪
Croatian National Theatre ⑰
Parliament Building ➓
Stone Gate ➎
Tower of Lotrščak ⑮

Parks and Gardens
Botanical Garden ㉑
Maksimir Park ㉖
Mirogoj Cemetery ㉗

The Gallery of Old Masters, home to major European works of art

GETTING AROUND
The districts of the old part, Kaptol and Gradec, are mostly pedestrian areas, as is the central Jelačić square, which is served by numerous tram routes connecting the eastern and western parts of the city *(see pp272–3)*. Many bus routes connect the squares around the "horseshoe" with all the suburban districts as well as Novi Zagreb, where there is also a racetrack, a large exhibition area and the Jarun sailing centre, which is situated on the other side of the River Sava.

Mirogoj
Cemetery

GORNJI GRAD

KAPTOL

DÓLAC

TRG
BANA JELAČIĆA

DONJI GRAD

ZRINJEVAC

STROSSMAYEROV
TRG

TOMISLAVOV
TRG

STARČEVIĆEV
TRG

Glavni
Kolodvor

OTANIČKI VRT

Maksimir
Park

VISITORS' CHECKLIST

Map D2. 710,000. at Velika Gorica, Pleso, (01) 626 52 22, 17 km (10 miles) SE. Glavni Kolodvor, (060) 333 444; Zapadni Kolodvor. Avenija Marina Drzica 4, (060) 313 333. **City:** Kaptol 5, (01) 489 8555; trg bana Jelačića 11, (01) 481 40 51. Smotra Folklora, Folklore Festival (Jul); Zagrebačke Ljetne Večeri, Zagreb Summer Festival. www.zagreb-touristinfo.hr

| 0 metres | 200 |
| 0 yards | 200 |

SEE ALSO

• **Where to Stay** pp225–6

• **Where to Eat** pp239–40

View of the city of Zagreb

KEY

- Street-by-Street *pp152–3*
- Railway
- Train station
- Funicular railway
- Tourist information
- Parking
- Church

Cathedral of St Stephen ❶
Katedrala Sv. Stjepana

Kaptol. ☏ *(01) 481 47 27.*
⏰ *8am–8pm daily.*

DEDICATED to the Assumption and the saints Stephen and Ladislaus, this is the most famous monument in the city. Its present appearance dates from renovations carried out by Friedrich von Schmidt and Hermann Bollé after the earthquake of 1880, which destroyed the dome, the bell tower and some of the walls. The rebuilding, which retained the medieval plan of the cathedral, was just the latest in a series of alterations the building had undergone in its long history. The building was already in existence in 1094 when King Ladislaus transferred the

Decorative detail of one of the spires of St Stephen

bishopric here from Sisak. Destroyed by the Mongols in 1242, the cathedral was rebuilt by Bishop Timotej a few years later. In the centuries that followed, the side aisles were added and the church was decorated with statues and reliefs.

The new Neo-Gothic façade (1880) is flanked by two twin spires. The façade has a large ornate doorway with sculpted decorations, a rose window and three high windows, the whole crowned by a tympanum.

The interior has three aisles and a polygonal apse. During a late 19th-century reorganization, the Baroque and Rococo altars were transferred to other churches in the diocese, and as a result only a few Gothic and Renaissance works remain. These works include a statue of St Paul (13th century), wooden statues of the saints Peter and Paul from the 15th century, a triptych entitled *Golgotha* (1495) by Albrecht Dürer and a 14th-century *Crucifixion* by Giovanni da Udine. The cathedral also contains the tombs and votive chapels of bishops and important personalities in Croatian history, such as Petar Zrinski, Krsto Frankopan and the blessed Cardinal Alojzije Stepinac, whose tomb behind the main altar is by Ivan Meštrović.

Of great interest are the frescoes from the Giotto-esque school in the sacristy: the oldest (12th century) in inland Croatia. In the basement of the bishop's sacristy, the **Cathedral Treasury**

The central nave in the Neo-Gothic Cathedral of St Stephen

preserves a rich collection of religious objects. These include illuminated manuscripts, finely crafted church ornaments from the 11th to the 20th centuries, and objects of veneration such as the Cloak of King Ladislaus (11th century), a bishop's veil from the 14th century and the so-called Sepulchre of God. This last was made by the embroiderers of the village of Vugrovec, where Bishop Petar Petraetić founded an embroidery school in around 1650. Among the oldest works are a 10th-century ivory diptych and a bronze Crucifix from the 11th–12th centuries.

Archbishop's Palace ❷
Nadbiskupska Palača

Kaptol. ◐ *to the public.*

THE ENORMOUS Baroque buildings comprising the Archbishop's Palace enclose the other three sides of the cathedral square. The building incorporates three of the five round towers and one square tower, which were part of the fortifications built from 1469 as defence against Turkish attacks. The present palace dates from 1730, when several buildings were linked and united by an imposing Baroque façade.

Inside the complex is the Romanesque chapel of

The tall spires of the Cathedral of St Stephen

St Stephen Protomartyr (13th century). This is the oldest building in Zagreb to have survived in its original form: the frescoes are from the same period.

In the square in front of the palace stands a fountain with a column crowned by a statue of Mary with four Angels, the work of the Viennese artist Anton Dominik Fernkorn (1813–78) in around 1850.

The moats that once surrounded the walls have been filled in and turned into the **Ribnjak Public Gardens**, with various statues including one called *Modesty* by Antun Augustinčić (1900–79). The defences were partially demolished in the 19th century, however. At No 18 Ulica Kaptol, opposite the cathedral, is the **Northeast Tower**, which is now a residence. At No 15 stands the **Northwest Tower** (Prišlinova Kula), now part of a 15th-century building.

The Archbishop's Palace by the Cathedral of St Stephen

Church of St Francis ❸

Sv. Franjo

Ulica Kaptol 9. ☎ *(01) 481 11 25.* ◻ *5–8pm daily.*

FOUNDED, according to legend, after St Francis' return from the East, this church in fact dates from the 16th century. After the earthquake of 1880, the church was rebuilt in the Neo-Gothic style. It was at

Stained-glass windows by Ivo Dulčić in the church of St Francis

this time that the Baroque altars were removed. Some of the side altars are Neo-Gothic, while on the main altar there is a fine painting of St Francis by Celestin Medović (1857–1920). The brightly coloured stained-glass windows were designed by Ivo Dulčić in the 1960s.

In the adjacent 17th-century **Monastery**, where the saint supposedly stayed, is the much-visited chapel of St Francis (1683), with ornate stucco decorations and Baroque paintings.

Church of St Mary ❹

Sv. Marija

Dolac 2. ☎ *(01) 481 49 59.* ◻ *for mass.*

OPATOVINA ULICA IS a narrow street where some of the houses were built using parts of the late-15th century fortifications. The street leads into the ancient district of Dolac, at the end of which stands the church of St Mary, which dates from the 14th century. It was rearranged in 1740 when several Baroque altars were built by Franjo Rottman, but its present appearance dates

back to rebuilding after the earthquake in 1880.

Near the church stands a statue by Vanja Radauš of the legendary wanderer and minstrel Petrica Kerempuh, playing to the figure of a hanged man.

The large, picturesque **Dolac Market**, which was first held in 1930, takes place around the church. This is a characteristic district of the city where Baroque houses face narrow streets and lanes. A historic pharmacy is at No 19 Ulica Kaptol and an ancient house at No 7.

Stone Gate ❺

Kamenita Vrata

Kamenita.

IN THE WALLS AROUND Gradec, the part of Upper Town built on a neighbouring hill to Kaptol, there were once five gates. Stone Gate is now the only one of these remaining. It was built in the 13th century, and stands beside a square tower from 1266. In 1731 a fire destroyed all the nearby houses, but a painting of Mary with Child on the gate was left undamaged. A chapel was established around this painting and a Baroque wrought-iron grille now protects the work, attributed to a local master from the 16th century.

On the west façade of the church is a statue of a woman, the work of the sculptor Ivan Kerdić in 1929.

On the other side of the gate, on the corner of Kamenita and Habdelićeva, stands an 18th-century building. On the ground floor of this building is a **Pharmacy** (Alighieri ljekarna) which has been in existence since 1350 and which, from 1399 onwards, belonged to Nicolò Alighieri, the great-grandson of the great Italian writer Dante.

The monument to Petrica Kerempuh, Dolac

Street-by-Street: the Upper Town (Gornji Grad)

I N THE UPPER TOWN there are various institutions which have played a significant part in the history of the city and of Croatia. They now house the political and cultural centres of the country: the presidency of the Republic, Parliament, the State Audit Court and several government ministries. All of these buildings were restored, repaired or rebuilt after the terrible earthquake of 1880. Some of the ancient noble palaces have been converted into museums. There are also three interesting churches: the ancient church of St Mark, the Baroque church of St Catherine built by the Jesuits, and the church of Saints Cyril and Methodius. The daily signal to close the city gates was rung from the medieval tower of Lotršcak (Turris Latruncolorum).

Pietà **by Ivan Meštrovic**

Natural History Museum
Created from three collections, the museum houses most of the finds from Krapina, which date human presence in Croatia back to the Palaeolithic era **7**

Ban's Palace
The building dates from the 17th century and was built after the city became the seat of the Ban (governor of Croatia) in 1621. It now houses the presidency of the Republic **11**

Croatian Historical Museum
This museum, housed in the splendid Vojkovic-Oršic palace, has works of art and documents collected since 1960 **12**

★ **National Museum of Naive Art**
Over 1,500 works of Naive art by the founders and followers of the Hlebine school are held here **13**

Church of SS Cyril and Methodius
Built by Orthodox Christians in the first half of the 19th century, the church, designed by Bartol Felbinger, has a fine iconostasis **14**

Tower of Lotršcak
At noon every day a cannon is fired from this tower, which dates from the 12th century **15**

KEY

– – – Suggested route

★ Meštrović Gallery
The great Croatian sculptor Ivan Meštrović lived in this 18th-century building from 1922 to 1941. About ten years before his death he donated his home and all the works of art in it to the state **⑧**

LOCATOR MAP

Parliament Building
This building dates from 1910, when the provincial administration offices were enlarged. The independence of Croatia was proclaimed from the central window of the building in 1918 **⑩**

★ Church of St Mark
The coloured tiles on the roof of this fine Gothic church form the coats of arms of Croatia, Dalmatia, Slavonia and Zagreb **⑨**

The Gallery of Contemporary Art in the Kulmer Palace puts on exhibitions by Croatian and foreign artists.

0 metres	50
0 yards	50

The Klovićevi Dvori, an important temporary exhibition site, has been housed since 1982 in a 17th-century Jesuit monastery.

STAR FEATURES

★ Church of St Mark

★ Meštrović Gallery

★ National Museum of Naive Art

Church of St Catherine
Built on the site of an ancient Dominican church, this is the city's most fascinating Baroque building **⑯**

City Museum ❻
Muzej grada Zagreba

Opatička ulica 20. **☎** *(01) 485 13 64.* **◯** *10am–6pm Tue–Fri; 10am–1pm Sat & Sun.* **▨** *by appt.*

THREE HISTORIC buildings (the convent of the nuns of St Clare from around 1650, a 12th-century tower, and a granary from the 17th century, now converted into a school) have been linked to form the City Museum. Its 12 collections, consisting of 74,000 pieces, illustrate the history and culture of Zagreb from its origins to the present day.

The exhibits include paintings, maps and views of the city, standards, flags, military uniforms, coats of arms and fragments of sculpture from civil and religious monuments, and also archaeological finds. Many of the exhibits were donated by the city's famous townsmen and women, including the actress Tilla Durieux, the musician Rudolf Matz, the composer Ivan Zajc, the soprano Milka Trnina and architect Viktor Kovačić.

Along the street is the 19th-century **Ilirska Dvorana Palace**, which houses part of the Croatian Academy of Arts and Sciences, and the **Paravić Palace** (19th century), with fine wrought-iron gates, now the Institute of Historical Studies.

Some of the statues on display in the City Museum

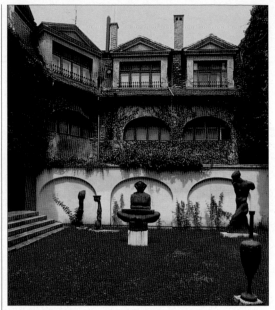

Sculptures in the garden of the Meštrović Gallery

Natural History Museum ❼
Prirodoslovni Muzej

Demetrova 1. **☎** *(01) 485 17 00.* **◯** *10am–5pm Tue–Fri, 10am–1pm Sat & Sun.* **ⓦ** *www.hpm.hr*

THE 18TH-CENTURY Amadeo Palace, a theatre from 1797 to 1834, has been the Natural History Museum since 1868, when collections from the Department of Natural Science at the National Museum were transferred here. At the end of the 19th century there were three museums of natural history: Mineralogy and Petrography, Geology and Palaeontology, and Zoology. These three museums merged in 1986 to form the present museum.

The over 2,500,000 exhibits include minerals from all over the world and the palaeontology collections include some of the material found in Krapina. The zoological collection documents every species of animal found in Croatia as well as many exotic species.

A mineral in the Museum of Natural History

Meštrović Gallery ❽
Atelje Meštrović

Mletačka 8. **☎** *(01) 485 11 23.* **◯** *10am–6pm Tue–Fri, 10am–1pm Sat & Sun.* **▨**

THE GALLERY BUILDING dates from the 17th century; the sculptor Ivan Meštrović himself modernized it to live in from 1922 to 1942. It now houses a collection of his work. It belongs to the Meštrović Foundation, which also owns the Gallery and the Kaštelet in Split, as well as the mausoleum in Otavice (*see p108*). There are almost 300 works on display, including exhibits in the courtyard – copies of *History of Croatia, Deposition* and *Woman in Agony*. The drawings, models, and sculptures in wood, stone and bronze testify to the great expressive ability and the technical skills of the great sculptor. His personal archives are also here, as well as photographic records and works by other artists associated with the master.

Ivan Meštrović

REGARDED as one of the most important sculptors of the 20th century, Ivan Meštrović was born in 1883 in Vrpolje, on the Pannonian Plain, where his parents had gone for the harvest from their native town of Otavice in the Dalmatian hinterland. As a young boy he delighted in making clay figures

Portrait of Ivan Meštrović

and his work was noticed by the town mayor and by Lujo Marun, an archaeologist, who sent him to Zagreb when he was 17 to study sculpture. Thanks to the Viennese industrialist Koenig, he was able to attend the Academy of Fine Arts in Vienna, where he designed works for later production. Here he met and became friends with

the great French sculptor, Auguste Rodin. In 1907 he moved to Paris and his first exhibition established his reputation. He worked in various cities, including Split – where he created many of the works now on show in the Meštrović gallery there – and Zagreb. Here he also took up politics: during World War II he was imprisoned by the Ustaše and freed on the intervention of the Vatican. He then sculpted the *Pietà Romana*, now in the Vatican Museum. After the war he taught at universities in the US, where he died in 1962. He was buried in the mausoleum in Otavice *(see p108)* that he designed for himself and his family.

Meštrović, intent on his work

Detail of the *Resurrection of Lazarus* (1944)

Woman on the Shore *is a splendid female figure in marble (1926) which seems to twist around on itself. The form of the body is vigorous and yet the hands are delicate and slender.*

THE SCULPTOR AT WORK

The speed at which Meštrović executed his works was proverbial, although the preparation time was lengthy. To satisfy demand, he duplicated his works in wood, marble and bronze. Three copies exist of the statue of the Bishop of Nin, in Nin, Split and Koprivnica.

Maternity *is a wooden sculpture from 1942 which demonstrates the artist's great expressive talent. The figure of the child is almost insignificant, leaving the face of the mother to play the main role.*

History of Croatia *is a work from 1932 of which there are three versions; one in bronze is in the Meštrović Galley in Zagreb. The woman's thoughtful gaze looks to the future, symbolizing expectations and hopes.*

The church of St Mark, with its colourful glazed tile roof

Church of St Mark ❾
Sv. Marko

Markov trg. ☎ (01) 485 16 11.
🕐 8am–8pm daily.

Today this is the Upper Town's parish church. St Mark's was first mentioned in 1256 when King Bela IV granted the town of Gradec permission to hold a market fair in front of the church. The fair lasted for two weeks and was held to celebrate the saint's day.

The church has undergone various alterations over the centuries. All that is left from the original construction is a Romanesque window and a splendid Gothic doorway, created by the sculptor Ivan Parler between 1364 and 1377. The 15 niches on the door contain statues of Jesus, Mary, St Mark and the 12 apostles. Some of these were replaced by wooden copies in the Baroque era.

On various occasions fires and earthquakes have been responsible for changes in the church's appearance. Its present look dates from 1882, when the coloured glazed tiles on the roof were added. The tiles bear the coats of arms of Croatia, Dalmatia,

Slavonia and the city of Zagreb. The church interior has been refurbished with several statues by the sculptor Ivan Meštrović. On the high altar is a large *Christ on the Cross*, a *Pietà* stands on the altar of the Holy Cross and a bronze statue of *Mary with Child* adorns an altar dedicated to the Virgin Mary. The modern frescoes depicting Croat kings in action were painted by Jozo Kljaković.

Parliament Building ❿
Sabor

Markov trg. ℹ (01) 456 92 22.
🕐 by appt.

Built in Neo-Classical style in 1908 after several 17th- and 18th-century Baroque buildings were razed, this building holds an important place in the story of Croatia. Historic proclamations have been issued from the balcony: the seceding of the nation from the Austro-Hungarian kingdom (29 October 1918) and independence from Yugoslavia after a referendum in 1991. Today the Sabor is still the centre of 21st-century Croat politics.

Mary with Child by Meštrović, St Mark's

Viceroy's Palace ⓫
Banski Dvori

Markov trg. ℹ (01) 456 92 22.
🕐 by appt.

The parliament chamber, the central archives, the law courts, the President of the Republic's residence and government offices are all housed in this building in front of St Mark's. The palace is similar in design to the parliament building and is made up of two long 18th-century structures. In the 19th century two two-storey wings were added.

Croatian Historical Museum ⓬
Hrvatski Povijesni Muzej

Matoševa ulica 9. ☎ (01) 485 19 00.
🕐 10am–5pm Tue–Fri, 10am–1pm Sat & Sun. ● public hols. 🖼 📷 🚫

A museum has been housed here since 1960, but it only became the Croatian Historical Museum in 1991 when several collections were merged. The museum illustrates the history of Croatia from the Middle Ages to the present day by means of all kinds of mementoes. These include documents and paintings of political, military and cultural events, as well as items such as firearms, flags and medals. There is also a well-stocked specialist library.

The museum is housed in the Baroque Vojković-Oršić Palace, which dates from the second half of the 18th century. The decorated ballroom is still preserved.

The Parliament Building (Sabor), built in Neo-Classical style in 1908

My Homeland by Ivan Rabuzin (1961), National Museum of Naive Art

National Museum of Naive Art ⓭

Hrvatski Muzej Naivne Umjetnosti

Ćirilometodska ulica 3. ⓒ (01) 485 19 11. ⬤ 10am–6pm Tue–Fri, 10am–1pm Sat & Sun. ⬤ public hols. 🎫 📷 🌐 www.hmnu.org

SINCE 1994, this 19th-century building with its beautiful Neo-Baroque façade has housed works from an exhibition of Naive painters which opened in Zagreb in 1952. The paintings are characterized by the use of vivid colour and a strong feeling for narrative. There are paintings by the founders of the Naive trend, Ivan Generalić and Mirko Virius, as well as by the Hlebine school *(see p19)*, where works by Ivan Večenaj and Mijo Kovačić stand out, and primitive artists from other regions (Ivan Lacković, Ivan Rabuzin, Stjepan Stolnik and Matija Skurjeni). Among the sculptures are several by Lavoslav Torti.

Church of SS Cyril and Methodius ⓯

Sv. Ćiril i Metod

Ćirilometodska ulica. ⓒ (01) 485 17 73.

FIRST BUILT IN AROUND 1830 in Neo-Classical style by the architect Bartol Felbinger (1785–1871), the church was rebuilt after the earthquake of 1880 in a Neo-Byzantine style designed by Hermann Bollé.

The interior has a large iconostasis painted by the Ukrainian Epaminondas Bučevski, and four large paintings by Ivan Tišov.

The adjacent Greek-Catholic seminary was built in 1774 and enlarged at the beginning of the 20th century.

Tower of Lotrščak ⓯

Kula Lotrščak

Strossmayerovo Šetalište. ⓒ (01) 485 17 68. ⬤ Apr–Oct: 11am–7pm Tue–Fri, 2–7pm Sat & Sun. 🎫

SINCE THE MIDDLE of the 19th century, the inhabitants of Zagreb have set their clocks at noon by the sound of cannon fire from this square tower. It dates from the 13th century and is one of the oldest buildings in the city.

At one time the tower also had a bell, which announced the closing of the city gates each evening. Anyone left outside at night ran the risk of being robbed by thieves.

The tower originally stood alongside the southern side of the walls of Gradec. Even at that time, the walls, nearly 2m (6 ft) thick, were built with chains inside them as an anti-earthquake measure.

The tower now houses a gallery. It is worth climbing to the top for spectacular views over the city.

Church of St Catherine ⓰

Sv. Katarina

Katarinin trg. ⓒ (01) 485 19 50. ⬤ 8am–8pm daily.

THE JESUITS BUILT this church in around 1630 on the site of a Dominican building. The church is considered to be one of the most beautiful religious buildings in Zagreb. The white façade has a doorway and four niches with statues and six prominent pilasters. Above is a niche with a statue of Mary.

The single-nave church is home to numerous Baroque works of art. Of particular interest are the stucco reliefs (1721–3) by Antonio Quadrio, the *Scenes of the Life of St Catherine* by the Slovenian artist Franc Jelovšek (1700–64) in the medallion on the ceiling, a beautiful *Altar of St Ignatius* by the Venetian sculptor Francesco Robba (1698–1757) and, on the main altar (1762), *St Catherine among the Alexandrian Philosophers* by Kristof Andrej Jelovšek (1729–76).

In the nearby square called Jezuitski trg, there is a fountain with a statue of a *Fisherman with a Serpent* by Simeon Roksandić (1908). Facing this is a Jesuit monastery (17th century) and a large building from the same period which was the Jesuit seminary and later, a boarding school for boys of noble parentage.

The rich Baroque interior of the church of St Catherine

The Neo-Baroque building housing the Croatian National Theatre

Croatian National Theatre ⑰

Hrvatsko Narodno Kazalište

Trg Maršala Tita 15. 🖀 *(01) 482 85 32.* ⭕ *for performances only.* ⬤ *Mon, 1 Jan, Easter, 1 May, 1 Nov, 25–26 Dec.* 🔲 *www.hnk.hr*

THE CROATIAN National Theatre stands in the square marking the beginning of a U-shaped series of parks and squares forming a "green horseshoe", the design of the engineer Milan Lenuci (1849–1924). The theatre, one of a number of imposing buildings in the square, was completed in 1895 and is a blend of Neo-Baroque and Rococo. It was designed by the Viennese architects Hermann Helmer and Ferdinand Fellner. The roof has two small domes at the front and a higher dome further back. The exterior is ornamented with two orders of columns running along its entire length.

The interior is richly decorated with works by Croatian and Viennese artists. Five stage backcloths include one called *The Croatian Renewal*, a splendid work by Vlaho Bukovac.

In the area in front of the theatre stands a masterpiece by Ivan Meštrović, *The Well of Life*: a group of bronze figures huddled around a well.

Museum of Arts and Crafts ⑱

Muzej Za Umjetnost i Obrt

Trg Maršala Tita 10. 🖀 *(01) 482 69 22.* ⭕ *10am–6pm Tue–Fri, 10am–1pm Sat & Sun.* 🈺 *by appt.* ⓘ 🅿 ∅ 🔲 *www.muo.hr*

A 19th-century clock, Museum of Arts and Crafts

THIS MUSEUM was first established in 1880 to house collections of artworks by craftsmen and artists. The building was designed by Hermann Bollé and was built between 1882 and 1892. More than 160,000 works of applied arts from the Gothic period to the present provide an overview of Croatia's cultural history and its close ties to the rest of Europe.

The collections include jewellery, fabrics (the famous embroidery from Varaždin, and 15th- and 16th-century tapestries from Tournai, Antwerp and Brussels), wooden sculptures, musical instruments, Austrian furniture, French ivory, 16th-century Italian paintings, and chandeliers from Murano, Germany and Bohemia (the section covering the era from the Biedermeier to the Viennese Secession style is particularly interesting). The ceramic collection has works from all the leading European manufacturers. The adjacent library has 50,000 books on arts and crafts.

Mimara Museum ⑲

Muzej Mimara

Rooseveltov trg 5. 🖀 *(01) 482 81 00.* ⭕ *10am–5pm Tue, Wed, Fri & Sat, 10am–7pm Thu, 10am–2pm Sun.* ⬤ *Mon.* 🈺

IN 1972, Ante Topić Mimara, a businessman who was also a collector, painter and restorer, donated his extensive collections to the city of Zagreb, and the Mimara Museum was set up for their display. The museum is housed in an enormous Neo-Renaissance building built in 1895 by the German architects Ludwig and Hülsner. It was formerly a grammar school.

The works are displayed chronologically from the prehistoric era to the present day. The archaeological section is particularly fascinating, with important finds from ancient Egypt, Mesopotamia, Persia, Pre-Columbian America, as well as the Middle and Far East (Japan, Cambodia, Indonesia and India are represented).

The icon collection not only contains Russian pieces, but also has icons from Palestine, Antioch and Asia Minor dating from the 6th to the 13th centuries. There are ancient Persian, Turkish and Moroccan carpets, and about 300 exhibits cover over 3,500 years of the development of Chinese art, from the Shang to the Qing dynasties.

The 550 glassware exhibits come from Europe, as well as Persia, Turkey and Morocco. About 1,000 objects and

The Bather by Renoir (1868) in the Mimara Museum

pieces of furniture give a good overall picture of European craftsmanship from the Middle Ages to the 19th century.

There is also a wide-ranging collection of 200 sculptures, which date from ancient Greece to the time of the Impressionists. They include works by the Italian sculptors Giambologna, the Della Robbias and Verrocchio, and the Frenchmen Jean-Antoine Houdon and Auguste Rodin. Italian painting is represented by, among others, Veronese, Paolo Veneziano, Pietro Lorenzetti, Raphael, Canaletto, Giorgione and Caravaggio.

Dutch Baroque painting is represented by Rembrandt, Jacob Van Ruisdael and Jan Van Goyen. Flemish masters here include Rogier van der Weyden, Hieronymus Bosch, Van Dyck and Rubens. Diego Velázquez, Bartolomé Esteban Murillo and Francisco Goya represent the Spanish painters.

The museum also has paintings by the English artists John Constable and J M W Turner and the French painters Edouard Manet, Pierre-Auguste Renoir and Camille Pissarro.

Ethnographic Museum ⑳
Etnografski Muzej

Mažuranićev trg 14.
🇮 (01) 482 62 20.
⏰ 10am–6pm Tue–Thu, 10am–1pm Fri–Sun. ⚫ public hols. 📷

T HIS IS THE MOST important museum of its kind in Croatia. It was founded in 1919 and set up in this harmonious domed building, constructed in 1902 in the Secession style by the architect Vjekoslav Bastl, for exhibitions held by the Chamber of Commerce. The statues decorating the central part of the façade are by the sculptor Rudolf Valdec and the frescoes on the dome inside were painted by Oton Iveković. Only a small

Traditional Croatian costumes on display, Ethnographic Museum

proportion (2,800 pieces) of the 80,000 exhibits which the museum possesses are on display. Croatian culture is illustrated through exhibits of gold and silver jewellery, musical instruments, splendid embroidery, furnishings, kitchen utensils, tools, beautiful traditional women's costumes embroidered in gold and men's ceremonial dress. Reconstructions of farmhouses and rooms illustrate the customs and way of life of Croat farmers and fishermen.

Putto by Verrocchio, Mimara Museum

There is also a fascinating collection of dolls dressed in traditional costumes, called the Ljeposav Perinić collection.

The valuable collection of pieces from non-European civilizations, including Latin America, Central Africa, the Far East and Australia, was assembled from donations made by scholars and explorers, among them Dragutin Lerman and brothers Mirko and Stevo Seljan.

Botanical Garden ㉑
Botanički Vrt

Marulićev trg 9.
🇮 (01) 484 40 02. ⏰ Mar–Sep: sunrise–sunset Tue–Sun.

P ART OF THE "green horseshoe" designed by Milan Lenuci is a large, English-style garden created in 1890 by Antun Heinz, a professor of botany, and entrusted to the faculty of Mathematics and Natural Sciences at Zagreb university.

The garden, covering an area of 50,000 sq m (540,000 sq ft), is an oasis of tranquillity in which to escape the bustle of the city, and for this reason it is a popular place in which to stroll. There are about 10,000 plant species here, including around 1,800 tropical plants from all over the world, with Asia particularly well represented.

Paths link the conifer woods, artificial ponds, the university pavilions and glasshouses. A wonderful display is provided by the different varieties of trees, shrubs and flowers which are grown here. Aquatic plants are cultivated in special ponds.

One of the many ponds in the Botanical Gardens

The Art Pavilion, venue for major exhibitions

Art Pavilion ㉒
Umjetnički Paviljon

Trg Kralja Tomislava 22.
📞 (01) 484 10 70.
🕐 11am–7pm Mon–Sat; 10am–1pm Sun. ♿
🌐 www.umjetnicki-paviljon.hr

IN 1896 the Art Pavilion represented Croatia at the international exhibition in Budapest. It was set up on this site in 1989 by Ferdinand Fellner and Hermann Helmer. Since then it has been used for art exhibitions. A work by Ivan Meštrović, a monument to the Renaissance painter Andrija Medulić, stands in front of the pavilion.

The pavilion faces onto a square, Trg Kralja Tomislava, dedicated to the first Croatian king, Tomislav. An equestrian statue by the sculptor Robert Frangeš-Mihanović stands here in commemoration.

Gallery of Old Masters ㉓
Galerija Starih Majstora

See pp162–3.

Gallery of Modern Art ㉔
Moderna Galerija

Andrije Hebranga 1.
📞 (01) 492 23 68. 🕐 10am–6pm Tue–Sat; 10am–1pm Sun. ● 1 Jan, Easter, 25, 26 Dec. ♿

SINCE 1973, Vraniczany Palace (1882) has housed works by the most eminent Croat painters and sculptors of the 19th and 20th centuries. The institution itself dates from 1902 when the first works of Ivan Meštrović, Mirko Rački and F Bilak were acquired. Later purchases and donations added to the gallery's extensive collections which now boast 9,500 paintings, sculptures, watercolours, drawings and prints.

At the entrance, the large painting, *Gundulić – Osman's Dream*, 1894 by Vlaho Bukovac, immediately establishes the standard of the collection. The gallery also has works by Ljubo Babić,

Miljenko Stančić, V Karas, M Mašić, Emanuel Vidović, C Medović, MC Crnčić, B Csikos-Sessia, Ivan Meštrović, Robert Frangeš-Mihanović, Josip Račić, Miroslav Kraljević, V Becić, O Hermann and Edo Murtić.

Archaeological Museum ㉕
Arheološki Muzej

Trg Nikole Šubića Zrinskog 19.
📞 (01) 487 30 00, 487 31 01.
🕐 10am–5pm Tue–Fri, 10am–1pm Sat–Sun. ♿ 🅿 by appt. 🛈
🌐 www.amz.hr

A LARGE 19th-century building, the Vraniczany-Hafner Palace, has housed the Archaeological Museum since 1945. The institution itself, however, was founded in 1846. The imposing rusticated façade has columns marking the entrance.

Around 400,000 pieces from all over Croatia, and particularly the area around Zagreb, are on display here.

Head of Plautilla, Archaeological Museum

There are five main sections: prehistoric, Egyptian, ancient and medieval, and a part devoted to coins and medals.

The first section covers the period from the Neolithic to the late Iron Age and includes

Gundulić - Osman's Dream **by Vlaho Bukovac, founder of modern Croat painting, Gallery of Modern Art**

An avenue in Maksimir Park, home of the Zoo

the famous *Vučedol Dove*, a pouring vessel shaped like a bird. Despite the rustic materials used, it nonetheless reveals the technical skills that the pre-Illyrian civilizations had acquired.

Another important exhibit is the bandage used to bind the Mummy of Zagreb. This bandage has mysterious origins and bears text in the Etruscan language, which has not yet been completely deciphered.

The ancient collection is the most important of all, and includes splendid painted Greek vases, inscribed stones and, in the Roman section, sculptures and metal objects from the numerous towns which were built during the Imperial Age. From Salona *(see pp114–5)* came the *Head of Plautilla*, one of the most valuable exhibits here. It is now an emblem of the museum.

The medieval collection begins with the "Great Migrations of the Peoples", documented by an inscription dating from 888 (the oldest in Croatia), which mentions Duke Branimir, an ancient prince of Croatia *(see p34)*.

The coin section is divided into Greek, Celtic, Roman (Republic and Imperial), Byzantine and modern.

The library next door houses 45,000 volumes, some of which are extremely rare.

Sword hilt decoration, Archaeological Museum

Maksimir Park ㉖
Maksimirski Perivoj

Maksimirska Cesta 125.
☐ *daily.*

THE LARGEST PARK in the city (covering over 3 sq km/ 1 sq mile), is considered one of Croatia's living monuments.

It is named after Bishop Maksimilijan Vrhovac, who initiated the project in 1794. The park was finally completed in 1843.

The park is landscaped in the English style with wide lawns and flower beds, small woods and lakes. Near one of the lakes is the **Zoo** (Zoološki vrt), with hundreds of different animal species. Among the follies scattered around the park is one called **Vidikovac** (Belvedere).

Mirogoj Cemetery ㉗
Groblje Mirogoj

Mirogoj. ☐ 7.30am–6pm daily, summer: 7.30am–8pm daily.

AT THE FOOT of Mount Medvednica, 4 km (2 miles) from the centre of the city, is the Mirogoj Cemetery, built in 1876 by Hermann Bollé. This great architect had already demonstrated his ability and talent with the building of the new city district. The cemetery covers

an area of 28,000 sq m (6.91 acres) and the tombs of the most illustrious figures in the political, cultural and artistic life of Croatia lie here.

An imposing façade covered in ivy forms the entrance to the Catholic and Orthodox chapels. From here branch two long Neo-Renaissance arcades which house the burial rooms of the most important families.

A long tree-lined avenue divides the area into two sections which in turn are divided into squares of trees and bushes. Among the areas of greenery stand funeral monuments by leading Croatian sculptors and engravers. There are works by Ivan Meštrović, Jozo Kljaković, Ivan Rendić, Antun Filipović, Antun Augustinčić, Edo Murtić, Markus Sutej, Dozo Dražić, Ivan Kerdić and Robert Frangeš-Mihanović.

As well as the tombs of notable personalities there is also a monument dedicated to the memory of the soldiers who died during World War I, by Juri Turkalj and V Radauš, and a monument dedicated to the Jews who died in World War II, by Antun Augustinčić. On one of the cemetery lawns there is a monument dedicated to the German soldiers killed in the war.

The well-preserved cemetery is a real open-air museum and is often visited by the local inhabitants, who regularly put fresh flowers and candles on the tombs of great Croats of the past.

Arcade in the Mirogoj Cemetery, one of the most beautiful in Europe

Gallery of Old Masters ㉓
Galerija Starih Majstora

IN 1876 JOSIP JURAJ STROSSMAYER, the rich and powerful Bishop of Æakovo and one of the leading proponents of a pan-Slav movement, had this gallery built to house the Academy of Arts and Sciences and later the Gallery of Old Masters, to which he donated his own collection of about 600 works of art.

The neo-Renaissance building has a large internal porticoed courtyard. Ten rooms on the upper floor house around a hundred works from the major European schools from the 14th to the 19th century. Opposite the entrance is a large statue of Bishop Strossmayer sculpted by Ivan Meštrović in 1926.

Virgin with Child and St Francis and St Bernard
This small painting is one of the few works by Bartolomeo Caporali (c.1420–1505) to be found outside Perugia in Italy.

Susanna and the Elders
The three figures depicted in the painting stand out against the landscape in the background. The faces of the two old men are very expressive; it is as though they are revived by gazing at the beautiful Susanna. The artist, Majstor Izgubljenogsina, demonstrates great technical skill and vivid use of colour.

Second floor

GALLERY GUIDE
The gallery is on the second floor of the building. Exhibits include works by important Italian, German, Flemish and French masters, representing schools and artistic trends from the 14th to the 19th century. Before visiting the gallery, note, in the entrance hall, the Baška Tablet, one of the oldest documents of Croat culture (11th century), written in Glagolitic script.

Bridge with Three Arches on the Cannaregio Canal
This painting, by Francesco Guardi (1712–93), is one of numerous views painted by the Venetian artist. The subject is one of the lesser known corners of his native city.

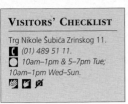

Virgin Mary with Jesus, John and an Angel
This tondo by Jacopo del Sellaio uses exuberant colour. The Tuscan artist belonged to the circle of Filippo Lippi and Sandro Botticelli.

Adam and Eve
This lively painting is by Mariotto Albertinelli (1474–1515), a Florentine painter who worked in Perugino's circle. It shows Adam and Eve being expelled from Earthly Paradise.

KEY

- Italian School 14th–16th century
- Italian School 16th–18th century
- Flemish and Dutch Masters and European School 15th–16th century
- Flemish and Dutch School 16th–17th century
- French Masters 18th–19th century

★ St Nicholas and St Benedict
The work reveals the expressive skill of the great Venetian master, Giovanni Bellini (1430–1516). The figures of the saints occupy simple niches.

★ St Sebastian
This delicate image of the saint by Vittore Carpaccio (1465–1525) was probably part of a polyptych. In this painting with its vivid colouring, the Venetian master expresses the drama of the martyrdom through the smile of the young man at the moment of his death.

Main entrance

STAR FEATURES

★ St Nicholas and St Benedict

★ St Sebastian

CENTRAL CROATIA

ENTRAL CROATIA IS BORDERED TO THE WEST *by the vine-covered hills of Samobor, which continue on towards Karlovac and Ogulin, and to the south by the Bosnia-Herzegovina border as far as Jasenovac. To the northeast is a stretch of fertile valley formed by the Sava river, which goes from Zagreb to the Lonjsko Polje Nature Park. These wetlands, south of Sisak, are home to all kinds of birds.*

This region of Croatia has long been a meeting point for different civilizations. Until the 12th century BC, this area was inhabited by the Illyrians, who were joined by Celts in the 4th century BC. The first Illyrian cities became Roman towns after the 1st century AD. The most important was Siscia (now called Sisak), which was destroyed by the Avars but repopulated by Slavic tribes called Sisak.

Head of Mitra, 2nd century AD, Sisak

The southern border with Bosnia, which dates back to 271 AD, was confirmed at the time of the division between the Western and Eastern Churches in 1054, and later re-confirmed when the Turks occupied the Balkans. To stop the continuous Turkish raids, in 1578 the Austrian Emperor established a *Vojne Krajine* (Military Frontier) in areas which had mostly been abandoned by the Croats, who had fled to the coastal cities for refuge. To help guard the borders, Serbian refugees were brought in, along with minorities of Vlachs, Albanians, Montenegrin and German-speaking groups. Villages sprang up which were inhabited by Catholics, Muslims and people of the Orthodox faith. These diverse communities lived together without any serious tension until the mid-19th century, when feelings of nationalism swept across Europe. The most recent war, fought in the name of nationalism, not only created widespread destruction but also "ethnic cleansing", resulting in the exodus of thousands of Serbs.

This part of Croatia is the area least visited by tourists, although it offers magnificent scenery with rivers and wood-covered hills and good Croatian cuisine. There is plenty to see, with ancient castles, churches, museums and nature reserves.

Horses grazing in the Lonjsko Polje Nature Park

◁ The *Assumption*, a fresco by Franc Jelovšek in the Franciscan church of St Anastasia, Samobor

Exploring Central Croatia

THREE DISTINCT AREAS make up this part of the country: the lowlands around the capital, with numerous 18th-century buildings constructed on the sites of ancient castles; the hilly area renowned for its wine production (Samobor and Karlovac), and the strip of border with Bosnia-Herzegovina, south of Sisak. The landscape of the area is varied, with areas of rolling plains alternating with vine-covered hills. Higher areas are covered in thick woods. In the cities and larger towns there are Baroque churches, monasteries, castles, fortresses and museums. Most suffered damage in the recent war. Some have now been repaired but others are still waiting to be restored.

Roman piece, Civic Museum, Sisak

Interior of the church of St Mary in Jastrebarsko

LADUČ
JANUŠEVEC
LUŽNICA ❷
NOVI DVORI
TOUR OF COUNTRY HOUSES
SAMOBOR ❶
A11
ZAGREB
ŽUMBERAK
OKIĆ ❸
KERESTINEC
BREZOVICA
Novo Mesto
JASTREBARSKO (JASKA) ❹
VUKOMERIČKE GORICE
VELIKA GORICA
31
30
OZALJ ❺
DONJA KUPČINA
6
36
Kupa
POKUPSKO
❻
KARLOVAC
DUGA RESA
31
Rijeka
GORA
GLINA
37
23
6
Rijeka
1
PETROVA GORA
❽
TOPUSKO TOPLICE
VELIKA KAPELA
❼ OGULIN
VELJUN
6
23
SLUNJ
Bihać
Senj
42
K O R D U N
1

GETTING AROUND

The road network which crosses central Croatia is good. From Zagreb the A11 motorway goes to Samobor and the Lonjsko Polje Nature Park, the A12 goes to Jastrebarsko and Karlovac. State road number 30 serves Sisak, while a secondary road network connects the other towns. All the main towns and cities are served by the Croatian railway system, except for the city of Samobor. Buses go to all villages, however small.

0 kilometres   20

0 miles   20

Sights at a Glance

Garić **15**
Jasenovac **11**
Jastrebarsko **4**
Karlovac **6**
Kostajnica **10**
Kutina **14**
Lonjsko Polje Nature Park **13**
Novska **12**
Ogulin **7**
Okić **3**

Ozalj **5**
Samobor **1**
Sisak **9**
Topusko Toplice **8**

Tour

Tour of Country Houses
pp170–71 **2**

Locator Map

See Also

- **Where to Stay** p226
- **Where to Eat** p240

The River Sava near Sisak

The vine-covered hills around Okić

Key

✈ International airport
▬ Motorway
▬ Major road
▬ Minor road
--- Railway line

The main altar in the church of
St Anastasia, Samobor

Samobor ❶

Map C2. ⌘ *35,000.*
☎ *(01) 336 66 34.* 🚌 *Trg kralja
Tomislava 5, (01) 336 00 44.*
🎭 *Carnival (Feb); Day of the city
(26–28 Jul).*

SAMOBOR IS BUILT below the
ruins of what was once a
large fort (Stari Grad). In 1242
it was granted the status of a
royal free town, and became
an important trading centre.
Today it is one of the capitals
of Croatian gastronomy.

In the central area
(Taborec) there are some
old wooden houses and
Baroque buildings as well as
the Gothic church of **St
Michael** (Sv. Mihovil), which
was remodelled in the
Baroque period. Dating from
the same time is the church of
St Anastasia (Sv. Anastazija)
and a Franciscan monastery:
the *Assumption* behind the
main altar was frescoed by
Franc Jelovšek in 1752, while
the altar on the left was

decorated by Valentin
Metzinger (1734). The
adjacent monastery is laid
out around a beautiful
quadrangular cloister and
has Baroque frescoes in the
refectory and library.

The history of the city and
local area is well documented
in the **Civic Museum** (Muzej
Grada Samobora), housed in
the 18th-century Livadić
Palace. The section dedicated
to the history of Croatian
mountaineering is especially
interesting.

🏛 **St Anastasia**
Ulica Sv. Anastazija. ☎ *(01) 336 38
61.* ◐ *by appt.*
🏛 **Civic Museum**
Livadićeva 7. ☎ *(01) 336 10 14.*
◐ *9am–2pm Tue–Fri; 9am–1pm
Sat, Sun.* 📷 🎥 ♿ 🔊 *English,
German.* 📷

Tour of Country Houses ❷

See pp170–71.

Okić ❸

Map C2.
🏛 **County:** *Remetinečka 75, Zagreb,
(01) 652 11 17.*

ON THE ISOLATED hilltop
above Okić stand the
ruins of a fortified town.
These consist of the remains
of a wall with round towers,
an entrance gate and a
Gothic chapel. The town,
mentioned in documents
from 1183, belonged to the
counts of Okić, Zrinski,
Frankopan and Erdödy. It

was destroyed by the Turks
and the town was eventually
abandoned in 1616.

In the village around the
foot of the hill is the church
of **St Mary** (Sv. Marija). It was
rebuilt in 1893 incorporating
a decorated doorway from
1691. Inside are some
Baroque altars, a splendid
pulpit and a font. In front of
the church is an octagonal
bell tower with a vestibule.

A painting by Metzinger in the
church of St Mary in Jastrebarsko

Jastrebarsko ❹

Map C2. ⌘ *17,000.* 🚆 *from
Zagreb.* 🚌 *from Zagreb.*
🏛 **County:** *Remetinečka 75, Zagreb,
(01) 652 11 17;* **Town Hall:** *Braće
Kazić 1, (01) 628 11 15.*
W *www.jastrebarsko.com*

AT THE FOOT OF the Plešivica
mountain chain, between
Samobor and Karlovac, stands
Jastrebarsko. The town
appears in documents of
1249. It assumed greater
importance in 1257 when it
was declared a royal free
town by Bela IV and became
a trading centre for timber,
livestock and the wine which
is still produced locally.

In the 15th century the
town was a feudal holding of
the Erdödy family, who built
an imposing **castle** on a
square ground-plan with
round towers at the corners
and an internal porticoed
courtyard. Two centuries later
it was altered and turned into
a residential building which is
now the town's **Civic
Museum** (Gradski Muzej).

The ruins of the fortified town of Okić, perched on a hilltop

The Baroque church of **St Nicholas** (Sv. Nikola; 1772–75) contains a fresco by Rašica and the tomb of Petar Erdödy (1567). In the church of **St Mary** (Sv. Marija; 1740), originally Dominican and later Franciscan, the altars are all Baroque. The painting on the altar dedicated to Mary is by Valentin Metzinger and dates from 1735.

Ozalj ❺

Map C2. 🏛 *1,200.* 🚇 *(047) 731 158.* 🚌 *Karlovac, (047) 614 701, Ozalj, (047) 731 107.* 🚉 *Kurilovac 1, (047) 731 196.* 🎭 *Day of the city (30 Apr); Summer evenings in Ozalj (15–20 Aug).*

A castle (Stari Grad) which belonged to royalty once stood on this rocky spur. It was built in the 13th century to monitor the roads and the traffic on the river Kupa which flows below it. The castle was strengthened by the Babonić counts and was also the property of the Frankopan family and, in the late 16th century, of Juraj Zrinski. After the Ottoman threat had passed, a village grew up around the castle which had become a residential manor.

Parts of the fortress remain visible: two encircling walls with five semi-circular towers. Next to these are some more recent buildings: the granary

Coat of arms, Civic Museum, Karlovac

Ozalj castle, once owned by the Frankopans and Juraj Zrinski

(palas) (16th century) and a Gothic family chapel. The main building, on several levels, was renovated in 1928 by the Thurn und Taxis family who had inherited it. For a time the building was abandoned but in 1971 it became a **Museum**. Exhibits explain the history of the fort and local area and there are some Glagolitic inscriptions.

♨ Castle and Museum
Ulica Zrinski Frankopana.
📋 *(047) 731 170.* 🕐 *9am–3pm Mon–Fri; 11am–5pm Sat, Sun.* 🈺 🔲

Karlovac ❻

Map C2.
🏛 *71,000.* 🚇 *(047) 432 233, (047) 600 740.* 🚉 **Local:** *Zrinski trg 3, (047) 615 115;* **Regional:** *A Vraniczanya 6, (047) 615 320.* 🌐 *www.karlovac-touristinfo.hr* 🎭 *Carnival (Feb); Summer in Karlovac (Jun); International folk festival (Aug).*

Today Karlovac is an industrial city and an important junction for roads to Slovenia. It originated as a bulwark against Turkish raids, but was actually founded in 1579 by the Archduke of Austria, Charles of Habsburg, from whom the town gets its name. The town was planned by the Italian N Angelini as a city-fort at the confluence of the rivers Korana and Kupa. The layout was based on a six-pointed star with bastions and moats which have now been transformed into public gardens. The interior contained 24 buildings, all similar, all of which are still preserved today – although they are used for different purposes.

The heart of the city is Strossmayer Square with the Baroque Frankopan Palace which houses the **Civic Museum** (Gradski Muzej). The archaeological and ethnographic collections document the city's history.

Clock tower of the church of the Holy Trinity in Karlovac

In the square Trg Bana Jelačića is a Franciscan monastery, with a **Museum of Sacred Art** in the cloisters.

The town is also the site of the Catholic church of the **Holy Trinity** (Sv. Trojstvo), mainly from 1683–92 with an 18th-century clock tower (1795). The church has an elaborate black marble altar made by Michele Cussa in 1698. The Orthodox church of St Nicholas (Sv. Nikola) dates from 1786.

To the east the city now extends as far as **Dubovac Castle**, a medieval construction with three towers, now a hotel.

🏛 Civic Museum
Strossmayerov trg 7.
📋 *(047) 615 980.* 🕐 *8am–4pm Mon–Fri; 10am–noon Sat & Sun.* 🈺 🔲 *by appt.*
🏛 Museum of Sacred Art
Trg bana Jelačića 7.
📋 *(047) 615 950/1.*
⬤ *for restoration.*
🔒 Holy Trinity
Trg bana Jelačića 7.
📋 *(047) 615 950/1.*
🕐 *for mass. Other times by appt.*

Tour of Country Houses ❷

To THE SOUTH AND WEST of Zagreb are several small towns which are easily reached from the A1 motorway, where there are numerous buildings of great architectural interest. Several of them are found along the road which goes from Zaprešić to the Zagorje hills. They were built by members of the Croatian aristocracy after the threat of Turkish invasion had passed and are mainly 18th- and 19th-century reconstructions of older houses. Almost all of the buildings were expropriated after World War II when the Croatian state was set up, and put to different uses. The interiors are not open to the public.

Lužnica ④
Built in the 18th century, this large building has two storeys and a U-shaped ground-plan. The central part is flanked by two round towers with conical roofs. The centre of the long façade culminates in a high tympanum and there are three arched windows on the upper floor above a splendid doorway.

Januševec ⑤
This building, 6 km (4 miles) from Zaprešić, is one of the most beautiful examples of Neo-Classical architecture in Croatia. It was built around 1830 and has three storeys and a rectangular ground-plan centred around a central hall lit by a lantern in the roof. In the centre of the Palladian façade is a three-arched portico with four columns above, crowned by a large tympanum.

0 kilometres   3

0 miles   3

Bregana   E70

Samobor   309

JASTREBARSKO

Laduč ⑥
This castle, 7 km (4 miles) west of Zaprešić, was constructed by the architect K Waidman in 1882 for Baron Vladimir Vranyczani. The pastel colour of the large two-storey building blends harmoniously with the deep green lawns in front. In the centre of the façade is a three-arched portico with an arched loggia above. Today the building houses a nursery school.

Novi Dvori ③

This Neo-Romanesque building near Zaprešić stands on the site of an older structure which was once the country residence of the Ban, Josip Jelačić (1801–59). The house, surrounded by a large park, was partly restored in 1991. The façade has a high stepped tympanum and in front of the entrance is an arched portico with a terrace above. The family tomb stands in the grounds.

TIPS FOR DRIVERS

Departure point: Brezovica.
Length of tour: 40 km (25 miles) one way.
Information: All the houses included in this tour can be seen from the outside. Some may be partially open for visitors.
🅘 Zagreb Tourist Office: Trg bana Jelačića 11, (01) 481 40 51, 481 40 52. *Stopping-off points:* Hotel Restoran Babylon, Betonska cesta 5 🄲 (01) 337 15 00, is an award-winning restaurant near Kerestinec. In Samobor, cheaper restaurants include the Samoborska Pivnica beerhall.

KRAPINA

③

Zaprešić

E59

Kerestinec ②

This villa, southwest of Zagreb, was built in 1575 over older buildings by the Erdödy family. It is famous as a place where many intellectuals were imprisoned in World War II. The square building stands in a lovely park and has four round corner towers, a fine doorway and an internal arcaded courtyard. Today it is used as a barracks.

KEY

▬ Tour route
▬ Motorway
⋯ Other roads

Bestovje

Sv. Nedjelja

ZAGREB

②

VARAŽDIN

E65

E71

①

KARLOVAC

Brezovica ①

The Drašković family built a house here in the 16th century. It was converted into a Baroque palace two centuries later and for some time has been a luxury hotel. The two-storey building has a U-shaped ground-plan and the façade has two round corner towers and a raised central section.

The 15th-century castle of the Frankopan counts in Ogulin

Ogulin ❼

Map C2. 🏰 *11,000.* 🚉 *(047) 542 421.* ℹ️ *Ulica B. Frankopana 2, (047) 532 278.* 🌐 *www.ogulin.hr*

WHEN MARSHAL TITO was imprisoned here in 1927 and 1933 *(see p40)* this town became well-known throughout Croatia. The prison was part of a castle built by the Frankopan counts in the 15th century. The castle walls enclosed a large building with two tall towers at the ends, a Gothic chapel and several houses which were built when Ogulin became a staging post on the *Vojna Krajina* (Military Frontier, *see p37*) in 1627. Part of the structure is given over to the **Regional Museum** which has sections on archaeology, folklore and mountaineering.

A short distance from the fortified town is the Old Castle (Zulumgrad) situated near the Dula abyss: a chasm formed by the Dobra river.

Topusko Toplice ❽

Map D2. 🏰 *4,400.* 🚌 *from Zagreb.* ℹ️ *Trg bana Jelačića 4, (044) 885 203.* 🎭 *A summer of sport (30 May–15 Sep).*

THE PRESENCE of a Cistercian abbey made this a centre for spreading Christianity in the Banovina area (a region of green valleys south of Sisak, between the Sava and Glina rivers). The abbey was founded in 1204 by King Andrew II and a village grew

up around it in the Middle Ages. The complex was destroyed but the foundations are now being excavated. The church, of which parts of the façade survive, surrounded by a dense wood, is also being uncovered. Incisions, difficult to decipher, have been discovered on the base of some of the columns.

The nearby hot water springs (up to 78°C/172°F) were used in Roman times and in the first half of the 19th century a thermal spa was established which was frequented by the Emperor Franz Joseph and other court dignitaries. Today the spa treats rheumatic and neurological problems, and the after-effects of incapacitating injuries.

Sisak ❾

Map D2. 🏰 *61,000.* 🚉 *(044) 521 157.* 🚌 *(044) 522 667.* ℹ️ *Rimska ulica, (044) 522 655.*

THE CITY OF SISAK stands at the point where the rivers Kupa and Odra flow into the Sava and has always played an important role in Croatian history. Its name has changed a number of times over the course of its 1,000 years of existence. It originated as the Illyrian Segestica, becoming Siscia with the Celts, and Colonia Flavia Siscia in the Imperial Roman period. Rome conquered the town after

Hercules (1st century AD), Sisak museum

a bloody battle in which Emperor Augustus was wounded. After the conquest of the Balkans, the emperor nominated it the capital of the Pannonia Savia province, making it an important trading centre.

It was destroyed by Attila in 441, and in the 6th century it was raided by the Avars and Slavs. The town was finally rebuilt by the Croats and became Sisak. It was from here that Prince Ljudevit began the conquest of Croatia in the 8th century. Sisak was destroyed again by the Hungarians in the 10th century, and was also abandoned by the bishop, who transferred the see to Zagreb, but built a fort here. In 1593 this fort was the site of a battle which resulted in the first Turkish defeat in the Balkans.

The town rose again nearby and began to enjoy a long period of prosperity, thanks to the tolls on river traffic. It still has some Baroque buildings, including the old and new town halls.

A park surrounds the **fortress** (Stari Grad) on the River Kupa, south of the city. The fortress was built in the 13th century and reinforced at the time of the Turkish invasions. It has a triangular ground-plan, with three large round brick towers (1544–55), connected by a high wall with openings for firearms. In the park is a beautiful traditional farmhouse. The **Civic Museum** (Gradski Muzej) has material from the Roman settlement.

⚓ **Fortress**
Brkljača Erdelja. ℹ️ *(044) 520 294.* ⚙️ *for restoration.*

🏛 **Civic Museum**
Kralja Tomislava 8. 🔑 *(044) 520 294.* 🕙 *10am–6pm Tue–Fri; 10am–1pm Sat & Sun.* 🎟 🚫

ENVIRONS: About 20 km (12 miles) southwest is **Gora** which, in the Middle Ages, was the centre of a Županija (county) of the same name. The county seat was a castle

Fortress of Sisak next to the Kupa river, built in the 13th century

which appears in documents in 1242, but which was destroyed by the Turks in 1578. The Gothic church of **St Mary** (Sv. Marija) was also badly damaged but survived and was restored in the 18th century in the Baroque style. The church has chapels on all corners and resembles a castle. Inside are traces of the original paintings, and a fine marble altar and pulpit.

Kostajnica ⑩

Map D2. 🏠 *2,700.*
🚉 *from Zagreb, Sisak.*
🚌 *from Zagreb, Sisak.*
ℹ️ *Vladimira Nazora, (044) 672 366.*

STANDING ON the left bank of the River Una which, for much of its length, marks the border between Croatia and Bosnia-Herzegovina, this village still bears the signs of damage from the recent war. On an island, near a destroyed bridge, is a castle built in the Middle Ages but frequently razed. Only three towers connected by a high wall remain in the wake of the last war. The church and monastery of **St Anthony of Padua**, built after the Turks left at the end of the 17th century, have been restored but are without furnishings (some of the Baroque altars were famous for their beauty).

ENVIRONS: Around 14 km (9 miles) to the southwest is **Zrin**, where the ruins of a castle built in the 14th century by the Babonić family stand on a hill. In 1347 it passed to the Bribir princes of Šubić. A

The tulip-shaped monument by Bogdanović in Jasenovac cemetery

branch of the family took the name of Zrinski after the village around the castle. It was occupied by the Turks from 1577 until the end of the 17th century when they destroyed it.

The Zrinskis played an important role in Croatia's history: as fierce defenders against the Turks; then as the authors of the failed attempt to free the territory from Habsburg rule *(see p175)*.

Jasenovac ⑪

Map E2. 🏠 *1,200.* 🚉 *from Sisak.*
🚌 *from Sisak.* ℹ️ *Trg kralja Petra Svačića 3, (044) 672 366.*

THIS TOWN IS notorious as the place where, during World War II, tens of thousands of prisoners of war, Jews, Gypsies, Serbs and Croats, perished in the concentration camp which was located here. In memory of this terrible genocide, a

large tulip-shaped monument, designed by the artist Bogdan Bogdanović, has been erected in the centre of the cemetery.

The church of St Luke in Novska

Novska ⑫

Map E2. 🏠 *8,000.*
🚉 *from Zagreb, Sisak, (044) 600 060.* 🚌 *from Zagreb, Sisak.*
ℹ️ *Trg Luke Ilića Oriovčanina 2, (044) 601 305.*

THE TOWN of Novska is the starting point for visiting the Lonjsko Polje Nature Park *(see p174)* and for excursions to the Psunj mountains.

The church of **St Luke** (Sv. Luka) has Gothic origins but was rebuilt in the Baroque style. It has a fine altar and a painting by the modern painter Z Šulentić.

In the **Bauer Gallery** there are many works by Naive and contemporary artists.

Novska's economy is based on industry and trade and rail and road links are good.

The castle of medieval origins in Kostajnica, on the banks of the Una

Nesting storks in the Lonjsko Polje Nature Park

Lonjsko Polje Nature Park ⑬

Map D2. **Park office (Jasenovac)**
🛈 *(044) 672 080. Entrance at Čigoč*
🛈 *(044) 715 115.* ⭘ *8am–4pm daily.* 🈳

THE WIDE BEND IN the River Sava between Sisak and Nova Gradiška has been a special ornithological reserve since 1963. It became a nature reserve in 1987 to protect an area of 506 sq km (195 sq miles). This vast area was regularly flooded by the river and its tributaries (Lonja, Ilova, Pakra and Čazma) during the thaw, and in the summer and early autumn the waters would recede. Since the 1960s parts of the wetlands have been drained and even though the area is now just a fraction of its original size (it now covers 6.5 sq km/ 2.51 sq miles), the park is still one of the most fascinating marshes in Europe.

Woods of oak, poplar, ash and willow trees grow along the banks of the river and on the higher ground, while the dry fields are used as grazing for sheep in the summer months. Wild boar live here, as well as deer, and there are also black Turopolje pigs and Posavina horses, both of which are protected species.

The park is an important stopping place for black storks, which arrive in spring and leave in autumn after nesting, for numerous species of heron, for egrets and a variety of birds of prey, including the rare harrier and white-tailed eagles.

Kutina ⑭

Map D2. 🏙 *15,000.* 🚍 *(044) 682 381.* 🚌 *(044) 682 605.* 🛈 *Hrvatskih branitelja 2, (044) 681 004.*

KUTINA, in the Moslavina region, was built over the ruins of a Roman *castrum* and numerous finds have been discovered. The town is linked to two castles; Kutinjac Grad, documented in 1256, and the fortress of Plodvin, however only ruins and parts of the walls remain.

Kutina flourished again in the 17th century, developing on the plain south of the fortress. It is here that the church of **Our Lady of the Snow** (Snježna Marija) was built by Count Karl Erdödy in around 1770. The church is surrounded by a covered portico and is decorated inside with stucco and *trompe-l'oeil* paintings by Josip Görner. The sculpture and the inlaid wooden furnishings which enclose the altar of the Holy Sepulchre are a unique example of Baroque composition.

Erdödy Castle, rebuilt in 1895, houses the **Museum of Moslavina** (Muzej Moslavine) which tells the history and folklore of Moslavina, through documents, objects and traditional costumes.

🏛 Museum of Moslavina
Trg kralja Tomislava 13. 🚹 *(044) 683 548.* ⭘ *8am–1pm Mon–Fri.*

Interior of the church of Our Lady of the Snow in Kutina

ENVIRONS: Around 50 km (31 miles) northwest of Kutina is **Ivanić-Grad** and the nearby towns of **Klostar Ivanić** and **Križ**. In Ivanić-Grad there are workshops making pretty flax and linen products, keeping local traditions alive.

In Klostar Ivanić there is a Franciscan monastery founded in 1508 and the church of St Mary (Sv. Marija), with collections of silver, paintings and richly illustrated music codices.

In Kriz, the parish church of the Cross was founded by the Knights Templar in the 11th century. The church has a richly decorated Baroque interior and a magnificent organ, built in 1787.

Some remains of the old fortifications around Garić

Garić ⑮

Map D2. 🏙 *76 (Podgarić).*
🛈 **Regional:** *trg kralja Tomislava 5, Bjelovar, (043) 241 680.*

ON A HILL in the Moslavačka chain (Moslavačka Gora) near Podgarić stand the ruins of the fortified town of Garić, noted as a *castrum* in 1256. In 1277, it was granted by the king to Timotej, Bishop of Zagreb, who entrusted its defence to the counts of Gardun, and later to the counts of Celje. Nearby, below Garić, the Pauline order founded the monastery of St Mary in 1295. In 1544 the town and the monastery were destroyed by the Turks.

The fortified town was protected by high walls and was an irregular shape. There was a moat with towers, and further towers inside the walls.

The Zrinski and Frankopan Dynasties

DUJMO, COUNT OF KRK, died in 1163 and his descendants took the name of Frankopan *(Frangere Panem)* after Venice confirmed the family's rule over Krk. They were allied with Venice until 1480 when they were forced to surrender the island. However, they still had vast estates given to them by the Hungarian kings. The Šubić family became counts of Bribir when they were granted the town by King Andrew II in 1290, and counts of Zrinski in 1347 when they were obliged to move to Zrin *(see p173)*. The execution of the Ban of Croatia, Petar Zrinski, and his brother-in-law Franjo Krsto Frankopan in 1671 ended the two most powerful Croatian dynasties. The Habsburgs confiscated their property and the Zrinski line died out. A branch of the Frankopan family still survives in Friuli, Italy.

Franjo Krsto Frankopan
(1645²–1671), great grandson of Krsto Frankopan and Mario Frangipane's heir (the Roman branch of the family), was publicly executed in Wiener Neustadt in 1671, for his part in a plot against the Empire.

Krsto Frankopan,
(1480²–1527), son of Bernard, Ban of Croatia, and Louise of Aragon, was Emperor Maximilian's general in the war against Venice in the early 16th century. He was imprisoned in Venice and died fighting for the independence of Hungary, of which Croatia was part.

Franjo Krsto — Frankopan awaiting execution

Petar Zrinski —

EXECUTION OF THE REBELS
On 30 April 1671, in the town square in Wiener Neustadt, the Ban of Croatia, Petar Zrinski, and his brother-in-law, Marquis Krsto Frankopan, were beheaded on charges of high treason on the orders of Emperor Leopold I. The two brothers-in-law had attempted to form a coalition of the Croatian feudal lords in order to limit Austro-Hungarian influence.

Nikola Zrinski fought against the Turks and was a defender of Christianity. He died in the Battle of Siget in 1566, after he refused the sultan's offer to make him Governor of Croatia if he abandoned the Emperor.

Petar Zrinski *was the Ban (governor) from 1664, and the leader of the movement which sought to limit Habsburg activity in Croatia. The attempted revolt was foiled by betrayals and the promise of a possible agreement. The two leaders went to Vienna to negotiate with the Emperor. When they reached the capital they were imprisoned, and a few months later were beheaded.*

SLAVONIA AND BARANJA

T HE EASTERNMOST PART OF NORTHERN CROATIA, *between Hungary, Serbia and Bosnia-Herzegovina, is one of the most fertile areas of Europe, known as "the granary" of Croatia. The landscape of Slavonia and Baranja is characterized by expanses of wheat and maize fields and hills covered with vineyards or ancient woods. The main city, Osijek, is famous for its fortified centre.*

First inhabited by the Illyrians, present-day Slavonia and Baranja came into contact with the Roman world in the 2nd century BC. It took the Romans more than 200 years to subdue the inhabitants of this region, which they referred to as Pannonia. From 402 Pannonia was invaded, first by the Goths, then the Huns, Visigoths, Burgundians, Gepids, Longobards, Sarmatians and finally the Avars. When the Slavs arrived, very little remained of Roman rule, and the land, ever since then called Slavonia, was practically uninhabited.

Fresco in the church of St Francis, Požega

In 925 the Kingdom of the Croat Sovereigns was set up and this lasted until 1097, when King Koloman conquered Slavonia and created the Hungarian-Croat kingdom. Following the Battle of Mohács in 1526, Slavonia became part of the Ottoman Empire, and remained so until 1689.

To confront the constant disputes between the Turks and the Holy Roman Empire, the Habsburgs set up a Military Frontier *(Vojne Krajine)*, which lasted until 1881, when Austria-Hungary took Bosnia-Herzegovina from the Turks. The frontier was abolished and absorbed into Croatia.

When war broke out in 1991, the presence of Serb villages was a pretext for the Serbian occupation of Slavonia. In 1995 the Croatians reconquered the area, forcing Yugoslav soldiers and Serbs to leave. Although war damage is still visible along the border, particularly in Vukovar, great efforts are being made with rebuilding and Slavonia is once again well worth visiting for its historical treasures. It is also an area of great natural beauty and includes the nature reserve of Kopački Rit, a wetlands sanctuary for wildfowl.

Local people in the typical traditional costumes of the region

◁ The tall spires of the Neo-Gothic cathedral in Osijek *(see p188)*, with the River Drava in the background

Exploring Slavonia and Baranja

SLAVONIA, the region between the rivers Sava, Drava and Danube, is made up of a vast rolling alluvial plain with chains of hills at its edges which are covered in woods and vineyards. At one time the rivers turned the area into an enormous swamp for many months of the year. Baranja is a triangular area of land in the far northeast, bordered at the extreme tip by the rivers Drava and Danube and the Hungarian border.

The plains are covered in fields of maize and the hills are given over to viticulture. In the southern corner, the Drava river regularly overflows from spring to autumn to create a broad area of marshland, now the Kopački Rit Nature Park. The park is an important wildlife sanctuary, a refuge for hundreds of different species of bird, including the rare black stork.

On the right bank of the Drava river is Slavonia's main city, Osijek. It has wide avenues, parks, and 19th-century, Viennese-style buildings, as well as an impressive Neo-Gothic cathedral.

The Baroque belfry of St Roch in Virovitica

SIGHTS AT A GLANCE

Varaždin

PODRAVINA

BILOGORA

VIROVITICA **㉖**

ČAĐAVICA

SLATINA

DARUVAR **❶**

VOĆIN

ORAHOVICA **㉕**

NAŠICE **㉔**

KUTJEVO **❺**

PAKRAC
LIPIK **❷**

POŽEGA **❹**

Zagreb

NOVA GRADIŠKA **❸**

POSAVINA

SLAVONSKI BROD **❻**

The countryside around Slavonski Brod

GETTING AROUND

For many years Osijek was a rail, road and river junction of
some importance. Since the recent war, rail and river traffic
has become less significant. However, Osijek is still the centre
of the road system in the area and, thanks to a good network,
the city can easily be reached from Slavonia and Baranja using
state road number 3 from Varaždin, or the number 7 road from
Vukovar and the E73 from Hungary. There is also an efficient
public bus service. About 7 km (4 miles) from Osijek there
is a domestic airport with daily connections to Zagreb.
Osijek itself has an excellent tram service which makes
it easy to get around the city.

LOCATOR MAP

SEE ALSO

• *Where to Stay* p227

• *Where to Eat* pp240–41

The traditional costumes of Bizovac

The ruins of Grad Ružica, near Orahovica

KEY

✈ Airport

▬ Motorway

▬ Major road

▬ Minor road

- - Railway line

�12 Viewpoint

Daruvar ❶

Map E2. 🏘 *10,000.* 🚊 *Osijek, 91 km (56 miles); Zagreb, 150 km (93 miles).* 🚌 🚃 ℹ️ *Julijev Park 1, (043) 331 215.* 🎎 *Wine exhibition (May).*

T HIS PLACE WAS KNOWN by the name of Aquae Balissae in the time of the Roman Empire for the quality of its hot water spring, the source of which is at the foot of the Papuk mountains.

The town developed from three medieval settlements. In 1760 the area was given to a Hungarian count, Antun Janković, who built a Baroque manor and the first **spa**. Today, Daruvar (meaning "city of the crane") has a hotel and a **Medical Centre** (Daruvarske Toplice), offering the spa waters.

There are two 18th-century churches in the town, one Catholic and one Orthodox. Daruvar is also a centre for the Czech people in Croatia, who maintain the Czech language and customs.

💧 Spa
Julijev Park. 📞 *(043) 331 215.*

Lipik ❷

Map E2. 🏘 *11,300.* 🚊 *Osijek, 93 km (58 miles); Zagreb, 155 km (96 miles).* 🚌 🚃 *from Pakrac.* ℹ️ *Ulica Marije Terezije 27, (034) 421 001.* 🎎 *Day of the city (4 Nov).*

T HE AREA (Aquae Balissae) was known in Roman times for its waters. In the early 19th century a hot water spring, rich in fluorine, sodium and calcium, was rediscovered and Lipik became one of the most famous spas in Croatia. It was especially popular between the two World Wars. Lipik was seriously damaged in the 1991 war, but a new **spa** has been built and the hotels and medical centres restored. Lipik is also known as a centre for breeding the famous Lipizzaner horses. The breed originated in the 16th century in Lipizza in Slovenia.

💧 Spa (Toplice)
Marije Terezije 5. 📞 *(034) 421 322.*

Baroque building in Požega's main square

Nova Gradiška ❸

Map E2. 🏘 *14,800.* 🚊 *Osijek, 93 km (58 miles); Zagreb, 155 km (96 miles).* 🚌 ℹ️ *Slavonskih graničara 15, (035) 361 494.*

I N 1725 THIS TOWN was founded as Fredrichsdorf by the Viennese, who planned to build a fortress here. The town, situated at the foot of Mount Psunj, is built on a fertile plain. An agricultural market is regularly held in the main square, which is lined with Baroque buildings.

The Neo-Classical church of St Stephen of Hungary (Sv. Stjepan Kralj) is now the **Immaculate Conception**. The Baroque **Sanctuary of St Theresa** (Sv. Terezija) dates from 1756.

🏛 Immaculate Conception
Aloizija Stepinca 1. 📞 *(035) 362 203.* 🕐 *8am–6pm daily.*

The Baroque Sanctuary of St Theresa in Nova Gradiška

Požega ❹

Map E2. 🏘 *21,000.* 🚊 *Osijek, 67 km (42 miles); Zagreb, 175 km (109 miles).* 🚌 🚃 ℹ️ **Local:** *Trg Sv. Trojstva 1, (034) 274 900.* **Regional:** *Županijska 7, (034) 272 505/668.* 🎎 *Feast of St Gregory (12 Mar), Music Festival Zlatne zice Slavonije (Sep).*

T HE ROMANS FIRST founded this town, a halfway settlement between the towns now called Sisak and Osijek, with the name of Incerum. In the 11th century it was one of the centres from which the heretical movement of the Bogomili spread; after their repression in the 12th century the city was granted to the Templars by King Bela IV.

In 1227 the Franciscans founded a monastery, the church of which was used as a mosque during the Turkish occupation. In the 18th and 19th centuries the town was called the "Athens of Slavonia" for the cultural events held to commemorate the expulsion of the Turks in 1691. The city took on a new look during this period: in the main square, Trg Sv. Trojstva, buildings with stucco and Baroque porticoes were built.

In the square stands a column, a memorial to plague victims made in 1749 by Gabrijel Granić. To one side of the square is the renovated 18th-century church of **St Francis** (Sv. Franjo). The monastery alongside still houses a community of Franciscan monks.

Interesting examples of Baroque architecture in the town include the Jesuit College (1711) and Gymnasium (1726), opened by the Jesuits who, in 1763, also founded the Požega Academy. Dating from 1763, the church of **St Theresa** (Sv. Terezija Avilska) became a cathedral in 1997. The frescoed walls are by Celestin Medović and Oton Iveković.

The church of **St Lawrence** (Sv. Lovro, 14th century) was renovated in Baroque style in the early 18th century. It still has some 14th-century frescoes. There are also tombstones testifying to the city's glory; one is for the poet Antun Kanižlić (1699–1777). In the square between the church of St Francis and the Jesuit College is a statue of Luka Ibrišimović, a Franciscan who distinguished himself in the battles against the Turks.

The **Civic Museum** (Gradski Muzej) contains an assortment of archaeological finds, Romanesque reliefs and Baroque paintings.

Every year on 12 March Požega holds an event called Grgurevo, to commemorate a local victory over the Turks won in 1688.

🏛 **Civic Museum**
Matice Hrvatske 1. 📞 (034) 272 130. ◯ 8am–3pm, Mon–Fri.
🛉 **St Theresa**
Trg Sv. Terezije 13. 📞 (034) 274 321. ◯ 8am–noon, 3–6pm daily.

14th-century fresco in the church of St Lawrence, Požega

Kutjevo ❺

Map F2. 🏘 7,400. 🛬 Osijek 62 km (38 miles). 🚆 Našice, 27 km (17 miles). 🛈 Republike Hrvatske 77, (034) 255 092/3. 🎉 Feast of St Gregory (12 Mar).

A N IMPORTANT wine-producing centre, the town is famous for a winery founded by the Cistercians. In 1232, the order built a monastery here and encouraged the cultivation of vines. After Turkish rule, at the end of the 17th century, Jesuits took over the monastery and wine-making resumed. The Cistercian cellars are still intact and wine is still an important industry. The Jesuits also built the church of **St Mary** (Sv. Marija) in 1732, which houses a painting of the Madonna with Child by A Cebej (1759).

Slavonski Brod ❻

Map F3. 🏘 70,000. 🛬 Osijek, 47 km (29 miles); Zagreb, 197 km (122 miles). 🚆 (060) 333 444. 🚌 Trg Hrvatskog proljeća, (035) 444 300. 🛈 **Local:** Trg Pobjede 28, (035) 447 721. **Regional:** Petra Krešimira IV 1, (035) 216 362. 🎉 Folklore Festival, Brodsko kolo (mid-Jun).

B UILT ON the site of the Roman town Marsonia, this town was placed so as to monitor the traffic on the river Sava, the border with

Baroque altar in Holy Trinity church in Slavonski Brod

Bosnia-Herzegovina. The town belonged to the counts Berislavić-Grabarski from the Middle Ages to 1526 when it was conquered by the Turks, who occupied it until 1691.

To defend the border, in 1741 the Viennese government built a fort with barracks, residences for governors and religious buildings. Damaged during World War II and again in the war in 1991, the buildings are under repair: some are used as schools and others house museums and galleries.

The town has grown beyond the original ramparts. Along the banks of the Sava is a **Franciscan Monastery**, dating from 1725, recently renovated, and the Baroque church of the **Holy Trinity** (Sv. Trojstvo) with many statues, paintings and magnificent altars.

The **Regional Civic Museum** (Muzej Brodskog Posavlja) contains historic documents and archaeological finds from the region.

The well-known Croatian writer, Ivana Brlić-Mažuranić (1874–1938), spent much of her life in this town. She wrote fairytales for children: among her most famous works are *Fisherman Palunco, Jagor* and *The Forest of Stribor*. The town is also known for its folklore festival (Brodsko kolo) which is held every year in June.

🏛 **Regional Civic Museum**
Ulica Ante Starčevica 40. 📞 (035) 447 415. ◯ 8am–4pm Mon–Sat, 10am–1pm Sun. ● 25 Dec, 1 Jan. 🗺

The cloisters in the Franciscan monastery, Slavonski Brod

View of the 19th-century red-brick Cathedral of St Peter in Đakovo

Vrpolje ❼

Map F3. 🏚 *2,200.*
🛬 *Osijek, 39 km (24 miles).* 🚌 *from Osijek.* ❶ **Regional:** *Sunčana ulica 39, Bizovac, (031) 675 897.*

A SMALL COUNTRY town, Vrpolje is known as the birthplace of the sculptor Ivan Meštrović (1883–1962) *(see p155).* Many of the artist's works, donated to the town he held in great affection, can be seen here. In the small parish church of **St Ivan** (Sveti Ivan Krstitelj, 1774) is his statue of St John the Baptist, a relief and a crucifix, while outside is a striking *Bust of a Woman.* The **Gallery** (Spomen Galerija) has 30 of his works on display: casts, bronzes and wooden sculptures.

Bust of a Woman by Meštrović, Vrpolje

Đakovo ❽

Map F2. 🏚 *25,000.* 🛬 *Osijek, 36 km (22 miles).* 🚉 *(031) 811 360.* 🚌 *(031) 811 390.* ❶ *Kralja Tomislava 3, (031) 812 319,* FAX *(031) 811 233.* 🎭 *Đakovo embroidery, Đakovački Vezovi (first week in Jul).*

IN MEDIEVAL TIMES this town was known by the name of Civitas Dyaco, and later as Castrum Dyaco. Late in the 13th century it became a bishopric, and its influence extended over most of Slavonia and Bosnia. Conquered and destroyed by the Turks in 1536, the town became a Muslim centre and a mosque was built. After Turkish rule, the city was renovated. Only the mosque, at the end of the central avenue, was retained. It was converted into the parish church of All Saints (Svi Sveti) in the 18th century.

The central square is dominated by the **Cathedral of St Peter** (Sv. Petar), built between 1866 and 1882 by Bishop Josip Juraj Strossmayer; the project was the work of the Viennese architects Karl Rösner and Friedrich von Schmidt. The imposing façade is flanked by two 84-m (275-ft) belfries. The interior has frescoes by Maksimilijan and Ljudevit Seitz, sculptures by Ignazio Donegani and Tomas Vodcka and decorations by Giuseppe Voltolini from the 19th century. The crypt houses the tombs of the bishops Strossmayer and Ivan de Zela. Next to the church is the 18th-century Bishop's Palace, which has an ornate Baroque doorway.

The Festival of Embroidery of Đakovo (Đakovački Vezovi) is held at the beginning of July with displays of traditional local costumes, folk dancing and wine tasting.

🏛 **Cathedral of St Peter**
Strossmayerov trg. 📞 *(031) 802 225.* ⏰ *6am–noon, 3–8pm daily.*

Novi Mikanovci ❾

Map F2. 🏚 *200.* 🛬 *Osijek, 50 km (31 miles).* 🚉 *Stari Mikanovci, 3 km (2 miles).* ❶ *(032) 203 137.*

THE VILLAGE is famous for the small Romanesque church of **St Bartholomew** (Sveti Bartol), from the first half of the 13th century, a rare example of architecture from before Turkish rule. The church stands in a cemetery and is called the "Tower of Pisa of Slavonia" because of its leaning bell tower, which appears to be held up by the façade. At the cemetery entrance is a colourful statue of St Bartholomew.

Županja ❿

Map F3. 🏚 *12,000.* 🛬 *Osijek, 67 km (41 miles).* 🚉 *(032) 831 183.* ❶ *Josipa Jurja Strossmayera 1, (032) 832 711.* 🎭 *Folklore Festival, Šokačko Sijelo (Feb).*

ON THE BORDER with Bosnia-Herzegovina, Županja lies along a wide bend in the Sava River. The area has been inhabited since ancient times; Bronze Age finds have been discovered in a necropolis. One of the first Croat settlements was set up here. After Turkish rule it became one of the military staging posts on the *Vojne Krajine* (Military Frontier) *(see p37)* and a trading centre.

The **Frontier House** is a wooden building originally from the early 19th century, used by tax collectors. Burnt

Embroidered head-dress in the Ethnographic Museum, Županja

down during the recent bombings and now rebuilt, it houses the **Ethnographic Museum** (Zavičajni Muzej "Stjepan Gruber").

🏛 **Ethnographic Museum**
Savska 3. ☎ *(032) 837 101.*
◯ *9am–1pm Mon–Fri; during exhibitions Sat & Sun 10am–noon.*

Vinkovci ⓫

Map F2. 👥 *36,000.* ✈ *Osijek, 43 km (27 miles).* 🚉 *(060) 333 444.* 🚌 *(032) 308 937.* ℹ **Local:** *Trg bana Josipa Šokčevića 3, (032) 334 653;* **Regional:** *Glagoljaška 27, (032) 344 034.* 📷 *Autumn in Vinkovci, Vinkovačke Jeseni (Sep).*

FOUNDED BY THE Romans with the name of Aurelia Cibalae, this was the birthplace of the Emperors Valens and Valentinian, and a bishop's see from the 4th century. In the Middle Ages it was called Zenthelye, because of the presence of the (now abandoned) church of **St Elias** (Sv. Ilija). The church dates from the 12th century, and is one of the oldest monuments in Slavonia.

The **Civic Museum** (Gradski Muzej), situated in the former 18th-century Austrian barracks in the main square, holds finds from the Roman necropolis and has a folklore collection. Large Roman sarcophagi are displayed in front of the museum.

Exhibit in the Civic Museum, Vinkovci

Facing the garden is the church of SS Eusebius and Pollio (Sv. Euzebije i Polion) from 1775, and the Town Hall, both under repair.

Each September a festival of music and popular traditions is held in the town and groups from all over the country take part. The streets are decorated, stallholders sell local produce, and musicians and jugglers perform.

🏛 **Civic Museum**
Trg bana Šokčevica. ☎ *(032) 332 504.* ◯ *10am–1pm, 5–7pm Tue–Fri; 10am–1pm Sat–Sun.* 📷 📷

The church of St Ivan, next to the fortified walls in Ilok

Ilok ⓬

Map G2. 👥 *6,800.* ✈ *Osijek, 62 km (38 miles).* 🚉 *Vukovar, 39 km (24 miles).* ℹ **Regional:** *Glagoljaška 27, Vinkovci, (032) 344 034.* 📷 *Grape harvest festival (Sep–Oct).*

OVERLOOKING a wide loop in the River Danube, Ilok is the easternmost city in Croatia and the centre of the region of Srijem, famous since Roman times for its wine production. In the late Roman era the city grew in importance and took the name of Cuccium.

In the Middle Ages it was a *castrum* with high walls, towers and fortified buildings. The defences were reinforced in 1365, and the town was given to Nikola Kont, whose family later acquired the title of Counts of Ilok.

Around the middle of the 15th century, the church and monastery of **St Ivan Kapistran** (Sv. Ivan Kapistran) were built inside the fort. St Ivan Kapistran was a Franciscan who was famous for uniting Christian forces against the Turks and who was buried here in 1456. When Ilok became a major Turkish administrative and military centre in the 16th century, mosques and baths were added to the fortress.

Both the church and the monastery have recently been renovated and between them, long stretches of the ancient walls can still be seen. Parts of one of the Turkish baths are still visible.

In 1683, after his role in winning the battle of Vienna, Commander Livio Odescalchi was given the town of Ilok by the Austrian Emperor. In this idyllic setting he built a U-shaped mansion, **Odescalchi Manor**. Today, the mansion houses the Odescalchi Collection, a restaurant, public offices and the **Civic Museum** (Gradski Muzej) with archaeological and ethnographic collections. The wines of Ilok are still produced here in the cellars, among them a dry white wine called Traminac.

⛪ **Church and Monastery of St Ivan Kapistran**
Fra Bernardina Lejakovića 13.
☎ *(032) 746 021.* ◯ *by appt or before mass.*
🏛 **Odescalchi Manor and Civic Museum**
☎ *(032) 529 088.*
◯ *7am–3pm, Mon–Fri, for wine tastings only.* **Civic Museum** ◐ *for restoration.*

The mansion built by Commander Livio Odescalchi in Ilok

Tabernacle in the Franciscan monastery in Šarengrad

Šarengrad ⑬

Map G2. 🏘 *100.* ⬛ *Osijek, 53 km (33 miles).* 🚉 *Vukovar, 30 km (19 miles).* ℹ️ **Local:** *(032) 746 076;* **Regional:** *Vinkovci, (032) 344 034.*

A MEDIEVAL FORT once controlled the heavy traffic along the river Danube at this spot. In the 15th century, Count Ivan Maroivički added a **Franciscan Monastery**. The fort, however, was destroyed during the war with the Turks and the area remained uninhabited until their departure late in the 17th century.

With the return of the inhabitants, the monks set up a school and collected archaeological items for a museum.

During the break-up of former Yugoslavia between 1991 and 1995, the area was heavily bombed. The church and monastery have since been restored and the statue of St Anthony of Padua has been put back in position. From the hill there are good views of the Danube.

Vukovar ⑭

Map G2. 🏘 *45,000.* ⬛ *Osijek, 23 km (14 miles).* 🚉 *Vinkovačka cesta.* 🚌 *from Vinkovci.* ℹ️ **Local:** *Vukovar, (032) 442 889;* **Regional:** *Vinkovci, (032) 334 653.*

THIS BAROQUE CITY was once known for its churches, elegant 18th-century buildings, numerous museums and art galleries. However, Vukovar has come to symbolize the war which raged in Slavonia in 1991, when it was bombed by the Serbs and the JNA (Yugoslav People's Army). The historic Baroque nucleus was almost totally destroyed. Plans for repair in collaboration with UNESCO are under way but hampered by the lack of international funds.

Vukovar has a very long history, as evidenced by the famous "Dove of Vučedol" from 2000 BC. This vessel was found 5 km (3 miles) from Vukovar and is now in the Archaeological Museum in Zagreb (*see pp160–61*).

The city, at the confluence of the Danube and the river Vuka, was known by the name of Vakovo in the Middle Ages. Later it was given to various families: the Horvat, the Gorjanski and the Talovci. Conquered by the Turks, Vukovar became a military garrison and a key trading centre. After liberation from the Turks in 1687, it resumed its role as an advance post of the Christian Catholic world against the Muslim and Orthodox religions.

In 1736, it was given to the Eltz counts, who called the town Vukovar. As the inhabitants were Catholics or of the Orthodox faith, churches were built for both religions, including a Franciscan monastery (1727).

The Dove of Vučedol, symbol of Vukovar

In 1751, the Eltz family built a huge Baroque mansion. It was nationalized after World War II and then housed the **Civic Museum** (Gradski Muzej). The palace was badly damaged in 1991 and the contents of the museum, along with the Bauer Collection and the Franciscan monastery treasury, were seized and taken to museums in Belgrade and Novi Sad. In December 2001 the collections were returned, and are gradually being restored. The Catholic church of SS Philip and James (Sv. Filip i Jakov) and the Orthodox church of St Nicholas (Sv. Nikola) were also badly damaged in 1991.

🏛 **Civic Museum**
L Ribara u. 2. 📞 *(032) 441 270.* ⬜ *8am–4pm Mon–Sat.*

Erdut ⑮

Map G2. 🏘 *1,500.* ⬛ *Osijek, 37 km (23 miles).* 🚌 *from Osijek.* ℹ️ **Regional:** *Sunčana ulica 39, Bizovac, (031) 675 897; Županijska 2, Osijek, (031) 203 755.*

THE TOWN OF ERDUT gained a place in history when, on 13 November 1995, an agreement between Croatia and Yugoslavia was drawn up here, setting out the return of Slavonia and Baranja to Croatia after almost four years of Serb occupation.

The town occupies an important strategic position overlooking the Danube, and a fortification was erected in Roman times. In the medieval period a **Castle** was built. It was damaged by the Turks, but then rebuilt by them. The castle was also used by the Habsburgs. Two towers, one circular and one square, survive from the old castle.

The large **Cseh Mansion**, where the 1995 agreement was drawn up, is now under repair. It was built in the 19th century by the Cseh family, lords of the manor in the area from the early 18th century.

The circular tower of the medieval castle, Erdut

Osijek ⑯

See pp188–91.

A naive outdoor sculpture,
Ernestinovo

Ernestinovo ⑰

Map F2. 🏠 200. ✈ Osijek, 20 km
(12 miles). 🚌 from Osijek.
🚩 **County:** Sunčana ulica 39,
Bizovac, (031) 675 897; Županijska 2,
Osijek, (031) 203 755. 🎨 Open-air
exhibition of sculpture (Aug).

FOR MANY YEARS, well-known
sculptors have been
meeting in Ernestinovo to
present their work in a
summer show. This small
village is now famous for its
open-air exhibitions. The first
exhibition was organized in
1976 by the sculptor Petar
Smajić. It took place in exile
from 1991 to 1996 and
returned to Ernestinovo the
following year. Many works
of art are displayed and
offered for sale in the village
galleries. Ernestinovo was
badly damaged during the
recent war, but the village
is now being rebuilt.

Kopački Rit Nature Park ⑱

See pp192–3.

Topolje ⑲

Map F2. 🏠 200. ✈ Osijek, 46 km
(28 miles). 🚆 Beli Manastir, 16 km
(10 miles). 🚌 from Osijek.
🚩 **Regional:** Sunčana ulica 39,
Bizovac, (031) 675 897.

IN 1687, AFTER the victory in
Vienna over the Turks,
Prince Eugene of Savoy,
commander of the Imperial

forces, decided to build a
church to commemorate the
victory in the countryside
surrounding Topolje. The
location has particular charm
as the church is set among
trees standing alone among a
patchwork of fields of maize
and tobacco. The church was
sacked, however, and nearly
completely destroyed in the
conflicts following the break-
up of former Yugoslavia.
The building is now
undergoing extensive
restoration although the
splendid furnishings have
sadly been lost.

Here, as in Darda, there
are several Hungarian
communities, who, together
with the Croats, are gradually
returning after their exile
during the Yugoslav
occupation. The Hungarian-
style houses with their
overhanging roofs add a
distinctive character to the
area. In the autumn, long
strings of chilli peppers
can be seen hanging out
to dry in the sun.

ENVIRONS: Around 10 km
(6 miles) east of Topolje is
the town of **Batina**. In Roman
times this was the site of a
fortress on the banks of the
River Danube and was known
by the name of Ad Militarae.
Until the war of 1991, which
depopulated this small town
set among hills and vineyards,
there was a bridge connecting
Baranja with Hungary and
Vojvodina, but since its
destruction, both river and
road traffic have stopped.

On one of the small hills,
a tall monument in white

Hungarian-style houses with chilli
peppers hanging to dry, Topolje

stone with a female figure in
bronze representing Victory
commemorates the fallen of
World War II. It is the work
of one of the great Croatian
artists of the 20th century,
Antun Augustinčić.

Mansion of the Esterházy barons,
now the Town Hall of Darda

Darda ⑳

Map F2.
🏠 6,700. ✈ Osijek, 15km (9 miles).
🚌 from Osijek.
🚩 **Regional:** Sunčana ulica 39,
Bizovac, (031) 675 897.

AN ELEGANT MANSION built by
the Esterházy barons in
the second half of the 18th
century, now renovated and
used as the Town Hall, is the
only evidence of Darda's
history. Darda was once a
fortified city, represented on
17th-century maps as a large
fortress, connected to Osijek
by the 8-km (5-mile) bridge
of Solimano. Built in 1566 to
cross marshland, the bridge
was destroyed in 1664 by
Nikola Zrinski (see p175) to
block the Turkish army. On
that occasion the city was
subsequently devastated.

In the recent war in the
1990s, two 18th-century
churches were destroyed: the
Catholic church of St John the
Baptist (Sv. Ivan Krstitelj) and
the Orthodox church of St
Michael (Sv. Mihajlo).

ENVIRONS: Bilje, 4 km (2
miles) south of Darda, is the
site of the information office
for the Kopački Rit Nature
Park (see pp192–3). It is
housed in a palace built by
Prince Eugene of Savoy, who
was granted the small town
of Bilje after the victory in
Vienna over the Turks (1687).

Osijek ⑯

THE CAPITAL OF SLAVONIA sits in the middle of a fertile plain. It is a centre of industry, a university town, and a lively Central European city with wide roads linking three districts: the Fort (Tvrđa), Lower Town (Donji grad) and Upper Town (Gornji grad). The city developed in 1786 when the three areas merged. Due to its position on the River Drava, Osijek has always played a strategic role. In 1806 Emperor Francis I declared it a Royal Free Town (this document is now in the Museum of Slavonia). In 1991, after the declaration of independence by Croatia, the city was bombed for over a year by Yugoslav forces and much of the old centre (Upper Town) was damaged. Liberated in 1995, in 1998 Osijek became part of the Croat state again.

View of the main square in the heart of Tvrđa

Exploring Osijek

The fort (Tvrđa) is the fortified centre of Osijek. It was constructed in the early 18th century after liberation from the Turks. Fortunately, Tvrđa did not suffer serious damage during the war in the 1990s. As a result it has preserved its Baroque architecture, which is characterized by simple, austere lines, unusual at this time. This lack of ornamentation was due to the fact that the buildings were intended for use by soldiers and office workers.

Facing Trg Sv. Trojstva, the central square of Tvrđa, named after the Holy Trinity, are various Baroque buildings, including the Building of the Guard, with an 18th-century clock tower, and the General Headquarters of Slavonia, which is now part of the university, and recognizable by its monumental Baroque entrance.

The heart of city life is the main square in the Upper Town, Trg Ante Starčevića.

With its shops, bars and restaurants, this is Osijek's modern face, dating back to the second half of the 19th century and the early 20th century. Facing the square is the County building, built in the early 20th century in the Renaissance style.

🏛 Museum of Slavonia
Muzej Slavonije
Trg Sv. Trojstva 6, Tvrđa. **(** (031) 208 501. **○** 10am–1pm Tue–Fri; 7–10pm Sat. **▨ ✔ ✗ ❑**
On the eastern side is the old Town Hall which has housed the Museum of Slavonia since 1946. Geological, prehistoric, Greek, Illyrian and Roman objects are on display here. One section is dedicated to ancient Roman Mursa with statues, tombstones, architectural pieces and a coin collection.

Other sections are dedicated to folklore with exhibits of richly decorated costumes. Today these clothes provide models for a flourishing handicrafts industry making golden silk fabrics.

⛪ Church of the Holy Cross
Sv. Križ
Franjevačka ulica, Tvrđa. **(** (031) 208 177. **○** 8am–noon, 3–8pm.
Northeast of the main square, on the site of a sacred medieval building, stands the church of the Holy Cross, built by the Franciscans between 1709 and 1720. Next to this is the monastery (1699–1767) which housed the first printing press in Slavonia (1735), and from the mid-18th century also housed schools of philosophy and theology. In the church is a statue of the Virgin from the 15th century and some liturgical furnishings.

⛪ Church of St Michael
Sv. Mihovil
Trg Jurja Križanića, Tvrđa. **(** (031) 208 990. **○** before mass.
Standing a little way back from the square is the church of St Michael, which was built by the Jesuits. The façade is flanked by two bell towers, and the monastery has a splendid doorway (1719). Below street level the foundations of the 16th-century Kasim-paša mosque are still visible.

War memorial in Kralja Držislava park

⚑ Europe Avenue
Europska Avenija
This is the main road of Osijek, linking the Fort (Tvrđa) to the Upper Town (Gornji grad). It crosses some of the city's parks, one of which is Kralja Držislava park, site of a striking bronze memorial to the fallen of the 78th Infantry Regiment (*Soldier in the Throes of Death*), by Robert Frangeš-

Interior of the Neo-Gothic
church of SS Peter and Paul

Mihanović (1898), which is
regarded as the first modern
sculpture in Croatia.

🏛 Gallery of Fine Arts
Galerija likovnih umjetnosti
Europska Avenija 9. 📞 (031) 213
587. 🕐 9am–noon, 5–8pm Mon–Fri;
10am–1pm Sat & Sun. 📷 🎬 by
appt. 🚫
The Gallery of Fine Arts,
founded in 1954, is housed
in an elegant 19th-century
house. There are collections
of paintings from the 18th
and 19th centuries, as well
as works by contemporary
Croatian artists. There is also
a section dedicated to the
"Osijek School".

🔒 Church and Monastery of St James
Sv. Jakov
Kapucinska ulica 41, Gornji grad.
📞 (031) 201 183. 🕐 8am–noon,
3–8pm.
The oldest building in the
city is the church of St James
(1702–27), with a Capuchin
monastery. In the sacristy are
mid-18th-century paintings
about the life of St Francis.

🔒 Church of SS Peter and Paul
Sv. Petar i Pavao
Trg Marina Držica, Gornji grad.
📞 (031) 369 626. 🕐 noon–3pm,
5–5.30pm.
This imposing Neo-Gothic
church is dedicated to St
Peter and St Paul. The church
is known as "Katedrala"
(cathedral) to the locals
because of its size: the façade
has towers 90 m (295 ft)
high. It was designed by
Franz Langenberg and
built in the late 19th
century. The 40 stained-
glass windows and some
of the sculptures are by
the Viennese artist
Eduard Hauser. Most of
the windows were
bomb-damaged but are
now being restored.

VISITORS' CHECKLIST

Map F2. 🏘 107,000. ✈ 5 km
(3 miles) Sv. Leopolda Mandića,
(031) 297 340. 🚆 Bartula
Kašića, (031) 214 355. 🚌 Trg
Ružičke, (031) 205 155.
🛈 **Local:** Županijska 2, (031)
203 755; **Regional:** Sunčana
ulica. 39, Bizovac, (031) 675
897. 🎭 Music Festival of the
Croatian Drum (May), City day (2
Dec), Summer Nights of Osijek.

🎭 Croatian National Theatre
Hrvatsko Narodno Kazalište
Županijska ulica 9, Gornji grad.
📞 (031) 220 700.
The Croatian National Theatre
was built in the Moorish style
in the early 19th century. Opera
and drama productions are
put on from September to May.

Interior of the Croatian National Theatre

OSIJEK CITY CENTRE

Church of the Holy Cross ②
Church of St James ⑥
Church of St Michael ③
Church of SS
  Peter and Paul ⑦
Croatian National Theatre ⑧
Europe Avenue ④
Gallery of Fine Arts ⑤
Museum of Slavonia ①

KEY

🟦 Street-by-Street pp190–91

🛈 Tourist information

🔒 Church

🅿 Parking

⊠ Post office

0 metres   500

0 yards   500

Street-by-Street: the Fort (Tvrđa)

Parchment with the title of "Royal Free Town"

T HE FORTIFIED CENTRE of Osijek (Tvrđa) was built on the site of the Roman settlement of Mursa, which, in 131 AD, became the capital of Lower Pannonia with the name of Colonia Aelia Mursa. Destroyed by the Avars and rebuilt by the Croats, it remained a military and administrative centre until it was attacked and burnt by the Turks in 1526. Making the most of the strategic position, the Turks rebuilt the Fort and, under Suleyman II, also constructed a bridge across the Drava. After the expulsion of the Turks in 1687, the Austrian Emperor destroyed the mosques and other reminders of Turkish rule. He then built a fortified series of buildings more like a city than a fort. Tvrđa now houses the Town Hall, the university faculties, and the Museum of Slavonia. The only remaining part of the ramparts is towards the river Drava and includes the "Water Gate" (Vodena Vrata).

★ Church of St Michael
Constructed by Jesuits in the first half of the 18th century, the church has a Baroque façade flanked by two towers.

Building of the Guard
On the western side of the square stands the Building of the Guard, with a clock tower from the 18th century and fine porticoes.

TRG J. KRIŽANIĆA

FRANJE

KAMILA FIRINGERA

PINTEROVIĆ

KUHAČA

TRG SVETOG TROJSTV

MARKOVIĆA

BOSKOVIĆA

KAMILA FIRINGERA

Croatian Academy of Science and Arts

Plague Column
The centre of the square is dominated by the "column of the plague", erected in 1729 in thanks for the ending of an outbreak of the disease.

KEY

- – – Suggested route

STAR SIGHTS

- ★ Church of St Michael

- ★ Museum of Slavonia

Church and Monastery of the Holy Cross
The church, erected by Franciscans between 1709 and 1720, is next to the monastery which housed the first printing press in Slavonia.

View of Osijek and the River Drava
Splendid views of the city can be enjoyed from the banks of the Drava. It was once important for river trading, but trade is now practically non-existent.

TANCIĆA

TRG VATROSLAVA
LISINSKOG

BOSENDORFERA

FRANJEVAČKA

FRAKULTETSKA

FRANJE

KUHAČA

JAGIĆA

FRANJEVAČKA

Darda
(see p187)

KNEZA TRPIMIRA

0 metres 100

0 yards 100

Đakovo
(see p184)

★ Museum of Slavonia
This museum contains interesting collections of geological, prehistoric, Greek, Illyrian and Roman material.

Headquarters of Slavonia
On the northern side of the main square of Tvrđa is the former Headquarters of Slavonia, now the University Rectorate, easily recognized by the imposing façade.

Kopački Rit Nature Park ⑱
Park Prirode Kopački Rit

THIS TRIANGULAR PIECE OF LAND is bordered by the final stretch of the river Drava before it meets the Danube. The landscape changes with the seasons and becomes flooded when the Danube overflows. The area covers 170 sq km (65 sq miles) and can turn into an immense wetland marsh. At other times it is a vast grassland plain with pools and ponds. There are also dry areas which support enormous willows and tall oak trees. A nature reserve since 1967, it has a rich and varied fauna and for many months of the year provides a sanctuary for hundreds of different species of bird, both migratory and domestic. A high embankment on the western side stops the further spread of the flood waters. On top is a road which allows cars to cross this part of the park.

White Storks
One of the park's symbols, the white stork is especially visible in the breeding season.

Park Entrance
The main entrance to the Kopački Rit Park is in the village of Bilje (see p187).

OSIJEK

| 0 kilometres | 2 |
| 0 miles | 2 |

Black Storks are rare; only a few dozen pairs of the bird inhabit the park.

Sakadaš Canal

Sarvaška Pond

Drava

Lakes
Forty different species of fish live in the lakes and ponds which form in the park.

Drava

White-Tailed Eagle
The many birds of prey maintain a balance among the bird population. The white-tailed eagle is the rarest eagle in Europe.

Waterfowl
Ponds and lakes provide an ideal habitat for the wading birds and swans which are present all year round.

Deer and Roe deer in their hundreds congregate in the flooded areas of the park, for brief periods of the year.

Great Crested Grebe
The mating display of these birds is one of the more spectacular sights in the park.

Ducks and Geese
The mallard duck is a much photographed bird for its bright plumage. There are also pochards, shovelers and tufted ducks.

Wild Boar
During the spring it is sometimes possible to see whole families of this shy animal in the oak woods.

Danube

Kopačko Lake

Bjelo Lake

Hulovski Canal

Danube

Drava

Cormorant
Usually found in colonies, cormorants build their nests in trees. Here, thousands of their nests can be seen in the tall willow and poplar trees.

KEY

━━ Major road

━━ Scenic road

ℹ Tourist information

The thermal spa in the village of Bizovac

Bizovac ❹

Map F2.
🏘 *5,000.* ✈ *Osijek, 20 km (12 miles).* 🚆 *from Osijek.* 🚌 *from Osijek.* 🛈 **Regional:** *Sunčana ulica 39, (031) 675 897.*

DURING THE SEARCH for petroleum in the middle of the 20th century, a hot water spring was discovered here. The water of the spring reaches a temperature of 90°C (194°F) and is rich in minerals. A few years later, the thermal spa of **Bizovačke Toplice** was built. The spa proved to be extremely successful and it is now an enormous complex including a hotel, two large swimming pools, and cabins for mud baths. Every day hundreds of guests come here to undergo thermal treatments which are helpful in treating rheumatic and respiratory illnesses, and in healing injuries.

The small centre of Bizovac is also well known in Slavonia for its exquisite gold and silver embroidery. The work is carried out by the young women of the area, usually to a commission.

🟦 **Bizovačke Toplice**
Suncana 39. ☎ *(031) 685 180.*
🌐 www.bizovacke-toplice.hr

ENVIRONS: Around 9 km (5 miles) south of Bizovac is the village of **Brodanci**, famous for the Olympics of Ancient Sports, held here in August every year. During the competition, athletes take part in some of the sports once practised by the peasants of Slavonia, such as tug-of-war, boulder-throwing, bare-back riding and other strenuous challenges and competitions.

A lively popular festival has developed around the event; musicians perform in the streets and there are displays of old crafts. Local handicrafts can be bought and regional food can be sampled.

Valpovo ❷❷

Map F2. 🏘 *8,200.*
✈ *Osijek, 30 km (18 miles).* 🚌 *(031) 651 185.* 🛈 *Ulica Matije Gupca 32, (031) 656 200.* 🎭 *Summer in Valpovo: dancing, folk music and theatrical shows (summer).*

THE CENTRE OF Valpovo stands on the remains of the fort of Lovallia, one of many fortified settlements which the Romans established on the Pannonian plain. In the Middle Ages, a castle was erected to keep a look-out over the nearby Drava river. The castle was later granted to the Morović, Gorjanski and Norman families. After the Turkish conquest in 1526, the castle was used as a garrison.

In 1687, after the expulsion of the Turks, the area was handed over to the Hilleprand Prandau family. At the beginning of the 19th century they demolished parts of the castle in order to construct the large building which today houses the **Valpovo Museum** (Muzej Valpovštine). The museum contains period furniture and interesting archaeological finds. The complex stands in a large

The imposing castle at Valpovo, now a museum

park and a moat surrounds the medieval walls, the tower, the new building and the church. A town developed around the fort, and with it the splendid Baroque church of the **Immaculate Conception** (Začeće Marijino) of 1722.

🏛 **Valpovo Museum**
Dvorac Prandan-Norman.
☎ *(031) 650 490.*
⚫ *for restoration. The old castle, park and tower can be visited.*

Majláth, a mock-medieval manor in the town of Donji Miholjac

Donji Miholjac ❷❸

Map F2. 🏘 *7,000.* ✈ *Osijek, 45 km (28 miles).* 🚆 *Valpovo, 20 km (12 miles); Našice, 30 km (18 miles).* 🚌 *(031) 631 207.* 🛈 *Kolodorska 2, (031) 633 103.* 🎭 *Miholjačko Sijelo: festival in costume (summer).*

ON THE BANKS of the Drava river, this small town lies on the Hungarian border. All traces of the past have been erased, except for the church of **St Michael** (Sv. Mihovil), which has Romanesque origins. The mock-medieval **Majláth Manor** was built at the beginning of the 20th century by the Majláth family. It has pinnacles and a tall tower on the façade. The manor is now the town hall.

🚪 **Majláth Manor**
Vukovarska 1. ☎ *Tourist Office (031) 633 103.* ⚪ *by appt.* 🎭

ENVIRONS: About 25 km (15 miles) west is the village of **Čadavica**. Traces from ancient Croatian settlements have been discovered near here. The Romanesque church of St Peter was used by the Turks as a mosque and was renovated in the 18th century.

Našice ❷

Map F2. 🏛 *8,300.* 🚉 *Osijek, 42 km (26 miles).* 🚌 *(060) 333 444.* 🚍 *(060) 313 333.* ❚ *Pejačevićev trg 4, (031) 614 951.*

A SMALL PLATEAU is the setting for the town of Našice, which is surrounded by vineyards and woods. Built on the site of an ancient settlement, it was referred to in the first half of the 13th century under the name of Nekche, as property of the Templar Knights. After the dissolution of this order in 1312, it passed to the Gorjanski nobles and, later, through marriage, to the counts of Ilok, before falling into the hands of the Turkish forces in 1532.

After the expulsion of the Turks, Našice's fortunes changed. The Franciscans returned and restored the church of **St Anthony of Padua** (Sv. Antun Padovanski). They also rebuilt their monastery, which had been founded here at the start of the 14th century. Both needed repairing after war damage suffered in 1991.

A short distance away is a large manor house, built at the beginning of the 19th century in Neo-Classical style by the Pejačević family, where the musician Dora Pejačević (1885–1923) lived. Situated in a large park, the two-storey building has recently been restored.

The church of St Anthony of Padua in Našice

This building is now the **Civic Museum**.

🏛 **Civic Museum**
Pejačevićev trg 5. ❚ *(031) 613 414.* ⬚ *8am–3pm Mon–Fri; 9am–noon Sat.* 🎦 ✔ ⚲

Orahovica ❷

Map F2. 🏛 *4,300.* 🚉 *Osijek, 62 km (38 miles).* 🚌 *(033) 646 079.* 🚍 *(033) 673 231.* ❚ *Kralja Zvonimira 5, (033) 673 270/ 414.* 🎪 *Spring in Orahovica: folklore event (Jun).*

T HE TOWN OF ORAHOVICA is well known in Croatia for its wines. It was a feudal estate in 1228, and later a Turkish garrison, acquiring its present-day look in the 18th century.

On one of the hills around the town stand the ruins of **Rosetta** (Ružica Grad), one of the largest of Croatia's medieval forts. The walls were 9m (29 ft) thick and enclosed military buildings, a church, and the governor's residence. The complex was so large it was often referred to as a city.

The Turks burnt down the fort, then partially restored it and used it as a military garrison. Liberated in 1690, the fort was once again used for defence, and a village, inhabited by Serbs, developed around its base.

ENVIRONS: Along the road to Kutjevo, 5 km (3 miles) south of Orahovica, near the village of Duzluk, is the Orthodox **Monastery of St Nicholas** (Manastir Sv. Nikola), which has ancient frescoes and illuminated manuscripts. Some 30 km (18 miles) from Orahovica, following the road to Virovitica, then turning left for Ceraljie, is **Voćin**, a small village where the destruction caused by the war in 1991 is still evident. The village lies at the foot of a large castle built in the second half of the 13th

century by the Aba counts. Today, the houses in Voćin are in ruins. All that remains of the church of **St Mary** (Sv. Maria), which was built by King John Corvinus in the first half of the 15th century, is part of the apse wall.

The ornate altar in the Baroque church of St Roch, Virovitica

Virovitica ❷

Map E2. 🏛 *16,000.* 🚉 *Osijek, 89 km (55 miles).* 🚌 *Ulica Stjepana Radića, (033) 730 121.* 🚍 *Trg Fra. B. Gerbera 1, (033) 721 113.* ❚ *Trg Kralja Tomislava 1, (033) 721 241.* 🎪 *Day of the City (16 Aug).*

D OCUMENTS from the end of the first millennium give the town its Hungarian name of Wereuche. It was declared a free town by King Bela IV in 1234 and it developed into an agricultural and trading centre. Later occupied by the Turks, it remained under their rule until 1684. When it later flourished, all Ottoman traces were destroyed.

The Baroque church of **St Roch** (Sv. Rok), decorated by the sculptor Holzinger and the painter Göbler, dates from the 18th century. On the site of the ancient Wasserburg Castle stands the imposing **Pejačević Manor** (1800–4), now the **Civic Museum** (Gradski Muzej) with archaeological and folklore collections and an art gallery.

🏛 **Civic Museum**
Palazzo Pejačević, Trg Bana Jelačića. ❚ *(033) 722 127.* ⬚ *9am–2pm Mon, Wed, Fri; 9am–7pm Tue, Thu; 9am–noon Sat.*

THE NORTHERN COUNTIES

THE LANDSCAPE IN THIS PART OF CROATIA *is made up of a variety of elements: the rolling hills of Zagorje with their therapeutic spring waters and thermal spas; the county of Prekmura, which is famous for its wines; the cities of Varaždin and Čakovec, which developed around ancient castles; Koprivnica, surrounded by lush countryside and vineyards, and Bjelovar and Križevci with their palaces.*

The principal towns in the area have ancient origins and two, Varaždin and Križevci, were also at various times the seat of the Sabor, the Croatian Parliament. Bjelovar is the most recent and largest city-fortress in the country. Even before the 1991 war which affected the south of this area, the wars of the second half of the 18th century had already destroyed all evidence of the Middle Ages and Turkish occupation.

However, there are many religious buildings in the area, including a number of Catholic Franciscan and Pauline monasteries in places once inhabited by Orthodox communities. Religious life is still very active here and church buildings are cherished.

Porcelain plate in the Naive Museum in Hlebine

The high hills of Zagorje are covered in forests, broken up only by the clearings created for imposing medieval castles, many of which have since been transformed into sumptuous Baroque residences. In Podravina, drained by the River Drava, which in some parts flows along the Hungarian border, the hills are lower and are characterized by vineyards and sparse woodland.

This part of Croatia has preserved all kinds of ancient customs and traditions, a source of inspiration for the Naive art movement. The home of Naive art is Hlebine, where artists such as Ivan Generalić encouraged and fostered the talent of local amateur painters.

Typical countryside between Belec and Marija Bistrica

◁ Café life in the pretty Baroque town of Varaždin

Exploring the Northern Counties

THIS IS AN AREA OF good, fertile agricultural land and the lush countryside produces an abundance of maize, tobacco and sunflowers. The hillsides are covered in vineyards as far as the eye can see and yield wines, good whites in particular, which can be bought along the Wine Road, from wineries or in the village shops. Despite these attractions, the region does not see a great deal of international tourism. This is particularly true of Međimurje, the valley crossed by the River Mura, granted to Croatia after World War I. Part of the population here is of Hungarian origin and the people have preserved their Hungarian customs and traditions.

A side chapel of St Mary of the Snows, Marija Bistrica

View of the castle in Veliki Tabor

ŠTRIGOVA

VINICA

Maribor

TRAKOŠĆAN

VINAGORA

VELIKI TABOR

KRAPINA   LEPOGLAVA

PREGRADA   SUTINSKE TOPLICE   BELEC

KRAPINSKE TOPLICE

MILIJANA   Z A G O R J E   TOUR OF THE THERMAL SPAS

KUMROVEC   TUHELJSKE TOPLICE

KLANJEC   BEDEKOVČINA

ZABOK

STUBIČKE TOPLICE   MARIJA BISTRICA   SVETI IVAN ZELINA

M E D V E D N I C A

Zagreb   Zagreb

0 kilometres   15

0 miles   15

SEE ALSO

• *Where to Stay* p227

• *Where to Eat* p241

SIGHTS AT A GLANCE

GETTING AROUND

New motorways connecting Zagreb to Maribor in
Slovenia, and passing through Krapina and Hungary
(and serving Varaždin), are currently being built. In the
meantime, cars have to use the state roads which run
more or less parallel to the two motorways. State road 3
goes from the Slovenian border, northwest of Varaždin,
and continues on towards Osijek. A railway line runs
alongside state road 3 and at Varaždin interconnects with
railway lines from Zagreb, Slovenia and Hungary. There
are also train connections to Slovenia and Hungary from
Čakovec and Koprivnica stations.

LOCATOR MAP

A Naive painting from the Hlebine Gallery

Varaždin Castle in winter

KEY

▬	Motorway
▬	Main road
▬	Minor road
---	Railway line
✹	Viewpoint

Varaždin ●

Door detail, church of the Assumption

Traces of occupation from the Neolithic age, the La Tene civilization and the Roman period have been found around Varaždin castle. Despite this, the first mention of the town is found in a document from 1181, when King Bela III confirmed the rights of the Zagreb Curia to the thermal spas in the area. In 1209, it was declared a free town by King Andrew II and it began to develop as a trading centre. In the late 14th century it passed into the hands of the counts of Celjski, followed by the counts of Frankopan, Brandenburg and Erdödy. In 1446, it was destroyed in a fire and in 1527 the Turks attacked. In 1776 another fire destroyed the houses, but the Baroque buildings, for which the town is famous, were fortunately spared.

Aerial view of the Castle, today home to the Civic Museum

🏛 Castle and Civic Museum
Stari Grad & Gradski Muzej
Strossmayerovo šetalište 7.
🄲 (042) 210 399. ◯ 10am–3pm Tue–Fri; 10am–1pm Sat & Sun. 🖾 🖪 🗷
This castle was built by the Zrinskis (the rectangular tower is from this period) over the ruins of an observation tower and, in the 15th century, two round towers were added. The castle was rebuilt in 1560 by the Italian architect Domenico dell'Allio, who created a Renaissance structure on two floors with arcades and corridors facing courtyards.

The castle's present look dates from the time of the Erdödy counts, who added the bastions and a moat. It is now the Civic Museum which has collections of weapons, porcelain, furniture, handicrafts, and a pharmacy from the 18th century. Remains of the wall and the Lisak tower, to the east of the castle, are the only evidence remaining of the ancient walls.

🏛 Gallery of Old and Modern Masters
Galerija Starih i Novih Majstora
Stančićev trg 3. 🄲 (042) 214 172.
◯ 10am–2pm Tue–Fri; 10am–1pm Sat & Sun. 🖾 🖪 by appt. 🗷
The gallery has a large collection of works from all over Europe, particularly landscapes by Flemish and Italian artists, and portraits by German and Dutch painters.

🏛 Tomislav Square
Trg Kralja Tomislava
Town Hall (Gradsk Vijećnica):
Trg kralja Tomislava 1. 🄲 (042) 210 985. ◯ by appt.
Drašković Palace (Dvor Drašković):
Trg kralja Tomislava 3. 🄲 (042) 210 985. 🖪 to the public.
This square is the heart of the town. Facing the square is the **Town Hall** (Gradska Vijećnica), the oldest building in Varaždin. Built in the Gothic style in the 15th century, it has since been altered and a clock tower added. It has been the Town Hall since 1523, when Prince George of Brandenburg gave

it to the city. It is guarded in summer by the Purgars, who wear richly decorated blue uniforms and bearskin hats.

To the east of the square stands **Drašković Palace** (Dvor Drašković), built in the late 17th century with a Rococo façade. The Croat Parliament met here in 1756–76. Opposite stands the Renaissance Ritz House, one of the oldest in the town, as evidenced by the date (1540) engraved on the doorway.

🏛 Cathedral of the Assumption
Uznesenja Marijina
Pavlinska ulica. 🄲 (042) 210 688.
◯ 8am–12.30pm, 4–6pm daily.
The church of the Assumption became a cathedral in 1997. Both the church and the annexed monastery were built in the first half of the 17th century by the Jesuits. Later, the Pauline order moved in.

The cathedral's tall façade is enlivened by pillars. The interior is a triumph of the Baroque. The main altar occupies the width of the central nave and has gilded columns, stuccoes and engravings. At the centre of the altar is an *Assumption of the Virgin*, reminiscent of Titian's work in Venice. Evenings of Baroque music concerts are held here.

The rich Baroque altar in the Cathedral of the Assumption

🏛 Church of St John the Baptist
Sv. Ivan Krstitelj
Franjevački trg 8. 🄲 (042) 213 166.
◯ 7am–noon, 5.30–7.30pm daily.
The church was built in 1650 in the Baroque style on the site of a 13th-century church. The façade has a Renaissance

The bell tower of St John the Baptist in Tomislav Square

doorway with a tympanum and two statues of St Francis of Assisi and St Anthony of Padua. The interior has eight side chapels and an ornate gilded pulpit from the late 17th century. The bell tower is 54 m (177 ft) high.

In front of the church is one of the copies of the *Monument of Bishop Gregory of Nin* by Ivan Meštrović. The adjacent pharmacy has many works of art, among them some allegorical frescoes by Ivan Ranger *(see p204)*.

🏛 Herzer Palace
Dvor Herzer
Franjevački trg 6. **(** *(042) 210 474.* ● *for restoration.*
Entomological Museum: (*(042) 210 474.* ○ *10am–3pm Tue–Fri; 10am–1pm Sat & Sun.* 🈂 📷 🚫
Built at the end of the 19th century (the founders' coat of arms is on the door), the palace has housed the well-organized **Entomological Museum** (Entomoloski Odjel) since 1954. The museum was founded thanks to the entomologist Franjo Košćec (1882–1968), who, in 1959, donated his natural history collection to the city. From 1962 to 1980, his work was carried on by his daughter Ružica, a biologist. As well as thousands of insects, the museum also has a herbarium. Periodically the museum organizes exhibitions on the effects insects have on the land and its inhabitants.

🏠 Church of the Holy Trinity
Sv. Trojstvo
Kapucinski trg. **(** *(042) 213 166.* ○ *10am–noon, 4–6pm daily.*
The church dates from the early 18th century and houses numerous Baroque paintings,

furnishings by local masters, and an organ with figures of angels playing instruments.

The neighbouring monastery, which dates from the same period, is famous for its library which contains many parchments, incunabula and manuscripts, and some of the oldest documents written in ancient Croatian *(kajkavski)*.

🏛 National Theatre
Narodno Kazalište
Ulica Augusta Cesarca 1.
(*(042) 214 688.* ○ *for performances only.*
Built by Hermann Helmer in 1873, this is one of the main cultural centres in the city. During the summer and autumn, theatre-goers from all over Europe come to attend the performances.

VARAŽDIN TOWN CENTRE

Castle and Civic Museum ①
Cathedral of
  the Assumption ④
Church of
  St John the Baptist ⑤
Church of the Holy Trinity ⑦
Gallery of Old
  and Modern Masters ②
Herzer Palace ⑥
National Theatre ⑧
Tomislav Square ③

KEY

🛈 Tourist information

✝ Church

🅿 Parking

🚌 Bus station

✉ Post office

MARIBOR
V. NAZORA
TRG BANA JELAČIĆA
ČAKOVEC
S. VRAZA
LI. GAJA
A. ŠENOE
A. ŠENOE
TRG M. STANČIČEV
LISINSKOG
URŠULINSKA
FRANJEVAČKI TRG
PAVLINSKA
A. STEPINCA
KAČIĆA MIOSIĆA
DRAŠKOVIĆA
GUNDULIĆA
CANKARA
KOPRIVNICA
railway station
IVANEČ
KAPUCINSKI TRG
A. CESARCA
ZRINSKIH I FRANKOPANA
KAPUCINSKI TRG

0 metres 200
0 yards 200

Vineyards in the countryside around Čakovec

Čakovec ❷

Map D1. 🏠 *16,000.* 🚉 *(040) 384
333.* 🚌 *Masarykova ulica, (040) 313
947.* 🛈 **Local:** *Kralja Tomislava 1,
(040) 313 319, 310 969;* **Regional:**
R. Boškovića 2, (040) 374 254.
🎭 *Croatian music (Carnival);
Founding of the city festival (29 May).*
🌐 *www.tourism-cakovec.hr*

In THE SECOND HALF of the
13th century, on a site
once inhabited by Romans,
Count Demetrius Chaky, a
magistrate at the court of King
Bela IV, built a tower here
which was called Chaktornya.
In the following century, the
main defensive structure in
Međimurje was built around
the tower. In 1547 Emperor
Ferdinand gave it to the Ban
(governor) of Croatia, Nikola
Zrinski *(see p175)*, together
with a large estate, as a
reward for the victory against
the Turks and to settle a debt.

Nikola Zrinski died heroically
while fighting against the
Ottomans in defending Siget,
and became a national hero.
On 29 May 1579, one of his
successors, a member of the
Zrinski family of Siget,
guaranteed tax privileges to
whoever went to live in the
city that was developing
around the fort. This date is
considered the founding of
the city and is celebrated with
a festival. Bastions and a moat
were added in this period as
defence against cannon fire.
Inside the walls, a four-storey
palace was built around a
square courtyard.
   In 1671 Petar Zrinski led a
plot to separate Croatia from
the Kingdom of Hungary.
The plot was discovered and
Zrinski and his co-conspirator
Franjo Krsto Frankopan were
beheaded on 30 April 1671.
Čakovec then came under the
direct rule of the Emperor.

The Renaissance "**Old
Castle**", of which only the
first floor remains, and the
Baroque "**New Castle**" with a
rectangular plan, face each
other inside the medieval
walls. For a long time the
Old Castle was used as a
prison. It is now being
restored and is to be used in
future for cultural activities.
The church has been
reopened for worship.
   The **Međimurje Civic
Museum** of Čakovec has on
display exhibits of prehistoric
material, many Roman finds,
and ethnographic collections.
There is also an exhibition
dedicated to the local
composer, J Slavenski
(1896–1955), who was known
for his love of the traditional
music of the region.
   Čakovec is the main
administrative centre of the
Međimurje, a frontier region
which borders Slovenia and
Hungary. The land in the
western part of the region is
hilly with broad valleys, and
is renowned for its wines,
while the fertile plains of
the eastern part produce
cereal crops.

🏛 **Međimurje Civic Museum**
Trg Republike 5. 📞 *(040) 313 285.*
🕐 *10am–3pm Tue–Fri; 10am–1pm
Sat–Sun.* 🈺 📷

ENVIRONS: In a small village
2 km (1 mile) from Čakovec
stands the church of **St Helen**
(Sv. Helena). What little
remains of its original Gothic

The Old and New castles of Čakovec

The frescoed façade of the church of St Jerome, Štrigova

form has been integrated into an overall Baroque appearance. The church is all that survives of the monastery founded by the Paulines in 1376. It has been rebuilt at various times, firstly after a Protestant revolt, then because of a fire and finally after an earthquake.

Inside the church are the tombstones of the powerful Zrinski family, the lords of Čakovec: that of Nikola Zrinski and his wife Catherine Frankopan, and also that of Petar Zrinski.

The church also contains several tombs of members of the Kneževič family, who became the successors to the Zrinskis.

Fresco on the door of the church of St Jerome, Štrigova

into a palace in the 17th century. At one time the palace was famous for its rich furnishings, its art collections, and for the fact that the Hungarian king, Matthias Corvinus, was often a guest here.

The church of **St Jerome** (Sv. Jerolim) stands on a hill at the edge of the village. Restoration has uncovered the frescoes above the doorway and in the niches on the façade, which is flanked by two harmonious bell towers and culminates in a curvilinear tympanum.

In the church are numerous *trompe-l'œil* paintings by the Tyrolean artist Ivan Ranger *(see p204)*, depicting *Angels*, the *Evangelists* and the *Life of St Jerome*. There are also statues representing the fathers of the Church.

Vinica ❹

Map D1.
🏃 1,200. 🚌 *from Varaždin.*
🛈 **Regional:** *(042) 394 000.*

THIS SMALL TOWN lies at the foot of vine-covered hills. It was first mentioned in documents in 1353 as the site of a medieval fortress. At one time it was known for the large palace built by the Patačić counts on the site of their old castle. The palace

is now in ruins, as is that of the Draškovič counts, which was situated in the centre of a large park.

In the late 19th century, Count Marko Bombelles created **Opeka Park**, 2 km (1 mile) south of Vinica. This large arboretum was at that time the only one of its kind in Croatia. Here Bombelles planted exotic trees and plants from around the world, including the Americas, Japan, Tibet and the Caucasus, over an area of flat and hilly ground.

Next to this wonderful park, declared a protected nature reserve in 1961, a School of Horticulture has been set up. This school has several glasshouses and a large garden of flowering plants.

🌷 **Opeka Park**
⬜ *at all times.*

One of the frescoes decorating the church of St Helen, Čakovec

Štrigova ❸

Map D1.
🏃 600. 🚌 *from Čakovec.*
🚌 *from Čakovec.* 🛈 **Regional:**
R Boškoviča 2, (040) 374 254.

NUMEROUS FINDS of Roman origin have been discovered here, leading historians to believe that this village was built on the site of the Roman city of Stridon, the birthplace of St Jerome.

The counts of Strigovcak lived here, but their castle was destroyed during a raid by the Turks. Nearby, the Bannfy counts also built a castle, which was transformed

Colourful floral display in Opeka Park, near Vinica

Choir stalls in the church of St Mary, frescoed by the artist Ivan Ranger

frescoes can be found here. Also of interest is the pulpit and the altar of St Anne by the Pauline monk and sculptor Aleksije Köninger.

🔒 **Church of St Mary**
Trg 1. hrvatskog sveučilišta 3.
📞 *(042) 791 128.*
⭘ *by appt.*

Lepoglava ❺

Map D1. 🏚 *38,000.*
🚉 *(042) 791 193.* 🚌 *for Ivanec.*
ℹ **Local:** *Trg 1. hrvatskog sveučilišta 5, (042) 791 670;*
Regional: *Varaždin, (042) 394 000.*
🎭 *Lace exhibition (Sep).*

THIS TOWN IS FAMOUS for the intricate lace which is made here, thanks to its Lace School, which was founded some centuries ago.

The town is also notorious in Croatia as being the site of a historic prison. At various times, Marshal Tito and Archbishop Stepinac, head of the church in Croatia in World War II, among others, were imprisoned here.

The prison building was formerly a Pauline monastery, built on the orders of the Count of Celje at the end of the 14th century. It was embellished and enlarged in the second half of the following century by King Matthias Corvinus. It was used as a school of theology, grammar and philosophy, as well as a secondary school open to lay pupils.

In 1854, after the dissolution of the Pauline order, the monks' cells became prison cells. Behind the large, ancient cloisters a more modern prison was built, but it is no longer in use and is awaiting repair.

However, restoration has been completed on the beautiful Gothic church of **St Mary** (Sv. Marija), which was

rebuilt in the Baroque style in the late 17th century. The church has a single nave and polygonal choir. The façade has prominent pilasters enclosing niches, and two tympana. Inside is 18th-century stuccowork by Antonio Giulio Quaglio alongside magnificent works by the fresco painter Ivan Ranger (of note is his *Apocalypse* in the choir stalls). Ranger's largest cycle of

Typical lace from Lepoglava

Trakošćan ❻

Map D1. 🏚 *30.*
🚌 *for Bednja.* ℹ **Regional:** *Varaždin, (042) 394 000.*
🌐 *www.trakoscan.net*

THE PRETTY surroundings of the **Castle of Trakošćan**, and its excellent state of conservation, make this one of the most visited tourist sights in Zagorje. The castle was built to guard the road which descends from Ptuj towards the valley of the River Sava. The castle was listed in 1434 as one of the properties granted by Sigismund of Austria to the Count of Celje. It was used for defence purposes until the

IVAN RANGER (JOHANNES BAPTISTE RANGER)

Born in Axams, today a suburb of Innsbruck in Austria, in 1700, Ivan Ranger joined the Pauline order at a very early age. Not much is known of his years as an apprentice, but it is certain that he lived for a time in Italy, where he encountered the Baroque style in Venice, Rome, Bologna and Mantua. At the age of 30 he was invited to Lepoglava, then the headquarters of the order, to which he remained loyal until his death in 1753. He also worked in nearby towns and in Slovenia (at the monastery of Olimje and the castle-monastery of Sveti Jernej in Rogatec). In line with Pauline principles, he created a school of fresco painters. With these artists he produced colourful fresco cycles which were full of expression (the *trompe-l'œil* paintings also reveal great technical skill). His themes were always religious, and he was much imitated.

Fresco painted by the Pauline monk Ivan Ranger

The Castle of Trakošćan, now a museum

end of Turkish rule. In 1568 it became the property of the Drašković counts.

During the second half of the 19th century, it was transformed into a splendid Neo-Gothic residence by Djuro Drašković. He also added an artificial lake, a park and gardens, while at the same time preserving some of the military aspects of the castle. It stands on a wooded hilltop and is surrounded by a high wall with a tower, which encircles the imposing palace.

In 1953, 25 of the rooms were turned into a **Museum** where furniture, armoury, vestments and paintings, as well as a rare series of portraits of the Drašković family, are on display.

⛪ Castle and Museum
【 (042) 796 422, 796 495.
⏱ Jun–Sep: 9am–6pm daily;
Oct–May: 9am–3pm daily. **▨ ▧**

Krapina **❼**

Map D1.
🏃 4,500. **🚉** Frana Galovića, (049)
371 012. **🚌** A. Starčevića, (049) 315
018. **🛈** Magistratska 11, (049) 371
330. **🎫** Week of music and
Kajkaviana culture (Sep).

T HE TOWN IS WELL-KNOWN in the scientific field because the remains of Krapina man, *Homo krapinensis*, who lived in the Palaeolithic age, were found nearby. The Neanderthal skeleton, discovered in 1899 in a hillside cave, is now in the Archaeological Museum in Zagreb. However, some of his possessions, such as utensils and weapons, have remained in Krapina, and are exhibited in the small **Museum of Evolution**.

Krapina is first documented in 1193 as the site of a castle, now destroyed, built to guard the river of the same name. After the danger of Turkish attack had passed, it was conceded to the Keglević counts and became an important administrative town.

It also became a religious centre. In the mid-17th century, a Franciscan monastery and the Baroque church of **St Catherine** were built. The sacristy and some of the monastery rooms are decorated with vivid frescoes by Ivan Ranger.

Bust of Ljudevit Gaj, Krapina

In one of the town squares is a monument to Ljudevit Gaj, born in Krapina in 1809. During the first half of the 19th century he was a prominent figure in the movement which promoted the revival of Croatian politics and culture.

🏛 Museum of Evolution
Šetalište V Sluge. **【** (049) 371 491,
371 161. **⏱** Jun–Sep: 8am–6pm
daily; Oct–May: 8am–3pm daily. **▨**
▧ by appt.

ENVIRONS: A short way northeast of Krapina is the sanctuary of the **Madonna of Jerusalem** in Trški Vrh, regarded as one of the most magnificent examples of Baroque art in Croatia. Built in 1750–61, on a square plan, the façade has a bell tower with an onion dome. Inside is an arched portico with rounded corners and four chapels similar to the tower. The walls, vaults, ceilings and dome of the church are covered with a cycle of frescoes of biblical subjects and scenes from Mary's life by the Styrian artist, Anton Lerchinger. The ornate main altar (with a statue of the Virgin brought from Jerusalem in 1669) is by sculptor Filip Jacob Straub of Graz, while the pulpit and the other three altars are the work of Anton Mersi, a gilder and sculptor.

Fresco in the Baroque church of the Madonna of Jerusalem in Trški Vrh

Pregrada ❽

Map C1. 🏯 *400.*
ℹ️ **Local:** *Trg Gospe Kunagorske 3, (049) 377 050;* **Regional:** *Zagrebacka 6, Krapinske Toplice, (049) 233 653.*
🎭 *Carnival (Feb), Branje grojzdja, grape harvest (Sep).*

THE VILLAGE CHURCH has ancient origins but now presents a 19th-century appearance, made distinctive by the façade flanked by two pointed bell towers. Inside, as well as the tombs of members of the Keglević and Gorup families, there is also a very large organ, which was at one time in Zagreb Cathedral.

On the site of a medieval castle, in the Hrvatsko Zagorje woods, along the Wine Road, stands **Gorica Castle**, once owned by the Keglević family and the feudal manor of the area. Two round towers frame the structure of the elaborate façade. Other buildings behind the towers are now used as a winery.

ENVIRONS: On a vineyard-covered hill, 7 km (4 miles) west of Pregrada, in **Vinagora,** stands an unusual sanctuary of ancient origins. This place of worship became the parish church in 1780. The church of St Mary of the Visitation (Sv. Marija od Pohoda) contains some Gothic statues and rich furnishings. The church is surrounded by walls which encircle the hill.

Two round towers guard the sanctuary entrance, which also once had a drawbridge. These towers are now used as chapels.

Inside the church of St Mary of the Visitation, Vinagora

Veliki Tabor ❾

Map C1.
🚌 *from Krapina or Zagreb for Desinić.* ℹ️ **Regional:** *Zagrebačka 6, Krapinske Toplice, (049) 233 653.*
🎭 *hunting tournament with falcons (Oct).* 🔳 *www.veliki-tabor.hr*

ONE OF THE MOST famous and best preserved castles in Croatia stands on a bare hilltop, making it visible from a great distance. It was royal property in the 14th century at the time of King Matthias Corvinus I (the fact that it was royal property justified its imposing appearance). It was granted to the family of the Ratkaj counts, who in the 16th century altered and softened its rather austere rooms, transforming it into a sumptuous residential palace.

Walls with four semicircular towers encircle the main body of the castle, which is built on a pentagonal ground plan. Two floors with porticoes face the central courtyard. The bastions (no longer extant), made Veliki Tabor a fortress to be feared. The castle is now a museum.

🏰 **Castle**
Desinić. 📞 *(049) 343 052.*
FAX *(049) 343 055.*
🕐 *10am–5pm Mon–Sun.* 📷

ENVIRONS: Miljana, just to the southwest of Veliki Tabor, is home to one of the most picturesque Baroque castles in Croatia. Construction began in the 17th century but was not completed until the mid-19th century. This time span resulted in a variety of styles; there are striking Rococo frescoes in some rooms.

Kumrovec ❿

Map C1.
🏯 *300.* 🏢 *(049) 553 129.*
🚌 *from Zagreb.* ℹ️ *(049) 553 131.*
🎭 *Marriage of Zagorje (Sep).*

THIS WAS THE BIRTHPLACE of Marshal Tito, born Josip Broz in 1892. His house, which dates from 1860, was turned into a museum in 1953. On display are the furniture and household goods which belonged to his family.

In the square in front of the house is a monument to Tito, the work of Antun Augustinčić in 1948. Along with other village houses, Tito's birthplace is now part of a folk museum, the **Ethnological Museum – Staro Selo**, which means "old village". The houses are furnished with utensils and household goods of the time. Reconstructed workshops

The Castle of Veliki Tabor, one of the best-preserved castles in Croatia

◁ **Vineyards around Kumrovec, in the hilly region of Zagorje**

Birthplace of Marshal Tito, part of the Staro Selo museum in Kumrovec

have been set up to demonstrate crafts such as hemp- and flax-weaving.

🏛 Ethnological Museum – Staro Selo
[(049) 553 107. **□** Jun–Sep: 9am–8pm daily; Oct–May: 9am–3pm daily. 🎦 📷

Klanjec ⑪

Map C1.
🏠 600. 🚉 (049) 550 404. 🚍 from Zagreb, Krapina, Zabok. **ℹ** Trg A. Mihanovića 3, (049) 550 144. 🎦 Carnival (Feb).

THE SCULPTOR Antun Augustinčić (1900–79) was born here, and the **Antun Augustinčić Museum and Gallery** has displays of his work. The artist was the co-founder of Zemlja (Union of Artists of the World), based on ideas of politically committed art.

Statue of Antun
Mihanović, Klanjec

Also of interest are the Franciscan monastery and the annexed church of St Mary, both built in the 17th century by the powerful Erdödy family, whose tombs lie here.

In the main square is a monument by Robert Frangeš-Mihanović, dedicated to the poet Antun Mihanović, who wrote the Croatian national anthem.

Another memorial dedicated to Antun Mihanović is the 9-m (29-ft) memorial stone which stands in Zelenjak, 3 km (2 miles) north of Klanjec, in the direction of Tuheljske Toplice.

🏛 Antun Augustinčić Museum and Gallery
Trg A. Mihanovića 10. **[** (049) 550 343. **□** 9am–4pm Mon–Sat.

Bedekovčina ⑫

Map D1.
🏠 3,500. 🚉 Trg A Starčevića 12, (049) 213 106. 🚍 from Zagreb. **ℹ** Regional: Zagrebacka 6, Krapinske Toplice, (049) 233 653. 🎦 Wine fair (Jun).

THIS TOWN is home to a particularly attractive castle and palace, one of many buildings erected over the ruins of ancient castles in the Zagorje hills. The majority of these were destroyed during the wars against the Turks. This particular castle was built in the early 18th century, and now houses public offices. The castle is built on a quadrangular plan, on two levels and with a sloping roof. Coats of arms are emblazoned above the two entrance doors.

Marija Bistrica ⑬

Map D1. 🏠 1,000. 🚉 Zlatar Bistrica, 5 km (3 miles). 🚍 from Zagreb. **ℹ** Zagrebacka, (049) 468 380. 🎦 Bistrica week (Jul).

THIS SMALL VILLAGE on the northern side of the Medvednica mountain is home to the **Sanctuary of St Mary of the Snows** (Sv. Marija Snježna), one of the best-known pilgrimage sites in Croatia. There has been a church on this site since 1334. In the mid-16th century, when a Turkish invasion seemed imminent, a wooden statue of the Black Madonna with Child was hidden in the church. Some decades later, it was miraculously rediscovered, to great joy and emotion. It still inspires tremendous devotion today.

The church has been enlarged several times and was the first to be declared a sanctuary of Croatia by Parliament (1715). It was rebuilt in 1883 by the architect Hermann Bollé. He adopted an eclectic approach, combining Romanesque, Gothic and Baroque styles. The church also has a large frescoed portico.

The sanctuary possesses a rich store of beautiful religious pieces: gold and silver pieces, furnishings and sacred vestments adorned with gold embroidery. Some objects are now on exhibit in the Diocesan Museum in Zagreb.

🔒 Sanctuary of St Mary of the Snows
Trg pape Ivana Pavla II 24.
[(049) 469 156. **□** 8–11am daily.

Sanctuary of St Mary of the Snows in Marija Bistrica, a place of pilgrimage

Tour of the Thermal Spas ⑭

BETWEEN VARAŽDIN AND ZAGREB are five thermal spas, dating from different eras. Set in a pleasant hilly landscape of vineyards and woods, the spas are popular with Croatians and visitors from German-speaking regions. As well as being attracted by the well-equipped thermal spas, visitors are also drawn by the cities and towns nearby. In addition there are numerous castles, sanctuaries, churches and museums, making this a very pleasant area to stay in.

Decorative detail from the Roman baths, Varaždinske Toplice

Krapinske Toplice ③

This thermal spa was built in the second half of the 19th century near a hot water spring rich in calcium, magnesium and carbonate. The hospital treats rheumatic, cardio-vascular and neurological illnesses with bathing in the pools (four outdoor and one indoor) and mud treatments.

Sutinske Toplice ④

Located 8 km (5 miles) northwest of Zlatar, at an altitude of 170 m (557 ft), this site has been famous since the 13th century for its curative waters, which are slightly radioactive and rich in minerals, particularly calcium and magnesium. Mud baths are particularly effective for the treatment of a variety of ailments. Outdoor pools only.

Stubičke Toplice ①

This spa is at the foot of Mount Medvednica, 3 km (2 miles) from Donja Stubica. The spa dates from 1776. There is a hotel with a pool, and a hospital specializing in the treatment of degenerative diseases of the joints and spine. The hot spa waters emerge at 69°C (156°F).

Tuheljske Toplice ②

This spa town is 46 km (28 miles) from Zagreb. At the hotel with its eight pools, rheumatic, respiratory, urological and gynaecological illnesses are treated.

0 kilometres 10

0 miles 10

TIPS FOR DRIVERS

Length of tour: 100 km (62 miles). **Stops:** Hotel Matija Gubec, V. Šipeka 31, Stubičke T., (049) 282 501/ 630; Hotel Minerva, Varaždinske T., (042) 630 431. **ℹ** Stubičke T., V. Šipeka 24, (049) 282 727; Krapinske T., Zagrebačka 2, (049) 232 106; Hotel Toplice, (049) 232 165; Tuheljske T., Gajeva 4, (049) 556 224; Sutinske T., (049) 439 226; Varaždinske T., (042) 630 000.

The decorated interior of the church of St Mary of the Snows, Belec

Varaždinske Toplice ⑤

The spa resort in Varaždin is one of the oldest in Croatia. The first baths were set up at the end of the 18th century and the first public spa was opened to the public in 1829. The thermal waters are used to treat rheumatic and orthopaedic conditions.

KEY

▬ Tour route

▬ Motorway

═ Other roads

ℹ Tourist information

Belec ⑮

Map D1.
🚶 500. **🚌** from Zabok.
ℹ Magistratska 11, Krapina, (049) 371 330.

AMONG THE HILLS of Zagorje is the village of Belec, much loved by art historians, because on its outskirts is the small church of **St George**, one of the few Romanesque buildings preserved in inland Croatia. The bell tower takes up nearly all of the façade (it resembles a defensive tower rather than a campanile). On the right is a small portico with two thin columns. This leads to the interior, where there is an ornate Gothic altar and interesting frescoes dating from the year of its construction.

Lower down the hillside is the church of **St Mary of the Snows** (Sv. Marija Snježna), constructed by the Keglević family in 1674. This church is considered a masterpiece of Croatian Baroque, because of its sumptuously decorated and ornamented interior. The monk and artist Ivan Ranger (*see p204*) painted some of his *trompe-l'œil* masterpieces here, including *Scenes from the Old Testament* and *Episodes of the Virgin Mary's Life*. The church also has a magnificent main altar, surrounded by cherubs and saints.

🏠 Church of St Mary of the Snows
📞 (049) 460 040. **⭕** by appt.

Varaždinske Toplice ⑯

Map D1. **🚶** 2,000. **🚊** from Zagreb and Novi Marof. **🚌** from Zagreb.
ℹ Trg Slobode 16, (042) 630 000.

THE WATERS that gush from a sulphurous spring at the foot of the hill south of Varaždin were known to the Jasi, an Illyrian tribe, in the 3rd century BC. The town was known as Aquae Jasae by the Romans, and the spa rapidly developed, as shown by the numerous archaeological finds discovered here. The baths were used until the area was invaded by the Goths. Later, a landslide buried the baths in mud and for centuries they were forgotten.

In the 12th century, under the rule of the bishop of Zagreb, a village was founded with the name of Toplissa and the inhabitants began to use the hot water from the spring once more. During the construction of the present-day resort, the Roman town was rediscovered.

Varaždinske Toplice also boasts a medieval district which includes a castle, part of which houses an **Archaeo-logical Museum**. Inside a small fortress is the parish church with an organ from 1766 and two carved altars made by Francesco Robba.

In a nearby park is Seoska Kuća, an 18th-century rural house with furniture and objects from the same era.

The sanctuary dedicated to the Trinity, Ludbreg

Ludbreg ⑰

Map D1.
🏛 *3,300.* 🚌 *from Koprivnica.*
🚉 *from Zagreb.* 🚩 *Trg Sv. Trojstva
14, (042) 810 690.* 📷 *Celebration of
Miraculous Blood (1st Sun in Sep).*

MANY TRACES from the
Roman era, such as
walls and baths, have been
found in this area. In
researching these finds, some
historians have identified
Ludbreg as being the Roman
site of Jovia.

The town later became one
of the first bishop's sees in
inland Croatia. In 1414,
during a mass, a priest saw
the wine in the chalice turn to
blood and the town chapel
where this miracle took place
became a destination for
pilgrims. In 1513 Pope
Leo X declared Ludbreg the
only **Sanctuary of the
Trinity** (Sv. Trojstvo) in
Croatia.

The church, originally
Gothic, was altered in 1829,
and now features a Baroque
altar and frescoes by M Racki
(1937). The portico is typical
of churches of pilgrimage
and dates from 1779.

In 1739, Parliament voted to
build a large chapel dedicated
to the Precious Blood of
Christ here, in order to
preserve the miraculous
chalice in an appropriate
place. The chapel was not
finally consecrated until 1994.

A manor house in Baroque
and Classical style, built by
the Battayany family in 1745,
today houses workshops
belonging to the Croatian
Restoration Institute.

Koprivnica ⑱

Map D1. 🏛 *24,000.*
🚉 *Kolodvorska 10, (048) 621 017.*
🚌 *Zagrebačka ulica, (048) 621 282.*
🚩 *Bana Jelačića 7, (048) 621 433.*
W *www.tz-koprivnicko-krizevacka.hr*
📷 *Podravski Motivi, Naive art
exhibition (first week of Jul).*

ANCIENT Kukaproncza, was
founded by the powerful
Ernust family, and a key
trading centre for the Podravina area as well as a royal
city from 1356. It was burnt
down by the Turks in the
16th century, destroying one
of Croatia's first free towns.

Slowly rebuilt in the 17th
century, the town took on a
Baroque appearance with a
wide avenue flanked by the
main public and private
buildings. At one end stands
the 19th-century County Hall
of Koprivnica and Križevci.
There are many Serbian
immigrants here, hence the
Orthodox Church of the Holy
Spirit (Sveti Duh), dating from
the late 18th century.

A significant event for the city
was the establishment in 1685
of a **Franciscan Monastery**
and the church of St Anthony
of Padua. The monastery
was a source of culture and
learning for the whole region
and it has resumed this role
in recent times.

Nearby is the **Civic
Museum** (Gradski Muzej)
with archaeological, historical
and cultural collections, and
the **Koprivnica Gallery** with
a collection of Naive works
linked to the Hlebine school
(*see p19*). Next door, in a
former old brewery, is the
beer hall Kraluš (*see p241*),
much loved by the locals.

🏛 **Civic Museum**
Trg Leandera Brozovića 1.
☎ *(048) 642 538.* ⏱ *8am–2.30pm
Mon–Fri; 10am–1pm Sat.*
🏛 **Koprivnica Gallery**
Zrinski trg 9/1. ☎ *(048) 622 564.*
⏱ *8.30am–3.30pm Mon–Fri,
9.30am–1pm Sat.* 📷

ENVIRONS: Hlebine, 13 km
(8 miles) east of Koprivnica,
owes its fame to the peasant
painters fostered by the artist
Krsto Hegedušić. In the 1930s
this group founded the so-
called "Hlebine school" (*see
p19*) of Naive art: the core
of a trend in painting which
represented the landscape
and people of this region in
a simple and original way.
Their work is exhibited in
both the **Hlebine Gallery**
and the Koprivnica Gallery.

🏛 **Hlebine Gallery**
Trg Ivana Generalića 15. ☎ *(048)
836 075.* ⏱ *10am–4pm Mon–Fri,
10am–2pm Sat.* 📷

A work of Naive art of the Hlebine school in the Koprivnica Gallery

The medieval castle in Đurđevac, today housing a gallery

Đurđevac ⑲

Map E1. 🏛 *7,000.*
🚆 *Kolodvorska 21, (048) 813 089.*
🚌 *(048) 812 002.* 🛈 *Stjepana Radića 1, (048) 812 046.*
🎭 *Đurđevo, City Day (23 Apr); Legend of the Picoki, culture and folklore show (last week of Jun).*

ALTHOUGH THE TOWN'S name derives from an ancient religious building dedicated to St George (Sv. Jurai), the town is now known for the **Castle** (Starigrad), whose ancient name is mentioned as Wasserburg, meaning castle on the water. In the Middle Ages the structure was much larger (excavations reveal a rectangular plan with a drawbridge and tower). All that remains now is a roughly octagonal building with an internal courtyard. A gallery occupies the upper floor and there is a restaurant on the ground floor.

Bjelovar ⑳

Map D1. 🏛 *27,000.*
🚆 *Masarykova ulica, (043) 241 263.*
🚌 *Masarykova ulica, (043) 241 269.*
🛈 *Local: Trg Eugena Kvaternika 4, (043) 243 944;* **Regional:** *Trg kralja Tomislava 5, (043) 241 680.* 🎭 *Terezijana, cultural display (Jun).*

IN THE MIDDLE AGES this town was called Wellewar. It acquired greater status in 1756, when Maria Theresa of Austria built a fort here. It became a military town, and was built on an octagonal layout, centred around two intersecting roads. These are now home to the church of

St Theresa, schools, the Orthodox church of the Holy Spirit and the barracks. The **Civic Museum** (Gradski Muzej) has a rich collection, donated by Count Barešić.

🏛 Civic Museum
Trg Eugena Kvaternika 1. 📞 *(043) 244 207.* ⏰ *9am–2pm, 5–7pm Tue–Fri; 8am–noon Mon & Sat.*

The iconostasis in the Church of the Holy Trinity, Križevci

Križevci ㉑

Map D1.
🏛 *12,000.* 🚆 *(048) 716 193.*
🚌 *(048) 681 149.*
🛈 *Nemčićev trg 6, (048) 681 199.*
🌐 *www.tz-koprivnicko-krizevacka.hr*
🎭 *Križevačko Veliko Spraviśće, cultural and gastronomic event (first week in Jun).*

REFERENCES TO this town are found in acts from the early 12th century. In 1252 it was declared a royal free town, and at various times it was chosen as the meeting place for the Croatian parliament. During a meeting in 1397 certain nobles

considered traitors to King Sigismund were massacred – one was the Prince palatine, Stjepan Lacković. The town was later fortified but after Turkish rule, only the towers' foundations and pieces of the wall remained.

The oldest building is the medieval **Church of the Holy Cross** (Sv. Križ), but only the side doorway dates from this period. The church was restructured in the Baroque style in the second half of the 18th century. The altar of the Holy Cross was sculpted by Francesco Robba in 1756 for Zagreb cathedral.

The Franciscan **Church of the Holy Trinity** (Sv. Trojstvo) has an iconostasis, frescoes by Celestin Medović and Ivan Tišov from the early 19th century, and a magnificent main altar, the work of 18th-century artist Sante Pardoni.

The attached monastery became the **Bishop's Palace** (Biskupski Dvor). It houses paintings, icons, manuscripts and holy objects, and a votive column dedicated to St Florian. The **Civic Museum** (Gradski Muzej) has archaeological and art collections.

🏛 Church of the Holy Cross
Ivana Dijankovečkog 1. 📞 *(048) 711 210.* ⏰ *by appt.*
🏛 Bishop's Palace
📞 *(048) 712 171.* ⏰ *by appt.*
🏛 Civic Museum
Šenoina 2. 📞 *(048) 711 210.*
⏰ *8am–3pm Tue–Fri; 10am–noon Sat & Sun.* 🎭

Altar by Francesco Robba in the church of the Holy Cross, Križevci

TRAVELLERS'
NEEDS

WHERE TO STAY

CROATIA has for some time been quite a popular holiday destination and with Germans, Austrians and Italians in particular.

Hotel sign at Bežanec, near Pregrada

Over the years facilities have improved and there are now more accommodation options available to visitors. Although the tourist industry suffered badly during the war of the 1990s, the damage has largely been repaired and resorts are able to offer a wide range of places to stay. There are plenty of modern hotels, apartments and holiday villages, especially along the coast. Simpler but perfectly acceptable facilities can be found on camping sites or when renting private rooms. Numerous tour operators and travel agencies offer package holidays to different resorts in Croatia, but it is not difficult to make your own travel arrangements. Accommodation is best booked in advance, and planning ahead is a good idea in the peak summer months of June, July and August, as hotels and camping sites get very busy.

The Hotel Palace-Bellevue in Opatija *(see p221),* on the Istrian coast

HOTELS

TOURISM BOOMED in Croatia in the 1970s and 1980s and most of the hotels, particularly those in the resorts along the coast, date from this period. Facilities are generally of a modern type although decor and furnishings can seem rather monotonous. This type of accommodation may not offer the charm of old-fashioned hotels elsewhere in Europe but service is usually good, rooms are clean and spacious and all the basic facilities (most rooms will have an en-suite bathroom) are provided.

Grander, turn-of-the-century hotels, built during the 19th and 20th centuries, are really only found in Zagreb, the capital, and in Opatija, in the Kvarner gulf. Opatija became a popular seaside resort at the time of the Austro-Hungarian Empire, when the Habsburgs were regular visitors, and it still has several hotels dating from this time. They offer a style and somewhat faded elegance not found in the more modern multistorey buildings along the coast.

Zagreb is also home to larger luxury hotels including several belonging to well-known international hotel chains, such as Sheraton. The facilities and services offered by these hotels are of a very high standard which is reflected in the prices.

PRIVATE ROOMS

A GOOD VALUE alternative to staying in a hotel is to look for accommodation in private lodgings *(privatne sobe).* This is not only cheaper, but it also gives you a chance to get to know the local people and understand their culture and way of life. Rooms offered in private accommodation are gradually being classified into three standards (the category of the room will also be reflected in the price).

The first and best category is three-star and this includes all rooms with a private bathroom. The two-star

The Hotel Fortuna *(see p222)* on the island of Sveti Nikola facing Poreč

The elegant lobby of the Hotel Esplanade in Zagreb *(see p226)*

category indicates rooms where the bathroom is shared with one other room. Lastly, the one-star category indicates the most basic level.

Private lodgings can be booked through the various agencies which can be found in all the tourist resorts. A tourist tax and commission are charged and in summer landlords may require stays of a minimum of four nights.

A cheaper way of finding rooms is by contacting local families directly. A good place to start is at your point of arrival or meeting places such as bus stations, ferry landing stages and at main cafés. These places are often frequented by landladies with rooms for rent. It is always a good idea to check the location and price before committing yourself.

Another way of finding accommodation without official help is by looking for the signs offering rooms – *sobe* in Croatian, *Zimmer* in German or *camere* in Italian – hanging outside the door. It is a good idea to begin looking fairly early in the day. If you find somewhere you like, you can ask to be shown the room and, if you are happy with what you see, you can arrange the terms and the price of your stay. It may even be possible to negotiate the price, especially out of season.

In general this kind of accommodation is offered on a room-only basis, though many rooms have a kitchen corner. Some families offer half-board or even full-board.

SELF-CATERING

Some of the larger hotel complexes on the coast offer self-catering apartments as well as hotel rooms. These can be an excellent solution for families or groups of friends travelling together, as prices are reasonable and you still have access to hotel facilities such as pools and restaurants.

GRADING

Croatia is moving towards adopting the star system common in other European countries, from one star for simple accommodation to five stars for a luxury hotel. However, you will still see the old Croatian classification by letter. According to this system, hotels are divided into five categories. The highest category is "L", the equivalent of a five-star. This

Sign indicating rooms for rent

indicates hotels offering a high standard and a wide range of services and facilities. This type of hotel will usually have one or more restaurants, a night club, sports facilities, a swimming pool, and on the coast, perhaps a private beach. There are not very many "L" category hotels in Croatia and most of them are in Zagreb.

Hotels belonging to category "A" (roughly four-star) offer facilities and services similar to the "L" category but the furnishings are somewhat simpler and more standardized.

Most of the hotels in Croatia fall within the "B" category, which indicates hotels offering a good standard of comfort, roughly equivalent to a three-star. Hotels in the "C" and "D" categories are cheaper but are generally more spartan in their furnishings and offer fewer services. Bathrooms are usually shared.

It is common practice in Croatia for hotels to offer half-board *(polupansion)*, with the price including bed and breakfast, as well as another meal (usually an evening meal). Prices for half-board are very reasonable; often not much more than you would pay for just the room. However, hotel restaurant food is often based on rather standardized "international" cooking, and may lack local character.

The entrance to the Hotel Opera in Zagreb *(see p226)*

Sign indicating a camping site, or **Autocamp** nearby

CAMPING SITES

THERE ARE PLENTY of camping sites in Croatia. These range from small, often privately run camping sites to the large *Autocamps*, which offer services and facilities such as restaurants and shops. Almost all Croatian camp sites are located in woods by the sea, so you can keep cool under shady trees on hot summer days. The majority of camping sites are located in Istria and the Kvarner area, and in Dalmatia.

All camping sites are open in the summer months of June, July, August and until the middle of September. However, it is best to check with the camping site itself if you are planning to stay in camping sites during May and late September, as the opening periods can vary from year to year.

Some of the loveliest camping sites, situated as they are in hidden-away spots, are those run by the naturist organization FKK *(see p259)*, which are for naturists only.

Camping outside designated areas is prohibited in Croatia so do not be tempted to stop overnight in the woods or forests, on the beaches or in any areas not specifically reserved for campers.

YOUTH HOSTELS

AN ECONOMICAL alternative for young people is to stay in one of the hostels run by the **HFHS** (the **Croatian Youth Hostel Association**).

There are six youth hostels in Croatia. Rates vary according to the season and a Youth Hostelling Card (available from the YHA in your home country) will entitle you to a discount.

PRICES

THE HOTELS and camping sites in the main tourist resorts, such as the coastal areas, the Plitvice lakes and the capital Zagreb, usually charge higher prices compared with similar hotels in other places in Croatia. Prices rise in the high season, particularly in the month of August, at least in the seaside resorts, regardless of a hotel's star rating. However, even these higher prices are still reasonable and visitors to Croatia will find that prices are about 10 per cent to 20 per cent lower compared with other parts of Europe for accommodation of a similar standard.

Prices in Zagreb stay the same all year round.

BOOKINGS

TOURISM IN CROATIA is very much a "do-it-yourself" affair. If you prefer not to opt for an all-in package holiday *(see p266)*, you can plan your excursions as you go along. Excluding the peak of the high season (August), rooms can usually be found without booking in advance.

The Croatian National Tourist Office *(see p259)* can supply information ahead of your trip. Local tourist offices (there is one in every town) will help you find a room or you can apply to a hotel directly to find out if there are rooms available.

The Hotel Dubrovnik in Zagreb *(see p226)*

DISABLED TRAVELLERS

CARE FOR the disabled in Croatia is good, for the grim reason that the numbers of disabled people have risen as a result of the recent war. However, despite renewed sympathy and consideration, it is taking time to improve disabled access to buildings such as hotels and restaurants. Many hotels can be unsuitable for persons with restricted mobility. This can often be the case with hotels built on steep slopes which are well provided with steps but not ramps or lifts. For further information, contact Savez Organizacija Invalida Hrvatske, the Association of Disabled Organizations of Croatia or RADAR in the UK *(see p259)*.

Outdoor pool at the Hotel Sol Elite Koralj in Umag *(see p223)*

Aerial view of the Sveti Andrija lighthouse near Dubrovnik

LIGHTHOUSES

A DELIGHTFUL and unusual accommodation option in Croatia is the chance to stay in one of the lighthouses which stand on strategic points on the islands and the promontories along the coast. The views can be breath-taking and the setting tranquil, far from the bustle of the tourist resorts.

At the moment it is possible to stay in 11 lighthouses.

Savudrija is 9 km (5 miles) from Umag, and is the oldest lighthouse in the Adriatic and is built in an ideal spot for windsurfers.

Rt Zub is on the Lanterna peninsula, 13 km (8 miles) from Poreč and Novigrad. Even though it is in a relatively isolated position, it is within reach of a number of tourist resorts.

Sveti Ivan na pučini is situated on an island which is part of the archipelago off Rovinj, which is 3.5 km (2 miles) away, ideal for those who love fishing or diving.

The **Porer** lighthouse, on the island of the same name, is 20 km (12 miles) from Pula. It offers truly spectacular views and is in a particularly isolated position. **Veli Rat** stands among pine trees on the northwestern promontory on the island of Dugi Otok,

35 km (22 miles) from Zadar, while at the entrance to the port of Makarska, near one of the most beautiful beaches in the Adriatic, stands the **Sveti Petar** lighthouse.

The lighthouse of **Sušac** was built in 1878 on the island of the same name, 40 km (25 miles) from Hvar. It stands 100 m (328 ft) above sea level and offers a wonderful view of the open sea. There are numerous paths on the island and it is possible to scuba dive near the rocks at the southern end of the island.

The lighthouse of **Pala-gruža** is situated 68 km (42 miles) from Split, between the Italian and Croatian coasts, while on the island of Lastovo, 80 km (50 miles) from Split, is the **Struga** lighthouse, dating from 1839. This is a great location for those who love fishing.

The **Sveti Andrija** lighthouse stands on the island of the same name and is 10 km (6 miles) from Dubrovnik. Finally, there is **Prišnjak** lighthouse on the island of Murter, surrounded by a thick pine wood.

The lighthouses contain one or two apartments, able to accommodate four or more people. For more information, contact **Adriatica.net**, who are based in Zagreb.

Choosing a Hotel

THESE HOTELS have been selected across a wide price range for their good value, facilities and location. They are listed by region, starting with Istria and the Kvarner area. Use the colour-coded thumb tabs, which indicate the areas covered on each page, to guide you to the relevant sections of the chart. For road map references, see the inside back cover.

	NUMBER OF ROOMS	CREDIT CARDS	RESTAURANT	PRIVATE BEACH	SWIMMING POOL
ISTRIA AND THE KVARNER AREA					
BRIJUNI ISLANDS: *Karmen* (Kn)(Kn) Veliki Brijuni. **Map** A3. ((052) 525 400. FAX (052) 212 110. W www.np-brijuni.hr This hotel offers a range of services including a swimming pool and a sports centre. TV Y P	54	●			▨
BRIJUNI ISLANDS: *Neptun-Istra* (Kn)(Kn)(Kn) Veliki Brijuni. **Map** A3. ((052) 525 100. FAX (052) 212 110, 521 367. W www.np-brijuni.hr This hotel is in a good harbourside location on the main island. Tennis, bowling, beach volleyball. Hairdressing salon. TV ▤ Y P	88	●			▨
CRES: *Cres* (Kn)(Kn) Riva Creških Kapetana, Cres. **Map** B3. ((051) 571 108. FAX (051) 571 163. A small, charming family-run hotel overlooking the picturesque harbour. Y	25	●	▨		
CRES: *Kimen* (Kn)(Kn) Riva Creških Kapetana, Cres. **Map** B3. ((051) 571 161. FAX (051) 571 513. W www.cresanka.hr Surrounded by woods, this comfortable hotel also has a sports centre. Y P	210	●	▨	●	▨
CRIKVENICA: *Kastel* (Kn)(Kn) Frankopanska 22. **Map** B2. ((051) 241 044. FAX (051) 241 490. W www.jadran-crikvenica.hr This hotel is in an old, renovated building which was once a monastery and later a castle. It has an old-world atmosphere and offers guests a range of services and facilities, including a night club. Y P	73	●	▨	●	
CRIKVENICA: *Omorika* (Kn)(Kn) M Muževića. **Map** B2. ((051) 785 023. FAX (051) 785 015. W www.jadran-crikvenica.hr This hotel by the sea has a night club, private beach and sports centre. Self-catering apartments are also available. Y P	115	●	▨	●	▨
KRK: *Marina* (Kn)(Kn) Obala hrvatske mornarice 17, Krk. **Map** B3. ((051) 221 128. FAX (051) 221 357. W www.hotelikrk.com A small, charming hotel in the centre of the town. Good service. Y P	18	●	▨		
KRK: *Koralj* (Kn)(Kn)(Kn) Vlade Tomašića, Krk. **Map** B3. ((051) 221 044. FAX (051) 221 063. Close to the sea, this hotel has good facilities for the young and the sporty: a pool, sports and fitness centres, sauna and night club. ▤ P	215	●		●	▨
LOŠINJ: *Alhambra* (Kn)(Kn) Mali Lošinj. **Map** B3. ((051) 232 022. FAX (051) 231 904. W www.jadranka.hr This comparatively small hotel stands surrounded by the pine woods of Čikat, right by the sea. P	40	●		●	
LOŠINJ: *Punta* (Kn)(Kn) Veli Lošinj. **Map** B3. ((051) 662 000. FAX (051) 236 301. W www.jadranka.hr This hotel complex stands on a headland stretching towards the sea. Accommodation includes apartments. ▤ Y P	350	●	▨	●	▨
LOŠINJ: *Aurora* (Kn)(Kn)(Kn) Sunčana Uvala, Mali Lošinj. **Map** B3. ((051) 231 324. FAX (051) 231 542. W www.jadranka.hr This large hotel is surrounded by woods in the bay of Sunčana Uvala (Sunny Bay). Pool, sauna, fitness studio. Near the nudist beach. TV ▤ Y P	404	●	▨	●	▨
LOŠINJ: *Bellevue* (Kn)(Kn)(Kn) Čikat, Mali Lošinj. **Map** B3. ((051) 231 222. FAX (051) 231 268. W www.jadranka.hr This modern hotel is set among the pine woods of Čikat, close to the sea. It is comfortable and well equipped, with good sports facilities including a sports and fitness centre. TV Y P	160	●	▨	●	▨

	NUMBER OF ROOMS	CREDIT CARDS	RESTAURANT	PRIVATE BEACH	SWIMMING POOL
LOŠINJ: *Vespera* (Kn)(Kn)(Kn) Sunčana Uvala, Mali Lošinj. **Map** B3. 〖 (051) 231 304. FAX (051) 231 402. W www.jadranka.hr Close to the sea, surrounded by a large pine wood. Water sports. ▤ ❒ P	404	●	■		■
LOVRAN: *Bristol* (Kn)(Kn) Maršala Tita 27. **Map** B2. 〖 (051) 291 022. FAX (051) 292 049. W www.liburnia.hr This attractive late 19th-century building on the seafront has good facilities including a dance hall. ▤ ❒	102	●	■		■
LOVRAN: *Excelsior* (Kn)(Kn)(Kn) Maršala Tita 15. **Map** B2. 〖 (051) 292 233. FAX (051) 291 989. W www.liburnia.hr A hotel located right by the shore, offering sport and fitness centres, swimming pool and night club. Sauna and massage. TV ▤ ❒ P	185	●	■	●	■
OPATIJA: *Istra* (Kn)(Kn) Maršala Tita 145. **Map** B2. 〖 (051) 271 299. FAX (051) 271 826. W www.liburnia.hr This classic hotel stands on the seafront. It has a health centre, a casino and shops. ▤ ❒ P	115	●	■	●	■
OPATIJA: *Palace-Bellevue* (Kn)(Kn) Maršala Tita 144-146. **Map** B2. 〖 (051) 271 811. FAX (051) 271 964. W www.liburnia.hr The Palace-Bellevue is a large late 19th-century hotel next to the beach. Swimming pool, sauna and disco. ▤ ❒ P	200	●	■	●	■
OPATIJA: *Admiral* (Kn)(Kn)(Kn) Maršala Tita 139. **Map** B2. 〖 (051) 271 533. FAX (051) 271 708. W www.liburnia.hr This large hotel is by the sea. Fitness studio, beauty parlour, massage centre, disco and marina. TV ▤ ❒ P	174	●	■		■
OPATIJA: *Ambasador* (Kn)(Kn)(Kn) F Peršića. **Map** B2. 〖 (051) 271 211. FAX (051) 271 772. W www.liburnia.hr The refurbished Ambasador stands on a quiet wooded promontory. Taverna, disco, pools, shops and sauna. TV ▤ ❒ P	215	●	■	●	■
OPATIJA: *Kvarner* (Kn)(Kn)(Kn) Park I Maja 4. **Map** B2. 〖 (051) 271 233. FAX (051) 272 202. W www.liburnia.hr This hotel, the oldest in Croatia, is by the sea. Antique furniture and a ballroom add to its character. TV ▤ ❒ P	50	●	■	●	■
OPATIJA: *Millennium* (Kn)(Kn)(Kn)(Kn)(Kn) Maršala Tita 109. **Map** B2. 〖 (051) 202 000. FAX (051) 202 020. W www.ugohoteli.hr A modern, stylish, luxury hotel, the Millennium stands in a seafront position. Extras include a pool bar and beauty parlour. TV ▤ ❒ P	95	●	■	●	■
PLITVICE: *Plitvice* (Kn)(Kn) Plitvička Jezera. **Map** C3. 〖 (053) 751 100. FAX (053) 751 1165. W www.np-plitvice.tel.hr Within the Plitvice Lakes Nature Park, this hotel is surrounded by lovely forests. TV ❒ P	51	●	■		
PLITVICE: *Grabovac* (Kn)(Kn)(Kn) Plitvička Jezera. **Map** C3. 〖 (053) 751 999. FAX (053) 751 892. W www.np-plitvice.tel.hr This recently constructed motel is a good choice for those travelling by car. Private garages are available. P	31	●	■		
PLITVICE: *Jezero* (Kn)(Kn)(Kn) Plitvička Jezera. **Map** C3. 〖 (053) 751 400. FAX (053) 751 600. W www.np-plitvice.tel.hr At the heart of the Plitvice park, recently refurbished. TV ▤ ❒ P	250	●	■		■
POREČ: *Diamant* (Kn)(Kn) Brulo. **Map** A2. 〖 (052) 451 566. FAX (052) 451 206. W www.riviera.hr A modern hotel in the resort of Brulo. It is near the sea and has good tennis courts and shops. Good value. TV ❒ P	274	●	■		■

For key to symbols see back flap

Price categories are for a standard double room for one night including tax, service charges and breakfast:
(kn) under 200 kuna
(kn)(kn) 200–300 kuna
(kn)(kn)(kn) 300–450 kuna
(kn)(kn)(kn)(kn) 450–600 kuna
(kn)(kn)(kn)(kn)(kn) over 600 kuna

CREDIT CARDS
American Express, MasterCard or Visa are accepted.
RESTAURANT
Restaurant within the hotel, usually also open to non-residents unless otherwise indicated.
PRIVATE BEACH
Private beach for hotel guests.
SWIMMING POOL
Hotel with an open-air or indoor swimming pool.

	NUMBER OF ROOMS	CREDIT CARDS	RESTAURANT	PRIVATE BEACH	SWIMMING POOL
POREČ: *Tamaris* (kn)(kn) Lanterna. **Map** A2. ((052) 401 000. FAX (052) 443 500. w www.riviera.hr This hotel near the beach offers guests good facilities. Swimming pool, children's pool and fitness centre. Y P	345	●	▦		▦
POREČ: *Fortuna* (kn)(kn)(kn) Otok Sveti Nikola. **Map** A2. ((052) 406 000. FAX (052) 451 119. w www.riviera.hr A well-equipped hotel situated on the small, charming island of St Nicholas facing Poreč. ▤ P	175	●	▦		▦
POREČ: *Mediteran* (kn)(kn)(kn) Plava Laguna. **Map** A2. ((052) 451 933. FAX (052) 451 838. w www.plavalaguna.hr The hotel, directly by the sea, is surrounded by a pine wood, just outside Poreč. ▤ P	345	●	▦		▦
POREČ: *Parentium* (kn)(kn)(kn) Zelena Laguna. **Map** A2. ((052) 411 500. FAX (052) 451 536. w www.plavalaguna.hr A modern hotel with lovely gardens, set on a wooded peninsula, 5 km (3 miles) from Poreč. Mini-market. TV ▤ Y P	340	●	▦	●	▦
PULA: *Histria* (kn)(kn)(kn) Verudela. **Map** A3. ((052) 590 000. FAX (052) 214 175. w www.istra.com/pula This large and comfortable hotel is located outside the city, at Punta Verudela. Views of the marina. TV ▤ P	225	●	▦	●	▦
PULA: *Park* (kn)(kn)(kn) Verudela. **Map** A3. ((052) 375 000. FAX (052) 375 018. This hotel at Punta Verudela is of a high standard and offers various facilities including a swimming pool and sports centre. TV ▤ P	120	●	▦		▦
RAB: *International* (kn)(kn) Obala K P Krešimira IV. **Map** B3. ((051) 724 266. FAX (051) 724 206. w www.imperial.hr This hotel stands in the town centre, and many rooms have harbour views. Indoor seawater pool and sun terrace. ▤	125	●	▦	●	
RAB: *Imperial* (kn)(kn) Palit. **Map** B3. ((051) 724 522. FAX (051) 724 126. w www.imperial.hr A classic hotel offering high standards of service. A short distance from the beach, it has a luxuriant garden. ▤ Y P	95	●	▦		
RAB: *Padova* (kn)(kn)(kn) Banjol. **Map** B3. ((051) 724 544. FAX (051) 724 418. This modern hotel has good facilities for the sports fan, including an indoor pool. It stands in the bay facing the old town. ▤ Y P	200	●	▦	●	▦
RIJEKA: *Jadran* (kn)(kn) Šetalište divizije, 46. **Map** B3. ((051) 216 230. FAX (051) 436 203. This fairly small hotel, outside the centre of the city and right by the sea, has a sports centre. Lovely views out to sea. TV Y P	35	●	▦		
RIJEKA: *Bonavia* (kn)(kn)(kn)(kn)(kn) Dolac, 4. **Map** B3. ((051) 357 100. FAX (051) 335 969. w www.bonavia.hr Modern, comfortable hotel in the centre of Rijeka; a good choice for business travellers. Internet access in every room. TV ▤ Y P	114	●	▦		
ROVINJ: *Montauro* (kn)(kn) A Smareglia. **Map** A3. ((052) 803 000. FAX (052) 813 287. The Montauro hotel is at Punta Corrente, outside the town centre, but close to the sea. Standards are very good. ▤ Y P	285	●	▦		▦
ROVINJ: *Valdaliso* (kn)(kn) Monsena. **Map** A3. ((052) 811 510. FAX (052) 811 541. w www.rovinjturist.hr By the sea, with an excellent water sports centre. Y P	165	●	▦		▦

ROVINJ: *Sol Club Istra* (Kn)(Kn)(Kn) | 411
Otok Sveti Andrija. **Map** A3. **C** *(052) 802 500.* **FAX** *(052) 813 484.*
W www.istra.com/jadranturist
This large hotel is on an island, 15 mins by boat from Rovinj. TV 目 Y P

ROVINJ: *Sol Park* (Kn)(Kn)(Kn) | 207
I M Ronjigova. **Map** A3. **C** *(052) 811 077.* **FAX** *(052) 816 977.* W www.istra.com/jadranturist
On the seafront, this hotel has a disco, gym, sauna, massage, shops and
pools. Many rooms have sea views. 目 Y P

ROVINJ: *Melia Eden* (Kn)(Kn)(Kn)(Kn) | 330
L Adamovića 66. **Map** A3. **C** *(052) 800 400.* **FAX** *(052) 811 349.*
W www.istra.com/jadranturist
A comfortable hotel outside the town. Bowling alley, mini-golf. TV 目 Y P

UMAG: *Aurora* (Kn)(Kn) | 206
Katoro. **Map** A2. **C** *(052) 741 346.* **FAX** *(052) 741 289.* W www.istra.com/istraturist
This hotel is in a pine wood near the sea and is a good choice for people
trying to keep costs down. P

UMAG: *Adriatic* (Kn)(Kn)(Kn) | 180
Jadranska. **Map** A2. **C** *(052) 741 644.* **FAX** *(052) 741 470.*
The Adriatic hotel is by the sea and offers, among other things, a fitness
centre, sports centre, night club, dance floor, pools and a casino. 目 Y P

UMAG: *Sol Elite Koralj* (Kn)(Kn)(Kn)(Kn) | 250
Katoro. **Map** A2. **C** *(052) 710 000.* **FAX** *(052) 701 999.* W www.istra.com/istraturist
Tourist hotel near the sea with swimming pools, fitness and sports centres.
Casino nearby. TV 目 Y P

VRSAR: *Belvedere* (Kn)(Kn) | 200
Vrsar. **Map** A2–3. **C** *(052) 441 118.* **FAX** *(052) 441 730.* W www.anita.hr
A holiday complex near the sea. As well as hotel rooms there are
comfortable villas to rent. P

VRSAR: *Pineta* (Kn)(Kn)(Kn) | 95
Vrsar. **Map** A2–3. **C** *(052) 441 131.* **FAX** *(052) 441 150.* W www.anita.hr
This hotel is a short distance from the sea and has a sports and fitness
centre, swimming pool and sauna. TV 目 Y P

DALMATIA

BRAČ: *Bretanide* (Kn)(Kn)(Kn) | 250
Put Zlatnog Rata, Bol. **Map** D5. **C** *(021) 740 140.* **FAX** *(021) 740 141.*
A large hotel complex near the sea, the Bretanide has everything you need
for a totally relaxing holiday. Y P

BRAČ: *Elaphusa* (Kn)(Kn)(Kn) | 160
Put Zlatnog Rata, Bol. **Map** D5. **C** *(021) 635 222.* **FAX** *(021) 635 477.* W www.bol.hr
This modern hotel stands in a prime position near the sea surrounded by
woodland, within reach of Bol. Internet café. Y P

CAVTAT: *Croatia* (Kn)(Kn)(Kn)(Kn)(Kn) | 500
Frankopanska 10. **Map** F6. **C** *(020) 475 555.* **FAX** *(020) 478 213.* W www.hoteli-croatia.hr
A huge deluxe hotel in a delightful position in the Bay of Cavtat, which has
recently been refurbished. A wealth of facilities, including private beaches
with restaurants. TV 目 Y P

DUBROVNIK: *Villa Dubrovnik* (Kn)(Kn) | 40
Vlaha Bukovca 6. **Map** F6. **C** *(020) 422 933.* **FAX** *(020) 423 465.*
W www.laus.hr/villa-dubrovnik
This hotel has its own beach. Dubrovnik is 2 km (1 mile) away. TV 目 Y P

DUBROVNIK: *Zagreb* (Kn)(Kn) | 18
Šetalište Kralja Zvonimira 27. **Map** F6. **C** *(020) 436 146.* **FAX** *(020) 436 006.*
This small, comfortable hotel is in a late 19th-century villa, 4 km (2 miles)
from Dubrovnik, next to a path leading through the pine woods of Lapad.
The restaurant menu includes vegetarian dishes. Y

DUBROVNIK: *Kompas* (Kn)(Kn)(Kn) | 110
Šetalište Kralja Zvonimira 56. **Map** F6. **C** *(020) 435 777.* **FAX** *(020) 435 877.*
W www.hotel-kompas.hr
This complex is on the Lapad peninsula and has excellent leisure facilities.
Fitness room, sauna, massages and shops. Seawater pool. TV 目 Y P

Price categories are for a standard double room for one night including tax, service charges and breakfast:
(Kn) under 200 kuna
(Kn)(Kn) 200–300 kuna
(Kn)(Kn)(Kn) 300–450 kuna
(Kn)(Kn)(Kn)(Kn) 450–600 kuna
(Kn)(Kn)(Kn)(Kn)(Kn) over 600 kuna

CREDIT CARDS
American Express, MasterCard or Visa are accepted.

RESTAURANT
Restaurant within the hotel, usually also open to non-residents unless otherwise indicated.

PRIVATE BEACH
Private beach for hotel guests.

SWIMMING POOL
Hotel with an open-air or indoor swimming pool.

DUBROVNIK: *Minceta*   (Kn)(Kn)(Kn)
Iva Dulčića 18. **Map** F6. ((020) 447 100. FAX (020) 447 603.
This large modern hotel is part of the Babin Kuk complex. Guests can make use of a well-equipped sports centre and shops. Y P

DUBROVNIK: *Argentina*   (Kn)(Kn)(Kn)(Kn)(Kn)
Frana Supila 14. **Map** F6. ((020) 440 555. FAX (020) 432 524. W www.hoteli-argentina.hr
In a waterside location with subtropical vegetation, the deluxe Argentina has pools, a fitness centre and sauna. TV ≣ Y P

DUBROVNIK: *Excelsior*   (Kn)(Kn)(Kn)(Kn)(Kn)
F Supila 12. **Map** F6. ((020) 353 353. FAX (020) 311 425. W www.hotel-excelsior.hr
This luxury hotel stands east of the city, and has lovely views of the old town. Many rooms have a sea view. TV ≣ Y P

HVAR: *Bodul*   (Kn)(Kn)
Hvar. **Map** D5. ((021) 741 744. FAX (021) 742 607.
A large hotel situated by the sea offering basic services and facilities. P

HVAR: *Adriatic*   (Kn)(Kn)(Kn)
Hvar. **Map** D5. ((021) 741 024. FAX (021) 742 866. W www.hoteli-maestral.com
This hotel stands in a charming harbour location. It is relatively small but facilities are good. Terrace restaurant. ≣ Y

HVAR: *Amfora*   (Kn)(Kn)(Kn)
Hvar. **Map** D5. ((021) 741 202. FAX (021) 741 711. W www.suncanihvar.hr
This hotel, on the beachfront a short distance from Hvar town, is popular with sports fans. Good diving centre. TV ≣ Y P

HVAR: *Palace*   (Kn)(Kn)(Kn)
Hvar. **Map** D5. ((021) 741 966. FAX (021) 742 420. W www.suncanihvar.hr
This hotel stands in a splendid position right in the centre of the picturesque town of Hvar. TV ≣ Y

KORČULA: *Bon Repos*   (Kn)(Kn)
Korčula. **Map** E6. ((020) 711 102. FAX (020) 711 122. W www.korcula.net
Set among cypresses, olive and pine trees, this large hotel offers rooms and also self-catering apartments. Choice of restaurants. P

KORČULA: *Liburna*   (Kn)(Kn)
Korčula. **Map** E6. ((020) 726 006. FAX (020) 711 746. W www.korcula.net
In a quiet, secluded seafront position with lovely views across the bay. There is a windsurfing school nearby. TV ≣ Y P

KORČULA: *Korčula*   (Kn)(Kn)(Kn)
Korčula. **Map** E6. ((020) 711 078. FAX (020) 711 746. W www.korcula.net
This traditional hotel, close to the harbour, is well placed for exploring the town. Terrace restaurant. TV Y P

KORČULA: *Marco Polo*   (Kn)(Kn)(Kn)
Korčula. **Map** E6. ((020) 726 100. FAX (020) 711 746. W www.korcula.net
With its well-equipped sports centre, this hotel is ideal for keep-fit fans. Situated right by the sea. TV ≣ Y P

MAKARSKA: *Biokovo*   (Kn)(Kn)(Kn)
Put Cvitačke 9. **Map** E5. ((021) 602 200. FAX (021) 611 753. W www.hotelbiokovo.hr
This centrally located hotel stands on the seafront with a tree-lined road separating the hotel from the bay. TV ≣ Y P

MAKARSKA: *Dalmacija*   (Kn)(Kn)(Kn)(Kn)
Kralja Krešimira. **Map** E5. ((021) 615 777. FAX (021) 612 211.
This hotel stands right by the sea, and front-facing rooms have fine views of the bay. Seawater pools. Jetskis for hire nearby. TV ≣ Y P

Hotel	Number of Rooms	Credit Cards	Restaurant	Private Beach	Swimming Pool
Dubrovnik: Minceta	340	●	■	●	■
Dubrovnik: Argentina	115	●	■		■
Dubrovnik: Excelsior	160	●	■	●	■
Hvar: Bodul	150	●			
Hvar: Adriatic	63	●			
Hvar: Amfora	235	●	■	●	■
Hvar: Palace	70	●	■		■
Korčula: Bon Repos	465	●	■		■
Korčula: Liburna	125	●	■		■
Korčula: Korčula	25	●	■	●	
Korčula: Marco Polo	115	●	■	●	■
Makarska: Biokovo	240	●	■	●	
Makarska: Dalmacija	190	●	■	●	■

PAG: *Pagus* (Kn)(Kn) · 70
Ante Starčevića 1, Pag. **Map** C4. 📞 *(023) 611 309.* **FAX** *(023) 611 101.*
Recently constructed, this hotel stands on the edge of the bay and offers
spacious rooms and a small private beach. 目 🍸 **P**

PRIMOŠTEN: *Zora* (Kn)(Kn)(Kn) · 385
Velika Raduća. **Map** D5. 📞 *(022) 581 111.* **FAX** *(022) 571 161.*
🔲 www.primostengunnernet.hr
An appealing hotel comprising several buildings, set in a dense pine wood
which entirely covers a peninsula stretching into the sea. 目 🍸 **P**

SPLIT: *Marjan* (Kn)(Kn)(Kn) · 190
Obala Kneza Branimira 8. **Map** D5. 📞 *(021) 399 211.* **FAX** *(021) 399 210.*
🔲 www.hotel-marjan.com
This modern hotel block lies along the coast towards Sustipan. Despite a
shabby exterior, rooms are very comfortable. 📺 目 🍸 **P**

SPLIT: *Split* (Kn)(Kn)(Kn) · 135
Put Trstenika 19. **Map** D5. 📞 *(021) 303 111.* **FAX** *(021) 303 011.* 🔲 www.hotelsplit.hr
This modern hotel overlooking the sea has a swimming pool and a sauna.
All rooms have balconies. 📺 目 🍸 **P**

SPLIT: *Hotel Consul* (Kn)(Kn)(Kn)(Kn) · 10
Tršćanska 34. **Map** D5. 📞 *(021) 486 080.* **FAX** *(021) 486 079.*
As well as the hotel rooms there are also three apartments. Rooms are
equipped with a minibar, telephone, TV and air conditioning.
📺 目 **P**

ŠIBENIK: *Ivan* (Kn)(Kn)(Kn) · 210
Hotelsko naselije Solaris. **Map** D5. 📞 *(022) 363 951.* **FAX** *(022) 361 801.*
🔲 www.solaris.hr
By the sea, this hotel has everything to keep you in good shape, with its
fitness centre, sauna, massage and sports facilities. 目 🍸 **P**

ŠIBENIK: *Jure* (Kn)(Kn)(Kn) · 210
Hotelsko naselije Solaris. **Map** D5. 📞 *(022) 363 999.* **FAX** *(022) 361 810.* 🔲 www.solaris.hr
Comfortable seaside hotel. 目 🍸 **P**

TROGIR: *Trogirski Dvori* (Kn)(Kn) · 16
Kralja Trpimira 245. **Map** D5. 📞 *(021) 885 444.* **FAX** *(021) 881 318.*
A very small but comfortable hotel with the added bonus of personal
service. 📺 目 🍸 **P**

TROGIR: *Medena* (Kn)(Kn)(Kn) · 650
Seget Donij. **Map** D5. 📞 *(021) 880 588.* **FAX** *(021) 880 019.* 🔲 www.hotelmedena.com
This enormous hotel complex stands in a pine wood near the sea and
offers good facilities. 目 🍸 **P**

VIS: *Issa* (Kn)(Kn) · 125
S A Zanelle 5, Vis. **Map** D6. 📞 & **FAX** *(021) 711 450.*
Situated near the coast, this modern hotel is well equipped. 目 🍸 **P**

ZADAR: *Novi Park* (Kn)(Kn) · 185
Majstora Radovana 7. **Map** C4. 📞 *(023) 206 200.* **FAX** *(023) 332 065.*
The Novi Park is surrounded by woodland, not far from the sea.
Extras include a casino. 目 🍸 **P**

ZADAR: *Zadar* (Kn)(Kn) · 80
Majstora Radovana. **Map** C4. 📞 *(023) 332 179.* **FAX** *(023) 332 065.*
This hotel is of a good standard and is situated next to a beach. A variety
of services is available to its guests. 目 **P**

ZADAR: *Kolovare* (Kn)(Kn)(Kn) · 220
Bože Peričića 14. **Map** C4. 📞 *(023) 203 300.* **FAX** *(023) 203 300.*
Surrounded by trees, near the sea and close to the old town, this hotel
offers all kinds of facilities for relaxation and recreation.
📺 目 🍸 **P**

ZAGREB

ZAGREB: *Central* (Kn)(Kn)(Kn) · 75
Branimirova 3. **Map** D2. 📞 *(01) 484 11 22.* **FAX** *(01) 484 13 04.* 🔲 www.hotel.central.hr
This modern hotel, close to the train station, offers good value for money.
Smallish but comfortable rooms. 📺 目 🍸

For key to symbols see back flap

Price categories are for a standard double room for one night including tax, service charges and breakfast:

(Kn) under 200 kuna
(Kn)(Kn) 200–300 kuna
(Kn)(Kn)(Kn) 300–450 kuna
(Kn)(Kn)(Kn)(Kn) 450–600 kuna
(Kn)(Kn)(Kn)(Kn)(Kn) over 600 kuna

CREDIT CARDS
American Express, MasterCard or Visa are accepted.

RESTAURANT
Restaurant within the hotel, usually also open to non-residents unless otherwise indicated.

PRIVATE BEACH
Private beach for hotel guests.

SWIMMING POOL
Hotel with an open-air or indoor swimming pool.

	NUMBER OF ROOMS	CREDIT CARDS	RESTAURANT	PRIVATE BEACH	SWIMMING POOL
ZAGREB: *Dubrovnik* (Kn)(Kn)(Kn) Gajeva 1. **Map** D2. ☎ *(01) 487 35 55.* FAX *(01) 481 84 47.* @ hotel-dubrovnik@hotel-dubrovnik.tel.hr This recently renovated, modern hotel is in the pedestrian area. Facilities are good. TV ≣ Y P	190	●	▨		
ZAGREB: *Laguna* (Kn)(Kn)(Kn) Kranjčevićeva 29. **Map** D2. ☎ *(01) 382 02 22.* FAX *(01) 382 00 35.* W www.hotel-laguna.hr A modern building just outside the centre but offering a higher standard compared with others in this category. TV ≣ Y P	275	●	▨		
ZAGREB: *Panorama* (Kn)(Kn)(Kn) Trg Sportova 9. **Map** D2. ☎ *(01) 365 83 33.* FAX *(01) 309 26 57.* W www.hup-zagreb.hr A modern skyscraper in the southwest part of the city. This hotel is of a very good standard. TV ≣ Y P	285	●	▨		
ZAGREB: *International* (Kn)(Kn)(Kn)(Kn) Miramarska 24. **Map** D2. ☎ *(01) 610 88 00.* FAX *(01) 615 94 59.* W www.hotel-international.hr This modern hotel is beyond the train station towards Sava. TV ≣ Y P	115	●	▨		
ZAGREB: *Esplanade* (Kn)(Kn)(Kn)(Kn)(Kn) Mihanovićeva 1. **Map** D2. ☎ *(01) 456 66 66.* FAX *(01) 457 79 07.* W www.esplanade.tel.hr A luxurious, historic hotel, in a beautiful 19th-century building near the station. Opulent decor and impeccable service. TV ≣ Y P	135	●	▨		
ZAGREB: *Opera* (Kn)(Kn)(Kn)(Kn)(Kn) Kršnjavoga 1. **Map** D2. ☎ *(01) 489 20 00.* FAX *(01) 489 20 01.* W www.opera-zagreb.com A modern hotel, part of the international group of the same name. Its guests are principally businessmen and wealthy tourists. TV ≣ Y P	225	●	▨		▨
ZAGREB: *Sheraton* (Kn)(Kn)(Kn)(Kn)(Kn) Kneza Borne 2. **Map** D2. ☎ *(01) 455 35 35.* FAX *(01) 455 30 35.* W www.sheraton.com This new building in the lower town offers all the comfort expected of a hotel in this international hotel chain. Gym and pool. TV ≣ Y P	310	●	▨		▨
CENTRAL CROATIA					
ČAKOVEC: *Park* (Kn)(Kn)(Kn) Zrinjsko Frankopanska. **Map** D1. ☎ *(040) 311 255.* FAX *(040) 311 244.* Located in the centre of the city, near sports facilities. TV ≣ Y P	80	●	▨		
SAMOBOR: *Livadić* (Kn)(Kn) Kralja Tomislava 1. **Map** C2. ☎ *(01) 336 58 50.* FAX *(01) 336 58 51.* W www.hotel-livadic.hr A traditional, family-run hotel offering spacious rooms and good service. TV	25	●			
SAMOBOR: *Samoborski Slapovi* (Kn)(Kn) Hamor 16. **Map** C2. ☎ *(01) 338 40 63.* FAX *(01) 338 40 62.* This small hotel, 3 km (2 miles) from Samobor, provides friendly service.	11	●			
SAMOBOR: *Babylon* (Kn)(Kn)(Kn) Betonska cesta 5. **Map** C2. ☎ *(01) 337 15 00.* FAX *(01) 337 10 44.* Hotel of a decent standard, probably the best in the area. There are also open-air spaces for sports. TV Y	19	●	▨		▨
SISAK: *Panonija* (Kn)(Kn) Ivana Kukuljevića Sakćinskog 21. **Map** D2. ☎ *(044) 515 600.* FAX *(044) 515 601.* A fairly large, modern hotel offering good facilities. P	45	●	▨		
SLUNJ: *Park* (Kn) Stara cesta 2. **Map** C2. ☎ *(047) 777 524.* FAX *(047) 777 524.* A hotel of a reasonable standard at good-value prices.	22	●			

SLAVONIA AND BARANJA

ĐAKOVO: *Blaža* Ⓚ Ⓚ Ⓚ | 23
A Starčevića 156a. **Map** F2. Ⓒ *(031) 816 760.* FAX *(031) 816 764.*
A modern, recently built hotel which offers travellers decent
standards of comfort. 📺 Ⓨ

DARUVAR: *Termal* Ⓚ Ⓚ Ⓚ | 100
Julijer Park 1. **Map** E2. Ⓒ *(043) 331 488.* FAX *(043) 331 455.*
This hotel is next to a thermal spa with hot springs. Facilities are excellent
and include sporting activities. 📺 ▤ Ⓨ

OSIJEK: *Mursa* Ⓚ | 125
Bartola Kašića 2a. **Map** F2. Ⓒ *(031) 207 640.* FAX *(031) 207 630.*
A 1970s hotel with good facilities. Good value for money. ▤ Ⓨ Ⓟ

OSIJEK: *Central* Ⓚ Ⓚ | 27
Trg A Starčevića 6. **Map** F2. Ⓒ *(031) 283 399.* FAX *(031) 283 891.*
Good, traditional 19th-century hotel situated in the centre of the city. ▤

OSIJEK: *Hotel Osijek* Ⓚ Ⓚ Ⓚ | 100
Šamacka 4. **Map** F2. Ⓒ *(031) 201 333.* FAX *(031) 212 135.*
Modern, high-rise waterfront hotel offering a good standard of facilities
with all the usual comforts. Ⓨ Ⓟ

VINKOVCI: *Cibalia* Ⓚ Ⓚ | 25
A Starčevića 51. **Map** F2. Ⓒ *(032) 339 222.* FAX *(032) 332 920.*
This small hotel provides all the basic facilities and offers travellers
good value for money.

VINKOVCI: *Gem* Ⓚ Ⓚ | 20
Kralja Zvonimira 120. **Map** F2. Ⓒ *(032) 366 912.* FAX *(032) 366 914.*
Small hotel with adequate facilities at a reasonable price.

VINKOVCI: *Slavonija* Ⓚ Ⓚ Ⓚ | 61
Duga ulica 1. **Map** F2. Ⓒ *(032) 342 555.* FAX *(032) 342 550.* Ⓦ www.son-ugo-cor.com
A smart, modern hotel of a high standard with a casino. 📺

VUKOVAR: *Dunav* Ⓚ Ⓚ | 35
Trg Republike 1. **Map** G2. Ⓒ *(032) 441 285.* FAX *(032) 441 762.*
This is a fairly small, neat hotel in a modern building offering good value
for money. Some rooms have pleasant views towards the river.

THE NORTHERN COUNTIES

KRAPINSKE TOPLICE: *Toplice* Ⓚ Ⓚ Ⓚ | 123
A Mihanovića 2. **Map** D1. Ⓒ *(049) 232 165.* FAX *(049) 232 322.*
This modern spa hotel offers its guests thermal pools (indoor and outdoor),
a sauna and sports facilities. 📺 Ⓟ

VARAŽDIN: *La'Gus* Ⓚ Ⓚ | 20
Varaždinbreg. **Map** D1. Ⓒ *(042) 652 940.* FAX *(042) 652 944.*
All the rooms in this renovated hotel are well equipped with en-suite
bathroom, TV, minibar and telephone. 📺 Ⓟ

VARAŽDIN: *Pansion Garestin* Ⓚ Ⓚ | 10
Zagrebačka 34. **Map** D1. Ⓒ & FAX *(042) 214 314.*
This is a small hotel with only ten rooms, all of which have an en-suite
bathroom, TV, minibar and telephone. 📺 Ⓟ

VARAŽDIN: *Turist* Ⓚ Ⓚ Ⓚ | 100
Kralja Zvonimira 19. **Map** D1. Ⓒ *(042) 395 395.* FAX *(042) 214 479.* Ⓦ www.hotel-turist.hr
A modern building, well-equipped with a sports centre, a games room,
a fitness centre and a sauna. 📺 ▤ Ⓨ Ⓟ

VARAŽDINSKE TOPLICE: *Tonimir* Ⓚ Ⓚ Ⓚ | 30
Kralja Tomislava 1. **Map** D1. Ⓒ & FAX *(042) 633 504.*
This is a motel, catering particularly for those travelling by car.
All the basic facilities.

VARAŽDINSKE TOPLICE: *Minerva* Ⓚ Ⓚ Ⓚ | 234
Trg Slobode 1. **Map** D1. Ⓒ *(042) 630 831.* FAX *(042) 630 431.*
A very large spa hotel offering its guests a wide range of
recreational facilities: thermal pools (indoor and outdoor),
sauna, sports centre. 📺 Ⓟ

For key to symbols see back flap

WHERE TO EAT

**Veljko Barbieri,
cook and writer**

THE FOOD in Croatia is very varied, from the fresh fish and seafood found in towns along the coast to the Central European dishes, such as goulash, offered in inland Croatia. Croatia has its own gastronomic traditions, but the coastal areas have been greatly influenced by the long years of Venetian rule and inland areas reflect the cuisines of Central Europe, in particular those of Vienna and Hungary. Pasta dishes and pizza (with a thin base, in the Italian style) can be found virtually everywhere. Croatian kitchens commonly make the most of a wide range of fresh produce including meat, fish and vegetables. The specialities include the famous sheep's milk cheese *(paški sir)* of Pag and air-dried hams called *pršut*. Prices are generally lower than in other western European countries, making eating out in Croatia a value-for-money experience.

**Sign for the Zlatna Guska
restaurant (see p241)**

**Sign of one of many *gostionica*
offering traditional cooking**

The Boban restaurant in Zagreb *(see p239)*

RESTAURANTS

THE CROATIAN WORD *restoran* generally means a formal restaurant, run as part of a hotel or large tourist complex. These establishments are characterized by a good level of service but they often offer so-called "international" cuisine. Although the food is usually perfectly good and satisfying, it has no regional flavour and is often rather standardized. Prices for a main meal in a place classed as a restaurant start from 190 kuna (about £16).

Less formal places to try out are the numerous *gostionica* or *konoba* (both are similar to a trattoria or taverna). These are often family-run businesses and they are good places to try good, traditional, local dishes. One of the drawbacks of these establishments, from a tourist's point of view, is that

they often do not display a menu outside indicating the kind of dishes on offer. If you are unsure about a place, it is best to go in and ask to see the menu (or get the owner or waiter to tell you the dishes of the day) and then decide whether to stay or not. Remember you are under no obligation and can feel completely free to leave if the food, the service or the prices on offer are not to your liking.

Most of the *gostionica* and *konoba* fall within the mid-price range and some offer very good value for money. The average cost of a meal is from around 120 to 200 kuna (from about £10–17). This sum would include a starter, a main course (always served with a vegetable) and a

dessert. Prices vary according to the standard of the place and its location. A *gostionica* or *konoba* along the coast will almost certainly be more expensive than those inland. Sometimes there is an extra charge for bread, but the service charge is usually included in the price of each single dish.

Along the coast, fresh fish is plentiful though not inexpensive. On menus, prices of fish and seafood are generally given by the kilo. A useful rule of thumb is that a good-sized portion of fish or seafood will usually weigh about 250 grams (10 ounces) and so you should be able to predict roughly how much you will be spending. The choice of fish and seafood on offer will vary daily depending on the catch.

Wine is often drunk with restaurant meals in Croatia (for an overview of Croatia's wines see pp238–9), but it is very common for restaurants to serve a drink consisting of a mixture of wine and water

Tables outside a pizzeria on the seafront in Umag

(bevanda), or *gemsit*, which is mineral water and local wine, brought to the table separately for you to mix.

PIZZERIAS AND BISTROS

PIZZAS ARE ALWAYS a good choice for the visitor travelling on a budget in Croatia. Croatian pizzas are very good and can compete with the best Italian tradition. The prices are always reasonable and are on average 30–40 per cent lower than similar meals in many other parts of Europe.

Another type of restaurant is the bistro, offering a range of straightforward dishes: from *rižot* (risotto) and spaghetti (regarded as *hors d'oeuvres* here), to simple basic dishes such as *ražnjići* (pork kebabs), *čevapčići* (meatballs) and seafood dishes such as fried octopus or squid rings *(lignje)*.

Beer, called *pivo*, is normally drunk with meals in pizzerias and bistros, but soft drinks, mineral water and wine are also available.

PICNICS AND SELF-CATERING

THERE ARE MANY temptingly beautiful places to visit in Croatia. If you are planning an excursion to one of the unspoilt but isolated spots where refreshment facilities will not be available, you can always take a picnic. Food can easily be bought from food shops, supermarkets or from one of the typical open-air markets where you can find a great variety of salami, cheeses, bread and olives, as well as fresh fruit and drinks.

Food prices are very reasonable and shopkeepers usually try to be helpful. It is common practice for staff to prepare rolls or sandwiches at the counter at no extra cost. Sometimes it is also possible to find some simple ready-made dishes such as *burek*. This is a type of savoury pastry, filled with meat *(meso)* or cheese *(sir)*, and baked in the oven. Buy *burek* in bakeries or small "fast food" shops.

Families or groups staying in self-catering apartments should also have no problem stocking up. Many hotel complexes with apartments also have mini-supermarkets.

VEGETARIAN FOOD

THERE ARE NO dedicated vegetarian restaurants in Croatia and even dishes that look vegetarian, like *manistra* (vegetable soup), may contain meat stock. However, restaurants, pizzerias and cafés serving Italian-style food will provide various options from pizzas with vegetable toppings to pasta dishes. Otherwise several side orders of vegetables are usually an option and omelettes *(omlet)* may be available in some places. The choice increases in autumn with the fresh mushroom season, especially in the Istria region.

PAYING

PAYMENT by credit card, normal enough in most European restaurants, small or large, is not really general practice in Croatia, except in the larger places and in hotel restaurants. Bills for meals are paid in cash in kuna.

Credit cards are often not accepted in the *gosttonica* and *konoba* or in smaller bars or cafés, so make sure that you carry enough cash with you.

OPENING HOURS

PLACES SERVING food and drinks have very flexible opening hours, and it is possible to eat at more or less any time of the day, especially in the tourist resorts. However the meal times of the local people do not vary much from other Mediterranean countries. Lunch is generally served from about noon to 2pm and dinner is served from around 8 to 10pm.

The elegant restaurant of the Hotel Esplanade *(see p226)* in Zagreb

What to Eat in Croatia

THE BASIS OF TRADITIONAL Croatian cuisine is Slavic, with influences from neighbouring countries which have played a part in forming the country's history in the distant or more recent past. Dishes in the inland regions are based on the produce from the land such as meat, pulses and cereals. These dishes often have a Central European flavour (influenced by Austro-Hungarian cuisine). On the coast, where fish, seafood and vegetables are widely used, the Mediterranean flavours of Italy and particularly Venice are dominant. An important part of traditional cuisine is the special dishes prepared for the various holidays, festivals and special occasions (harvest time, grape picking, weddings, baptisms, etc) and the religious holidays of different kinds (Christmas, Easter, and also saints' days, for example, St Martin's day).

Buzara *is a typical Dalmatian speciality. Scampi are gently simmered in a sauce of tomato, onion and herbs. The sauce can also be served with pasta.*

CUISINE OF THE ADRIATIC COAST

Fresh fish *(riba)* is one of the main specialities on the coast. When it is freshly caught, it is usually served simply grilled *(na žaru)*. Popular choices are red mullet, gilthead bream, sole and John Dory. Seafood of all kinds is also available, from mussels and squid to oysters and even lobster.

Sarma *is a dish which reveals Turkish origins. These stuffed cabbage leaves are filled with minced meat, herbs and spices.*

Oysters *are eaten raw with just a squeeze of fresh lemon juice or vinegar and shallots. Limski Channel and Ston oysters are famous.*

Chips

Assorted grilled meats

Salad (lettuce, raw onions and tomato)

A Mixed Grill *is a very common menu item in Croatia. Several pieces of meat (pork or veal) are chargrilled and may be served with ražnjići, tasty kebabs made with pork, and the ever-present čevapčići, meatballs flavoured with onions and a mixture of herbs. Grilled meat is usually served with chips and garnished with a fresh salad made of tomatoes, raw onions, lettuce and perhaps peppers too.*

Rižot *is a rice-based dish (similar to Italian risotto), made with mussels and other kinds of seafood. Rižot originates from Venice.*

Sheep's cheese from the island of Pag, or *paški sir*

Dalmatinski pršut, seasoned and smoked Dalmatian ham

Dalmatinski pršut a paški sir *is ham with sheep's cheese. Dalmatian ham is air-dried and smoked, and has a distinctive taste. It is often served with the famous sheep's cheese from the island of Pag. This combination is typically served as a starter with olives.*

Manistra, *also called menestra, is made with pulses and vegetables and is similar to the Italian minestrone. A winter version called* jota *is made with cabbage and beans.*

Pašticada *is a slow-cooked stew of beef. It is often served with Italian-style* gnocchi, *clearly demonstrating the blend of Hungarian and Italian influences seen in Croatian cuisine.*

Grilled fish and seafood *is of very good quality along the coast. Choose from sea bass, gilthead bream (shown here), or sea bream, or seafood such as squid, scampi, mussels, crayfish or even lobster.*

Soya bread   Bread with sesame seeds

Bread (kruh) *is always fresh and often home-made, even in restaurants. All kinds can be found, some made with soya, some with sesame seeds.*

Rožata *is a typical Dalmatian dessert. It is similar to crème caramel and is made with caramel, eggs, milk and bitter liqueur. It is served cold.*

Palačinka *is perhaps the best-known dessert in Croatia. It consists of a folded pancake filled with jam, melted chocolate or crushed walnuts.*

CUISINE IN INLAND CROATIA

The colder climate of the inland areas means that dishes served here are often heartier, especially in winter. Meat dishes are often prepared with rich, tasty sauces cooked in pans or under the *peka*, a type of metal bell. The red pepper condiment paprika, familiar from Hungarian cooking, makes an appearance here, as does goulash.

Kulen *is hot, spicy salame from Slavonia. This sausage is flavoured with chilli pepper and is served with soft cheese, bell peppers, tomatoes and pickled vegetables.* Kulen *salami are produced and smoked using traditional methods.*

Fiš paprikaš *is a stew of fresh-water fish (usually carp) flavoured with paprika. This dish undoubtedly originates from Hungary.*

Štrukli *are large, home-made ravioli (stuffed pasta parcels), made using different types of wheat, and baked in the oven. Savoury* štrukli *are filled with cheese; sweet versions can also be found.*

Zagorje Štrudel *consists of a roll of flaky pastry which encloses a filling of fresh soft cheese, honey and nuts. Its origins probably lie in Austrian cuisine.*

What to Drink in Croatia

A WIDE VARIETY OF LOCALLY made drinks is available throughout Croatia, from beers to wines to fiery fruit brandies. Croatian beer is usually of the lager type but dark beers can also be found. Foreign brands such as Stella Artois, Tuborg and Kaltenberg are brewed in Croatia under licence, and there are Irish pubs selling Guinness and other Irish beers. Croatia's vineyards yield all kinds of red and white wines, most of which are rarely seen outside the country. Spirits based on grapes are popular as aperitifs rather than after-dinner drinks, as are other fruit brandies made from plums or pears. Brandies flavoured with herbs, walnuts or even honey are also popular. Tap water is safe to drink but if the taste does not appeal there is a wide range of bottled mineral waters, both sparkling and still.

Typical sign for a pub, *pivnica* in Croatian

Traditional utensils for the preparation of strong Turkish coffee

COFFEE AND TEA

C OFFEE *(kava)* is drunk throughout Croatia. All over the country it is served very strong and black, in little cups, like an *espresso* coffee. If it is too strong you can add a little milk or order a *cappuccino* (freshly ground coffee with frothy hot milk). Strong Turkish coffee is also available in some places. Herbal teas *(čaj)* are sold everywhere. Indian teas can also be found, usually served with lemon, but you can ask for milk.

BEER

A NOTHER very popular drink sold in cafés and pubs is beer *(pivo)*, which is always served very cold. Most bottled beers are of the lager-type, but some darker beers can be found. The most well-known brands of lager beer are Ožujsko, made in Zagreb and Karlovačko (Karlovac). Another common brand is Pan. Well-known international beers such as Stella Artois are also widely available (some brewed under licence in Croatia), but tend to be more expensive.

Karlovačko beer

Ožujsko beer

SPIRITS

Pelinkovac liqueur   **Zrinski brandy**

A WIDE VARIETY of spirits is available in Croatia, demonstrating the nation's fondness for strong alcoholic drinks, in particular fruit-based eau-de-vie. One of the most popular spirits is a plum brandy originating in Slavonia called *Šljivovica*. It is found all over the country. *Loza* is a grape-based eau-de-vie with a high alcohol content, and *Travarica* is a herb-based spirit. *Vinjak* is a brandy, *Pelinkovac* is a herb liqueur, and *Maraskino*, a liqueur from Zadar, is flavoured with maraschino cherries.

Many spirits are drunk as aperitifs. A spirit called *Berme* is produced in Samobor, near Zagreb, and is made according to an ancient, well-guarded recipe. It is drunk as an aperitif, served with ice and a slice of lemon.

Šljivovica eau-de-vie

Some bottles of eau-de-vie with fruit, made at home all over the country

MINERAL WATER, SOFT DRINKS AND FRUIT JUICES

ALL BARS AND CAFÉS offer a wide range of fruit juices, as well as internationally known brands of soft drinks and fizzy drinks like cola. Tap water is safe to drink everywhere in Croatia and bottled mineral waters *(mineralna voda)* are also widely available. The two most common brands of mineral water in Croatia are Studena and Jamnica but there are also a great many imported brands available as well.

Mineral water

Orange juice

Pubs and bars with live music: a popular way to socialize

DRINKING CUSTOMS IN CROATIA

Pubs, bars and cafés are not only places to stop at various times of the day for refreshment, but also places to meet friends and socialize. For visitors this can also be a good way of meeting and getting to know local people.

One tradition found in Croatia is that of mixing wine with other drinks such as mineral water or even cola. A *bevanda* is red or white wine with plain water, while *gemišt* is white wine mixed with sparkling mineral water. One of the most popular summer drinks is red wine and fizzy cola, a drink called *bambus*.

Croatians like a drink or two, as is demonstrated by the custom in the Slavonian region of wine drinking with friends. This traditional ritual should only be undertaken by people with a very strong head for alcohol. It begins with the first phase, which is before any wine is consumed, known as the *Dočekusa*. This is then followed by the *Razgovoruša*, during which you chat while sipping at least seven glasses of wine. The final phase is called the *Putnicka*, reserved for the leave-taking, when yet more glasses are emptied before people say their final farewells.

WINES

CROATIA is also a land of vineyards, with vines grown on rolling hills inland and in pockets of stony soil on the coast and islands. Production varies in quantity and quality but standards are improving and there are some very decent wines around. From the Kvarner area come the white wine Žlahtina (from Vrnbik on Krk), red Cabernet (from Poreč) and Teran (from Buzet), a light red. Dalmatia is known for Pošip and Grk from Korčula (both white wines), Dingač (one of the best Croatian reds) and Postup from the Pelješac peninsula. Plavac (red) comes from Brač and Malmsy from Dubrovnik. Finally, from Slavonia come Kutjevačka Graševina, Kutjevo Chardonnay and Riesling, and Krauthaker Graševina.

Žlahtina

Dingač   **Postup**

WHERE TO DRINK

THERE ARE VARIOUS TYPES of establishments which serve drinks and it is useful to know a few of the basic categories. A *kavana* is equivalent to a café, and serves both alcoholic and non-alcoholic drinks, while a *pivnica* serves mainly beer. Irish pubs can also be found, selling Guinness and other Irish beers. Wine is generally drunk in a *konoba*. In the larger towns you can have a snack with your drink in one of the *bife*, the Croatian equivalent of a snack bar. However, there are not really rigid distinctions between the types of drinks served in one or other of these places. Cafés open very early and close late (usually around 11pm).

Drinks of various kinds (though rarely alcoholic) are also served in pastry shops – *slasticarna*. The close links that Croatia's gastronomic tradition has with Austria, and in particular with Vienna, has influenced the production of delicious cakes and pastries as well as excellent *sladoled* (ice cream). Pastry shops close earlier than cafés in general.

A snack bar with outdoor tables in Fažana, a coastal resort

Choosing a Restaurant

THESE RESTAURANTS have been selected across a wide price range for their good value, facilities and location. They are listed by region, starting with Istria and the Kvarner area. Use the colour-coded thumb tabs, which indicate the areas covered on each page, to guide you to the relevant sections of the chart. For road map references, see the inside back cover.

	CREDIT CARDS	CROATIAN CUISINE	INTERNATIONAL CUISINE	OUTSIDE DINING

ISTRIA AND THE KVARNER AREA

CRES: *Gostionica Belona*　　　　　　　　　　　　Ⓚ Ⓚ
Šetalište 23 travnja 20, Cres. **Map** B3. ☎ *(051) 571 203.*
This restaurant is popular with the locals and is particularly lively in the evenings.
The menu includes typical meat and fish dishes and also pasta.
○ *Easter–Sep: 9am–midnight daily; Oct–Easter: 9am–10pm daily.* 🍷

| ● | ▦ | ● | ▦ |

CRES: *Riva*　　　　　　　　　　　　　　　　　Ⓚ Ⓚ Ⓚ
Obala Creskih Kapetana 13, Cres. **Map** B3. ☎ *(051) 571 107.*
Riva has a pretty terrace overlooking the port, where you can enjoy good pasta
dishes and fresh fish. ○ *Easter–Sep: noon–11pm daily.* 🍷

| | ▦ | | ▦ |

KASTAV: *Kukuriku*　　　　　　　　　　　　　Ⓚ Ⓚ Ⓚ
Kastav 120. **Map** B2. ☎ *(051) 691 417.*
Offers original "slow-food" cooking. The menu changes daily and you can choose
from fish, meat or game. Follow the cook's recommendations.
○ *11am–midnight Tue–Sun.* P ☰ 🍷

| ● | ▦ | ● | ▦ |

KRK: *Konoba Šime*　　　　　　　　　　　　　　　Ⓚ
Ulica Antuna Mahnića 1, Krk. **Map** B3. ☎ *(051) 220 042.*
A good restaurant on the port serving traditional dishes. The atmosphere is
reminiscent of a medieval tavern. ○ *10am–11pm daily.* ☰ 🍷

| | ▦ | ● | ▦ |

KRK: *Galeb*　　　　　　　　　　　　　　　　　Ⓚ Ⓚ
Krk. **Map** B3. ☎ *(051) 221 261.*
Pizzeria set in a splendid location, with a large terrace
overlooking the harbour.
○ *Easter–Sep: 10am–10pm daily.*

| ● | ▦ | | ▦ |

KRK: *Konoba Nono*　　　　　　　　　　　　　Ⓚ Ⓚ
S J Štrossmayera 39, Krk. **Map** B3. ☎ *(051) 222 221.*
This restaurant in the centre specializes in local dishes (including meat dishes);
try the *surlice*, ribbon pasta served with goulash sauce.
○ *Easter–Sep: 9am–midnight daily.*

| ● | ▦ | | |

KRK: *Marina*　　　　　　　　　　　　　　　Ⓚ Ⓚ Ⓚ
Puntica 9, Punat. **Map** B3. ☎ *(051) 854 132.*
Near one of the most beautiful marinas in Croatia, this restaurant is renowned for its
good food, one of the best. ○ *11am–11pm Mon–Fri; 8am–11pm Sat & Sun.* P ☰ 🍷

| ● | ▦ | ● | ▦ |

LIMSKI CHANNEL: *Viking*　　　　　　　　　　　Ⓚ Ⓚ
Limski Kanal 1. **Map** A3. ☎ *(052) 448 223.*
On the Limski Channel, where mussels are farmed. You can eat excellent seafood,
including oysters, to your heart's content.
○ *11am–3.30pm, 6.30–11pm daily.* ● *Jan.* P ☰ 🍷

| ● | ▦ | ● | ▦ |

LOŠINJ: *Lanterna*　　　　　　　　　　　　　　　Ⓚ
Sv. Marije 71, Mali Lošinj. **Map** B3. ☎ *(051) 233 625.*
Far from the crowds which fill the town, particularly in summer, this small
establishment is a little off the beaten track and offers meat and fish dishes.
○ *Easter–Sep: 9am–11pm daily; Oct–Easter: 9am–10pm daily.* P

| ● | ▦ | ● | ▦ |

LOŠINJ: *Villa Diana*　　　　　　　　　　　　　Ⓚ Ⓚ
Baia di Čikat, Čikat 13, Mali Lošinj. **Map** B3. ☎ *(051) 232 055.*
This restaurant is located on a beautiful part of the coast and the menu is geared
around fish dishes.
○ *Easter–Sep: 10am–midnight daily; Oct–Easter: 10am–10pm daily.* P ☰ 🍷 🎵

| ● | ▦ | | ▦ |

OPATIJA: *Madonnina*　　　　　　　　　　　　　Ⓚ
Pava Tomašića 3. **Map** B2. ☎ *(051) 272 579.*
Pizzas and pasta are on offer in this pizzeria, which is in a central position
and offers good value for money. ○ *9am–midnight daily.* ☰

| ● | | | ▦ |

Price categories are for a complete meal with drinks (except wine), including service (a tip is recommended):
(Kn) under 100 kuna
(Kn)(Kn) 100–150 kuna
(Kn)(Kn)(Kn) 150–200 kuna
(Kn)(Kn)(Kn)(Kn) over 200 kuna

CREDIT CARDS
Major credit cards are accepted: American Express, Visa, MasterCard.

CROATIAN CUISINE
Restaurants which serve typical, traditional cuisine.

INTERNATIONAL CUISINE
Restaurants which serve dishes common to European cuisine.

OUTSIDE DINING
The option of eating outside, in a garden or on a terrace, often with a pleasant view.

	CREDIT CARDS	CROATIAN CUISINE	INTERNATIONAL CUISINE	OUTSIDE DINING
OPATIJA: *Amfora* (Kn)(Kn)(Kn) Crnikovica 4, Volosko. **Map** B2. (051) 701 222. This pleasant restaurant, a little outside the city, offers national cuisine, but also Istrian specialities (particularly fish dishes). noon–midnight daily.	●	■	●	■
OPATIJA: *Elita* (Kn)(Kn)(Kn) Maršala Tita 156. **Map** B2. (051) 271 014. At all times of the day or night (or nearly), good grilled food and also pizza is served. 9am–1am daily.	●	■	●	
OPATIJA: *Bevanda* (Kn)(Kn)(Kn)(Kn) Maršala Tita 62. **Map** B2. (051) 712 772. This restaurant, in Volovsko, 3 km (2 miles) from Opatija, offers scampi, squid and fish, always fresh and simply cooked. noon–11pm daily. 15 Jun–15 Jul.	●	■		■
OPATIJA: *Plavi Podrum* (Kn)(Kn)(Kn)(Kn) Obala Frane Supila 4. **Map** B2. (051) 701 223. A good choice of restaurant for those who like fish. Musical evenings. noon–midnight daily.	●	■		
POREČ: *Nono* (Kn) Zagrebačka 4. **Map** A2. (052) 453 088. Probably the best pizza in Croatia: choose from dozens of different toppings. Popular and always busy. noon–midnight daily.	●		●	■
POREČ: *Istra* (Kn)(Kn)(Kn) Milanovića 30. **Map** A2. (052) 434 636. A popular place with the locals. Typical local cuisine, try the *mučkalica*, a stew of chicken and vegetables with herbs. 11am–midnight daily.	●	■		
PULA: *Delfin* (Kn)(Kn) Kandlerova 8. **Map** A3. (052) 222 289. Typical Istrian specialities, not just fish dishes, are served on a pleasant terrace. Try the *manistra*, a kind of vegetable soup. 11am–midnight daily.	●	■		■
PULA: *Milan* (Kn)(Kn)(Kn) Stoja 4. **Map** A3. (052) 210 200. A good restaurant with traditions dating from 1967; situated in Stoja, near the beach. 11am–midnight Mon–Sat. Jan.	●	■	●	
PULA: *Valsabbion* (Kn)(Kn)(Kn)(Kn) Pješčana Uvala IX/26. **Map** A3. (052) 218 033. Voted one of the best restaurants in Croatia by local food critics. Traditional dishes are presented in a new way and there is also good international cuisine. noon–midnight daily. 31 Dec–31 Jan.	●	■	●	■
RAB: *Zlatni Zalaz* (Kn)(Kn) Supetarska, Rab. **Map** B3. (051) 775 150. Located in the beautiful bay of Biskupica, surrounded by woods, this restaurant offers typical Dalmatian cuisine as well as international dishes. There is a splendid view from the terrace. 11am–3pm, 6–11pm daily.	●	■	●	
RAB: *Ali Baba* (Kn)(Kn)(Kn) Srednja ulica 30, Rab. **Map** B3. A bonus at this small restaurant is the pretty terrace-garden. Excellent fish dishes. noon–3pm, 5.30pm–midnight Mon–Sat.	●	■		■
RIJEKA: *Bonavia* (Kn)(Kn)(Kn) Dolac 4. **Map** B2. (051) 357 100. Hotel restaurant of well-deserved fame, offering meat, fish, international cuisine. noon–midnight daily.	●	■	●	■

For key to symbols see back flap

	CREDIT CARDS	CROATIAN CUISINE	INTERNATIONAL CUISINE	DINING OUTSIDE

Price categories are for a complete meal with drinks (except wine), including service (a tip is recommended):
(Kn) under 100 kuna
(Kn)(Kn) 100–150 kuna
(Kn)(Kn)(Kn) 150–200 kuna
(Kn)(Kn)(Kn)(Kn) over 200 kuna

CREDIT CARDS
Major credit cards are accepted: American Express, Visa, MasterCard.

CROATIAN CUISINE
Restaurants which serve typical, traditional cuisine.

INTERNATIONAL CUISINE
Restaurants which serve dishes common to European cuisine.

OUTSIDE DINING
The option of eating outside, in a garden or on a terrace, often with a pleasant view.

RIJEKA: *Feral* (Kn)(Kn) M Gupca 5. **Map** B2. (051) 212 274. There is a wide choice of fish in this restaurant with typical marine decor. A pianist plays at weekends. ◗ *10am–11pm Mon–Sat.* ● *public hols.* ▤ ▮ ♫	●	▦	●	
RIJEKA: *Korkyra* (Kn)(Kn) Slogin Kula 5. **Map** B2. (051) 339 528. One of the best restaurants in Kvarner, renowned for its fish and good service. ◗ *9am–10pm Mon–Sat.* ▣ ▤	●	▦		▦
RIJEKA: *Municipium* (Kn)(Kn)(Kn) Trg Riječke Revolucije 5. **Map** B2. (051) 213 000. This restaurant near the town hall offers carefully prepared seafood specialities, home-made bread and cakes. Also vegetarian dishes. ▤ ▮	●	▦	●	▦
ROVINJ: *Veli Jože* (Kn)(Kn) Svetoga Kriza 1. **Map** A3. (052) 816 337. At this restaurant you can try Istrian dishes such as *bakalar* (salt cod) with a white sauce or lamb with potatoes. ◗ *Easter–Sep: 10–3am daily.* ▮		▦		
ROVINJ: *Amfora* (Kn)(Kn)(Kn) Rismondo 23. **Map** A3. (052) 816 663. Elegant surroundings, excellent service, and the flawless preparation of the dishes make this restaurant one of the best in town. ◗ *11am–11pm Tue–Sun.* ▮	●	▦		▦
UMAG: *Badi* (Kn)(Kn)(Kn) Umaška, Lovrečića bb. **Map** A2. (052) 756 293. A good place to eat fish and other seafood: the dish named after the restaurant is excellent. ◗ *Easter–Sep: 11am–11pm daily; Oct–Easter: noon–3pm, 6–11pm Mon–Thu, 11am–11pm Fri–Sun.* ▣ ▮	●	▦		▦
VRSAR: *Kool Ilva* (Kn)(Kn) Obala M Tita 1a. **Map** A3. (052) 441 987. Produce from the sea and inland is on offer in this restaurant: excellent fish as well as delicious dishes with mushrooms and truffles. ◗ *noon–midnight daily.* ▣ ▮	●	▦	●	▦

DALMATIA

BRAČ: *Gušt* (Kn)(Kn) Frane Radića 14, Bol. **Map** D5. (021) 635 911. A comfortable tavern-style place where you can eat simple but well-prepared meat and fish dishes. ◗ *Easter–Sep: noon–2am daily.* ▤ ▮	●	▦		▦
BRAČ: *Ribarska Kućica* (Kn)(Kn) Kućica, Bol. **Map** D5. (021) 635 144. From the terrace there are beautiful views of the sea. There is a wide choice of fish and a fixed price menu after 8pm every evening. Pizza. ◗ *Easter–Oct: 11–2am daily.* ▮	●	▦		▦
BRAČ: *Taverna Riva* (Kn)(Kn) Frane Radića 5, Bol. **Map** D5. (021) 635 236. This restaurant has tables inside as well as outside on a terrace with a view of the sea. ◗ *8am–midnight daily.* ▤ ▮	●	▦	●	▦
CAVTAT: *Kolona* (Kn)(Kn) Put Tiha 2. **Map** F6. (020) 478 787. The terrace is surrounded by greenery and has views of the sea. Try one of the many risottos, followed by freshly-caught fish, simply grilled. ◗ *Easter–Sep: 9am–midnight daily.* ▮	●	▦	●	▦
DUBROVNIK: *Tabasco* (Kn) Ispod Žičare 16. **Map** F6. (020) 429 595. This is a pizzeria situated in a charming position within the walls of the old city. It also serves *panzerotti*. ◗ *11am–midnight daily.* ▣ ▤	●			▦

DUBROVNIK: *Ragusa2*　　　　　　　　　　(Kn)(Kn)
Zamanijna 12. **Map** F6. **(** *(020) 321 203.*
At this family-run restaurant you can try the real local specialities. In the old part of
Dubrovnik. ◯ *10am–midnight daily.*

DUBROVNIK: *Jadran*　　　　　　　　　(Kn)(Kn)(Kn)
Poljana Paška, Miličevića 1. **Map** F6. **(** *(020) 323 403.*
Local and international cuisine with the setting an added bonus; it is located in the
cloister of the convent of St Clare. ◯ *Easter–Oct: 10am–midnight daily.* ▯

DUBROVNIK: *Konavoka*　　　　　　　　(Kn)(Kn)(Kn)
Setalište Kralja Zvonimira 38. **Map** F6. **(** *(020) 435 105.*
There is a charming atmosphere in this place, filled with potted plants, located in
Lopud. Traditional Croatian dishes and also good pizza. ◯ *noon–midnight daily.*

DUBROVNIK: *Orsan*　　　　　　　　　(Kn)(Kn)(Kn)
Ivana Zajca 2. **Map** F6. **(** *(020) 435 933.*
Orsan serves mainly fish, which is accompanied by Croatian wine. Guests sit out
on a terrace facing the sea. ◯ *8am–midnight daily.* ▯ ▤ ▯ ♬

DUBROVNIK: *Rosarij*　　　　　　　　(Kn)(Kn)(Kn)
Prijeko 2. **Map** F6. **(** *(020) 321 257.*
This restaurant, located in a quiet, peaceful corner of the old part of the city, serves
only the freshest fish and seafood. ◯ *11am–midnight daily.*

DUBROVNIK: *Nautika*　　　　　　　(Kn)(Kn)(Kn)(Kn)
Brsalje 3. **Map** F6. **(** *(020) 442 526.*
This is probably the most elegant restaurant in the city, and offers a lovely view of
the sea. The food matches the elegance of the restaurant and mainly consists of
fish dishes, quite expensive but worth trying. ◯ *noon–midnight daily.* ▯ ▤ ▯ ♬

DUGI OTOK: *Tamaris*　　　　　　　　(Kn)(Kn)
Obala Kralja Tomislava 17, Sali. **Map** C4. **(** *(023) 377 377.*
This restaurant serves fresh fish: spaghetti with fish sauce
and the grilled scampi are among its specialities. ◯ *10am–midnight daily.*

HVAR: *Eremitaž*　　　　　　　　　　(Kn)
Priko, Stari Grad. **Map** D5. **(** *(091) 542 83 951.*
Located in what was once a hospital for sailors in quarantine, the restaurant serves
fish specialities and has a terrace overlooking the sea. Romantic atmosphere.
◯ *Easter–Oct: noon–3.30pm, 6.30pm–midnight daily.* ▯

HVAR: *L'Antica*　　　　　　　　　　(Kn)
Stari Grad. **Map** D5. **(** *(098) 171 74 91.*
Well-known bar-restaurant in the centre of Hvar, a haunt of artists and intellectuals.
Excellent cocktails are served at the bar. ◯ *Easter–Sep: 9am–2pm, 6pm–1am daily.* ▯

HVAR: *Jurin Podrum*　　　　　　　(Kn)(Kn)
Donja Kola, Stari Grad. **Map** D5. **(** *(021) 765 804.*
The restaurant is in a small street. Fish dishes, good cheese and wine. A family-run
business. ◯ *Easter–Sep: noon–3am daily; Oct–Easter: noon–11pm daily.* ▤

HVAR: *Hanibal*　　　　　　　　　(Kn)(Kn)(Kn)
Pjaca, Hvar. **Map** D5. **(** *(021) 742 760.*
Scampi, prawns, lobster, but also meat and mushrooms are on offer in this popular
restaurant, which has tables inside and also outside in the square. It is best to book
in advance. ◯ *11am–11pm daily.*

HVAR: *Macondo*　　　　　　　　(Kn)(Kn)(Kn)
Groda, Hvar. **Map** D5. **(** *(021) 741 851, 742 850.*
Sample excellent fish cuisine here in elegant surroundings. The spaghetti
with lobster is very good. ◯ *Easter–Oct: 1pm–midnight daily.* ▯

HVAR: *Palača Paladini*　　　　　　(Kn)(Kn)(Kn)
Petra Hektorovića 4. **Map** D5. **(** *(021) 742 104.*
A pleasant restaurant with a lively atmosphere which offers good, typical Croatian
cuisine as well as international fare. ◯ *Easter–Sep: noon–midnight daily.* ▯

HVAR: *Paradise Garden*　　　　　　(Kn)(Kn)(Kn)
Hvar Groda, Hvar. **Map** D5. **(** *(021) 742 834.*
This restaurant near the cathedral serves a dish which stands out from the rest:
spaghetti with seafood. Here they make it without tomato, unlike everywhere else
along the coast. ◯ *Easter–Oct: noon–midnight Mon–Sat.* ▯

Price categories are for a complete meal with drinks (except wine), including service (a tip is recommended):

(Kn) under 100 kuna
(Kn)(Kn) 100–150 kuna
(Kn)(Kn)(Kn) 150–200 kuna
(Kn)(Kn)(Kn)(Kn) over 200 kuna

CREDIT CARDS
Major credit cards are accepted: American Express, Visa, MasterCard.

CROATIAN CUISINE
Restaurants which serve typical, traditional cuisine.

INTERNATIONAL CUISINE
Restaurants which serve dishes common to European cuisine.

OUTSIDE DINING
The option of eating outside, in a garden or on a terrace, often with a pleasant view.

	CREDIT CARDS	CROATIAN CUISINE	INTERNATIONAL CUISINE	DINING OUTSIDE

HVAR: *Panorama*   (Kn)(Kn)(Kn)(Kn)
Smokovnik, Hvar. **Map** D5. ((021) 742 515.
Located in a small Austrian fort with a terrace and a wonderful view of the bay, 2 km (1 mile) from Hvar town. One of its specialities is kid cooked in a metal bell: it must be ordered in advance. ○ *Easter–Oct: noon–1am daily.* **P**

| | | ■ | ● | ■ |

KORČULA: *Adio Mare*   (Kn)(Kn)
Svetoga Roka, Korčula. **Map** E6. ((020) 711 253.
Close to the reputed birthplace of the traveller, Marco Polo. The restaurant offers excellent fish dishes and a good atmosphere. ○ *Apr–Oct: 3am–midnight daily.* ▤

| | | ■ | | ■ |

KORČULA: *Morski Konjic*   (Kn)(Kn)
Stari Grad 47a, Korčula. **Map** E6. ((020) 711 642.
Pleasant surroundings and excellent fish dishes and shellfish; prepare to queue in the high season. ○ *Easter–Dec: 7am–midnight daily.* ▤

| | ● | ■ | | ■ |

MAKARSKA: *Jež*   (Kn)(Kn)
Petra Krešimira IV 90. **Map** E5. ((021) 611 741.
Traditional Dalmatian cuisine served in a modern way. Excellent fish and Croatian and Slovenian wines. ○ *Dec–Oct: 2pm–midnight daily.* **P** ▤

| | ● | ■ | ● | ■ |

MAKARSKA: *Riva*   (Kn)(Kn)
Obala Kralja Tomislava 6. **Map** E5. ((021) 616 829.
Good value for money. The restaurant offers delicious octopus and scampi. Eat outside on the terrace or in the garden under the trees. ○ *Easter–Oct: 11am–midnight.*

| | ● | ■ | ● | ■ |

METKOVIĆ: *Villa Neretva*   (Kn)(Kn)
Krvavac 2. **Map** E5. ((020) 672 200.
Located in the heart of the valley of the River Neretva, on the road from Opuzen to Metković, this is one of the best restaurants in Croatia. The menu offers fish, seafood, including scampi, and meat. One of its specialities is eel.
○ *Dec–Oct: 9am–midnight daily.* **P** ▤

| | ● | ■ | ● | ■ |

PAG: *Biser*   (Kn)(Kn)(Kn)
A G Matoša 8, Pag. **Map** C4. ((023) 611 333.
This hotel restaurant is near the sea and you can enjoy the view from the beautiful winter garden. ○ *7am–midnight daily.* **P** ▤

| | ● | ■ | ● | ■ |

PELJEŠAC: *Kapetanova Kuća*   (Kn)(Kn)(Kn)
Mali Ston. **Map** E6. ((020) 754 264.
This restaurant is known for its excellent seafood. ○ *9am–midnight daily.* ▤

| | ● | ■ | | ■ |

ŠIBENIK: *Forum*   (Kn)
Vladimira Nazora 7. **Map** D5. ((022) 218 646.
A good pizzeria, popular with the locals. The menu also includes some alternative hot dishes. ○ *7am–11pm daily.* ▤

| | ● | | | ■ |

ŠIBENIK: *Stari Grad*   (Kn)(Kn)
Obala Oslobođenja 12. **Map** D5. ((022) 219 330.
One of the few restaurants in the city with reasonable prices, near the port, where you can try spaghetti with seafood and fresh fish.
○ *Easter–Oct: 9am–3pm, 6pm–midnight daily.* ▤

| | ● | ■ | | |

SPLIT: *Galija*   (Kn)
Tončićeva 12. **Map** D5. ((021) 347 932.
Probably the best pizza in the city is found in this good-value restaurant.
○ *9am–11pm Mon–Sat, noon–11pm Sun.* ▤

| | ● | | | |

SPLIT: *Ponoćno Sunce*   (Kn)(Kn)
Teutina 15. **Map** D5. ((021) 361 011.
A restaurant serving tasty and well-prepared vegetarian dishes, together with specialities of Dalmatian cuisine.
○ *Easter–Sep: 10am–midnight Mon–Sat.* ▤

| | ● | ■ | ● | |

SPLIT: *Re di Mare*   Ⓚ Ⓚ
Lučića 4. **Map** D5. 【 *(021) 386 789.*
Located on the marina. Excellent fish dishes. ○ *11am–midnight daily.* 🅿 ▤ 🍷

SPLIT: *Sarajevo*   Ⓚ Ⓚ
Domaldova 6. **Map** D5. 【 *(021) 347 454.*
An unusual restaurant in a city centre, offering traditional Croatian fish
and meat dishes. Try the *pašticada*, a type of meat stew
served with gnocchi. ○ *10am–11pm daily.* ▤ 🍷

SPLIT: *Boban*   Ⓚ Ⓚ Ⓚ
Hektorovićeva 49. **Map** D5. 【 *(021) 543 300.*
A classic, elegant restaurant, patronized by the well-to-do of the city: meat and fish
are on the menu, and prices reflect the style. ○ *10am–midnight daily.* 🅿 ▤ 🍷

SPLIT: *Šumica*   Ⓚ Ⓚ Ⓚ
Put Firula 6. **Map** D5. 【 *(021) 389 897.*
This restaurant overlooking the sea is a fish lover's delight. Dalmatian food – the
scampi with *buzara* (garlic, tomatoes and white wine) is particularly good.
○ *9am–midnight daily.* 🅿 ▤ 🍷

TROGIR: *Fontana*   Ⓚ Ⓚ Ⓚ
Obrov 1, Trogir. **Map** D5. 【 *(021) 884 811.*
This pretty terrace overlooks the sea. The menu includes pizza, pasta and meat
dishes, and especially excellent fish. ○ *7am–midnight daily.* 🅿 ▤ 🍷

VIS: *Villa Kaliopa*   Ⓚ Ⓚ Ⓚ Ⓚ
V. Nazora 32, Vis. **Map** D6. 【 *(021) 711 755.*
A restaurant set in the middle of an exotic garden with statues and unusual plants.
Typical Dalmatian cuisine. ○ *5pm–midnight daily.* 🅿 🍷

ZADAR: *Albin*   Ⓚ
Put Dikla 47. **Map** C4. 【 *(023) 331 137.*
This restaurant, 5 km (3 miles) outside the centre in the tourist district of Borik,
offers well-prepared fresh fish dishes. ○ *8am–11pm daily.* 🅿 ▤ 🍷

ZADAR: *Foša*   Ⓚ Ⓚ
Kneza Dmitra Zvonimira 2. **Map** C4. 【 *(023) 314 421.*
Set in a beautiful bay, this restaurant offers fresh fish. ○ *Easter–Sep: 10am–midnight
Mon–Sat, 5pm–midnight Sun; Oct–Easter: 10am–midnight Mon–Sat.* ▤ 🍷

ZAGREB

Boban   Ⓚ
Gajeva ulica 9. **Map** D2. 【 *(01) 481 15 49.*
Modern Italian cooking, with tables in the basement or on the terrace outside.
Owned by the Croatian footballer Zvonimir Boban. ○ *10am–midnight daily.* ▤ 🍷

Dubravkin Put   Ⓚ Ⓚ Ⓚ
Dubravkin Put 2. **Map** D2. 【 *(01) 483 49 75.*
A good restaurant just outside the centre. The owner, who is from Dubrovnik, gets
daily deliveries from Dalmatia, guaranteeing the freshness. ○ *11am–midnight.* 🅿 ▤ 🍷

Gračanka   Ⓚ Ⓚ
Gračanska cesta 48. **Map** D2. 【 *(01) 467 40 89.*
On Mount Medvednica, this place is popular with the locals. Meat dishes and also
excellent mushrooms in season. ○ *noon–midnight Tue–Sun.* 🅿 🍷

Kaptolska Klet   Ⓚ
Kaptol 5. **Map** D2. 【 *(01) 481 48 38.*
This restaurant in front of the cathedral, on a covered terrace, serves mainly meat
dishes, well-prepared and good value for money. ○ *10am–midnight daily.* 🅿 ▤ 🍷

Mimice   Ⓚ Ⓚ
Jurišićeva ulica 21. **Map** D2. 【 *(01) 481 45 24.*
A popular restaurant with the local people, offering simple hot and cold dishes.
Crowded at any time of the day. ○ *7am–10pm Mon–Fri; 7am–6pm Sat.*

Okrugljak   Ⓚ Ⓚ
Mlinovi 28. **Map** D2. 【 *(01) 467 41 12.*
This rustic restaurant on the road between Zagreb and Mount Medvednica has a
garden for children. At simple wooden tables you can try the specialities of the
house: lamb, duck and turkey, always served with *mlinci*, a mix of oven-baked
pasta. ○ *11–1am daily.* ● *31 Dec.* 🅿 ▤ 🍷

For key to symbols see back flap

Price categories are for a complete meal with drinks (except wine), including service (a tip is recommended):
ⓚ under 100 kuna
ⓚⓚ 100–150 kuna
ⓚⓚⓚ 150–200 kuna
ⓚⓚⓚⓚ over 200 kuna

CREDIT CARDS
Major credit cards are accepted: American Express, Visa, MasterCard.

CROATIAN CUISINE
Restaurants which serve typical, traditional cuisine.

INTERNATIONAL CUISINE
Restaurants which serve dishes common to European cuisine.

OUTSIDE DINING
The option of eating outside, in a garden or on a terrace, often with a pleasant view.

	CREDIT CARDS	CROATIAN CUISINE	INTERNATIONAL CUISINE	OUTSIDE DINING
Pavljon ⓚⓚⓚⓚ Trg Kralja Tomislava 22. **Map** D2. 📞 *(01) 481 30 66.* This yellow Art Pavilion in the park in front of the station houses a restaurant serving Italian-inspired cuisine. Good service. ⏲ *10am–midnight Mon–Sat.* 🅿 ▤ 🍷	●	▪	●	▪
Pizzicato ⓚ Gundulićeva ulica 4. **Map** D2. 📞 *(01) 483 15 55.* This busy pizzeria offers pizza with a thin base and a variety of toppings at competitive prices. ⏲ *8am–midnight daily.* ▤				▪

CENTRAL CROATIA

JASTREBARSKO: *K Lojzeku* ⓚ Strossmayerov trg 12. **Map** C2. 📞 *(01) 628 11 29.* A restaurant with rustic furnishings offering home cooking. The menu lists typical Croatian dishes and meat. ⏲ *8am–11pm daily.* ● *1–15 Aug.* ▤ 🍷	●	▪	●	▪
KARLOVAC: *Žganjer* ⓚ Jelaši 41. **Map** C2. 📞 *(047) 641 333.* This is the restaurant of a motel with ten rooms, on the road to Plitvice. Croatian specialities and grilled meat, particularly lamb. ⏲ *always.* 🅿 ▤ 🍷	●	▪	●	▪
KUTINA: *Gradski Podrum* ⓚ Trg Kralja Tomislava 2. **Map** D2. 📞 *(044) 684 010.* Situated in the centre of the town, this simple restaurant has a large dining room with seating for 100 people. ⏲ *7am–10pm daily.* 🅿 ▤ 🍷	●	▪	●	▪
SAMOBOR: *Pri staroj uri* ⓚⓚ Giznik 2. **Map** C2. 📞 *(01) 336 05 48.* In a cottage in this charming village you can try traditional dishes such as *Hrvatska pisanica* (steak with mushrooms, onions, tomatoes and red wine sauce). ⏲ *11am–11pm Mon–Sat; 11am–6pm Sun.* ● *25 Dec.* 🅿 ▤ 🍷	●	▪	●	▪
SAMOBOR: *Samoborska Pivnica* ⓚⓚ Šmidhenova 3. **Map** C2. 📞 *(01) 336 16 23.* Near the town park, this pub-restaurant offers good food at reasonable prices, all day long. ⏲ *9am–11pm Mon–Fri; 9am–midnight Sat & Sun.* 🅿 🍷	●	▪		▪
SISAK: *Cocktail* ⓚⓚ Dr A Starčevića 27. **Map** D2. 📞 *(044) 549 137.* A restaurant in the centre of Sisak, near the town museum, serving traditional Croatian and Italian cuisine. Good wine selection. ⏲ *11am–11pm daily.* ▤ 🍷	●	▪	●	▪

SLAVONIA AND BARANJA

ĐAKOVO: *Croatia–tourist* ⓚ Preradovića 25. **Map** F2. 📞 *(031) 813 391.* Good meat dishes are served here. Try the *čobanac*, a type of goulash. ⏲ *6am–11pm daily.* 🅿 🍷	●	▪	●	▪
DARUVAR: *Terasa* ⓚ Julijev park 1. **Map** E2. 📞 *(043) 331 705.* Located near the thermal spas of Croatia, this restaurant has Baroque furnishings and serves Croatian, Hungarian, Czech and Italian cuisine. ⏲ *9–1am daily.* 🅿 ▤ 🍷	●	▪	●	▪
KUTJEVO: *Schön Blik* ⓚ Zagrebačka 11, Vetovo. **Map** F2. 📞 *(034) 267 108.* Situated by a lake, 8 km (5 miles) from Kutjevo, this place offers typical cuisine. It is on the Kutjevo to Velika road. ⏲ *10am–midnight daily.* 🅿 🍷		▪		▪
LIPIK: *Lipa* ⓚ Marije Terezije 5. **Map** E2. 📞 *(034) 421 244.* At Lipa you can try the typical cooking of Slavonia. ⏲ *7am–10pm daily.* 🅿 ▤	●	▪	●	▪

NAŠICE: *Ribnjak* (Kn)
Stjepana Radića 1, Ribnjak, Našice. **Map** F2. ☎ *(031) 607 006.*
This restaurant, 10 km (6 miles) from Našice, on the road for Osijek, offers
Slavonian cuisine and fish specialities. ◯ *7am–midnight daily.* **P** ☰ **▮**

NOVA GRADIŠKA: *Slavonski Biser* (Kn)
Teslina 2. **Map** E2. ☎ *(035) 363 259.*
Near the train and bus station, this restaurant offers Croatian cooking and
international dishes. ◯ *6am–midnight daily.* **P** ☰ **▮**

OSIJEK: *Bastion* (Kn)
Vatroslava Lisinskog. **Map** F2. ☎ *(031) 207 800.*
This is a café and restaurant. Its strong point is the distinctive atmosphere
created by its setting in an ancient tower. ◯ *8am–midnight daily.* **▮**

OSIJEK: *Slavonska Kuća* (Kn)
Firingera 26. **Map** F2. ☎ *(031) 208 277.*
An old house with rustic furnishings serving ancient traditional dishes, to be eaten
with the good local wine. ◯ *9am–11pm Mon–Sat.* **P** ☰ **▮**

OSIJEK: *Bijelo Plavi* (Kn)(Kn)(Kn)
Martina Divalta 8. **Map** F2. ☎ *(031) 571 000.*
Located near the swimming pool and stadium, this restaurant offers typical dishes
of the region. ◯ *7am–midnight daily.* **P** ☰ **▮**

SLAVONSKI BROD: *Slavonski Podrum* (Kn)(Kn)
Andrije Štampa 1. **Map** F3. ☎ *(035) 444 856.*
Typical Croatian cuisine is offered at this restaurant. ◯ *noon–11pm daily.* **P** ☰ **▮**

THE NORTHERN COUNTIES

KOPRIVNICA: *Kraluš* (Kn)(Kn)
Zrinski trg, 10. **Map** D1. ☎ *(048) 622 302.*
Traditional beer hall serving hot and cold local dishes in a charming old building.
Excellent choice of beers. ◯ *8am–11pm Sun–Fri; 8am–midnight Sat.* ☰

KOPRIVNICA: *Podravska klet* (Kn)(Kn)
Starogradska Cesta (4 km/2 miles from Koprivnica). **Map** D1. ☎ *(048) 634 069.*
Rustic-elegant atmosphere, offering good fresh food, just outside the town.
Music on Saturdays. ◯ *10am–10pm Sun–Thu; 10am–midnight Fri & Sat.* **P** **▮**

KRAPINSKE TOPLICE: *Zlatna Lisica* (Kn)
Martinišče 38a. **Map** D1. ☎ *(049) 236 527.*
An open-air restaurant offering simple, home-made cooking. **P** **▮**

STUBIČKE TOPLICE: *Slamnati Krovovi* (Kn)
Babića Đalskog 1. **Map** D1. ☎ *(049) 282 569.*
This restaurant is situated in the centre of the town and offers typical cuisine of the
region. The meat and the *štrukli* dessert are excellent. ◯ *6am–11pm daily.* **P** **▮**

TRAKOŠĆAN: *Coning* (Kn)
Trakošćan 5. **Map** D1. ☎ *(042) 796 224.*
Near a lake and the medieval castle of Trakošćan, this restaurant serves Croatian
specialities from the Zagorje hills. ◯ *6am–11pm daily.* **P** **▮**

VARAŽDIN: *Pivnica Raj* (Kn)
Gundulićeva 11. **Map** D1. ☎ *(042) 213 146.*
Traditional dishes of the region are served in this restaurant which has live music
on Saturdays and Sundays. ◯ *8am–10pm Mon–Sat; 8am–9pm Sun.* ☰ ♫

VARAŽDIN: *Zlatna Guska* (Kn)(Kn)
Habdelića 4. **Map** D1. ☎ *(042) 213 393.*
Set in a vaulted brick cellar, this very pleasant restaurant serves a range of meat
and fish dishes and offers a salad bar. ◯ *8am–11pm daily.*

VARAŽDIN: *Royal* (Kn)(Kn)(Kn)
Uska ulica 5. **Map** D1. ☎ *(042) 213 477.*
In the town centre, this restaurant offers grilled food and good Croatian wines.
◯ *9am–10pm Mon–Thu; 9am–midnight Fri & Sat; 9am–4pm Sun.* ☰ **▮**

VELIKI TABOR: *Grešna Gorica* (Kn)
Habdelića 6. **Map** C1. ☎ *(049) 343 001.*
This farmhouse on a hill facing Veliki Tabor, near Miljana castle, offers typical Croatian
dishes. ◯ *10am–10pm Mon–Fri; 9am–10pm Sat & Sun.* **P** ☰ ♫

SHOPPING IN CROATIA

CROATIA DOES its best to encourage its visitors to go shopping (indeed it is a significant factor in local economies) and there is a range of traditional and typical crafts, which are excellent souvenirs. The prices are by and large very reasonable too. Shoppers can choose from a variety of products from works of creative handicraft such as handmade lace or hand-painted ceramics to jewellery.

Doll in costume, Osijek

On the island of Pag, exquisite lace is made and in Osijek, where beautiful embroidery is a proud tradition, you can also buy pretty costume dolls. Ties and fountain pens, both of which originated in Croatia, also make good purchases. In some resorts, local artists make a living by selling their watercolours. Visitors can also buy all sorts of delicious Croatian consumables from honey to plum brandy.

Jars of various types of honey, a speciality on the island of Šolta

OPENING HOURS

SHOPS AND DEPARTMENT stores are usually open from 8am to 8pm from Monday to Friday (but some stores may open at 7am and close at 9pm) and from 8am to 2 or 3pm on Saturdays. However, it should be remembered that smaller shops often close at lunchtime, usually from noon to 4pm. Shops are generally closed on Sundays and holidays but in the high season in the tourist resorts many shops stay open for business as usual.

PRICES

THE PRICES ARE FIXED in the shops and it is not generally done to haggle over prices. However, in the markets and the street stalls it is acceptable practice, and it can also be fun, to negotiate a good price. The prices are

often displayed in the markets, but it should be remembered that at times the prices displayed are not always the same as those applied to the local people. The spending power of foreign visitors is frequently much greater than that of the local Croats and can occasionally result in pricing variations for locals.

PAYING

IN DEPARTMENT stores, shopping centres and the major chain stores, it is only possible to pay in local currency or by using one of the main international credit cards. In the smaller shops and in places such as markets, payments should be made in cash, in kuna.

VAT REFUNDS

TOURISTS IN CROATIA who spend more than 500 kuna on a single item are entitled to a refund of the Value Added Tax (VAT), which is called PDV in Croatia. When making your purchase, you should ask the sales assistant for the appropriate form (PDV–P), which should be properly filled in and stamped, on the spot.
  This document should be handed to the customs authorities on departure from Croatia, thus verifying that the item bought is genuinely destined for export.
  A PDV refund in kuna can be obtained within six months,

either at the same shop where the goods were purchased (in which case the tax is refunded immediately), or by posting the verified receipt back to the shop, together with the number of the bank account into which the refund should be paid. In this case the refund is dealt with within 15 days of receipt of the claim.

MARKETS

THE STREET MARKETS of Croatia are colourful, lively places to stroll around.
  In Zagreb, the Dolac (see p151) is a daily market where food is sold under colourful red umbrellas. There is also an underground area here where other products such as household articles and furnishings are sold.
  In Split there is a morning market which is held every

Fruit and vegetables on sale at the Dolac market in Zagreb

day on Pazar, just east of the palace walls. This market sells absolutely everything: fruit, vegetables, flowers, shoes, clothes and a vast assortment of souvenirs. There is a local saying which has it that if you cannot find what you are looking for at this market, it probably does not exist (at least not in Split).

SHOPPING CENTRES

LARGE SHOPPING CENTRES can also be found in Croatia, mainly in the larger towns and cities. Here you will find a number of shops selling assorted merchandise under one roof, usually including a large department store or supermarket.

In Zagreb the busiest and best-known department store is **Nama**, which is right in the centre of the city. Another useful shop, also in the city centre, is **Importanne**, which also has a pharmacy which is open 24 hours a day and sells cigarettes and newspapers. The **Importanne Galerija** is only open on weekdays.

Another useful store is **Plaza** which is open from Monday to Saturday. The **Rotonda** is also open from Monday to Saturday.

TRADITIONAL HANDICRAFTS

THERE ARE PLENTY OF opportunities for the visitor to buy a variety of typical Croatian handicrafts and produce, which make very tempting souvenirs.

The country has a long tradition of skilled production of a rich range of handicrafts and typical produce. Production of these crafts is encouraged and supported by the local authorities, who see it as a good way of preserving the cultural heritage and the ancient traditions and crafts of the country.

In Zagreb, you can buy handicrafts, embroidered articles, dolls in traditional costume, terracotta, ceramics, wooden objects and many other similar items at **Rokotvorine**.

Decorated ceramic objects on display in a shop

In Split you can find a large assortment of souvenirs, including objects clearly inspired by maritime themes. You can also buy good reproductions of objects from the era of Roman rule in the underground area of Diocletian's Palace *(see p117)*.

In Osijek, many shops in the centre of the city sell typical locally made handicrafts. Here you can also find dolls dressed in beautifully made costumes, packages of special lace and in particular fabrics finely embroidered with gold and silver thread.

EMBROIDERY AND LACE

ONE IMPORTANT typical Croatian craft is the art of embroidery, which is carried out more or less everywhere.

Gold thread embroidery produced in the town of Osijek

A characteristic design is a red geometric pattern stitched onto a white background. This design is used to decorate table linen, pillowcases and blouses.

The lace of Pag is justly famous and widely admired. The origins of the lace date back to the Renaissance period, when it was used to decorate the blouses of the ladies of the island of Pag.

However, it was not until the beginning of the 20th century that this particular handiwork assumed its well-deserved fame, thanks to a beautifully decorated blouse given by a noblewoman to the Archduchess of Austria Marie Josephine. This gift was so greatly appreciated and admired that the archduchess went to Pag in person to order more items of clothing. At that time, the Austrian court set trends for others to follow, and this was enough to guarantee the future success for the production of this lace.

The lace is made on a long cylindrical cushion by lacemakers of great skill and tremendous patience. The lace patterns produced are the lacemaker's interpretation of patterns and designs which have been passed down from generation to generation. In this way, the pieces of lace that are produced can often be very different from one another. However, all the patterns originate with the same geometric structure which forms the base.

Lacemaker working on a piece of Pag lace

Pag lace is surprisingly light but at the same time strong. If at all possible, pieces of the lace should be bought in Pag itself. Not only can you be sure of paying a better price than elsewhere but you will be helping to keep alive a tradition which is over a century old.

Prices vary according to the size of the piece you buy, but if you consider that a table centrepiece measuring 10 cm (4 in) in diameter takes a good 24 hours to make, you will have some idea of the labour involved.

Lace is sold in the shop adjacent to the **Pag Museum** (summer opening hours are from 6 to 9pm), but the best buys to be had may be found on the same road as the museum and along the ulica Tomislava, where every morning you can find women at their work, selling their lace directly to the public.

LUCKY JEWELLERY

THERE IS ONE ITEM of jewellery which can only be found in Croatia or, more precisely, only in Rijeka. This is the *morčić* or small Moorish figure. The figurine, in the form of a black character wearing a turban, was originally produced as earrings but today you can also find tie-pins and brooches. The *morčić* has become the symbol of the city and, in 1991, it was proclaimed the mascot of Rijeka. A legend dates the origins of the figurine to the

city's unexpected liberation from a Turkish siege during the 16th century. It was shown that a determining factor in the victory was the contribution of the women of Rijeka and it is said that their men decided to give them a gift of special earrings made to represent the invaders who had been forced to flee for their lives.

In fact, it seems more likely that the *morčić* originated in the 17th and 18th centuries as a local reproduction, made from decidedly poor materials, of a figurine set with stones which was very popular with the Venetians. The figurine represented the connections between Venice and the East and the mystery that this part of the world symbolized for them at the time.

The figure soon became a symbol of good luck among the Istrian people and since that time it has become more lavish and elaborate, so much so that its production has become the preserve of goldsmiths. The body of the figure is traditionally glazed ceramic. On request, precious stones may be used to decorate this figure. The best place to buy a *morčić* in Rijeka is the **Mala Galerija**.

CURIOSITIES

CROATIA CAN CLAIM to have invented one of the most well-known of men's accessories, the tie, or cravat. The tie actually originates from a type of scarf worn by Croatian cavalrymen to distinguish them from other soldiers during the bloody 30-year war which devastated Europe in the 17th century.

The French took to referring to this particular way of tying the scarf as "*à la cravate*", meaning "in the Croatian way". Since that time the tie, or cravat, has become a standard symbol of smart, elegant dressing for hundreds of millions of men in the world.

An earring with the *morčić* of Rijeka

The production of ties in Croatia today is still of a very high standard, and a tie would make a highly appropriate choice for a souvenir of your visit.

There are some very good clothes shops in the centre of Zagreb where you can buy an assortment of ties, and these

One of many jeweller's shops in Croatia

include **Follow Me**, **Heruc Galeria** and **Jobis**.

Another little-known fact is that the inventor of the fountain pen was an engineer from Zagreb. In 1906, one Eduard Slavoljub Penkala patented a mechanical pencil and a year later a pen with a reservoir of ink, called the "mechanical pen", which revolutionized the way people wrote.

The inventor opened the first factory for the production of fountain pens in Zagreb in 1911. Within a short space of time it became an enormous success and developed into one of the most important manufacturing centres for writing instruments, producing fountain pens which were exported all over the world. There could not be a more appropriate place to buy this everyday item than Zagreb itself.

Elegant ties on display in a shop in the centre of Zagreb

LOCAL PRODUCE

THE GASTRONOMIC specialities and local produce of Croatia are as varied as the landscape of Croatia.

Among the country's best-known natural products, one of the most important is lavender. Lavender is sold dried in small bags or as essence in bottles. It can be found more or less all over the country but is particularly linked with the island of Hvar (*see pp124–5*), where its colour and scent can nearly

Paški sir, the sheep's cheese of Pag, sold on the island

overwhelm the senses when the shrubs are in flower. The scent is particularly pungent when you browse the lavender stalls near the port, where you can buy any number of cosmetic products made with lavender.

The gastronomic specialities of Croatia also make excellent souvenirs. Many places have their own particular speciality. Among many items worthy of mention are the mustard (in traditional containers) made in Samobor, near Zagreb, the honey from Grohote, on the island of Šolta, and *cukarini* biscuits from Korčula.

Another unmissable delicacy is the delicious truffle found around Buzet, over-looking the Mirna valley in Istria (although these are only available in season).

However, the most highly valued of all delicacies is cheese. Croatia produces a range of its own cheeses, and the most well-known is *paški sir*, a mature cheese made from sheep's milk, produced on the island of Pag (*see pp100–101*). It is still made according to traditional methods and the grazing pasture for the sheep, full of aromatic herbs, is said to give it a distinctive flavour.

To buy the cheese on the island just look for signs with the name of the cheese, "*paški sir*" outside the farmhouses, or go to the well-stocked shop of **Tonći Buljanović**.

Seller of essence and lavender bags on the island of Hvar

ENTERTAINMENT IN CROATIA

A VARIETY OF entertainment is available in Croatia, for residents and visitors alike. Traditional, cultural centres of entertainment include the theatres which put on plays and ballet (in summer, performances are sometimes held outdoors in places with a particularly pretty setting), and cinemas, offering the chance to see international films in the original language. Music lovers will find a wide range of concerts, from contemporary to classical, as well as lots of opportunities to listen to Croatian folk music and dancing, which have a long tradition. There are night clubs, particularly in the larger cities and in major coastal resorts, where you can dance and listen to music til late, and casinos to try your luck at the gaming tables. In addition, visitors can go to sporting events such as football or basketball games, both of which are hugely popular sports. Croatia offers something for everyone, and also, just as importantly, for all age groups.

Classical ballet, National Theatre in Zagreb

The ornate interior of the National Theatre in Zagreb

INFORMATION AND TICKETS

F OR INFORMATION concerning dates, times, prices and booking details of the various festivals, shows, theatre performances and musicals, it is best to get in touch with the relevant local tourist information office in Croatia. All these offices can provide details about the cultural events happening in their part of the country.

Posters announcing forthcoming events are often displayed all over the cities and towns and these are a good way of finding out about the more important or more popular shows.

For information concerning theatre performances, you can also go to the theatre box office itself, where you can usually buy tickets on the spot.

THEATRE AND DANCE

T HE THEATRE IN CROATIA has a long tradition. The average foreign visitor is of course at a linguistic disadvantage when it comes to plays, in that performances are in Croat, a language which is not easily or widely understood by foreigners. However, there should be no barrier to appreciation of performances of opera, classical or modern music concerts and ballet.

Folk music and dance performances are very popular with visitors and give a fascinating glimpse of the country's traditions through the dances, songs and costumes of the performers.

Theatre performances usually take place in the evening. A typical starting time is 7.30pm. You can normally choose from a seat in the *parter* (stalls), *lože* (a box) or the *balkon* (the gallery). Different prices are charged for different seating areas, but in general theatre tickets are usually very reasonably priced.

Many theatre and musical performances are staged in lovely old buildings. A neo-Baroque building in Zagreb houses the **Croatian National Theatre**, which is used principally for opera and ballet.

A somewhat more unusual form of theatre is the puppet show put on at **Zagrebačko Kazalište Lutaka**; performances are only held at the weekends.

Rijeka can also offer a variety of options for theatre-goers, with classic programmes of opera, ballet and plays. These take place in the **Ivan Zajc Theatre**, which is over a hundred years old (it was actually founded in 1895).

Classical performances in Split are staged at the

Costume drama in Dubrovnik, at the Rector's Palace

Musicians playing traditional Croatian music

National Theatre, founded
in 1891 and completely
renovated in 1979. Every year
a special programme called
"Summer in Split" is put on.

In Zadar, the **National
Theatre** presents a varied
programme of events.

Music

THERE ARE numerous
opportunities to listen to
live music in Croatia. Events
vary with the season, but
the seasonal festivals of live
music are particularly
enjoyable. Try to get tickets
for these annual events if they
coincide with your stay in the
country. The theatres of the
principal cities offer varied
musical programmes.

In the resorts along the
coast, many of the larger
hotels hold musical evenings.
These events range from
traditional, local music to
international classics and are
organized to entertain guests
in the summer evenings.

In Zagreb, there is a wide
choice of concerts to choose
from. Go and see the shows
at the **Kontrapunkt**, which
started up in 1999 at the
Aquarius Club. They take a
global approach to music,
with styles ranging from disco
to jazz to folk. They also put
on photographic exhibitions
and other shows.

Classical music concerts are
usually held in the two rooms

of the **Vatroslav Lisinski**
theatre. Also in Zagreb,
operetta, musicals and
programmes of folk music
and dance are usually put
on at the **Komedija** in the
Kaptol area.

In Pula, try to get to some
of the performances held
in the ancient, but well-
preserved, **Roman
Amphitheatre**. In summer
this is the venue for festivals
of music, film and art. For
further information
concerning these events,
contact the local tourist
information office.

Dubrovnik offers a
particularly varied panorama
of musical events. These
include folk performances
in May, June, September
and October on Sundays
at 11am in front of the
church of St Blaise.

Concerts by the local
philharmonic orchestra are

held in the atrium of the
Rector's Palace, and on
Thursdays in the autumn,
classical music is performed
in the church of St Blaise
by the String Quartet of
Dubrovnik.

The most traditional event
is the **Dubrovnik Summer
Festival**, which has been
held in the Dalmatian capital
for 50 years. The programme
of theatre, music and dance
lasts for five weeks between
July and August. The
repertory is very wide and
has something to suit
everybody's taste. The
opening of the festival
invariably begins with a
celebration with bands and
fireworks in Luža Square.

Tickets can be bought at
the festival office or directly
at the site where the
performance is to take place,
one hour before the start.

Night Clubs

EVENINGS USUALLY start in the
cafés, bars and pubs
which often have live music,
and then continue at the
night clubs and discos, which
remain busy until the early
hours of the morning.

New multipurpose
entertainment centres have
been established in the larger
cities such as Zagreb and
Split. They have café-bars
with music, cinemas, music
rooms, dancing and discos.
These places offer fun for all
ages, but are mainly geared
to younger people.

There are many night clubs
in Zagreb. The **Sokol Club** is
open until 4am (closed
Mondays and Tuedays) and
offers rock concerts every

The amphitheatre in Pula, summer venue for various concerts

A late-night bar in Dubrovnik

Sunday and free entry for women before midnight. The famous **Saloon** (open from Tuesday to Saturday until 4am) attracts a mixed crowd, while **The Best**, also open until 4am (closed Mondays and Tuedays), is one of the most popular places for young people. Finally, the **Kulušić** (open from Thursdays to Sundays until 4am) is currently one of the most "in" places, attracting fans of funk and disco music. Live gigs are put on here from time to time.

In Rijeka, a good place to go for a drink and dancing is the **Palach Club**. In Zaton, 18 km (11 miles) north of Zadar, one of the largest discos in Croatia is the **Saturnus**, which throngs with Croats and foreigners alike. It is open every night in July and August and at weekends during the rest of the year.

In Split, popular places for dancing are the **Discovery**, and the **Night Café Metropolis**, which also has live concerts nearly every day of the week. If you prefer dancing under the stars in summer, choose the **Shakespeare**; in winter the **Masters** is an option.

For dancing in Pula, the best-known spots are the **Rock Club Uljanik** and the **Disco Piramida**.

In Dubrovnik, a place with a long tradition of providing lively entertainment every night, there are the **Esperanza**, and the **Divine Folie** with the latest techno music. Another popular Dubrovnik spot is the **Latino Club Fuego**.

CINEMA

CINEMA-GOING is a real passion in Croatia as is evident from the many cinemas, particularly in the larger towns and cities. The cinemas show international films and all the latest box office hits. In Croatia, films in foreign languages are not dubbed but are shown in their original language with Croatian subtitles, which obviously can make life a lot easier for foreign visitors.

The choice is widest in the capital, Zagreb, where you can see all kinds of films, from the latest Hollywood releases to experimental and cult films. The 20 cinemas in Zagreb include the **Zagreb** and **Kic Art**. The **Kinoteca** is one place that shows seasons of cult, arthouse and experimental films.

In Zadar, the **Gotham** multimedia centre offers various kinds of entertainment with cinemas, which are busiest from 7 to 9pm, a night

club open from 11pm to 4am in the morning and a café with restaurant service which is open from 3pm to midnight.

CASINOS

IF YOU ENJOY a spot of gambling, whether it be betting at the traditional gaming tables of roulette, baccarat or blackjack, or just playing on the ever-popular slot-machines, you will find various opportunities in Croatia. There are casinos in most of the larger towns and cities, often within hotels.

The capital offers the widest choice in its hotel casinos: those of the **Hotel International**, the **Hotel Esplanade** and the **Royal**, in the Hotel Panorama. All stay open until the early hours.

In Pula, a favourite casino is in the **Hotel Histria**, in Punta Verudela.

SPECTATOR SPORTS

THIS IS A country with a prestigious sporting tradition, despite its relatively short history as a nation.

Football is universally loved and the Croats are very proud of the fact that the Croatian national football team reached a well-deserved, if somewhat unexpected, third place in the World Cup held in France in 1998.

Basketball is also an immensely popular sport. The basketball teams such as Cibona of Zagreb or the Split team have won numerous European trophies. Croatia

The Hotel Esplanade in Zagreb, home to a casino

has produced basketball champions such as the great Toni Kukoč, still playing and a star in the American professional league.

However, even if emigration of the best talent to more lucrative markets in other countries has undoubtedly made itself felt, it is still rewarding to go to a stadium or a sports hall to watch a national or even an international game.

In Zagreb there are lots of opportunities to watch a live game. For football fans there is the **Maksimir Stadium**, in the eastern part of the city, home of the local Dinamo Zagreb football team. (The other main football club is Hajduk Split.) The stadium is easily reached by all the trams going in the direction of Bukovacka. Championship games are held here more or less all year round on Sunday afternoons – except for the usual summer break of a couple of months.

Then there is basketball at **Cibona Centar**, which hosts the championship games of the Cibona team from October to April; these are usually held on Saturday evenings.

Tickets for sporting events are sold direct to the public at the ticket offices at the relevant stadium or hall.

The Cibona basketball team from Zagreb during a match

OUTDOOR ACTIVITIES

THE JAGGED COASTLINE, which twists and turns over some considerable distance, is fringed by over a thousand islands (of which only 67 are inhabited), making Croatia a real paradise for people who love being in, on or by the sea. Opportunities for sailing, fishing, diving, windsurfing and all kinds of water sports are abundant and facilities for the experienced and the beginner alike

from yacht-charter companies for sailors to windsurfing schools for the novice are available. Many of the large hotels on the coast have swimming pools and many have several, some with a shallow pool for children. Other sports such as tennis, climbing and hiking are also well catered for. Croatia can offer several thermal spa centres, perfect retreats for relaxing and unwinding *(see pp210 and 253)*.

Sailing school along the coast

Sailing along the Croatian coast

SAILING

THE CROATIAN COAST has many natural harbours, ports and marinas, making it a real haven for sailors.

Experienced sailors can enjoy sailing or cruising by hiring a yacht or catamaran. In Croatia there are at least 75 officially registered associations which offer charter services, and more than 1,400 boats are available for rent.

It is possible to hire a boat with or without a crew. If you want to sail the boat yourself you must have a skipper's licence that is valid for the type of boat you choose. You must also be able to demonstrate that you have passed an exam which testifies that you are competent in the use of equipment for VHF radio communications. In addition, you must inform the port authorities of the exact number of guests and crew members on board and again if there are any changes to these figures.

People sailing to Croatia in their own boat should be aware that any boat over 3 m (10 ft) in length and with an engine over 4 kW must be reported to the nearest Harbour Master's Office on arrival. The Harbour Master must also be informed of the number of people on board, including crew. The craft has to be registered and a tourist tax is charged.

Croatia also offers a range of marine support services which is growing every year in response to increasing demand. Facilities at marinas include refuelling points, repair services, water and electricity hookups, medical assistance, and surveillance. Accommodation in apartments is also available. There are 48 marinas in Croatia offering a total of over 12,000 berths for boats in the water and over 7,000 on dry land.

Marinas are classified according to the level of services they offer and berths are charged accordingly.

The Adriatic Croatia International Club, better

known as **ACI**, is the leading association for marine tourism and operates a chain of 21 marinas stretching from Umag, on the far north of the Croatian coast, to Dubrovnik in the south. These places are well-equipped, with modern equipment and easy access to technical support as well as to various other services such as restaurants, cafés, shops and laundries.

Visitors can take out a yearly contract with ACI which entitles them to use facilities reserved for members and also gives them a special discount on berths at the other ACI marinas.

Coastal radio stations broadcast information on the weather on a daily basis and provide a 24-hour forecast in Croatian and English. Useful sources are Radio Rijeka UKW channel 24, Radio Split UKW channels 07, 21, 23, 81, and Radio Dubrovnik UKW channels 07 and 04.

Mooring in the harbour at Makarska

WINDSURFING

IT IS POSSIBLE to hire boards and sails and sign up for lessons in this energetic sport at nearly all coastal resorts. However, surfers agree that the best place for windsurfing in Croatia is Bol on the island of Brač *(see p122)*. A northwest wind blows steadily here from April to October. It is normally at its most intense in the early afternoon and then gradually subsides towards sunset.

Experts consider the best time of year to practise this sport is around the end of May and the beginning of June, and also at the end of July and the beginning of August.

Windsurfing is not permitted in harbours, or in national parks.

Windsurfing, a very popular sport along the Croatian coast

DIVING

ALTHOUGH the Croatian Adriatic may not be able to compete with other decidedly more exotic destinations such as the Red Sea or the Maldives, the diving in Croatia attracts an ever growing number of tourists who have a passion for the underwater world.

Those who intend to make diving a part of their holiday in Croatia must have a special permit which can be obtained from diving clubs and authorized tourist agencies. The permit is valid for one year and costs 100 kuna. The permit is only issued to those who have diving

The sea off Croatia, rich in marine life and coral

qualifications from one of the internationally recognized diving organizations (BSAC, CMAS, IANTD, NAUI, PADI, SSI). Temporary diving qualifications are not valid.

Diving is allowed in most areas except places where there is a particular prohibition, such as a nature reserve or a military zone. In some areas it is only possible to dive with special permission, which must be obtained beforehand.

Areas that are off-limits include the parks of Krk and Brijuni *(see pp56–7)*, the nature reserves in the bay of Ston and the Lemski Channel, the park of Telašcića, ports and harbour entrances, areas of heavy maritime traffic and anywhere within a 100-m (328-ft) radius of military ships and installations.

The areas requiring special authorization are the Kornati National Park *(see pp96–7)*,

the islands of Mljet *(see pp134–5)*, Vis, Biševo, Svetac, Brisnik, Sušac, Kopiste, Lastovo, Donji Skoji, Vrhovnjaci and Palagruža.

Underwater photography and the use of video cameras is allowed everywhere except for around submerged archaeological remains. For this, permission must be obtained from the Ministry of Culture.

FISHING

THE ADRIATIC SEA is one of the richest in Europe and draws all kinds of fishermen. In order to go fishing, you will need a licence which is issued by tourist offices, authorized agencies and those diving centres and clubs which have an arrangement with the Ministry of Agriculture and Forestry.

The cost of the licence depends on its duration. Licences valid for 1 day cost 60 kuna, 3 days cost 150 kuna, a week, 250 kuna and 30 days, 500 kuna. The licences permit fishing with a rod and line or a spear gun and it is possible to fish everywhere except in the protected areas of the marine parks (that is, Kornati, the Brijuni islands, Krk and Mljet).

Along with the licence you will receive a list of the areas which are off-limits, indications of the quantity that you are allowed to catch of each fish species, and a list of the fishing techniques which are permitted.

Fishing in clear waters off the coast

HIKING IN THE MOUNTAINS

THE MAGNIFICENT coast of Croatia is known all over the world, but what is not so well known is that there are also numerous mountain peaks in the hinterland where you can go climbing.

It was in Croatia in fact, in 1874, that one of the first seven mountaineering associations in the world was founded.

There are many mountain areas all over the country. The Velebit massif *(see p99)* is a chain which extends for almost 150 km (93 miles) east of the central part of the coast. Other areas which are good for climbing are the Cicarija chain, which is 40 km (25 miles) in length and encloses the Istrian peninsula, and Mount Učka, near the eastern coast of Istria, which is over 1,400 m (4,592 ft) in height. In addition the Gorski Kotar covers an area of 35 km (22 miles) between the northern coast and the beginning of the Pannonian Plain (Karlovac) and probably offers the best opportunities for mountain hiking in the whole country, particularly in the area of the Risnjak National Park *(see pp72–3)*.

The trail signs are those used internationally and they are maintained by the local mountaineering clubs. These clubs also run shelters, with the exception of the Velebit massif which is directly administered by the Croatian Mountaineering Association (Hrvatski Planinarski Savez) known as **HPS**.

However, on the more isolated peaks, where there are no shelters, signs may often be missing. This is due to the lack of frequent checks and the destruction of signposts by the weather, animals or careless climbers.

A mountain rescue service is of fundamental importance in the mountains, where accidents can occur. In Croatia this service is run by the Mountain Rescue Service which offers free assistance to all.

You can telephone the **Mountain Rescue Service** direct, but it is probably better to call the nearest police station (call number 92).

If climbing is too strenuous, there are ranges of hills which

Abseiling down a rock face in summer

make excellent rambling territory; for example the Samobor hills and Mount Medvednica in particular, where there are clearly marked trails.

FREE CLIMBING

LOVERS of this sport will find there are many rock faces suitable for free climbing in various parts of the country. The Paklenica National Park has over 400 routes, suitable for any level of ability. Near Baška, on the island of Krk, and at Brela, on the Dalmatian coast, near Makarska, it is possible to combine the sea and the mountains in the same day in the warmer weather.

The rock faces present varying levels of difficulty, but all are usually accessible all year round. Do remember, however, that in autumn and winter, climbers should be extremely wary of the strong bora wind *(bura)*, which can make climbing conditions extremely difficult.

WINTER SPORTS

ALTHOUGH THE country has all the topographical and climatic conditions suitable for the development of winter sports, facilities are still comparatively under-

Hikers on one of the paths in Paklenica National Park

Clay court tennis, a popular sport in Croatia

developed. However, there are skiing facilities in Platak and on the Medvednica and Bjelolasica mountains.

TENNIS

THIS IS ONE OF the most popular sports in the whole country: almost every town can count one or two tennis courts among its sports facilities and the same is true of all the larger hotels, tourist resorts and the larger camping sites. The sport was given a great boost when Goran Ivanisevic won the Men's Singles at Wimbledon in 2001. When the player returned to his native city, Split, he was given honours normally reserved for conquering heroes.

The tennis courts in Croatia are generally surfaced with clay or a synthetic material, as found elsewhere in continental Europe. There are also tennis clubs which, as well as being somewhere to play the sport itself, also offer refreshment facilities, tennis instruction and sometimes gyms and swimming pools. Two of the best-equipped clubs are the **Tennis Club Pecine** in Rijeka and the **Tennis Club Smrikve** in Pula.

WHITEWATER RAFTING

WHETHER you want to shoot rapids or just enjoy rafting down a river this is an activity that has a growing

attraction. Some agencies (for example, **General Turist**) organize trips to rivers where conditions are suitable such as the Kupa and Cetina. Gentler rafting can be found on the river Srmanja near Zadar.

GOLF

GOLF is not a traditional Croatian sport, but interest is developing and Croatia now has two courses. **Dolina Kardinala**, near Karlovac, is an 18-hole course, and there is a 9-hole course on the island of Brijuni, near Pula.

To play at one of the Croatian golf clubs you may need to show a membership card issued by the national federation from your home country, which also shows your handicap.

RELAXATION

SEVERAL EXCELLENT spa resorts offer natural thermal springs and treatments, as well as providing ideal places to relax and regain a sense of well-being (see *Thermal Spas Tour pp210–11*). There is also a useful website with links to resorts, descriptions and prices.

A golfer on a practice course

DIRECTORY

SAILING

ACI
M Tita 151, Opatija.
℡ *(051) 271 288.*
ⓦ www.aci–club.hr

DIVING

Croatian Diving Federation
Dalmatinska 12, Zagreb.
℡ *(01) 484 87 65.*
Ⓕ *(01) 484 91 19.*
ⓦ www.diving–hrs.hr

Pro Diving Croatia
Bulevar Oslobodenja 23, Rijeka.
℡ *(051) 219 111.*
ⓦ www.diving.hr

HIKING & CLIMBING

HPS
ⓦ www.hps.inet.hr

Mountain Rescue Service
℡ *(01) 482 41 42.*

TENNIS

Tenis Centar Alplan
Av. Dubrovnik 15, Zagreb.
℡ *(01) 652 14 22.*
ⓦ www.alplan.hr

Tennis Club Pecine
Setaliste XIII Divizije 33, Rijeka.
℡ *(051) 421 782.*

Tennis Club Smrikve
Stinjanska cesta 91, Pula.
℡ *(052) 517 011.*

Tennis Club Split
Put Firula 18, Split.
℡ *(021) 389 576.*

WHITEWATER RAFTING

General Turist
Praska 5, Zagreb.
℡ *(01) 48 10 033.*

GOLF

Dolina Kardinala Golf Course
℡ *(047) 731 100.*

Brijuni Golf Course
℡ *(052) 525 888.*

SPAS

ⓦ www.spas.about.com

SURVIVAL
GUIDE

PRACTICAL INFORMATION

Tourism is an important source of revenue and every effort is being made to foster the growth and development of the industry. Since independence in 1991, a number of measures have been introduced to encourage visitors, including simplifying border formalities and introducing tax reductions on items destined for export. Hotels and historic buildings damaged in the war have been rebuilt and there are also

Logo of the Croatian National Tourist Board

programmes in place to improve road and maritime links, both internally and also with neighbouring countries. Public services are also being improved. The country is rapidly reaffirming itself as a popular holiday destination, able to offer tourist facilities of international standard at quite competitive prices. Croatia is not yet a member of the European Union, but many of its regulations and practices already fall in line with EU standards.

The busy embarkation point for the Brijuni islands at Fažana

WHEN TO GO

The busiest, most popular times to visit the Croatian coastline are the summer months of July and August. With its crystal clear seas, combined with thousands of islands and bays for exploration or swimming, the coast is a major attraction. In addition, the summer weather is reliably sunny, another important aspect for many. The island of Hvar, for example, can count on over 200 days of sunshine a year.

In the peak season, hotels and resorts are at their busiest, so if in fact a quieter holiday is preferred it would be better to choose the months of May, June or September, when the weather is still fine but resorts are not quite so crowded.

Another advantage of travelling out of peak season is that much lower prices are

on offer. The countryside, with its countless beauty spots, offers breathtaking scenery all year round but spring and autumn are the best months for hunting or fishing in the many lakes and rivers.

Inland Croatia is also home to a number of thermal spas, and it is possible to combine a few days of therapeutic treatment or relaxation (*see pp210–11*) with visits to cities and towns with their rich historical and artistic heritage.

Unlike nearby Slovenia, Croatia's facilities for winter tourism are not yet well-developed, although there are a few ski slopes, for example in Platak and the Medvednica and Bjelolasica mountains. Zagreb, the capital, offers numerous attractions the whole year round.

Bottle of Croatian wine

TRAVEL DOCUMENTS

To enter Croatia, visitors need to be in possession of a valid passport. People from countries in the European Union, the US, Canada, Australia and New Zealand do not need a visa to enter Croatia and may stay for up to 90 days.

To check whether you require a visa, visit the website of the Croatian Ministry of Foreign Affairs (www.mvp.hr) for a list of countries whose citizens require visas. Information is in Croat and English. If you do need a visa, seek advice from the Croatian Embassy in your home country.

The Croatian authorities have formed a bilateral agreement with Italy, according to which Italian citizens need only carry an identity card.

All foreign citizens must register with the local police within 48 hours of arrival. Failure to do so may result in a fine or even expulsion from the country. In practice, if you are staying in a hotel, the reception staff will take care of this procedure for you.

People travelling with pets (dogs or cats) must have an International Certificate and the necessary documents demonstrating that vaccinations are up to date, particularly with regard to rabies.

CUSTOMS INFORMATION

THERE ARE NO restrictions on personal effects brought into Croatia by travellers and customs regulations are harmonized with the standards of EU member states. It is also possible to bring into the country or export 200 cigarettes or 50 cigars, 1 litre of spirits, 1 litre of wine, 500 grammes of coffee and 50 millilitres (one bottle) of perfume or essence.

On entering the country, any major, high-value items such as radio equipment, computers, photographic equipment, video cameras, recorders and any other recording equipment and portable televisions must be declared.

If you are arriving by boat you must report your arrival to the Harbour Master's Office and register the number of people on board and all equipment.

There is no limit to the import and export of foreign currency. The limit for the export of local currency is 2,000 kuna.

TOURIST INFORMATION

EVERY TOWN and city has a tourist offfice, called Turisticki Ured, Turisticki Zajednica, Tourist Information Centar, or, usually in the smaller towns, by the name of Turist Biro. These offices provide information on excursions and transport and will often help visitors to find accommodation in hotels or private rooms (see p217).

There are also county and regional tourist offices, managed by the Ministry of Tourism, which are divided according to their administrative territories. These offices can provide information about the whole county.

Another way of finding out about the country is to contact the Croatian National Tourist Board in your own home country before leaving. The Croatian Ministry of Tourism is very aware of the important role the tourist offices play in encouraging

Tourist asking for help and directions

visitors to Croatia and has set up information offices in all the major countries, with the aim of publicizing the attractions that Croatia has to offer. The Internet is also a very useful source of all kinds of relevant information. One particularly helpful website is run by the Croatian National Tourist Board (www.croatia.hr).

OPENING HOURS

PUBLIC OFFICES OPEN from 8am to 4pm on weekdays, and most other kinds of office business more or less follow these standard opening times. These hours may vary and can sometimes be extended (or even reduced) for other businesses, for example banks (see p264) and post offices (see p262), which are also open on Saturdays. Shops are usually open

early in the morning (see p242), as are cafés, sometimes as early as 6am.

DISABLED TRAVELLERS

IN CROATIA there is a great awareness of the problems faced by the disabled, emphasized by the country's recent history and the fact that the country now has many more people with disabilities caused by the civil war. Stations, airports, larger hotels and restaurants above a certain standard and the main public offices in the larger towns are accessible to those in wheelchairs.

However, facilities are not so good at the ports and the disabled may have difficulty getting on and off ferries.

For further information on this subject, contact the **Savez Organizacija Invalida Hrvatske**, the Croatian organization for the disabled, which has its main head-quarters in Zagreb. **RADAR** in the UK may also have details.

TRAVELLING WITH CHILDREN

TOURIST COMPLEXES such as large hotels and resorts, particularly those on the coast and in the larger towns and cities, usually provide facilities for children, such as playgrounds, children's pools and baby-sitting services.

In smaller towns and inland regions less visited by tourists it is usually more difficult to find facilities provided especially for the very young.

Children at play in one of the larger tourist resorts

Enjoying outdoor café life in Varaždin

LANGUAGE

IN THE NATIONAL language, which is *hrvatski* or Croatian, Croatia is called Hrvatska. It is not a particularly easy tongue to learn but since most people in Croatia have studied at least one other foreign language, visitors should be able to make themselves understood in most circumstances. Italian, German and English are widely spoken, particularly in the coastal tourist resorts and by those who often have contact with foreign visitors, such as in hotels, restaurants and shops. French is less common. Young Croatians generally speak very good English, so if you need to ask for help in English, seek out a younger person or a student.

FORMS OF GREETING

CROATIANS tend to be quite reserved with strangers, particularly in the interior regions which see fewer tourists. Attempting a few words of the country in which you are a guest is good manners and will be appreciated. The forms used vary according to the person you are addressing: he or she may be a *gospodin* (a man), a *gospodja* (a married woman) or a *gospodjica* (a young single woman).

Greetings vary for the different times of the day: *dobro jutro* (good morning), *dobar dan* (good afternoon,

but also, in a broad sense, good day), *dobra večer* (good evening), *laku noć* (good night). *Ciao* is an informal greeting used by youngsters or people with whom you have become familiar.

Words that can be used for everyone are *zbogom* or *dovidenja* (goodbye) or *zdravo* (hello). For polite requests use *molim* (please) and *hvala* (thank you). For more vocabulary, see the Phrase Book (*pp287–8*).

DRESS

ALTHOUGH IT IS not necessary to dress formally, clothes which are neat and tidy will be appreciated. For example, trainers are not suitable for dining in restaurants.

CUSTOMS

WOMEN, particularly those travelling alone, face no particular risks when travelling in Croatia, though single women are likely to attract attention. However, this is more likely to be of a gallant and courteous nature rather than a real nuisance. Making it clear that attention is unwanted is sufficient to deter someone.

Women, and particularly foreign women, may feel free

to wear any type of clothing. It is not frowned upon to wear skimpy bikinis or even go topless on the beaches.

However, it should be remembered that certain places, particularly bars and pubs, are usually frequented predominantly by men, and a woman alone in these places may feel a little embarrassed by the attention, and even the curiosity with which she is observed.

Croatia is a very tolerant country. An example of this is the complete acceptance of topless bathing or even nudism on the beaches.

Homosexuality is not illegal, although up to now no real gay communities have emerged as they have in other countries.

TIPPING AND BARGAINING

THE PRACTICE of tipping, usually calculated at ten per cent, is widespread in Croatia, even in restaurants, where a service charge is normally included in the price. When paying in bars or in taxis it is expected that at least the sum will be rounded up. Another customary practice is the tipping of tourist or museum guides after a tour.

In department stores, supermarkets and shops the prices for goods are fixed but elsewhere, particularly in the

Strolling down the street, a safe enough activity everywhere in Croatia

street markets that are held in the town squares, or at stalls along the road, it is possible to haggle over prices.

SMOKING

SMOKING is very common in Croatia, and in most public places there is a very lenient attitude towards smoking. No-smoking regulations are applied with a certain flexibility, and only in smarter hotels and restaurants will you find special areas for smokers and non-smokers.

NATURISM

CROATIA IS A popular country for naturism, where it is practised freely at designated places and resorts which are outstanding for their quality and high standards. Defined by the International Naturist Federation as "a way of living in harmony with nature, characterized by the practice of communal nudity", naturism has a very long tradition in Croatia. In fact, it was back in 1934 that the first vacation resort for naturists was opened in Rajska plaza (Paradise beach), on the

island of Rab. Among early visitors were the Duke of Windsor and Mrs Simpson.

Today, naturism is widely practised. There are about 30 naturist centres along the Croatian coast, and some have Blue Flag (clean beach) status. These places are appropriately screened, allowing guests to enjoy the absolute freedom and peace the surrounding nature has to offer in total relaxation.

The beaches that are reserved for naturism are flanked, in some places, by tourist resorts with holiday villages and camping sites.

UK tour operators offering naturist holidays in Croatia include **Dune Leisure** and **Peng Travel**.

ELECTRICITY

THE ELECTRIC CURRENT is 220V, 50Hz all over the country. Throughout Croatia, standard European two-pin plugs are used.

TIME

CROATIA is one hour ahead of Greenwich Mean Time (GMT) in winter, and two hours ahead in summer.

A beach on the Dalmatian coast

Health and Personal Safety

CROATIAN PUBLIC HEALTH services meet the standards of those elsewhere in Europe, and in general visitors to Croatia run no serious health risks. There are no endemic diseases. Tap water is drinkable all over the country, and the most common ailments that visitors are likely to suffer are those caused by over-exposure to the sun and insect bites. Travellers in inland regions should be aware that de-mining along former lines of confrontation is not complete. Do not be tempted to stray from known safe routes in these zones. Crime rates are comparatively low, and there is little street crime, although visitors should take the usual precautions in busy places to protect valuables.

VACCINATIONS AND MEDICAL ASSISTANCE

VISITORS TO CROATIA do not require any particular vaccinations unless they are coming from an infected area (check with the health authorities beforehand in the country of departure).

There are hospitals and clinics (*bolnica* or *klinički centar*) in all the major towns in Croatia and health centres and pharmacies (*ljekarna*) in all the smaller towns.

Foreign tourists do not pay for medical services if the Health Care Convention has been signed between Croatia and the country they come from. This applies to most countries in the European Union including the UK, Ireland and Italy. If you come from a country which has not signed the Convention, you have to pay for health services, according to a standardized price list.

It is however advisable to take out an insurance policy to cover medical assistance. The policy should also include repatriation by air-ambulance, as well as the refunding of any medical expenses that are necessary. The insurance company will want to see supporting documents and receipts.

All visitors have a right to emergency medical assistance, but certain medical services must be paid for (the fees are reasonable).

Certain activities, for example diving and rock climbing and in some cases, even hiking or motorcycling,

are often not included in travel insurance cover, as they are regarded as dangerous activities. Check the insurance policy details; it may be necessary to pay a surcharge to cover these kinds of sports.

Sign for a private health clinic in the city of Osijek

PHARMACIES AND MEDICINES

ALTHOUGH IT IS EASY to find all the more common over-the-counter medicines in pharmacies without too much difficulty, it is best to carry an adequate supply of any prescription medicines.

Some medicines are not known by the commercial names given to them in their country of origin, but by the active ingredients contained in them. This may cause difficulty for a pharmacist trying to comply with the request of a foreign visitor. In any event, it is useful if you

can produce a legible prescription written by your own doctor as proof that you are authorized to take a particular medicine.

Pharmacies are usually open from 8am to 1pm and from 3 to 7pm.

AILMENTS AND ILLNESS

MOST OF THE PROBLEMS that visitors suffer from in Croatia are those common to tourists anywhere.

Over-exposure to the sun can cause various problems, from severe burns to sunstroke and dehydration. Sun creams with a high protection factor should be used and it is advisable to wear a hat.

To prevent sunstroke you should drink a lot of liquids and avoid doing very strenuous sports or activities at the hottest time of the day.

A change in diet can cause stomach upsets, which are often a nuisance but can usually be treated quite quickly. In Croatia there is no risk of dysentery or similar illnesses.

On the beaches and near the coast the most common problem is probably irritating insect bites, particularly from mosquitoes, and it is a good idea to take some anti-histamine cream and insect repellent with you.

For hikers and climbers venturing inland there is the possibility of encountering snakes, so take the appropriate serum with you if you are planning such a trip.

People sunbathing on a Dalmatian beach

Travelling by ferry along the coast

Generally however, most minor ailments and disturbances can usually be avoided with a minimum of care and common sense.

Boat travel is a common means of transport for connections between the coastal towns and cities and obviously the only means of getting to virtually all the islands. Unfortunately many people suffer from seasickness, even when the sea conditions are not particularly rough. People who are susceptible should take some kind of travel sickness pill before embarking. It is advisable to keep to the central areas of the boat where any pitching and rolling is felt less and go on deck where fresh air and a visible horizon may help.

PUBLIC CONVENIENCES

THE GENERAL STANDARD of hygiene in Croatia is good. There are plenty of public toilets and they are usually clean. There is a charge (2 kuna) for public conveniences in bus and train stations, while those provided for customers in restaurants and cafés are free.

PERSONAL SAFETY

THE LEVEL OF SAFETY on the roads and in public places is good, and the police (*policija*) are deemed responsible for the protection and safety of the country's visitors as well as its citizens. Croatia has a relatively low crime rate, and violent crime is comparatively rare. If petty theft occurs, it is more likely to happen in crowded bus and railway stations.

It is highly unlikely that the police will create any problems for foreign visitors on holiday in Croatia unless, of course, the law is broken in some way. However, it is advisable to carry your identification documents, such as a passport, with you as the police have the right to ask for identification.

According to an international agreement, if a tourist is held for questioning or detained for whatever reason, he or she has the right to contact a diplomatic representative of his or her country (an embassy or consulate) and receive assistance in appointing a local lawyer, preferably English-speaking (*see p259*).

Any eventual costs and the lawyer's fee are the responsibility of the accused.

DIRECTORY

EMERGENCY SERVICES

Police
℡ 92.

Fire
℡ 93.

Ambulance
℡ 94.

Rescue Service
℡ 985.

Breakdown Service
℡ 987.

Information
℡ 981.

Automobile Club
w www.hak.hr

THEFT AND LOSSES

PRECAUTIONS for avoiding theft and loss of documents and personal belongings are the same as in any other country, so use your common sense. You should avoid leaving objects of value and money unattended, keep an eye on your luggage and bags, particularly in crowded areas, and do not wear showy, expensive jewellery which could attract the wrong kind of attention.

When you travel, it is always a good idea to make a photocopy of your personal documents and keep them in a separate place: in this way it will be much easier to obtain a duplicate. In the event of loss, report the circumstances to the police immediately.

A Croatian policeman with a police car

Communications

A Croatian postbox

THE COMMUNICATION SYSTEMS of the country are of a good standard and the public services, such as the post and telecommunications, function well. The news and information network is well-organized, although most visitors (unless they speak Croatian) will face the obvious obstacle of the language barrier. However, foreign television programmes can be received via satellite and it is also easy to find foreign newspapers and magazines in the newsagents, even if they appear a little later than they would at home.

Using a mobile phone, increasingly common in Croatia

Entrance to the Post Office (HP) in Dubrovnik

POSTAL SERVICES

IN JANUARY 1999, the national post and telecoms company HPT Hrvatska was divided into HP (postal services) and HT (telecommunications). HP operates a network of post offices, with branches in all towns, and offers a wide range of services, including the sale of stamps and telephone cards, and postal services of all kinds. It is also possible to send faxes from post offices. It is worth remembering that if you are sending ordinary post, such as postcards, stamps (*marke*) can also be bought at newsagents (*tisak*).

Letters and cards can be posted at post offices or in the yellow post boxes which are located at roadsides. The costs vary according to the type of correspondence and the destination. The stamp for a card to another European country costs much the same as elsewhere in Europe. Outside Europe costs extra.

Post offices are open from 7am to 7pm from Monday to Friday, and from 7am to 1pm on Saturday. During the summer period the post offices in the tourist resorts extend their opening times until 10pm.

A practical way to receive post while on holiday is to use the poste restante service. Any correspondence sent to the following addresses will be held until it is collected by the addressee. In Zagreb, the address is Poste Restante, 10000 Zagreb, Croatia and in Split, Poste Restante, Main Post Office, 21000 Split, Croatia. Holders of American Express cards and cheques can use a similar service, whereby their post can be addressed to branches of the Atlas travel agency, which has offices in the main towns.

PUBLIC TELEPHONES

PUBLIC TELEPHONES are found everywhere in Croatia. It is cheaper to telephone from a public phone rather than from your hotel, as hotels generally apply a supplement to any calls which are made. There are 10,000 pay phones in Croatia, operated by telephone cards.

Calls cost less if they are made at particular times of the day within certain time bands. The cost decreases by 25 per cent compared with the full price for calls made between 4 and 7pm and there is a 70 per cent

reduction on calls made during the night and on public holidays.

The telephones use phone cards (*telekarta*), with cards of 50, 100, 200 and 500 units, which can be bought at tobacconists, newsagents and news kiosks.

MOBILE PHONES

IN CROATIA several companies offer mobile phone services (GSM network): HTcronet, whose numbers are all preceded by the code 098, HTmobitel, with the code 099, and Vipnet, with the code 091. The HT GSM network covers approximately 98 per cent of the country.

Check with your mobile phone service provider before you leave to see whether they have an agreement of roaming with the Croatian networks.

As elsewhere, do not use mobile phones while driving.

INTERNATIONAL CALLS

CALLING CROATIA from abroad is very easy: after dialling the international code (00 in the UK), you then dial the international country code (385), followed by the area code without the initial zero (Croatia is divided administratively into counties, each with a corresponding code) and finally the number of the subscriber. To telephone abroad

Croatian telephone card of 100 units

from Croatia, dial the international code (again 00), followed by the international code of the country (for the UK it is 44), then the area code (excluding the initial zero) and finally the subscriber's number. The international codes for other English-speaking countries are as follows: the US and Canada, 1, Australia, 61, New Zealand, 64 and Ireland, 353.

Numbers beginning with the code 060 are information services. These services can be dialled up from anywhere within Croatia, using the same code.

An Internet Café in Dubrovnik, popular with younger people

THE INTERNET AND E-MAIL

THE USE OF the Internet and electronic mail is spreading rapidly in Croatia, and it is now easy to find Internet cafés in most places, even on the islands.

If you have a laptop computer which you want to use, the main internet service provider is HThinet (the telecoms service). The service is subject to a monthly fee, plus a subscription charge.

The lines can be fairly slow, but new optical cables are being introduced.

TELEVISION AND RADIO

THE CROATIAN radio and television company is Hrvatski Radio i Televizija (HRT). There are three national TV channels. Channel One broadcasts domestic news and documentaries, Channel Two foreign programmes and comedy, and Channel Three sport and music. Almost all programmes including films and other foreign productions are broadcast in their original language, with Croatian subtitles. The radio has daily news in English and German.

Many hotels have satellite television and hotel guests will have access to a wide range of European stations.

Croatian radio stations broadcast in Croatian only, apart from some traffic reports. On the Second Channel (at RDS-HRT2), reports on road and weather conditions are given in English, German and Italian.

NEWSPAPERS

THE MAIN NATIONAL daily newspapers are called *Vjesnik* and *Jutarnji List* and there is an evening paper, *Večernji List*. The satirical weekly, the *Feral Tribune*, is also widely read. All of these are published in Croatian, but British, Italian and German papers and magazines can often be found at news stands in major resorts and cities.

DIRECTORY

AREA CODES

Bjelovarsko-Bilogorska: 043
Brodsko-Posavska: 035
Dubrovačko-Neretvanska: 020
Istarska: 052
Krapinsko-Zagorska: 049
Ličko-Senjska: 053
Karlovačka: 047
Koprivnicko-Križevačka: 048
Medjimurska: 040
Osječko-Baranjska: 031
Požeško Slavonska: 034
Primorsko-Goranska: 051
Šibensko-Kninska: 022
Sisačko-Moslavačka: 044
Splitsko-Dalmatinska: 021
Varaždinska: 042
Virovitičko-Podravska: 033
Vukovarsko-Srijemska: 032
Zadarska: 023
Zagreb: 01
Zagrebačka: 01

USEFUL NUMBERS

Information for International Calls
📞 902.

International Operator
📞 901

Local Telephone Numbers
📞 988.

Speaking Clock
📞 95.

Telegrams
📞 96.

Telephone Numbers in other Counties
📞 989.

Wake-up Call
📞 9100.

Weather Forecast and Traffic Conditions
📞 060 520 520.

POST OFFICES

Dubrovnik
Dr A Starcevica 2.
📞 (01) 411 265.
FAX (01) 411 265.

Zagreb
Jurisiceva 13.
📞 (01) 48 11 090.

Typical newspaper kiosk in Valpovo

Banking and Currency

THE CROATIAN CURRENCY is the kuna, which in May 1994 took the place of the dinar (a descendant of the currency used in former Yugoslavia). Although it has only been in use for less than a decade, the kuna is in fact a very old currency; coins displaying the kuna (meaning marten – the pelts were once used for barter) were known to be in use in Slavonia in 1256. It is not difficult to change money into kuna at bureaux de change and banks throughout the country. Croatia is not yet part of the European Union but the euro is already accepted in many places.

BANKS AND EXCHANGE OFFICES

MONEY CAN BE CHANGED in banks and authorized bureaux de change or exchange offices. Banks are usually open from Monday to Friday from 8am to 7pm and on Saturday from 8am to 1pm. However, in the smaller towns, some banks may close in the middle of the day from noon to 3pm and on Saturdays a little earlier, at noon.

The exchange offices have much more flexible opening hours and are open until late in the evening in tourist areas. A commission is charged on the exchange which varies from 1 to 1.5 per cent at the exchange offices. These charges are smaller or non-existent if you change money at a bank.

You can also change foreign currency in post offices and tourist agencies. If

One of the many ATMs found in all main towns and cities

at all possible, avoid changing money at hotels or camping sites where the exchange rates are decidedly less favourable.

Do not be tempted to change money at stations and ports or along the roads with people who are not authorized. It may look like a good deal but there is always the risk that you might be given counterfeit banknotes. Finally, if you hold on to your original receipts you can re-convert any unused kuna banknotes back to the original currency at the end of your stay.

This exchange service is, however, only offered by banks.

Note that foreign currency can be imported into and exported freely out of the country.

The Zagrebačka Banka, with offices in Zagreb

ATMs

IN THE CITIES and main towns, cash can be withdrawn from Automated Teller Machines (ATM) by using internationally recognized cards. Check that the logo of the card you want to use is on the machine (*bankomat*) before making a withdrawal. ATMs of Zagrebačka banka accept Eurocard/MasterCard and Euronet ATMs accept Diners, American Express and Visa cards.

TRAVELLER'S CHEQUES

TRAVELLER'S CHEQUES can only be exchanged in a bank, while American Express card holders can get cash advances through branches of the Atlas travel agency which can be found in all the main cities in the country (Zagreb, Pula, Poreč, Zadar, Opatija, Split).

CREDIT CARDS

THE MOST COMMONLY accepted credit cards are Visa, MasterCard, American Express, Diners and Sport Card International. These can be used in the larger resorts, especially on the coast and in big hotels and restaurants. In the event of the loss or theft of your credit card, it is extremely important to report it immediately so that the card can be blocked. This can be done by phoning the relevant

---

DIRECTORY

LOST OR STOLEN CREDIT CARDS

American Express
📞 (01) 612 44 22.
🌐 www.amex.hr

Diners Club
📞 (01) 492 05 01.
🌐 www.diners.hr

Eurocard–MasterCard
📞 (01) 480 82 22
(Zagrebačka Banka, which is an intermediary for blocking the card).

Visa
📞 (021) 342 944.

card's emergency number (which is usually a number providing a 24-hour service, seven days a week).

CURRENCY

THE KUNA is divided into 100 lipa (the word lipa means a linden tree). The Central Bank issues banknotes of 500, 200, 100, 50, 20, 10 and 5 kuna, featuring Croatian heroes. Coins come in denominations of 5, 2 and 1 kuna, and 50, 20, 10, 5, 2 and 1 lipa. The local abbreviation for kuna is kn, but the international abbreviation is HRK.

The Croatian currency was formerly closely linked to the German mark and until 31 December 2001, prices for accommodation, especially private rooms, were always quoted in marks. However, the mark was replaced by the euro in January 2002. The government tries to keep rates of exchange steady, which helps travellers and also helps to present an overall image of stability to potential foreign investors.

In most towns, particularly along the Adriatic coast, the euro is increasingly accepted in banks and bureaux de change.

Banknotes
The Central Bank issues banknotes of 500, 200, 100, 50, 20, 10 and 5 kuna. Notes bear the portraits of famous Croats such as Stjepan Radić and Josip Jelačić.

5 kuna

20 kuna

50 kuna

100 kuna

200 kuna

Coins
The kuna is divided into 100 lipa. The coin denominations are 5, 2 and 1 kuna and 50, 20, 10, 5, 2 and 1 lipa. The 20 lipa coins are a silver colour and the 10 lipa coin is bronze-coloured.

1 kuna

2 kuna

5 kuna

1 lipa

2 lipa

5 lipa

10 lipa

20 lipa

50 lipa

TRAVEL INFORMATION

Road sign indicating customs

M OST VISITORS FROM THE UK arrive in Croatia by direct air connection from Britain, landing at Zagreb, Split or Dubrovnik. During the summer months, numerous charter flights operate and smaller airports in Croatia open. Almost 70 per cent of tourists visiting the country come from Germany, Italy and Austria, relatively near countries which are all well connected by road or sea. These visitors often use their own transport, usually car or motorbike, and travel directly by road or by using one of the ferry services. A great deal has been done to develop and improve all means of transport and the country now has good connections to the rest of Europe and the world. It is also possible to get to Croatia by train, for those who prefer this form of transport, although this is a slower method.

ARRIVING BY AIR

T HE NATIONAL airline company, **Croatia Airlines**, links the main airports of Croatia with the rest of Europe and the Mediterranean basin. The main European destinations are Amsterdam, Berlin, Brussels, Düsseldorf, Frankfurt, Istanbul, London, Mostar, Munich, Paris, Prague, Rome, Sarajevo, Skopje, Vienna and Zurich.

Other European airlines offering scheduled services to Croatia include British Airways, Lufthansa, Austrian Airlines, Air France, Lauda Air, SAS and KLM. Flying time from London is 2 hours 10 minutes, from Frankfurt 1 hour 30 minutes.

The low-cost airline Ryanair flies to Ancona on the Italian Adriatic coast, where there are good ferry links with the Dalmatian coast, and to Trieste in northeast Italy, which is very close to the Istrian border and offers train links to Croatia.

There are no direct flights from Ireland, the US or Canada. Travellers from these countries will need to change at one of the main European hubs such as London, Frankfurt or Rome, and take a connecting flight to Croatia. There is a daily flight to Zagreb from Rome Fiumicino, for example, as well as five flights a week to and from Split, and two flights a week to and from Dubrovnik.

There are also flights to Zagreb from Australia or New Zealand with Malaysia Airlines, with a stopover at Kuala Lumpur.

AIRPORT CONNECTIONS

C ROATIA HAS THREE main airports. Zagreb airport is 17 km (10 miles) from the centre of the city and is connected by a bus service to the central bus station in Držićeva; the journey takes about 25 minutes and runs from the city to the airport from 6.30am to 8pm and in the opposite direction from 4am to 8pm. The airport at Split is 24 km (15 miles) from the centre of the city and is also connected by a regular bus service. Dubrovnik airport is 18 km (11 miles) from the city and is also connected by a regular bus service. The journey time is about 20 minutes.

AIR FARES

F ARES ON SCHEDULED flights to Croatia vary according to the airline and the time of year. Fares tend to be higher in the summer. From the UK there are regular scheduled flights from Heathrow to Zagreb, with connections to Pula, Split, Rijeka and Dubrovnik, and in summer, direct flights to Dubrovnik from Gatwick and Manchester. There are charter flights to Croatia from a wide range of UK regional airports during the summer months. Contact the Croatian National Tourist Office in your own country for details.

PACKAGE HOLIDAYS

A NUMBER OF TOUR operators offer package holidays to Croatia where the price includes flights (usually charter flights) and accommodation. Among the UK tour operators offering package holidays are **Holiday Options**, **Balkan Holidays**, **Transun Holidays**, **Thomson Holidays** and **Cosmos Holidays**. **Saga**

A Croatia Airlines plane in flight

Driving along the Magistrala coastal road

Holidays cater for the
50-plus age group. **Adriatic
Holidays** offer sailing
holidays including 7- and 14-
day trips along the Dalmatian
coast, taking in a number of
the islands and Dubrovnik.

ARRIVING BY TRAIN

THE NETWORK on which
the Croatian railways is
based today was designed in
the 19th century, when the
country was part of the
Austro-Hungarian Empire.
The best railway services
today are still those offering
links with Central Europe.

However, you can travel
from London to Zagreb by
train, via Paris, Milan and
Venice, a trip of around 30
hours. An alternative route
goes via Brussels and
Ljubljana in Slovenia. **Rail
Europe** and **European Rail**
can supply information.

Connections from other
European cities include the
Intercity Munich–Zagreb (9
hours); the Eurocity "Mimara"
which covers the Berlin–
Leipzig–Munich–Salzburg–
Ljubljana–Zagreb route and
the Intercity "Croatia" takes
the route Vienna–Maribor–
Zagreb (6 hours 30 minutes).
Vienna–Rijeka takes 8 hours.

There are also rail
connections from Italy. From
Trieste Centrale, there is one
direct train to Zagreb, a
sleeper. There are also regular
trains to Zagreb from Belgrade
(four a day) and Budapest
(three a day).

The head office of **Croatian
Railways (Hrvatske
Željeznice)** is in Zagreb.

ARRIVING BY COACH

CROATIA is also well
connected to other
countries by coach. International coaches connect
Croatia with the bordering
states and also with France,
Switzerland, Germany and
Slovakia. There are good
connections with Austria
(there are services from
Vienna twice a week to
Rijeka, Zadar and Split, and
daily connections to Zagreb)
and Bosnia. From Dubrovnik

**Road sign for the Slovenian
border**

there are three services a
day to Mostar, and two to
Sarajevo. From Split there
are seven buses a day to
Mediugorje, 11 to Mostar and
six to Sarajevo. Four buses a
day depart from Zagreb to
Mostar and six to Sarajevo).

From Germany there are
almost daily services from
Berlin, Cologne, Dortmund,
Frankfurt, Mannheim, Munich,
Nuremberg and Stuttgart to
Zagreb and the coastal cities,
covering the stretch from
Rijeka to Split.

Many Italian cities are
connected to Zagreb by
coach: there is at least one
weekly service between the
Croatian capital and Bergamo,
Bologna, Florence, Milan,

Rome, Turin, Verona and
Venice, while there is a daily
service from Trieste.

The main bus station in
the country is **Autobusni
Kolodvor Zagreb** in the
capital. The Autoservizio
Friuli Venezia Giulia SAF
Trieste runs services four
times a day in the summer
and twice in winter to Pula.
From Trieste you can also get
to Rijeka and then from there
to Split five times a day and
and there are daily services to
Buzet and Labin. In Istria,
these services are run by the
Italian company SAITA
Autolinee, in collaboration
with Croatian companies.

ARRIVING BY CAR
OR MOTORBIKE

TRAVELLING TO CROATIA by car
(or by motorbike) is
popular with tourists from
neighbouring countries. There
are six main border crossings
between Croatia and
Hungary, 23 frontier points
between Croatia and Bosnia-
Herzegovina, ten frontier
points between Croatia and
Yugoslavia and 29 frontier
points between Croatia and
Slovenia.

Traffic coming overland
from Italy enters Croatia via
border crossings with
Slovenia, all classified as
international and open 24
hours a day, all year round.
Rabuiese-Muggia, towards
Savudrja, is the crossing point
for Istria; Basovizza-Pesek, for
Rijeka and Dalmatia; Fernetti-
Villa Opicina, for those going
towards Zagreb.

People driving to Croatia
need to carry a valid driving
licence, the car's log book (if
appropriate) and a green
card. On entering the country
drivers must also declare any
prior damage to the car which
has not yet been repaired. This
procedure is for insurance
purposes.

ARRIVING BY SEA

THE MAIN INTERNATIONAL ferry
connections are with Italy
via the ports of Trieste,
Ancona, Pescara and Bari.

The main Croatian maritime
company is **Jadrolinija**. This

company runs services between Ancona and Split (four times a week all year round and daily in the summer). The crossing takes nine hours. Ancona–Zadar runs twice a week, an eight-hour journey, and Bari–Dubrovnik runs twice a week all year (eight hours). In summer there are also connections to and from the islands of Korčula and Hvar (from Split), with services twice a week.

SEM Marina is another Croatian company which runs a daily service between Ancona and Split (nine hours).

Adriatica Navigazione is an Italian company running regular ferry services between Ancona and Split, more or less daily in the months of July and August; three times a week in June and September and twice weekly during the rest of the year. The crossing takes nine hours. Adriatica Navigazione also runs a service called "Linea della Costa Istriana" in the summer months. This links the Italian

One of the ships operated by the Jadrolinija company, connecting Croatian ports with the rest of the Adriatic

ports of the upper Adriatic (Grado, Trieste) with destinations in the north of Croatia such as Rovinj and Brijuni. For information and tickets contact the agencies at the ports of embarkation.

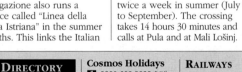

JADROLINIJA

Symbol of the maritime company, Jadrolinija

The Croatian company **Lošinjska Plovidba** runs a ferry between Koper in Slovenia and Zadar twice a week in summer (July to September). The crossing takes 14 hours 30 minutes and calls at Pula and at Mali Lošinj.

There are also hydrofoil passenger services from Italy run by **Agenzia Marittima Sanmar** from mid-June to mid-September. There are departures from Pescara every Monday and Saturday for the islands of Hvar and Brač, and Split, and every Tuesday for Split and the islands of Vis and Korčula. Hydrofoils also run every Friday to the islands of Korčula, Hvar and Split.

The Italian company **SNAV** runs daily catamaran services from Ancona to Split from mid-June to late September.

DIRECTORY

Croatian National Tourist Office
162–64 Fulham Palace Road, London W6 9ER.
☎ 020-8563 7979.
FAX 020-8563 2616.
W www.croatia.hr

AIRLINES

Croatia Airlines
☎ 0800 77 77,
(01) 481 96 33 (Cro).
W www.croatiaairlines.hr

PACKAGE HOLIDAYS

Adriatic Holidays
☎ 01865-516577 (UK).
W www.adriaticholidays
online.com

Balkan Holidays
☎ 0845-130 1114 (UK).
W www.balkan
holidays.co.uk

Cosmos Holidays
☎ 0800-093 3922 (UK).
W www.cosmos-
holidays.co.uk

Holiday Options
☎ 0870-013 0450 (UK).
W www.holidayoptions.
co.uk

Saga Holidays
☎ 0800-300 600.
W www.saga.co.uk/
travel

Thomson Holidays
☎ 0870-165 0079 (UK).
W www.thomson-
holidays.com

Transun Holidays
☎ 0870-44 44 747 (UK)
W www.transun.co.uk

COACHES

Autobusni Kolodvor Zagreb Information
☎ (060) 313 333 and
(060) 340 340 (Cro).

RAILWAYS

Croatian Railways
☎ (060) 333 444 (Cro).
W www.hznet.hr

European Rail
Tavistock Square,
London WC1H 3HR.
☎ 020-7387 0444.
FAX 020-7387 0888.
W www.europeanrail.com

Rail Europe
179 Piccadilly,
London W1V 0BA.
☎ 0870-584 8848.

FERRY SERVICES

Adriatica Navigazione
Ancona, Italy.
☎ 071 204 915-6-7-8.
FAX 071 202 296.

Agenzia Marittima Sanmar
Pescara, Italy.
☎ 085 652 47, 451 08 73.
FAX 085 451 08 82.

Jadroagent
Borisa Papandopoula,
Split.
☎ (021) 460 556.
FAX (021) 460 848.

Jadrolinija
Riva 16, Rijeka.
☎ (051) 666 100.
FAX (051) 211 485.

Lošinjska Plovidba
Splitska 2/4, Rijeka.
☎ (051) 319 000.
FAX (051) 319 003.

P Amatori
c/o Stazione Marittima,
Ancona, Italy.
☎ 071 204 305.
FAX 071 200 211.

SEM Marina
Gat Sv. Duje, Split.
☎ (021) 338 292.
FAX (021) 333 291.

SNAV
Ancona, Italy.
☎ (071) 207 6116.

Getting Around Croatia

THE TRANSPORT SYSTEM within the country is reasonably efficient, particularly if you are travelling by road or by sea. The connections between the mainland and the islands are excellent, and thanks to an extensive bus network, even the smaller, lesser known towns can be easily reached by bus. Although using air travel to get around the country is not that common, domestic flights link the major towns. Travelling by train is fine only if you have plenty of time, because the rail network is in need of modernization, resulting in very long journey times compared with the time it takes to cover the same distance by road.

DOMESTIC FLIGHTS

THERE ARE regular connections between the three major airports in the country, Zagreb, Split and Dubrovnik. There are also connections between these main airports and other secondary airports, such as the airport of Osijek, which is only 3 km (2 miles) from the city and connected by a regular city bus service. There is also a small airport at Zadar which is 15 km (9 miles) from the centre and the bus connection to the city takes about 15 minutes. Rijeka airport is 27 km (17 miles) from the city and, despite its name, is actually situated on the island of Krk, at Omišalj. The airport is connected to Rijeka by a bus service and the journey takes about 35–40 minutes.

The airport of Pula is just 7 km (4 miles) from the centre of the city and there is a bus service to and from Pula with a journey time of about 10 minutes.

Finally, the airport of Brač is a small airport on the island of the same name. It is only open in the summer months.

DRIVING AROUND CROATIA

THE CROATIAN road network is very extensive and road surfaces reasonably good. Cars drive on the right in Croatia and safety belts should be worn at all times, in both the front and back

The logo of AVIS, the car rental company

seats. Children under 12 must sit in the back of the car.

The speed limits are 50 km/h (30 mph) in towns, 80 km/h (50 mph) outside built-up areas, and 130 km/h (80 mph) on the motorways. Cars towing caravans must not exceed 80 km/h (50 mph).

Road signs are generally more or less identical to those found in the rest of Europe.

On certain stretches of motorway drivers pay a toll: Zagreb–Karlovac, Zapresic–Krapina, Varaždin–Gorican, Zagreb–Oprisavci and Rijeka–Delnice. There is also a toll to pay for the bridge to the island of Krk and the Ucka Tunnel.

Town traffic in the charming city of Osijek

The most scenic road of all is the road which winds along the Adriatic coast, the Magistrala (E65). Great care should be taken when driving along this road, however, particularly during the summer months. The road itself is quite demanding and it gets extremely busy.

In the larger towns and cities you can park in the public car parking areas or along the roads. Where indicated, a parking ticket must be clearly displayed inside the windscreen. If you park in a no-parking area, your vehicle can be forcibly removed by officials.

Service stations are open daily from 7am to 7 or 8pm, but in summer the opening times are extended until 10pm. On the main roads in the larger towns and cities and on major international routes you can find service stations open 24 hours a day. All kinds of petrol are available: Eurosuper 95 and Eurosuper 98, normal un-leaded and Super 98, as well as Eurodiesel.

The Croatian authorities are very tough on drink driving: it is illegal to drive with a blood alcohol level exceeding 0.5 ml per thousand.

BREAKDOWN ASSISTANCE AND TRAFFIC INFORMATION

EMERGENCY ROAD services are provided by the local **Automobile Club**, **HAK**, which can be reached 24 hours a day all year round by simply dialling 987 (preceded by the numbers 01 for calls from a mobile phone). The service provides repairs on the spot or in a garage (subject to transport), the removal of damaged cars and transport up to 100 km (62 miles) distance and is run by the local automobile club and local firms, which operate under the direct control of the automobile club.

HAK also provides information on road and maritime traffic, motorway tolls, any temporary diversions, the prices of petrol, ferry times, possible alternative routes and general assistance for those travelling by car, 24 hours a day, 365 days a year, on (01) 464 08 00. If you have access to the Internet, the website www.hak.hr is full of useful information and links.

CAR RENTAL

IT IS STRAIGHTFORWARD to hire a car in Croatia and car rental agencies can be found in all the main towns and cities, holiday resorts, and at the airports. Besides the well-known large multinational rent-a-car companies such as Avis and Hertz, there are many local independent companies offering competitive prices for similar types of vehicle and insurance cover.

One of the advantages of renting a car through the larger companies, however, is having the option of leaving the car in a different town from the collection point. Not all rental companies are able to offer this flexibility and there is always an extra charge for this service.

BUSES

BUSES ARE USED a great deal by the local population and are a valid means of transport for visitors as well, although communication with ticket offices and drivers may be difficult unless you speak a little Croatian. It will help to learn a little basic vocabulary and some useful phrases before setting out to use the buses.

The bus service covers an extensive network across the country with numerous connections and destinations,

Travelling by coach in the city of Dubrovnik

The entrance to the large railway station in Zagreb

although the tickets will be more expensive than on equivalent trains.

Services are divided into "intercity" (direct connections between the larger cities) and the regional services (with connections between the smaller towns and the main cities). Intercity services mean shorter travelling times, but ticket prices are the same.

There are daily connections between the towns and cities of Croatia and night buses cover the longer routes.

For information go to the local bus station (*Autobusni Kolodvor*) and consult the timetable. *Vozi svaki dan* indicates the daily services, while *ne vozi nedjeljom ni praznikom* shows which services do not run on Sundays and public holidays. The main bus station in the country is the **Autobusni Kolodvor Zagreb**, which is in Zagreb.

TRAINS

THE TRAIN is not widely used for travelling within Croatia: the railway network has not yet been adequately modernized and this is particularly apparent in the very long journey times. However, all the main Croatian towns and cities are linked by rail with the exception of Dubrovnik, where there is no railway station at all.

The hub of the Croatian railway network is the main station in the capital (Zagreb Glavni Kolod). There are trains to Rijeka with connections to the Istrian

towns; to Split, with a branch line for Zadar and Šibenik, serving the Dalmatian coast; to Varaždin, to the north; and to Osijek, to the east.

The following journey times can be expected: the minimum time is four hours for Zagreb–Rijeka, seven and a half hours from Zagreb to Split, two hours for Zagreb–Varaždin and four hours for Zagreb– Osijek. Croatian Railways – **Hrvatske Željeznice** – has its main office in Zagreb.

FERRIES SERVING THE COAST

THE FERRY SERVICES are very good and probably the best option when travelling down the entire coastline, even though it is not the cheapest way to travel.

Fairly large ships which provide good facilities connect the main towns along the Adriatic coast. Accommodation is available in cabins or there are seats inside and on deck (the cheapest). These ferries also transport cars, motorbikes, caravans and campervans.

The routes cover the entire Adriatic coast from Rijeka down to Dubrovnik, with stops in the main towns and also on the larger islands. After Rijeka, stops are made at Zadar, Split, Starigrad on Hvar, Korčula, Sobra on Mljet and Dubrovnik. The full trip lasts one day and usually involves sleeping overnight for the northern part of the journey, while the southern part takes place during the day, in both directions.

ISLAND FERRIES

THERE IS ALSO a wide network of connections between the islands and the mainland. The Croatian ferry network is divided into five districts and services are on ships which can transport both passengers and vehicles.

In the Rijeka district the islands of Cres and Lošinj are connected to the mainland by the Valbiska–Merag and Brestova–Porozina routes.

The island of Rab is connected to the coast by the Jablanac–Mišnjak route and with the island of Krk by the Lopar–Baška route. Finally, the island of Pag is connected to the coast by the Prizna–Žigljen route.

In the district of Zadar there are connections to Preko, on the island of Ugljan, Bribinj and Zaglav, on the island of Dugi Otok and from Biograd to Tkon on the island of Pašman.

In the district of Šibenik, the town is connected to the islands of Zlarin and Prvić.

In the Split district there are connections between Split and the island of Brač (Supetar), the island of Korčula (Vela Luka), the island of Hvar (to Starigrad), the island of Šolta (Rogač), the island of Vis (to the port of the same name) and the island of Lastovo (to Ubli).

There are also connections between Makarska and Sumartin (island of Brač), between Ploce and Trpanj on the Pelješac peninsula, between Orebić and Domince

(on the island of Korčula), between Drvenik and Korčula (on the island of the same name) and between Drvenik and Sućuraj (island of Hvar). Finally, in the district of Dubrovnik, the main connection is between Dubrovnik and the island of Mljet (Sobra).

For all the routes mentioned above, services run frequently in the high season (July and August), but services are significantly reduced outside the summer months. On some short routes, such as Jablanac–Misniak and Drvenik–Sućuraj, ferries sail non-stop so as to cope with the long queues which tend to form in the middle of the day.

For those travelling without a car or motorbike, there are some passenger-only services. These catamarans connect Split to the surrounding islands in the months from June to September only. There are also connections to the islands of Brač, Hvar, Vis, Korčula and Lastovo. The crossing times range from 45 minutes to Hvar to two and a half hours to Lastovo, the most distant. These services do not always run daily, particularly to the islands that are furthest away from the mainland.

Finally, a hydrofoil service also covers the routes from Split to Vis (the port on the island of the same name) and back with a daily service in the summer. For further information on hydrofoils, contact **SEM Marina**.

Ferry waiting to depart for the islands

DIRECTORY

AIRPORTS

Brač [(021) 648 615.
Osijek [(031) 514 400.
Pula [(052) 530 105.
Rijeka [(051) 842 132.
Zadar [(023) 313 311.

DRIVING

Automobile Club, HAK
[987 (preceded by 01 from mobile phones).
[(01) 464 08 00 (traffic information).

CAR RENTAL

Avis (in partnership with Autotehna)
[(01) 483 60 06.
w www.avis.com

Budget
[(01) 455 49 36.
w www.budgetrentacar.com

Hertz
[(01) 484 72 22.
w www.hertz.com

BUSES

Autobusni Kolodvor Zagreb
Information
[060 313 333, 060 340 340.

TRAIN TRAVEL

Hrvatske Zeljeznice
Mihanovićeva 12,
HR-10000 Zagreb.
[014 577 111,
FAX 014 577 730.

FERRIES

Jadrolinija
Riva 16, Rijeka.
[(051) 666 100.
FAX (051) 211 485.

Jadrolinija
Zrinjevac 20, Zagreb.
[(01) 487 33 07.
FAX (01) 487 31 41.
w www.jadrolinija.hr

SEM Marina
Gat sv. Duje, Split.
[(021) 338 292.
FAX (021) 333 291.
w www.sem-marina.hr

Getting Around Zagreb

T HE CITY OF ZAGREB has developed a good, efficient transport network which, by means of trams, buses and a funicular railway connecting the Lower and Upper Towns, ensures good connections between all the central and suburban districts. Trams run at regular intervals and there are also some night services. Gradec, the old town, has many areas which are pedestrianized and closed to ordinary traffic, making this a pleasant, fume-free zone to stroll around. There is no underground system in Zagreb.

WALKING

Z AGREB is a very large city and most visitors will need to use some form of public transport as a means of gettting around. However, the best way to visit the centre, that is the areas of Kaptol and Gornji Grad (Upper Town), is on foot. Walking gives visitors the chance to observe buildings and sights from close quarters, an especially rewarding experience in the old centre of Zagreb with its venerable churches and imposing buildings.

It is a good idea to get a map of the city from a tourist office. If need be, you can always ask the locals for directions because they are generally helpful to tourists, although the Croatian language may present a barrier to understanding.

TRAMS

T HE COMPANY WHICH runs the capital's public transport is the Zagrebački Električni Tramvaj, known as **ZET**. The network of electric trams is efficient, with frequent services covering a wide area.

A total of 15 tram routes run during the day (starting at around 4am and ending at midnight) and four lines run at night (covering the early hours from midnight to 4am).

The routes operating during the day are: 1 Zapadni kolodvor–Borongaj; 2 Crnomerec–Savisce; 3 Ljubljanica–Zitnjak; 4 Savski most–Dubec; 5 Jarun–Kvaternikov trg; 6 Crnomerec–Sopot; 7 Savski most–Dubrava; 8 Mihaljevac–Zaprude; 9 Ljubljanica–Borongaj; 11 Crnomerec–Dubec; 12 Ljubljanica–Dubrava, 13 Zitnjak–Kvaternikov trg; 14 Mihaljevac–Zaprude; 15 Mihaljevac–Dolje; 17 Precko–Borongaj.

All the lines run frequently during the day at intervals of six to ten minutes between trams, depending on whether it is a weekday or public holiday. On Sundays and other holidays tram numbers 3 and 8 do not run.

The four tram lines which run at night pass every 20 to 40 minutes on the following routes: 31 Crnomerec–Savski most, 32 Precko–Borongaj; 33 Dolje–Savisce and 34 Ljubljanica–Dubec.

The main hub for tram stops is Trg bana Jelačica, where seven different routes intersect.

BUSES

T HERE IS an intricate network of bus connections with numerous routes branching out to the various termini: Britanski trg, Jandriceva, Jankomir, Savski most, Ljubljanica, trg Mazuranica, Crnomerec, Mandalicina, Zapresic, Kaptol, Petrova, Svetice, Dubrava, Kvaternikov trg, Glavni kolodvor, Zitnjak, Sesvete, Borongaj, Mihalievac and Velica Gorica.

One of many tram lines serving the entire city

TICKETS

Tickets for both buses and trams can be bought in newsagents or kiosks (if need be, also on board, but the price is higher). The basic ticket is for a single journey. It must be punched in the machine as soon as you get on board and is valid for 90 minutes from that time. The tickets cost 6 kuna each (or 7 kuna from the driver on the bus). There is also a one-day ticket which costs 16 kuna, a good idea if you intend making various trips during the day (these tickets are valid until 4am on the following day). Monthly season tickets are also available. A useful website is www.zagreb-touristinfo.hr.

Funicular connecting the Lower and Upper Towns of Zagreb

Travelling without a ticket is punishable by a fine. If you are caught, the fine is 150 kuna if it is paid immediately or within eight days, but it can rise to 900 kuna if left unpaid.

FUNICULAR RAILWAY

An interesting method of transport is the *uspinjača*, a steep funicular railway that has been in operation since 1890. This trip is one of the shortest climbs in the world at 66m (216 ft) long and takes a little less than a minute to climb up from the Lower Town to the Upper Town,

Traffic in Zagreb city centre outside the railway station

arriving close to the Lotrscak tower. Departures are from Tomićeva street right in the centre, and leave every ten minutes from 6.30am to 9pm. The price of a single ticket is 2.5 kuna.

CABLE CAR

The **Žičara** is a cable car which connects Zagreb with Sljeme, the highest peak of the Mount Medvednica range, in a journey time of 20 minutes. The system has been in operation since 1963 and cabins can carry up to four people. Departures are every 20 minutes past the hour from 8am to 8.30pm daily. Return tickets cost 15 kuna.

TAXIS

In Zagreb, as in any other large city, taxis can be found. All taxis have a meter on board and fares start from 25 kuna as the basic rate and then 7 kuna for every kilometre of your journey. There is an extra charge of 20 per cent for journeys made on Sundays and public holidays and from 10pm to 5am every day, and there is also a charge of 5 kuna for luggage. If a taxi has to wait there is a further charge of 40 kuna an hour.

Yellow taxi sign

There are numerous taxi ranks (identified by a typical blue sign). Croatian speakers can call a taxi by phoning 970, and asking the taxi driver to come and collect you.

CAR RENTAL

In the capital it is also possible to rent a self-drive car by contacting one of the main car rental companies such as **Budget**, **Adria Plus**, **Kompas Hertz** and **Avis**. Assistance while you are on the road is provided by the Croatian Automobile Club, which can also offer advice on routes (*see p269 and p271*).

(*see p269 and p271*)

DIRECTORY

USEFUL NUMBERS

ZET
℃ (01) 365 15 55.

Žičara Cable Car
℃ (01) 458 03 94.

Taxi
℃ 970.

CAR RENTAL

Adria Plus
Zagreb Airport.
℃ (01) 626 52 15.
FAX (01) 625 60 75.

Avis
c/o Hotel Opera,
Kršnjavoga, Zagreb.
℃ (01) 483 60 06.
FAX (01) 483 62 96.

Budget
Praška 5, Zagreb.
℃ (01) 455 49 36.
FAX (01) 455 49 43.

Kompas Hertz
Mažuranićev trg 2, Zagreb.
℃ (01) 484 72 22.
FAX (01) 481 29 25.

General Index

Acknowledgments

FABIO RATTI EDITORIA would like to thank the following staff at Dorling Kindersley:

MAP CO-ORDINATOR
Dave Pugh.

SENIOR DTP MANAGER
Jason Little.

PUBLISHING MANAGER
Anna Streiffert.

MANAGING ART EDITOR
Marisa Renzullo.

PUBLISHER
Douglas Amrine.

DORLING KINDERSLEY would also like to thank all those whose contribution and assistance have made the preparation of this book possible.

PRINCIPAL AUTHOR
LEANDRO ZOPPÉ was born in Venice and graduated in Political Science from Padua University. At present he lives in Milan where, as a historian, he works as a freelance journalist and writer of tour guides and historical, artistic or naturalistic books.

CONTRIBUTORS
BOŽIDARKA BOZA GLIGORIJEVIĆ, Public Relations Manager for the Croatian National Tourist Board in Milan.

TEXT REVISION
Sanja Rojić (University professor),
Iva Grgic (University professor).

CHECKING OF PRACTICAL INFORMATION
Lucia Čutura, Viktor Jovanović Marušić, Jane Foster.

SENIOR EDITOR, UK EDITION
Jacky Jackson.

PROOF READER
Stewart J Wild.

INDEXER
Hilary Bird.

SPECIAL THANKS
Croatian National Tourist Board, Zagreb, in particular the director Niko Bulić; Croatian National Tourist Board, Milan, in particular the director Klaudio Stojnic and the public relations manager Božidarka Boza Gligorijević; the regional and local tourist boards of Croatia; Vinko Bakija (director of the tourist office, Supetar, island of Brač); Zdravko Banović (tourist office, Split); Daniela Barac (tourist guide in Crikvenica); Nikša Bender (marketing manager of the tourist office of Dubrovnik); Maja Boban (tourist guide of the environs of Zagreb); Ankita Boksic Franchini (tourist office, Split); Tanja Bunjevac (tourist office, Varaždin) Rujana Bušić (tourist guide in Vinkovci); Vanja Dadić (tourist guide in Šibenik); Mirjana Darrer (public relations manager of the tourist office in Dubrovnik); Marchese Doimo Frangipane di Aiello del Friuli; Danijela Duić (tourist guide in Karlovac); Jurica Duževic (director of the tourist office in Stari Grad, island of Hvar); Daniela Fanikutić (tourist office, Poreč); Ennio Forlani (director of the tourist office of Vodnjan); Vesna Gamulin (tourist guide in Dubrovnik); Miljenko Gašparac (guard of the Risnjak National Park); Boris Gržina (front office manager of the Hotel Esplanade in Zagreb); Vesna Habazin and Snježana Hrupelj (tourist guides in the area of the thermal spas); Mladenka Jarac-Rončević (Croatian Consul in Italy); Zoran Jelaska (tourist guide in Split); Vesna Jovičić (tourist guide in Pula); Darko Kovačić (tourist guide in the Lonjsko Polje Nature Park); Darko Kovačić (director of the tourist office, Omiš); Stanka Kraljević (director of the tourist office in the town of Korčula); Vlasta Krklec (Museum of Krapina); Tonći Lalić (tourist guide in Makarska); Damir Macanić (director of the tourist office in Osijek); Damir Mihalić (tourist office, Varaždinske Toplice); Josip Mikolčić (tourist office, Virovitica); Danijela Miletić (tourist office, Zagreb); Smiljan Mitrović (tourist guide in Zadar); Franjo Mrzljak (director of the National Museum of Naive Art, Zagreb); Andro Krstulović Opara (former Croatian Consul in Italy); Ottone Novosel (tourist guide in Križevci); Ankica Pandzic (director of the Museum of Croatian History in Zagreb); Danika Plazibat (Meštrović Gallery, Zagreb); Gordana Perić (tourist office, Zadar); Ante Rendić-Miočević (director of the Archaeological Museum, Zagreb); Mladen Radić (Director of the Museum of Slavonia, Osijek); Ljubica Ramušćak (Civic Museum of Međimurje, Cakovec); Ljiljana Sever (tourist guide in Varaždin); Josipa Šipek (director of Hotel Coning in Trakošćan); Doris Staničić (tourist guide in Osijek); Alka Starac (Archaeological Museum of Istria, Pula); Branka Tropp (director of the tourist office in Varaždin); Đuro Vanđura (director of the Gallery of Ancient Masters, Zagreb); Klara Vedriš (Gallery of Modern Art, Zagreb); Vjenceslav Vlahov (tourist guide in Zagreb); Igor Zidić (director of the Gallery of Modern Art, Zagreb); Marko Zoričić (director of the tourist office in Opatija).

Dorling Kindersley wishes to thank Lady Beresford-Peirse of the International Trust for Croatian Monuments for her time and invaluable suggestions.

PHOTOGRAPHY PERMISSIONS
The publisher would like to thank all the museums, the local corporations and associations, hotels, restaurants, shops and other places of interest for their co-operation and their kind permission in allowing their establishments to be photographed.

ADDITIONAL PHOTOGRAPHY
LUCIO ROSSI.

PICTURE CREDITS
Key to positions: t = t;
tl = top left; tlc = top left centre;
tc = top centre; trc = top right centre; tr = top right; cla = centre left above; ca = al centre above; crb = centre right above; cl = centre left; c = centre;
cr = centre right; clb = centre left below; cb = centre below; crb = centre right below; b = below; bl = bottom left; bcl = bottom centre left; bc = bottom centre; bcr = bottom centre right; br = bottom right;
(d) = detail.

While every effort has been made to contact the copyright holders, we apologize for any omissions and will be happy to include them in the following editions of this publication.

The publisher would like to thank the following individuals, associations and photograpic agencies for permission to reproduce their photographs:

DORLING KINDERSLEY ARCHIVES: 10bl, 230cr.

THE CROATIAN NATIONAL TOURIST BOARD ARCHIVES, Milan: 1c, 2–3, 17bl, 18bc, 19tc, 19cl, 21cl, 22tc, 22br, 23tl, 24–25 (all), 26, 30t, 31bc, 32bc, 36tc, 41tc, 44tr, 65t, 96crb, 97tl, 104cla, 105cr, 110br, 111tl, 113cl, 122 (all), 128t, 129tr, 129br, 131 (all), 132cr, 132bl, 133tl, 133c, 134tr, 134bl, 135tl, 135cra, 135br, 136–137, 138c, 141ca, 142tl, 144c, 144br, 145 (all), 150bl, 156tl, 173bl, 178, 184tl, 192br, 198cl, 199br, 200cl, 210c, 211tr, 217br, 219tl, 228tc, 244tl, 245tc, 247br, 249tr, 250tc, 251cl, 251br, 253bc, 256tc, 265 (all), 266bl, 268cl, 269cl, 270bl.

MONDADORI ARCHIVES: 9 (frame), 16bcl, 19cr, 28tl, 29tr, 29bc, 35 (all), 36cr, 36bc, 37 (all), 38tl, 38bl, 38br, 39bc, 40tl, 43 (frame), 119tl, 155tc, 155cl, 175ca, 190tl, 192tr, 193cra, 193crb, 193bl, 204br, 215 (frame), 230c, 231tl, 231bl, 233tlc, 251tc, 255 (frame).

ADRIANO BACCHELLA: 17bcr, 44clb, 49cr, 54c, 82–83, 84tr, 84bl, 85tl, 85br, 89crb, 94cl, 96cla, 214–215, 232br.

DOIMO FRANGIPANE: 175cla, 175cr.

GALLERY OF MODERN ART, Zagreb: 8–9, 160b.

GALLERY OF OLD MASTERS, Zagreb: 162–163 (all).

MEŠTROVIĆ GALLERY, Zagreb: 18tr, 152tl, 155cr, 155bl, 155br.

IMAGE BANK, Milan: 54br, 65br, 84cl, 85tr, 89tl, 143br, 149crb, 158tl.

MARCO LISSONI: 18br, 68cr, 104tl, 112cl, 130tl, 245br, 246br.

ARCHAEOLOGICAL MUSEUM, Zagreb: 27tc, 27br, 160c, 161c, 165c, 186c.

MUSEUM OF CROATIAN HISTORY, Zagreb: 38cb, 39tc, 39clb, 40cb, 152cl.

NATIONAL MUSEUM OF NAIVE ART, Zagreb: 19bl, 152bl, 157tl.

PAKLENICA NATIONAL PARK: 16cl, 99c, 99b, 252 (all).

ALDO PAVAN, AURA AGENCY, Milan: 13tc, 22cl, 44cb, 66br, 95crb, 110cla, 130cl, 130cr, 132tl, 133b, 134cl, 134cr, 135clb, 233cl, 242cl, 246tc, 246cl, 247tl, 248tl.

ANDREA PISTOLESI: 109tr.

LUCIO ROSSI: 3 (frame), 34bl, 176–177, 262bc.

THE ART ARCHIVE: 31br.

LEANDRO ZOPPÈ: 16bcr, 20cr, 23br, 28br, 29c, 31tr, 32–33c, 32cl, 32bl, 33cr, 33b, 41clb, 45tr, 45cr, 55tl, 56cla, 62cla, 62br, 63tr, 66tl, 66tr, 66cl, 67 (all), 77tr, 79c, 97clb, 98 (all), 99tr, 100–101 (all), 108 (all), 109cl, 109bc, 114–115 (all), 116cl, 161br, 175clb, 175bc, 181 (all), 184c, 184br, 185tc, 187 (all), 190tr, 191bl, 191br, 192cl, 192bl, 193tl, 193cr, 194cr, 202bl, 203cl, 203br, 204c, 205tl, 208bl, 209c, 210tr, 211cl, 213tl, 242tc, 243bc.

JACKET
Front - DK PICTURE LIBRARY: Lucio Rossi bl, cb, clb: GETTY IMAGES: Robert Everts main image. Back – CORBIS: Hans Georg Roth t; DK PICTURE LIBRARY: Lucio Rossi bl. Spine – GETTY IMAGES: Robert Everts.

All other images copyright © DORLING KINDERSLEY. For further information: www.dkimages.com

Phrase Book

PRONOUNCIATION
c – "ts" as in rats
č – "chi" as in church
ć – "t" is a soft t
d – "d" is a soft d
g – "g" is a hard g as in get
j – "y" as in yes
š – sh
Ž – shown here as "zh", sounds like the "J" in the French name, Jacques
"aj" – shown here as "igh", sounds like "I" or the "igh" in night.

IN AN EMERGENCY
Help!	Pomoć!	pomoch
Stop!	Stani!	stahnee
Call a doctor!	Zovite doktora!	zoveetey doktorah
Call an ambulance!	Zovite hitnu pomoć!	zoveetey heetnoo pomoch
Call the police!	Zovite policiju!	zoveetey poleetseeyoo
Call the fire brigade!	Zovite vatrogasce!	zoveetey vatrohgastsay
Where is the nearest telephone?	Gdje je najbliži telefon?	gdyey yey n-igh-bleezhee telefon
Where is the nearest hospital?	Gdje je najbliža bolnica?	gdyey yey n-igh-bleezhah bolnitsa

COMMUNICATION ESSENTIALS
Yes	da	dah
No	ne	ney
Please	molim vas	moleem vas
Thank you	hvala	hvahlah
Excuse me	oprostite	oprosteetey
Hello	dobar dan	dobar dan
Goodbye	dovidenja	doveedjenya
Good night	laku noc	lakoo noch
Morning	jutro	yootroh
Afternoon	popodne	popodney
Evening	večer	vecher
Yesterday	jučer	yoocher
Today	danas	danas
Tomorrow	sutra	sootrah
Here	tu	too
There	tamo	tahmoh
What?	što?	shtoh
When?	kada?	kada
Why?	zašto?	zashtoh
Where?	gdje?	gdyey

USEFUL PHRASES
How are you?	Kako ste?	kakoh stey
Very well, thank you	Dobro, hvala	dobroh, hvahlah
Pleased to meet you	Drago mi je!	dragoh mee yey
See you soon	Vidimo se	veedeemoh sey
That's fine	U redu	oo redoo
Where is/are…?	Gdje je/ su?	gdyey yey/ soo
How far is it to…?	Koliko je daleko do…?	kolikoh yey dalekoh doh…
How can I get to…?	Kako mogu doći do…?	kakoh mogoo dochee doh…
Do you speak English?	Govorite li engleski?	govoreetey lee engleskee
I don't understand	Ne razumijem	nay razoomeeyem
Could you speak more slowly please?	Molim vas, možete li govoriti sporije?	moleem vas, mozhetey lee govoreetee sporiyey
I'm sorry	Žao mi je	zhaoh mee yey

USEFUL WORDS
big	veliko	veleekoh
small	malo	mahloh
hot	vruć	vrooch
cold	hladan	hlahdan
good	dobar	dobar
bad	loš	losh
enough	dosta	dostah
well	dobro	dobroh
open	otvoreno	otvohrenoh
closed	zatvoreno	zatvohrenoh
left	lijevo	leeyevoh

right	desno	desnoh
straight on	ravno	ravnoh
near	blizu	bleezoo
far	daleko	dalekoh
up	gore	gorey
down	dolje	dolyey
early	rano	ranoh
late	kasno	kasnoh
entrance	ulaz	oolaz
exit	izlaz	eezlaz
toilet	WC	Vey tsey
more	više	veeshey
less	manje	manyey

SHOPPING
How much does this cost?	Koliko ovo košta?	kolikoh ovoh koshta
I would like…	Volio bih…	volioh bee…
Do you have…?	Imate li…?	eematey lee…
I'm just looking	Samo gledam	Samoh gledam
Do you take credit cards?	Primate li kreditne kartice?	preematey lee credeetney carteetsey
What time do you open?	Kad otvarate?	kad otvaratey
What time do you close?	Kad zatvarate?	kad zatvaratey
This one	Ovaj	ov-igh
That one	Onaj	on-igh
expensive	skupo	skoopoh
cheap	jeftino	yefteenoh
size (clothes)	veličina	veleechinah
size (shoes)	broj	broy
white	bijelo	beeyeloh
black	crno	tsrnoh
red	crveno	tsrvenoh
yellow	žuto	zhootoh
green	zeleno	zelenoh
blue	plavo	plavoh
bakery	pekara	pekarah
bank	banka	bankah
book shop	knjižara	knyeezharah
butcher's	mesnica	mesnitsah
cake shop	slastičarna	slasteecharnah
chemist's	apoteka	apohtekah
fishmonger's	ribarnica	reebarnitsah
market	tržnica	trzhneetsah
hairdresser's	frizer	freezer
newsagent's/ tobacconist	trafika	trafeekah
post office	pošta	poshtah
shoe shop	prodavaonica cipela	prodavaonitsa tseepelah
supermarket	supermarket	soopermarket
travel agent	putnička agencija	pootneechka agentseeyah

SIGHTSEEING
art gallery	galerija umjetnina	galereeyah oomyetneenah
cathedral	katedrala	katedralah
church	crkva	tsrkvah
garden	vrt	vurt
library	knjižnica	knyeezhneetsah
museum	muzej	moozey
tourist information centre	turistički ured	tooreesteechkey oored
town hall	gradska vijećnica	gradskah veeyeechneetsa
closed for holiday	zatvoreno zbog praznika	zatvorenoh zbog prazneekah
bus station	autobusni kolodvor	aootoboosnee kolodvor
railway station	željeznički kolodvor	zhelyeznichkih kolodvor

STAYING IN A HOTEL
Do you have a vacant room?	Imate li sobu?	eematey lee soboo
double room	dvokrevetna soba	dvokrevetnah sobah
single room	jednokrevetna soba	yednokrevetnah sobah
room with a bath	soba sa kupatilom	sobah sah koopateelom

shower	**tuš**	toosh
porter	**portir**	portir
key	**ključ**	klyooch
I have a reservation	**Imam**	eemam
	rezervaciju	rezervatseeyoo

EATING OUT

Have you got a table for…?	**Imate li stol za…?**	eematey lee stol zah
I want to reserve a table	**Želim rezervirati stol**	Zheleem rezerveeratee stol
The bill please	**Molim vas, račun**	moleem vas, rachoon
I am a vegetarian	**Ja sam vegeterijanac**	yah sam vegetereeyanats
waiter/waitress	**konobar/ konobarica**	konobar/ konobaritsah
menu	**jelovnik**	yelovneek
wine list	**vinska karta**	veenskah kartah
glass	**čaša**	chashah
bottle	**boca**	botsah
knife	**nož**	nozh
fork	**viljuška**	veelyooshkah
spoon	**žlica**	zhleetsah
breakfast	**doručak**	doroochak
lunch	**ručak**	roochak
dinner	**večera**	vecherah
main course	**glavno jelo**	glavnoh yeloh
starters	**predjela**	predyelah

MENU DECODER

bijela riba	beeyelah reebah	"white" fish
blitva	bleetvah	Swiss chard
brudet	broodet	fish stew
čevapčiči	chevapcheechee	meatballs
crni rižot	tsrnee reezhot	black risotto (prepared with cuttlefish ink)
desert	desert	dessert
glavno jelo	glavnoh yeloh	main course
grah	grah	beans
gulaš	goolash	goulash
jastog	yastog	lobster
juha	yoohah	soup
kuhano	koohanoh	cooked
maslinovo ulje	masleenovoh oolyey	olive oil
meso na žaru	mesoh nah zharoo	barbecued meat
miješano meso	meejeshanoh mesoh	mixed grilled meats
na žaru	nah zharoo	barbecued
ocat	otsat	vinegar
palačinke	palacheenkay	pancakes
papar	papar	pepper
paški sir	pashkih seer	sheep's cheese from Pag
pečeno	pechenoh	baked
piletina	peeleteenah	chicken
plava riba	plavah reebah	"blue" fish
predjelo	predyeloh	starters
prilog	preelog	side dish
pršut	prshoot	smoked ham
pržene lignje	przhene leegnyey	fried squid
prženo	przhenoh	fried
ramsteak	ramsteyk	rump steak
ražnjići	razhnyeechee	pork kebabs
riba na žaru	reebah nah zharoo	barbecued fish
rižot frutti di mare	reezhot frootee dee marey	seafood risotto
rižot sa škampima	reezhot sah shkampeemah	scampi risotto
salata	salatah	salad
salata od hobotnice	salatah od hobotneetsey	octopus salad
sarma	sarmah	cabbage leaves
sir	seer	cheese
sladoled	sladoled	ice cream
slana srdela	slanah srdelah	salted sardines
škampi na buzaru	shkampee nah boozaroo	scampi in tomato and onion
školjke na buzaru	shkolkay nah boozaroo	shellfish in tomato and onion

špageti frutti di mare	shpagetee frootee dee marey	spaghetti with seafood
sol	sol	salt
tjestenina	tjesteneenah	pasta stuffed with meat and rice
ulje	oolyey	oil
varivo	vareevoh	boiled vegetables

DRINKS

bijelo vino	beeyeloh veenoh	white wine
čaj	ch-igh	tea
crno vino	tsrnoh veenoh	red wine
gazirana mineralna voda	gazeeranah meeneralnah vodah	sparkling mineral water
kava	kavah	coffee
negazirana mineralna voda	neygazeeranah meeneralnah vodah	still mineral water
pivo	peevoh	beer
rakija	rakeeyah	spirit
tamno pivo	tamnoh peevoh	stout (dark beer)
travarica	travareetsah	spirit flavoured with herbs
voda	vodah	water

NUMBERS

0	**nula**	noolah
1	**jedan**	yedan
2	**dva**	dvah
3	**tri**	tree
4	**četiri**	cheteeree
5	**pet**	pet
6	**šest**	shest
7	**sedam**	sedam
8	**osam**	osam
9	**devet**	devet
10	**deset**	deset
11	**jedanaest**	yedanest
12	**dvanaest**	dvahnest
13	**trinaest**	treenest
14	**četrnaest**	chetrnest
15	**petnaest**	petnest
16	**šestnaest**	shestnest
17	**sedamnaest**	sedamnest
18	**osamnaest**	osamnest
19	**devetnaest**	devetnest
20	**dvadeset**	dvahdeset
21	**dvadeset i jedan**	dvahdeset ee yedan
22	**dvadeset i dva**	dvahdeset ee dvah
30	**trideset**	treedeset
31	**trideset i jedan**	treedeset ee yedan
40	**četrdeset**	chetrdeset
50	**pedeset**	pedeset
60	**šezdeset**	shezdeset
70	**sedamdeset**	sedamdeset
80	**osamdeset**	osamdeset
90	**devedeset**	devedeset
100	**sto**	stoh
101	**sto i jedan**	stoh ee yedan
102	**sto i dva**	stoh ee dvah
200	**dvjesto**	dveestoh
500	**petsto**	petstoh
700	**sedamsto**	sedamstoh
900	**devetsto**	devetstoh
1,000	**tisuću**	teesoochoo
1,001	**tisuću i jedan**	teesoochoo ee yedan

TIME

One minute	**jedan minuta**	yedan meenootah
One hour	**jedan sat**	yedan saht
Half an hour	**pola sata**	polah sahtah
Monday	**ponedjeljak**	ponedyelyak
Tuesday	**utorak**	ootorak
Wednesday	**srijeda**	sreejedah
Thursday	**četvrtak**	chetvrtak
Friday	**petak**	petak
Saturday	**subota**	soobotah
Sunday	**nedjelja**	nedyelyah